Masters, lackeys and serfs

Why authoritarianism persists
in the 21st century and how to oppose it

Carlos Viniegra

Masters, lackeys and serfs

Why authoritarianism persists
in the 21st century and how to oppose it

COMPLEXITY BOOKS

D.R. © Carlos Viniegra, 2017

First edition in Spanish 2017
Amos, lacayos y vasallos
Por qué el autoritarismo persiste en el siglo XXI y cómo enfrentarlo.
Copyright © 2017, Editorial Paralelo 21, S.A. de C.V.

Masters, lackeys and serfs
Why authoritarianism persists in the 21st century and how to oppose it
First edition in English 2018
Copyright © 2018, Carlos Viniegra Beltrán

Design & cover: Bruno Pérez Chávez
Translators: Rafael Aguirre Ponce (Chapters: 13, 14, 15, 17, 18)
                   Andrea Dabrowski (Chapters 1, 2, 10, 11, 12, 16)
                   Elizabeth Polli (Chapters 7, 8, 9)
                   Beatriz Ramírez Cuevas (Chapters: 1, 2, 3, 4, 5, 6)
Editors: Tom Johnson
                   Marilyn Ward

ISBN: 978-607-7891-36-9

For Mateo & María:
May the words of your old man
help you have a future to be reached

But man is not made for defeat. A man
can be destroyed, but not defeated.
Ernest Hemingway,
The Old Man and the Sea

Good artists copy; Great artists steal.
Pablo Picasso

Acknowledgments

Acknowledgments are the book's cliché, and this is understood until one needs to write its own. The first lesson learned when moving forward with the personal "I'm going to write a book" statement, until reaching the writing of these words — the last ones to be written — is that books are made possible by team effort, shared and sustained by the people who are close to the author. This means that when a friend tells you that he is going to write a book, it is likely that at some point he will recruit you to help the project bear fruit. So, to keep in line with the tradition, I want to acknowledge and give credit to the team that these past years have given me their talent, intelligence, love, time, and the effort to make this project a reality.

Above all to Angie, my wife, accomplice, and friend, whose loyalty has never flinched. As well as to Mateo & María, who during this period spent countless afternoons by my side, with my physical presence but in complete mental absence in front of the keyboard. Love you, guys! Also, to my septuagenarian father, with whom I can remember more than 30 years of conversations and discussions related to this book's topics, and that at times were rough and complicated. Although the discussion process made us clash, it also brought us closer and demonstrated that when there's integrity and intellectual curiosity, people at any age can change the way of looking at things and become open and generously accept new ideas. I specially want to give credit to his contribution and pen — the only one different from mine — in the Gibbs-Pareto section from chapter 10, which solidified the methodological framework of this work.

Secondly, I want to thank the heterogeneous group of co-conspirators and the project's friends who studied the first drafts and gave me support with their comments, opinions, and suggestions. Among them stands out the academic, material support, and friendship from Dr. Jaime Cervantes de Gortari, Professor from the Engineering Faculty at UNAM (National Autonomous University of Mexico) as well as the rest of the complexity science crew, doctors José Luis Fernández Zayas and Enrique Guzmán, both researchers from the Engineering Institute at UNAM. They were open to the possibility that an economist from the social sciences could use the advanced ideas from science and engineering to analyze the contemporary problems of society.

In the same order of first readers and experimental subjects we have my "compadres" Rolando Flores and Antonio Díaz, together with Pepe Levy and Juan Manuel Acuña, along with my "comadre" Ana Paula Hernández, who guided me to Hannah Arendt, and Rafael Aguirre, whose erudition always brought forward some interesting insight. I also include the friends and colleagues who — in epigraphs, anecdotes, and phrases — can confirm that I was always aware of their words and that during years I collected, developed, and made my own, the juiciest parts from our most interesting conversations.

Without a doubt, the masters, lackeys and serfs who I've gotten to know across my life also deserve a lot of credit. Some are even close and dear. They are the ones who, in their pavlovian authoritarian consistency, have shown, illustrated, and inspired me with vivid anecdotes about the regular patterns of human behavior.

In the end, but not the least, there's the dedicated editorial team that cleaned, straightened, and simplified the text. What stands out is the meticulous copy editing done by Andrea Torres, as well the technical and administrative team from the Mexico City publishing house Paralelo 21. Without a doubt, in these complicated times for the publishing industry, making a serious book for serious readers wouldn´t be possible without publishers like Luis Jorge Arnau and stubborn and decided editorial directors like Alejandro Toussaint, who strive to put the best of the country in the hands of their readers.

Acknowledgments to the English edition

The serendipity of random network effects creates opportunities where once there were none. In the summer of 2017, the Spanish edition was finished, and its design process had started. I attended Santa Fe Institute's 2017 Complexity Science Summer School in Santa Fe, NM. There I became part of an amazing international community of scientists and thinkers. The experience convinced me that to reach a wider audience, an English version of this book was needed. Once again, with Angie's decisive support and a set of lucky random connections, this new project came together. It all started when I met Frank and Billie Chambers in Santa Fe. For almost a year, Frank´s selfless generosity made him keep the project in mind and continued to make connections for it to move forward. Months after we met, he introduced me to Tom Johnson, this book's editor and SFI alumnus from the '90s. Together, we pulled together an amazing international team that translated, edited, and designed this new edition in record time. The translation team was led by Andrea Dabrowsky, who collaborated with Beatriz Ramírez and was later reinforced by Elizabeth Polli and Rafael Aguirre, who joined to meet a shortened and ambitious deadline. On the editing front, the always energetic team of Marilyn Ward and Tom Johnson burned the midnight oil for several weeks to produce a terrific manuscript in challenging circumstances. Bruno Pérez single handedly designed and produced the new edition just a few days after the editing process was completed. I want to thank them from the bottom of my heart for coming onboard and working so hard. Kudos to all!

We were able to move faster with this edition thanks to the generosity — as has become customary — of Paralelo 21, which made available the art from the Spanish edition. Carla Shedivy and Paul Hooper from SFI also played a small part in this serendipity that allowed this edition to reach a starting point. Once again, my gratitude to both!

Summary

I. The world as it is

II. The world that will cease to be

III. The world as it can be

Annexes

List of graphs, tables, and figures

Graphs

Tables

Figures

Page intentionally left blank.

I

The world as it is

1. Introduction

Objective

The contemporary world is like a coin. One side is open and technologically advanced, and the other, is closed and backward. Regardless of how one measures the differences, and despite all the progress made, most of humanity — nearly 7.5 billion people — live on the closed side. This means, in Thomas Hobbes'(1) famous words, that even in this century "life is solitary, poor, nasty, brutish, and short" for most people on the planet.

One cannot underestimate that, unlike the era in which Hobbes stated this famous phrase, the current world is better, particularly in the brutish and short aspects of life, thanks to the reduction of homicidal violence and the improvement of public health in the last 100 years. However, the disparities between those who live on the "open" side of the coin and those who live on the "closed" side can still be measured in orders of increasing magnitude. Today, the trend of long-term improvement for the population that is disadvantaged does not seem very encouraging. In addition to the historical challenges of lifting most of civilization to a better reality, there are new economic, political, social, and environmental challenges that make the situation more difficult.

Although every day millions of people try to tackle these problems, the world is at a stage in which it is no longer possible to address many topics in an isolated and specialized manner. Despite our best efforts, when confronting problems individually, we do not find answers to the new challenges emerging from the connections, the overlaps, and the contradictions among the different concerns. One example of this is the inextricable connection between economic development, the environment, and politics that we observe when addressing climate change. In the face of this and other problems, our most specialized scientific and technological tools seem useless to alleviate the vast array of human hardships. Consequently, we are forced to seek new ideas and solutions with the potential to produce progress in the tasks still pending.

The differences, which metaphorically are the coins' bright and open side and the dark or closed one, are related to two opposite cultural models whose origin is as ancient as civilization itself. Today, we know the models as the democratic and the authoritarian parts of the world. This work aims to explore, through a new scientific perspective, the operational mechanisms of both parts of the world and suggest tools and solutions that, despite the new challenges, will allow us to move away from the shadows.

The book is divided into three parts: 1) "The world as it is"; 2) "The world that will cease to be"; and 3) "The world as it can be." The first part analyzes the current condition of the world from the new viewpoint of complexity science — a conceptual framework based on the idea of cultural evolution. This idea follows an approach that studies human society as a complex adaptive system used to describe the enduring authoritarian world, whose main characters provide this book's title — *Masters, Lackeys, and Serfs* — as well as interpret the operational rules of the democratic world. In each case, we explain how the interaction rules that define each social system also determine the behavior of the different players or agents that in turn give rise to each type of social system through emergence. Emergence is a phenomenon characteristic of complex systems with which it is possible to explain some of the most difficult and evasive categories of social sciences, such as power and violence. Moreover, it opens the discussion over the merit figures or performance variables that are equal to value or what is valuable, and that encourage the evolutionary and persistent direction of each social system.

The first part provides an updated and simplified approach to the classic problems of the social sciences, and provides the basis to address two new problems, whose effects will entirely transform humanity. The first challenge that is analyzed in the second part is the integration of environmental protection to the framework of social architecture such as laws, the rights of present and future generations, the future development of advanced and emergent nations, and the relationship of said framework with the conservation of nature. The second challenge concerns changes driven by the digital revolution, whose axis is the disintermediation of everything it encompasses and that has already upset the economic, political, and social networks in a process that technically is known as the change of the network's topology. This produces and will produce new winners and losers that will confront each other, providing new possibilities for the generation of value, and at the same time, instability and systemic changes.

Finally, the third part of this book synthesizes the governing rules of the authoritarian world and the democratic one described in the first part, coupled with the challenges laid out in the second part, and presents the design parameters required to build next generation solutions. Under this third part we also describe some of the pioneer projects that show promise for lifting millions of people out of the shadows, making the open society grow and effectively oppose authoritarianism that unfortunately still prospers and is being renewed in the 21st century.

Postcards

We are all a product of our time and our circumstances. When writing this book, it seemed interesting to reflect and share the circumstances and context that in one way or another lie behind the ideas. Just like reality is complex and disorganized, the circumstantial context that led to my writing is not an articulated history, but rather a varied collection of postcards compiled throughout my life. Two of them are not my own, but have become mine as part of the family heritage.

I. Juanita Viniegra

Although the family has no written document of this anecdote, Uncle Roberto (Roberto Viniegra Osorio) always told us that in the 1940s, within the infamous Lecumberri prison in Mexico City — which today houses the National General Archives — marijuana was known among the prisoners as "Juanita Viniegra." In this respect, some historians(2) rediscovered in the last few years that Leopoldo Salazar Viniegra, a prominent psychiatrist from the first half of the 20th century, proposed the decriminalization of narcotics during a session of the Mexican Academy of Medicine in 1938. Without the attendees' knowledge or consent, he had distributed cannabis cigarettes for their consumption and no problems nor disturbances took place. The fact, published in the newspapers, convinced Academy members and Mexico's president Lázaro Cárdenas of the psychiatrist's proposal to legalize drug sales. So, on February 17, 1940, the norm that decriminalized drug consumption in Mexico through the *Federal Drug Abuse Manual* was published in the *Federal Official Gazette*.

The matter ran counter to international opinion, which aimed to formalize the worldwide prohibition of the sale and consumption of drugs. The new measure led the United States to exert its influence and put pressure on Mexico by issuing an embargo of analgesics and anesthesia. This forced president Lázaro Cárdenas to suspend the implementation of the *Drug Abuse Manual* on July 3, 1940, and normalize the flow of medicines into the country. As a result, an administrative investigation began at the psychiatric hospital founded by Salazar Viniegra and his colleagues (a model of psychiatric care also ahead of its time). When it ended, Leopoldo Salazar Viniegra, whose calling was medicine, not management, was accused of malfeasance. This plunged him into a deep depression that, according to Uncle Robert, led him to commit suicide.

Reviewed by Juan Alberto Cedillo in the book *La Cosa Nostra en México*, this is the story of a physician intent on eliminating the influence that "Lola la Chata," the main drug distributor in Mexico City, had over his patients. That's why more than 70 years ago, Salazar Viniegra pleaded with the United States government officials "...that there was only one way to stop drug traffic in Mexico; the State should create a monopoly for the sale of prohibited drugs to drug addicts..."(3). Today, the topic's discussion is still a taboo in Mexico, even though for decades drug trafficking and the violence related to prohibition have ravaged the country, while in the United States there is already a tacit acknowledgment of the famous doctor's ideas. At state level, a process to decriminalize marijuana for medical and recreational use is already taking place.

II. The loggers and power

My father says that when he was a very young child, something happened that led my grandfather to teach him and his brother to handle a gun to protect the family. In 1929, high school students — among them Miguel Alemán Valdés (future president of Mexico) and Gustavo Viniegra Osorio (future physician and grandfather of our clan)— mobilized in favor of the university's autonomy. In response, government officials sent the fire department to disperse the multitude. The family legend says the tension due to the conflict was such that at one point during the upheaval a firefighter brandished an axe against a group of students. Grandfather Gustavo confronted and disarmed him, and his action left an indelible remembrance in the memory of the young Miguel Alemán.

Years later, the main scandal in city newspapers was the clandestine tree logging in the woods close to the country's capital, near the Zempoala lagoons. Miguel Alemán, then Mexico's president, decided to take matters in hand and commission someone, whose courage he trusted since the 1929 disturbances, to create the country's first forest ranger corps, and bring those responsible to justice. The president summoned grandfather Gustavo to organize the forest rangers. Grandfather accepted with two conditions: to have full freedom of action and the guarantee that the law would be enforced against whomever was responsible of the illegal logging. Soon after, the new ranger corps found and arrested the criminal gang. To everyone's surprise, it turned out that the leader behind the criminal gang was a friend of the president, who ordered the man's immediate release. Grandfather angrily resigned his position.

But the matter did not end there. The people affected by the discovery of the illegal logging network threatened Gustavo Viniegra Osorio and his family, who had no government protection due to the conflict with the president. In line with the character of his youth, grandfather decided to be ready to face any situation by preparing his two small children for an armed aggression that fortunately never took place. However, to this day, clandestine logging in the forests surrounding the Zempoala lagoons is still recurring news in the media.

III. Space civilization

My grandmother Emma was born in 1898 and died in 1992. She never ceased to be amazed by mankind's landing on the moon. Her grandchildren, most of them born in the 1970s, remember her enthusiasm when she told us that our generation would get to travel and live in space.

For people born at the end of the 19th century, the things they saw and the events they lived through during the 20th century — the rise of the automobile, the 1910 Mexican Revolution, the First and Second World Wars, the nuclear bomb, the discovery of antibiotics, the generalized use of vaccines, commercial aviation and the space age — were sufficient assurance that the 1970 generation would make the great leap forward for humankind. My grandmother was fully convinced of this, together with other adults at the time, and for many years she made sure to let us know.

Today, we are still waiting to drive our first flying car, we long for the return of the Concorde supersonic commercial flights (inaugurated in

5

1973 and cancelled in 2003), and we wish to find the means to fulfill our generational calling, so humanity can move forward toward that better future our grandparents predicted.

IV. Epitaph for a killer

My grandmother Emma's house was a collection of the most diverse 20th century objects. The relics of her early adult life as a landowner in Zacatecas before the Mexican Revolution coexisted with the inherent objects of urban life during the second half of the 20th century. To me, the most interesting of all was the *National Geographic* magazine collection that took up a considerable number of bookshelves in the house. Many a time during our visits, we, as grandchildren, spent hours poring over the treasure trove of the magazine's maps, photographs, and articles (the *Wikipedia*, *Google*, and *YouTube* of our childhood).

It was not until the 1980s that I ran across a 1978 article that seemed to me moving and significant. Titled "Smallpox: Epitaph for a killer?"(4), it told the story of the first great triumph of mankind as a whole: the worldwide defeat and eradication of smallpox. The most gripping part of the article describes the culmination of the uphill battle of millions of people against this disease, which even managed to prompt cease-fires in several wars to find those affected including the population and the soldiers. The article starts with the telegram received by the paladin of smallpox eradication, Dr. Donald A. Henderson: "...April 17, 1978, Nairobi, Kenya. Search complete. No cases discovered. Ali Maow Maalin is the world's last known smallpox case."

In my family's history, the account takes on special meaning, since it was grandpa Gustavo who organized and launched the smallpox eradication campaign in Mexico; he was public health director general of the Ministry of Health at the time.

V. TI-99/A

One of the happiest expressions I recall seeing on my father's face was in 1983 when I came home while he was unpacking the first family computer: a Texas Instruments TI-99/A. This event epitomized the starting point of our journey into the space age. At long last, computers were tangible, and it was also possible for a mere mortal to access the unimaginable programming and computing power of a 16-bit microprocessor with a speed of 3MHz and 16kb of memory.

VI. Nine-to-five worker. Five-to-nine activist.

In Mexico, the generation born during the 1970s may well be called the "crisis generation," for instead of experiencing a time of stability and development, this generation weathered more combined economic and social crises than any other contemporary generation to date. These critical events forced us to adopt one of two stances: either growing a thicker skin to isolate us from the world or seeking out options for change. Those of us who decided on the more challenging road, that of change and participation, did so at a time when it was still dangerous to do so and when being part of the opposition in Mexico meant opting for marginalization.

In 1996, I went knocking on the door of the XVII district of the National Action Party (PAN) in Mexico City not knowing what to expect. To my surprise, I found a mature and friendly group of neighbors, lawyers, doctors, businessmen, and housewives, who from 9:00 a.m. to 5:00 p.m. were devoted to their professional activities and from 5:00 p.m. to 9:00 p.m. became political activists, concentrating on important neighborhood issues. If one has not experienced this form of citizenship, no longer in existence, one might be easily led to believe that in an authoritarian nation, building citizenship is impossible. But, as the philosophical precept dictates: "If it exists (or existed), it's possible."

The final consideration of this postcard, which became a harbinger of what would later come to pass, took place in the summer of 1996, when a young militant returned to our district after being away for a long time and who justified his absence from the district's activities by claiming he held a position in the party's headquarters. The project of the group to which he belonged was to ensure that Felipe Calderón, a party leader of the National Action Party (PAN), would become the first opposition president before 2012.

VII. PAN (National Action Party) Assembly

Being part of a genuine citizens' organization implies that its members, regardless of their seniority, are shareholders and acquire full rights from the moment they become affiliated. During the 1990s, the PAN in Mexico was such an organization. As soon as I joined the party, I started receiving the notices to participate in the meetings where the decisions regarding political leadership and election of candidates and members of the board were made.

The first assembly I attended in my capacity as delegate coincided with an electoral campaign. It was significant because of a strong disagreement between the assembly delegates and the party leaders concerning one of the items in the political platform. Felipe Calderón Hinojosa, future president of Mexico, was on the side of the party's leadership whose proposal was defeated by the assembly's delegates even though he made it very clear he was upset and publicly manifested his annoyance. But at the time, the democratic culture of the PAN was such that the decision of the assembly, which was vociferously held, was approved and recorded in the party's political platform. The latter, which is commonplace in democratic systems, was the first sign of true democracy that I had ever witnessed and constitutes the benchmark against which I am able to measure the level of democracy of any given situation.

Overtime, the PAN's practices changed. We militants stopped being the actual shareholders of the organization, and the control and ownership of the party were conveyed to the leaders backed by Felipe Calderón. As president of the country and with his administration, he crushed and debased the democratic machinery of the organization, which for decades had allowed PAN to endure authoritarian harassment as one of the few bastions of democracy in Mexico. Today, as is the case in other organizations, politics and political parties in Mexico do not belong to the citizens. The control of these organizations is in the hands of a cartel made up by the upper echelons of management.

VIII: Custodians of the city

Back in the 1970s, during a field trip, a young member of Scouts Group 76 of the Benito Juárez delegation in Mexico City was seriously injured. True to the tradition established by Baden Powell, the founder of the scout movement, the participants of the outing attempted to help their companion. Lacking the knowledge, tools, or means to provide assistance, the group realized it was inadequately prepared to deal with emergencies and decided to receive training, obtain equipment, and establish a first responder, rescue, and medical emergencies professional team. Years later, under scout leader Miguel Ángel Tena Salim, this Scout Group became the "Escuadrón SOS" (SOS Squad). This organization became bigger and more prestigious and managed to appeal to young people in the city to train in medical emergency services and to provide said services to others in a free and voluntary manner.

Early one morning in 1998, upon getting out of the ambulance and after a year's training and practice as an emergency medical technician, I arrived at the scene of a gruesome traffic accident for the very first time as a paramedic. I cannot forget the look on the onlookers' faces, the policemen and bystanders, all speechless and expressing the anguish roused by the scene, and at the same time the high expectations they anticipated from our service. Knowing that at any one time you are the last resort in solving a serious problem unquestionably constitutes a momentous rite of passage. The experiences and lessons learned during my time in the "Escuadrón SOS" are numerous and still prevail; that is where I found the love of my life and some of my closet friends.

However, the "Escuadrón SOS" where I trained as a paramedic no longer exists today. It fell prey to the usual vices and evils to which civil organizations are exposed to in a toxic authoritarian atmosphere, especially when the lives of their founders come to an end. With the disappearance of the SOS, new generations of young people have missed the opportunity to grow as individuals, to know and experience what it's like to be of service to others. They have also been deprived of a meeting point in which to come together with their peers, and without it, or any other similar meeting places, it is more likely that active and participative individuals will remain neutralized and diluted in the sea of contemporary apathy.

IX. July 2, 2000

On July 2, 2000, Mexican society decided to leave the 20th century behind and take a long stride into the future by voting on a massive scale to put an end to more than 70 years of revolutionary authoritarianism. At that time, the most viable organization to assume public trust was PAN, the political party that undertook society's mandate in the same way as a paramedic who is entrusted with rights and responsibilities to act in favor of others.

Those of us who were part and parcel of said change are probably not capable of fully expressing what we experienced that day. It was phenomenal! Everyone who had enlisted in the democratic struggle prior to 2000 was more accustomed to defeat than success. And even though we strove daily to bring about change, a part of us thought that it would still take years, even decades, to attain that democratic goal. The fact is that experience teaches us that in politics things that are unimaginable at some point sometimes suddenly change and are achieved sooner that we had anticipated.

X. What do we do now?

July 3, 2000, was a completely different day. We needed to come back to the reality of the post-election process. That morning, in the office of the secretary general of PAN for Mexico City, I soon came across two friends with whom I constantly discussed the country's future. In this group, I was treated as a tenderfoot, despite a long-standing family history of political involvement — my great-grandfather gave up his medical practice in the city to join the Zapatistas during the Revolution, my grandfather was a civil servant and Lázaro Cárdenas' personal physician, and my father is a left-wing scholar forged amid the hippie movement of 1968 at the University of California, Berkeley. So, about belonging to an economically liberal and socially conservative party, I was a feral militant fledging my wings and learning on my own.

The obvious question was: "What do we do now?" And the laconic answer of one of my colleagues was: "...once political alternation comes about, there are no roadmaps, and it is up to us to shape and set the course for what lies ahead." And he was right! Even though PAN was founded in 1939 and came to power in 2000, irrespective of democracy and electoral alternation, the organization only had a series of guiding principles, but lacked a nation-building project. Maybe this postcard is the one that is more closely linked to the conception of this book, since from that moment on, just as the Scouts experienced when founding the "Escuadrón SOS," it became clear that to rule it was necessary to learn and acquire training to fulfill the task entrusted to us by the people.

In generational terms, several of my peers got involved in politics before completing their professional education. In 2000, they had incomplete degrees, had not learned another language, and lacked the independent professional development that the senior militants of the PAN had. This situation remained unchanged as the years went by and, consequently, they were not invited to participate in government, despite belonging to the ruling party. Furthermore, this coincided with a period when, for age reasons, the group that had safeguarded PAN's democracy for many decades stepped down and passed on the torch to the generation that came to power. Seventeen years later, PAN is defeated and its mission shattered. Authoritarianism was democratically reinstated by the PRI (Revolutionary Institutional Party), and Mexico failed to take that significant leap forward. The country stumbled upon its own elite, who discovered it was easier to become part of authoritarianism than to build democracy. PAN failed to understand the domestic and international time and circumstances of the moment, or *Zeitgeist*, to articulate a new nation-building project that would make the most of the trust conferred upon it by the citizens on July 2, 2000. That trust was miserably wasted due to incompetence, which, in historic terms, turned out to be epic for the country. In other words, every iconic event in a nation, such as July 2 in Mexico, will always be followed by a July 3 that, just as in medical emergencies, requires preparedness and knowledge of what to do before establishing eye contact with the event.

XI. Retired unionized worker
In December 2007, after having acquired public office experience at the Ministry of the Environment, I embarked upon a new mission at the Ministry of Agriculture, one of the "hot spots" of the frayed authoritarian system. One of the most interesting experiences in my working life took place during my first day there. A worker had been timidly hovering around the door of my office for hours until, by the end of the day, he mustered enough courage to express his concern. The message enthusiastically conveyed by that thin and gray-haired man was that he had waited months for someone to take on my position because, having the necessary seniority to retire, he found it necessary, imperative even, to tell him face-to-face that he had succeeded in reaching the finish line.

As this was my first experience with a retiring employee, it seemed appropriate, even if we didn´t know each other, to say something encouraging along the lines of hoping that the considerable time he had spent in the ministry had brought him fulfillment, satisfaction and personal growth. I wanted him to feel he had accomplished interesting things throughout that time, now that the most productive chapter of his professional life was ending. It really surprised me to see that, as my improvised monologue went on, the cheerful look on his face turned into a gloomy and dispirited expression. This, of course, prompted me to try to find more positive things to say, but they only added to the individual's dismay. Shortly thereafter, the conversation was over, and my crestfallen interlocutor left the office looking down at the floor.

It took me a while to understand that in the cultural rationale of authoritarian unionism, the goal is to reach retirement age without generating value. This man had kept on "working" several more months than was necessary because he needed to brag to the boss about the fact that he had succeeded in showing up to work for 30 years without getting fired or generating any actual benefit for the organization (and by the same token, for Mexico). What he failed to consider, up until the day we had this conversation, was that making retirement an end had meant wasting the best 30 years of his life, having nothing to show for it except for the meaningless feat of reaching retirement age. This is, undoubtedly, one of the worst manifestations of collectivizing authoritarianism I have ever come across. It imposes a huge existential cost on those that follow this model in exchange for the promise of achieving very little, like a meager monthly retirement check.

XII. H1N1 and Google Earth

April 2009. Mexico's president addressed the nation regarding the outbreak caused by a new influenza, a virus subtype known as H1N1. Soon after, a high-level emergency group was created and joined by the deputy secretary for Energy Planning, a friend of the president, and, at the time, my boss at the Ministry of Energy. A few hours later, the information disseminated by the media became more and more alarming and by nightfall of the first day of the outbreak, I got a call from my boss: "We need to see the cases on a map, and things are moving very slowly here. Please see what you can do. We'll send the information to your e-mail address."

My previous experience with geographical information systems suggested that, if an epidemiological data processing platform was not available at this point, setting up whatever was required would entail funds, a sizeable team, and a couple of days to encode the data onto a visualization platform. At the time, the resources I had at hand were: a laptop and a team of one. The first choice was starting to recruit specialists, establishing a center of operations at the Ministry of Agriculture or the Ministry of the Environment, and find the hardware and specialized software for the task at hand. The other alternative was to opt for something completely different: *Google Earth*. This meant starting from scratch and learning to program in Keyhole Markup Language (KML), the platform's language. No one I knew had any such experience, which meant going it alone to find a solution. So, I studied and worked with KML all through the night and by dawn, the first data set had been uploaded to the platform and it was now possible to follow the outbreak with animations that represented the location, progress, and spreading of cases on a time line.

In the morning, I presented the results at the Ministry of Energy, and a call was immediately placed through the executive encrypted telephone system. Half an hour later, I was sitting in the situation room of the Secretary of Health to show him the visual progress of the outbreak he was responsible for controlling. Around the table, various epidemiological information experts, graduates from some of the world's most prestigious universities, were squirming in their seats and scowling because they could not understand how a team from the Ministry of Energy had managed to process the data in less time and without the proper resources. Once the meeting was over, we were invited to the outbreak's operational control room, where it took one more day to install a full conventional visualization platform, which, up until then, only showed a simple map of the country.

Things *had* changed. The cloud-computing era was real, showing that one individual with a laptop could access more resources on Internet-public platforms than those available in-house at any public institution. A door was opening to different ways of generating value and the government model centered on the institution was being called into question. To me, it was clear that from that moment on, generating public value would depend less on millionaire resources to access technological tools and more on the creative capabilities of individuals.

XIII. It was reality that failed, not the model

In 2009, several officers from the Ministry of Energy, including me, were summoned to a high-level meeting with officials from PEMEX, the state-owned oil monopoly. They were going to explain to us how the expensive modeling and planning platforms of the national energy system worked. These had been first installed in the 1980s, and for reasons unbeknown to us, had proliferated over the years. After a lengthy explanation of the characteristics of each of the seven platforms dedicated to do the same task, the obvious issue was finding out whether the company, after decades of experience and having invested hundreds of millions of dollars to purchase and use this type of technology, had managed to improve its forecasting capacity regarding the variables of the national energy system, and hence, the planning and decision-making processes. PEMEX delegates were completely baffled by the question. Their answer was that these systems were not used to improve planning or decision making, since their intended purpose was to officially justify the company's decisions. In other words, decisions in PEMEX were made first and foremost based on intuitive executive criteria and then, the technology of the modeling systems was used to justify the adopted decisions, not to inform them.

This, incredible as it may seem, was just the preamble to what happened next. In response to the inconceivable statement made by the company's representatives, I ventured an acrimonious statement: clearly this was one of the reasons why energy planning had been unsuccessful in our country. As an example, I brought up the fact that, at the time, Mexico had a 50% reserve capacity for electricity generation, which was equal to a 25% over-investment in infrastructure vis-à-vis the whole system, which represented a waste and a colossal and unnecessary financial expenditure. The counter-claim was not made by the oil company but by one of my colleagues from the Ministry of Energy, who categorically stated that planning had not failed since a technically correct process had been followed, and then elaborated on the subject by stating that what had failed was reality, which had not complied with the model.

Back in college, to caution us about the risk of falling prey to technocratic arrogance, professors would joke about economists who condemn reality for failing to conform to a given model. Suddenly, the joke had turned into a true story. Even now, upon reminiscing about this postcard, I still find it hard to believe that there are people out there who, through their actions, turn fables and their morals into actual stories while they hold strategic positions in a country. This dual story depicts a sign of the times: many of the people who are technically qualified to make decisions suffer from ethical, not technical, incompetence because they are indifferent or incapable of being critical and reasonable. They believe that these attributes stand in the way of the fulfillment of their personal ambitions.

XIV. Sick and tired of rationality

During the preparatory period for the COP15 (15th Conference of the Parties) climate change summit — held in 2009 in Copenhagen — Mexico undertook various endeavors to become part of the international climate change momentum. One such endeavor was to identify projects that could result in financial incentives by exchanging CO_2 (carbon dioxide) emission reductions for carbon credits. The list included the renewal of several petrochemical and hydrocarbon production industrial facilities, whose modernization was estimated at a cost of $10 billion, and would generate a return of less than $1 billion through the carbon credits mechanism. Modernizing the industrial facilities was necessary in and of itself and would improve the sector's security, productivity, and quality. Including carbon credits in the rationale of the project made it look better, but if the revenue from this scheme was the only factor considered, it was impossible to consider it as a profitable transaction.

The debate was taken before a committee from the President's office headed by a key government advisor and a top executive of the Ministry of the Treasury. I was asked to outline the topic of the meeting, which was simply: carbon credits would generate less than $1 billion in revenue; a $10 billion investment was needed, and the Ministry of Energy, considering the quality, productivity, and security benefits, was in favor of modernizing the industrial facilities, provided the Ministry of the Treasury consented to the investment of resources. The rest of the meeting was surreal. The official from the Treasury wanted to make use of the carbon credits without making the necessary investments to obtain them; the president's advisor wanted to inform the media about the reduction of CO_2 emissions, but was not interested in modernizing the industrial facilities. The critical point of the meeting came when the presidential advisor, at the end of his tether because he could not achieve short-term emission reductions without investing in the modernization of the energy infrastructure, "lost it" and vociferated: "We are sick and tired of you and your boss' rationality in analyzing these matters!" Currently, both characters are alive and well in the public arena of Mexican society despite their fondness for irrationality in the making of strategic decisions.

The tragedy associated with this postcard is that similar characters, known as technocrats during the administrations of presidents Carlos Salinas de Gortari (1988-1994) and Ernesto Zedillo (1994-2000); as "amigos de Fox" during Vicente Fox's administration (2000-2006); and renamed non-partisan technocrats in Felipe Calderón's administration (2006-2012), abound in the scene of decision-making bodies. They are the invisible cogwheels of the system that operates outside the political spectrum and thrive despite election alternation and government changes. They are not accountable to the citizens for their decisions and, as Trojan horses, only benefit themselves and their backers, who are also shielded from public scrutiny. They have no scruples when it comes to making, influencing or applying technical makeup to poor decisions, which are the source of the countless tragedies and corruption scandals currently swamping the media.

XV. COP15

Several events that could be regarded as the end of the modern era and the beginning of a new one, the postmodern era, occurred between 2007 and 2011. One such decisive event was the 2009 climate change summit, where I was able to attest to the obsolescence and incompetence of the multilateral system in addressing the complexity of global issues. As I walked down the hallways of the COP15 convention center, I witnessed various signs of collapse.

The perambulating entourages of presidents and prime ministers were everywhere. On one side, an African dictator in military garb laden with medals was striving to appear modern and respectable to the eyes of the world. On the other, Nicolas Sarkozy, the French president, was exclusively interested in garnering the media's attention. There were also small groups of youngsters who, enabled by digital technology, posted all sorts of news to their virtual followers and demanded action from the grownups. But upon asking them about their ideas, an authentic sense of ownership regarding the issues at hand was sorely lacking; they had no solutions of their own to propose. In the working rooms, where the substantial part of the undertaking was supposed to take place, activities were at a standstill because the architects of the summit were only concentrated on upholding the false promise that everything that thousands of individuals had failed to achieve in 20 years of negotiations would be resolved at the last minute in the final panel, in which "the masters of the world" would participate.

The members of the Mexican delegation decided to take standby shifts to always maintain the country's presence in the plenary room, which for days served as the showcase for world leaders. One of the shifts during the early morning hours, however, turned out to be entertaining due to the histrionic performance of Hugo Chávez, president of Venezuela. The truth is that, despite the best intentions of the "masters of the world," the COP15 summit failed. More than 100 presidents and prime ministers arrived at the meeting that was supposed to be the momentous turning point of international cooperation with great zeal and left feeling frustrated, having nothing new to show the world.

XVI. Arab Autumn

Late one night, after a long flight across two continents, I was riding in a van that was rushing to cross the bridge across the Nile to avoid the mob that had gathered at Tahrir Square. Four hundred meters ahead, the hotel guards were opening the stronghold to let us through. It was the autumn of 2011 and I had travelled to Egypt as part of an OECD (Organization for Economic Co-operation and Development) mission that, only a few months after the Arab Spring, was analyzing the future of the improved governance and the role of information technology in that country. At the time, a transitional government, made up mostly by former officials of Hosni Mubarak's administration, was in power.

Next morning, the news of the day was that the uprising of the previous night in Tahrir Square had been due to the execution of 27 Coptic Christians the day before. Later, the members of the mission were sitting in front of a group of serious-looking men wearing sunglasses indoors, with bushy mustaches and wearing double-breasted suits and wide ties, who reminded me of the Mexican politicians of the 1970s. After the formal introductions and a lengthy account of the changes the revolution implied and what the new government wanted to achieve, our first question was, given the country's change in context after the revolution, what strategic changes have been envisaged? The answer was clear, prompt and unexpected. *"A change of context does not compel us to change our strategy."* So, we decided to devote that week to performing an extensive series of interviews with Egypt's most diverse figures. Regardless of whether it was a former Mubarak associate or a member of the revolution, one by one, most of the interviewees emphatically "put down" their opponents and maintained that Egypt was a proud and ancient nation that needed a strong-handed leader, a pharaoh that could subdue its enemies.

Halfway through the process — which lasted a week — we were informed that the transitional government had announced that it was stepping down because of the massacre of Coptic Christians, so we didn't know if we were going to be able to continue with our mission's work plan. Immediately, the OECD's Secretariat explained that, should a major breakdown of the situation occur, we might be asked to swiftly get to the airport to leave the country and, should this be impossible, the contingency exit plan would be to move the team to the Italian embassy from where other evacuation alternatives would be considered. Luckily, none of the members of the mission — an Italian, a British national, a Mexican, and the members of the OECD Secretariat — were apprehensive, and in view of the alternatives, we decided to go on with the work plan while more information became available. Meanwhile, our interpreter, a Coptic Christian, used the pauses between interviews to pray to God for the safety of his community and the salvation of his people. Soon after, we learned that the Egyptian Supreme Council of the Armed Forces had refused to accept the government's resignation and had instructed the officials to remain in place, which they did. This made it clear to us that the first digital revolution in history was very much like the analog revolutions that came before it.

XVII. Shut up!

In 2013, I attended a conference on transparency and open government in the city of Beirut, Lebanon. After my presentation, an elegant female academician, whose air and demeanor reminded me of Sophia Loren of the 1970s, approached me to further discuss the subject. The professor from the Lebanese American University was interested in open government and was soon explaining the challenges faced by Lebanon on this subject matter. Before long, one of the conference organizers joined the conversation and immediately disagreed with the professor, who held her ground firmly and politely, as is customary during this type of conferences anywhere in the world.

I did not anticipate that the organizer, who was Lebanese and a member of an international organization, would resort to a local statement to win the argument: "Shut up! In any case, that's a woman's opinion and it carries no weight here." I am certain that this would have led to a major scandal and the end of the professional career of any man who would do this anywhere else in the world, but here its only impact was making a Mexican feel shocked and appalled, apart from the evident and silent resentment of the scholar. This simple anecdote illustrates the backwardness, impunity, and violence to which women are exposed every day in the authoritarian world, even those who are scholarly and cosmopolitan.

The series of topics addressed in these postcards attest to contemporary reality, which imposes upon us a tangled web of challenges, problems, and intertwined changes that go from the local to the global arenas and which we face daily when we step outside the door of our homes. Even if this reality may seem too wide-ranging and hard to face, the postcards deal with five key issues:

1. The difficulty in building democratic solutions in authoritarian systems.
2. The democratic model and the way it creates value.
3. The multiple facets of contemporary authoritarianism that need to be understood.
4. The importance of environmental challenges and the changes brought about by the digital revolution.
5. Incompetence as the main obstacle in building the democratic model.

Marginal Citizen

In May 2014, the CNN news station broadcast a chapter on Mexico of *Parts Unknown*(5), the series led by the famous American chef, Anthony Bourdain. At the same time, Bourdain, who is also a blogger, published an article called "Under the Volcano"(6), which caused an uproar in Mexico's social media. In both presentations, he first provides a first-hand testimony on the breakdown of daily life that is caused by the violence and its impunity, which are enabled by the corruption and complicity of government officials. Then he goes on to recognize the heroic resistance of some Mexican individuals, who, stubbornly, refuse to accept the sad reality.

"Under the Volcano" was published on the Internet in defense of Mexico, but its intention did not counteract the devastating effect of the blog's last paragraph:

> *"The received wisdom is that Mexico will never change. That it is hopelessly corrupt, from top to bottom. That it is useless to resist — to care, to hope for a happier future. But there are heroes out there who refuse to go along. On this episode of Parts Unknown, we meet a few of them. People who are standing up against overwhelming odds, demanding accountability, demanding change — at great, even horrifying personal cost. This show is for them..."*

The most difficult part to digest for those of us who have devoted an important part of our lives to improve Mexico's situation through organized civic participation is not that violence and corruption are pointed to, once again, as our country's most serious problems — something that, undoubtedly, hurts and today is a registered trademark in the world. But rather, as the chef accurately points out, it is that "the hope of a happier future" only has room in the heroic dimension, since the possibility of constructing a better situation today through the citizens' millions of small, ordinary and daily actions, has been cancelled. The discomfort provoked by Bourdain's acute perception of Mexico stems from its veracity, and as psychologists colloquially like to say, "If you can't bear it, you get it."

If we follow Bourdain's description in a literary train of thought, the current situation of countries like Mexico constitutes a tragedy and the hero is the only character who remains standing against the plot becoming a reality. Nevertheless, the hero is not there to prevent the story's fatal outcome, but rather as the counterpoint that underscores the play's tragic character.

The Recipe

It is not necessary to delve much further before reaching the conclusion that there is practically no citizenship in Mexico. In fact, it is possible to declare in advance what this book documents: that, among other things, Mexico and similar nations suffer high levels of economic, social and cultural inequality, endemic violence and corruption, a poor rule of law and justice, high levels of economic free riding, low entrepreneurship, low levels of social mobility, and high costs of access to the middle class. All are a result of the high cost of access to quality education and healthcare, credit, utilities like electricity and telecommunications — and a large share of the economy being informal(7). At the same time, there is a strong elite, a more prosperous one than that in more productive nations, and that is not built through democratic or meritocratic means(8), coupled with low levels of social engagement, philanthropy and the development of civil society organizations(9).

This panorama is replicated throughout the world, particularly in those places where poverty and violence are endemic, both today and throughout history, so that topics such as the genesis and reproduction of violence, authoritarianism, and extreme inequality have caught the attention of countless authors who have developed their own ideas to clarify what seems to be a recipe. That recipe is not in writing, is not taught in universities, nor is it being disseminated as a legitimate ambition. And yet, it reappears with undue success in the hands of many, even an ignorant who with the help of some followers manages to find themselves in the position, even fortuitously, to put it into practice.

The paradox is that the main aspiration of Western civilization during the modern era revolved around the construction of societies of citizens, but the average configuration of today's world, according to the indicators of income, poverty, democracy, education and health, reveal the persistence of a social architecture that is more feudal than modern, and which allows the existence of masters, lackeys and serfs[1]. It does not contemplate the existence of citizens as a central and ubiquitous element of society.

Graph 1 uses *The Economist's* democracy index classification of types of regimes, and compares population, gross national product, and poverty for each type of system. The data shows that only ≈12% of the world's population lives in full democracies. Moreover, it is clear that full democracies hold a greater share of the world income, with 55% of the total, and practically have no people living in poverty, in other words, with an income of less than $2 a day (< 1%).

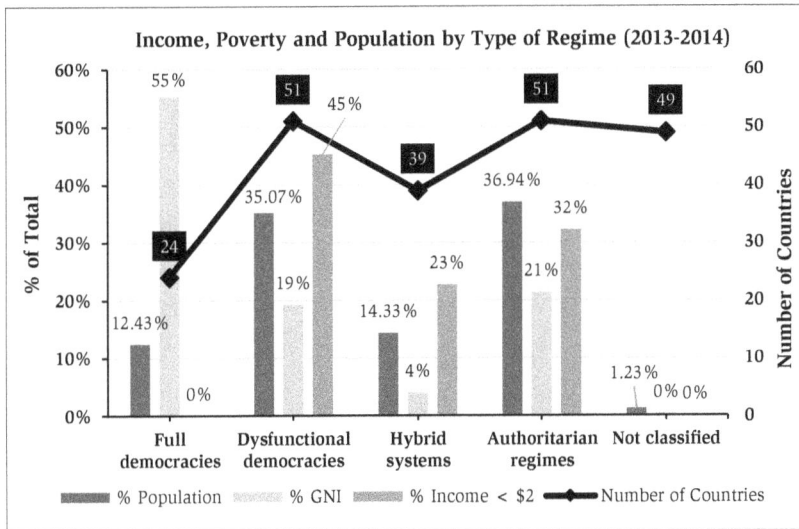

Graph 1: Population, Income and Poverty by Type of Regime. Sources: For population and income, the World Bank's data bank (2014), the democracy index is from *The Economist* (2014) and the data on poverty are published in Wikipedia (2014) and were collated with different sources.

---

1 In the Middle Ages, Masters, Lackeys and Serfs were well known and established social hierarchies and identities. The meaning of these identities within this work have a different hermeneutic root based on the Cultural Evolution Model. However, these terms are used to make a metaphorical connection between contemporary and medieval attitudes.

On the other hand, 45% of the rest of the world's income is divided unequally among ≈88% of the population. It stands out that well-established authoritarian systems restrain poverty better. With ≈37% of the world's population and 21% of the income, they hold 32% of people living in poverty. Dysfunctional democracies, with ≈35% of the world's population and 19% of income, hold 45% of the poor. The most serious situation is in hybrid systems that have ≈14% of the world's population, 4% of income and 23% of the poor. All combined, dysfunctional democracies, hybrid systems, and authoritarian regimes account for 99% of the poor, whose income is less than $2 a day.

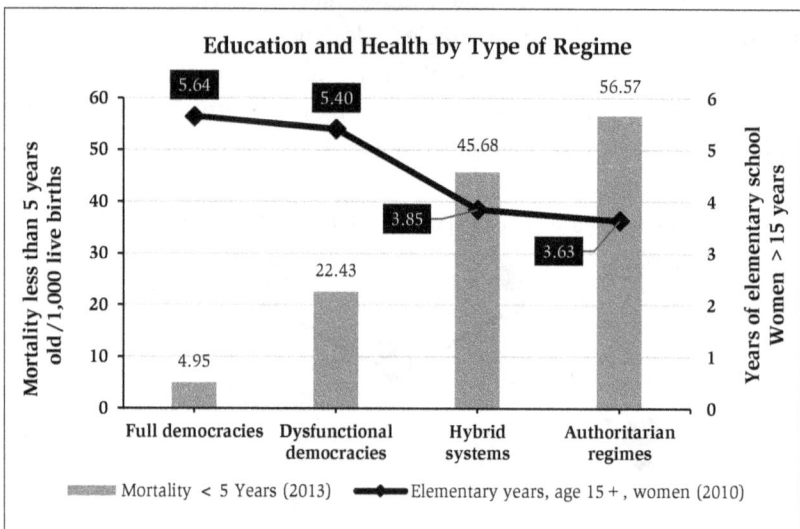

Graph 2: Education and Health by Type of Regime. Source: The World Bank's data bank (2014).

In the case of education and health, Graph 2 shows the indicator of deaths of children under five years old for every 1,000 live births, which is considered to be the base indicator to assess a country's general health, and the indicator of years of primary education in women over 15 years of age, which indicates women's general access to education, one of the main challenges for better education.

This shows once again that as far as health is concerned, full-fledged democracies are the systems with the best probabilities of survival of children under five years of age, but the mortality rate rises by 450% when they live in a dysfunctional democracy, by 922% in hybrid systems, and by 1,100% in authoritarian systems. Conversely, in education, both full-fledged democracies as well as dysfunctional ones provide better educational opportunities for women, since the number of years of primary education for women in those systems is more than five years. This is both the number required to achieve the universal primary level and a necessary condition for educational continuity. The hybrid and authoritarian systems still show that women's average education is less than four years.

Graph 3 is included to complement this information. It illustrates the income level and type of system that corresponds to every country with its name label. Graph 4 shows the same distribution, but without labels. In the upper part you can observe a U-shaped distribution and a high scattering of dots on the graph's left side (authoritarianism) that starts to diminish as you move towards the right side of the plot (democracy).

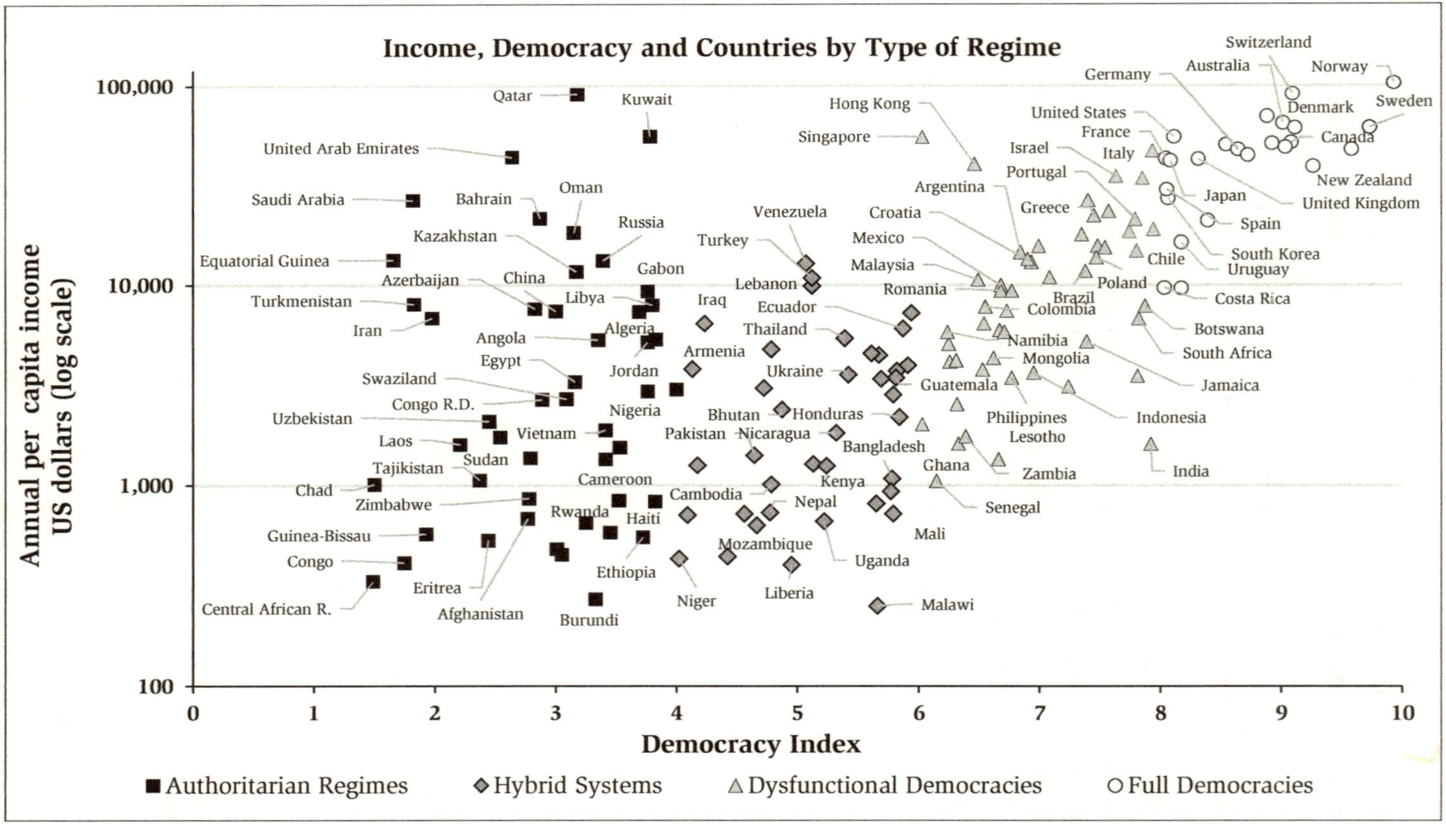

Graph 3: Income, Democracy and Countries by Type of System. Source: *The Economist's* Democracy Index, Income from the World Bank.

Income, Democracy and Countries by Type of Regime

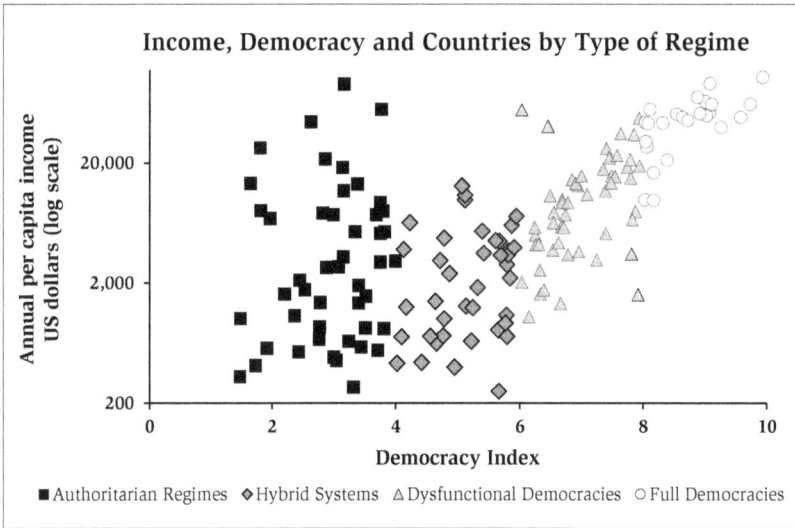

Graph 4: Income, Democracy and Countries by Type of System (without labels).

Given that the authoritarian-democratic division is the point of departure for this analysis, it is worthwhile to note that in the literature many are the authors who, having analyzed data sets like those presented in Graph 1 and Graph 2, also chose to classify nations into democratic and authoritarian ones. The classic example of this type of division is that of Karl Popper, who in 1945 explained this difference in two volumes entitled *The Open Society and its Enemies*. A more recent work that validates this approach is that of Douglass C. North and his colleagues. In *Limited Access Orders in the Developing World: A New Approach to the Problems of Development*(10), they define the division of the democratic-authoritarian world as Limited Access Orders (LAO) that are connected to the authoritarian systems, and Open Access Orders (OAO) that are related to democratic models.

For those of us who are interested in clarifying these topics, it is evident that the traditional approach is already neither productive nor viable. Any category, such as economic inequality or rule of law, becomes a body of knowledge so large and complex that some philosophers have decided to call those problems hyperobjects(11), issues that are too difficult to work with individually and become impossible and elusive when we try to study them in an aggregate manner. Nonetheless, while it became exponentially harder to understand the ever-growing complexity of human society, new and promising scientific and methodological approaches have been developed. One of them is *Complexity Science*(12), a discipline that makes it easier to find and describe the inner workings of complex systems such as the ones that emerge from social interaction in our vast and diverse human community.

2. Complex systems

What are complex adaptive systems?

S ystems, understood as a set of components that relate and interact among themselves and produce new things called results, can be classified in two broad categories: deterministic linear systems and complex adaptive systems.

- **Deterministic linear systems.**
  These systems are made from components and rules. The interaction among components in these types of systems takes place through fixed and linear rules. For example, machines are deterministic systems because the interaction between gears, pulleys, and mechanisms is fixed. Every time the switch is turned on, it allows the system to operate in a predetermined mode. If an engine drives the machine, the relationship between the speed of the engine and the speed of the system is linear and predictable. If the engine runs slowly, the system, too, will run at a low speed, and if the engine runs a bit faster, the system's speed will increase.

  If these systems are very large with thousands of components and rules, they are called complicated systems. In both cases of the simple or complicated linear systems, the components and the rules are hierarchically equal. For example, components of a car such as the steering wheel and wheels are as important as the mechanical coupling rule that connects them, known as the steering mechanism. The lack of any of these elements, including the connection rule, causes the system to fail; in short, the car breaks down.

  The interaction rules are driven by simple algorithms or formulas that prevent components from operating beyond what is defined by the rules. In the car example, the wheels turn left or right according to the mechanical coupling rule; there is no possibility for something different to happen. This condition is fundamental because it determines that the complicated systems' operations are reliable and predictable; when the driver turns the steering wheel to the left, the wheels turn in that direction, and when the driver steps on the gas pedal, the car also speeds up. Any other type of behavior would convert the car into an impractical artifact, a chaotic system.

- **Complex adaptive systems.**

  These systems consist of diverse and autonomous components, or so-called agents, whose configuration evolves in an emergent fashion based on a set of simple interaction rules and the systems' initial operating conditions. Unlike the deterministic linear systems, changes in the interaction rules have a greater effect on the systems' behavior. They are hierarchically more important than changes made to the components or agents. An ant colony, for example, does not cease to work when some of them die, even if it's the queen, but it can stop working entirely if one interaction rule changes, as it would happen, if the ants lose the instinct to care and feed the larvae.

  Another difference with deterministic linear systems is that the interaction rules give agents degrees of freedom, meaning that they allow agents to have an autonomous response. Thus, the agents' behaviors can adapt to changes in the systems' environmental and operational conditions, which leads the system to develop behaviors and properties not predetermined within the interaction rules. This process is known as emergence. A type of an adaptive behavior is a beehive's ability to search and feed from a varied array of flowering species as the seasons change. An example of emergence is the similar vascular or tree-like patterns made by water effluents all around the planet without the existence of a construction entity that determines the form's similarity. This means that to learn how a complex system works, we must first know the initial operating conditions, and particularly, the interaction rules that the agents follow among themselves and in relation to the environment where they develop.

Some problems solved with the complex systems theory are the whimsical movement patterns created by animals that live in groups, such as the ones made by flocks of birds and schools of fish. For decades, there was an effort to explain these phenomena through complicated models founded on collective action and coordination theories. That turned out to be unfeasible due to the high level of intelligence the animals would require to reproduce the workings of those models. But thanks to complexity science, whose work is to find and understand the simple interaction rules that define each complex system such as what each bird and each fish does when they move as a group, it was possible to explain the emergence of these phenomena through an agent-based model made by a simple set of rules and behaviors(13).

Likewise, in the case of persistence, emergence, and the reproduction of authoritarianism, what stands out is that the autonomous interaction of millions of people and human groups in different nations, eras, and social and cultural systems, have created similar authoritarian config-urations across the world. This signals the possible existence of simple interaction rules (a recipe) that, when used time after time, produce the similar authoritarian results that are observed around the world. Accord-ing to complexity scientists, the repetition of the phenomenon points to the existence of an initial default state, a situation also identified by Douglass North regarding the abundance and persistence of limited ac-cess orders [LAO](10).

This logic is contrary to the top-down historical explanations that give all the weight to the genius (or malice) of the great orchestrators of so-cial changes — the theories of the madman or the solitary hero — and reinforces the idea that the bottom-up emergent social construction is more influential than was previously thought. In the complex systems model, the emergence phenomenon indicates that authoritarianism or democracy are largely built from the bottom-up, and this points towards various questions, such as: Does the leader make the group or does the group make the leader? What happens with the leader who transgress-es the group's interaction rules? Does the leader's way of being reflect the personality of the group members? and What responsibilities do the group members have regarding the leader's actions?

To answer to these and other questions from the approach of com-plex adaptive systems, first, it is necessary to identify the components or agents, and then the interaction rules that define the system. Since the objective of our study is human society, identifying the agents is not a problem; they are all the human beings that are part of society and act within it. Conversely, discovering or identifying a set of interaction rules — be they few, elemental, and simple and that contemplate the development of the adaptation and emergence phenomena in the sys-tem, and ultimately explain the current configuration of authoritarianism or democracy — is a task that requires starting with a discussion of the traditional method's limits within which the foundations of the social sciences took shape.

The problem of social sciences

The paradox of social sciences is that when we investigate and delve into the subject of interest, we are simultaneously judging what we are a part of, which makes it impossible to observe without bias. Nonetheless, it, too, is — and will be — impossible for us to abandon the effort to understand ourselves. It is intrinsic to our condition of owning a self-aware consciousness that nourishes an insatiable curiosity.

The effort that was made to tackle this problem, being part of the object of study itself, is the use of rational and evidence-based methodologies in the social sciences. But the proliferation of different theories — philosophical, behavioral, historical, economic, and sociological analysis — shows us that, contrary to the hard sciences, the ever-increasing schools of thought for understanding people and society does not help us to see beyond our prejudices. Moreover, they prevent us from developing sound social knowledge.

It's likely that this situation, which seems impossible to resolve, will improve if we pay attention to the part of the research process in which, and despite the scientific method, it has been permissible for researchers to bring their biases into the social inquiry. I am referring to the moment prior to identifying a problem or formulating the research question when we make the first taxonomic organization of a phenomenon. These are the "eureka" moments when researchers realize intuitively that a social matter can be separated into different components such as rich and poor, capitalists and workers, innovators and investors, rural inhabitants and urban ones, and that conclude with the definition of taxonomies with which we build the analytical approach that circumscribes and limits the explicative capabilities of any research effort.

The decomposition of reality in taxonomic structures is one of the ways in which the human mind works. An example of this is the perception of color. Since ancient times, there has been an ongoing debate questioning whether the colors each one perceives are the same. The strange concept here is that there is no way to know because, through physics, we have learned that colors don't exist in nature. There is no such thing as red, yellow, or blue because there is no physical property that determines that the electromagnetic radiation with a wave length of 570-590 nanometers (nm) should be perceived as "yellow." Therefore, the decomposition of the visual information in discreet or taxonomic categories like the colors that we all say we see is an artificial and idiosyncratic construction generated by the neuroplasticity of the human mind(14). Perceptual science that explores phenomena such as color perception is starting to provide us with new clues about the mechanisms for acquiring and processing information in the human brain. Thus, we can say that human cognition has the native and subconscious capacity to group information with similar characteristics — perceived by the senses — in discreet categories and patterns. From this ability to classify emerges the idiosyncratic taxonomies or models that facilitate the interpretation of reality.

This cognitive process, that in principle is an evolutionary advantage, allows us to include biases, in a regular and subtle fashion, as a stage prior to the formulation of the research questions. Consequently, it skews the results according to the idiosyncratic characteristics of each researcher. Therefore, we have many and contradictory theories to explain the same phenomena in the social sciences.

When building taxonomies, such as the classification of proletarians and capitalists, the information we obtain is filtered and analyzed under the light of each model. The quality of our decisions and actions depend on the quality of the model and the prejudices we use to filter and interpret the information we obtain from reality. As the popular phrase says, "He who only has a hammer will begin to look at everything like a nail." Hence, we must find new and better ways to build foundational taxonomies for those disciplines aimed at learning about society and the human being.

Social sciences and philosophical fiction

Perceptual science affirms that, essentially, there is a difference between reality as we perceive it and reality such as it is. We fail to perceive reality in its entirety because nature must optimize between the cost of perceiving a larger measure of reality and the evolutionary advantages derived thereof. For example, a visual system capable of perceiving infrared, visible, and ultraviolet light would entail having visual processing centers that would alter the size and anatomy of the brain and head, and such changes would affect the entire anatomy of the human body.

This leads us to wonder if by having a limited perception of reality, do we only see a fraction of reality such as it is, or do we see an interpretation of reality as we need it to be to survive? Based on the latest evolutionary research(15), perceived reality, in all cases, is optimized and adjusted to achieve evolutionary fitness, not a factual reconstruction of reality or a part of it.

Consequently, if our perception of reality is limited and filtered to achieve evolutionary fitness and through this perceived reality, we come to understand, imagine, and construe the interpretation of the world, is all that we are able imagine part of a reality that we cannot perceive, or, whatever the reality, is it possible for us to imagine things beyond it? The answer to this question lies at the heart of the philosophy of science: yes, it is possible to think and imagine things beyond reality, which can be easily demonstrated.

Figure 1 illustrates a Penrose's impossible stairs diagram, made popular by Maurits Cornelis Escher (1898-1972), in his famous *Ascending and Descending* illustration, in which the celebrated graphic artist drew an unreal circuit of descending staircases that always lead back to the starting point. In this case, the artist imagined and designed something that misleads us and goes beyond possible reality. The same thing happens with countless artistic endeavors that are impossible to create.

Figure 1: Penrose impossible stairs.

With this third assumption, it is possible to state that even if we have a perception of reality that is conditioned and mediated by evolutionary pressure, we also can imagine things beyond reality. From an evolutionary standpoint, that gives us the power to break through the barrier of perceived reality, though the very same ability deceives us and makes it hard for us to separate possible reality from fantasy. That is perhaps why our foothold — possibly the only one where our mind somehow meets reality — is the part of scientific knowledge that lets us clearly know and differentiate when it is that we are trying to broaden our perception through art and when we are using scientific laws that conform to reality (Figure 2). In fact, this boundary is nothing new or unusual; it is clearly established in realms as diverse as theology and cosmology. Both disciplines focus on providing an answer to the same questions: What is the origin of the universe? How was it created? Is it finite? But theology continues to be open to any kind of imaginable response (*mythos*: combination of fantasy and reality) while cosmology remains circumscribed to the answers that may be construed on mathematics and the laws of physics (*logos*).

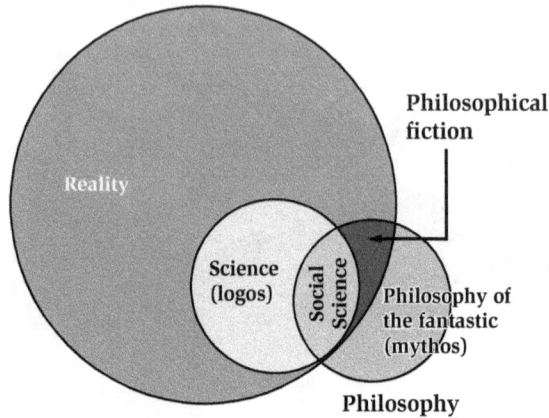

Figure 2: Reality, science, and philosophy.

Within the disciplines that comprise modern social science, the separation between science and art remains unresolved since we still haven't found the tools that explain the emergence and evolution of human culture based on hard scientific facts. However, it is possible to separate the art of philosophical fiction and the philosophy of the fantastic from what, strictly speaking, formal social science should be, by circumscribing social sciences within the boundaries of thermodynamics, evolutionary theory, and information theory. In fact, these are the boundary conditions of complexity science. Furthermore, an unexpected byproduct of this approach is that it is neither necessary nor desirable to integrate or subordinate science and art for there are communicating vessels that allow art to inspire science ('eureka' moments) and new scientific knowledge to motivate art.

As soon as the human mind managed to break free from the constriction of the senses and the literal interpretation of perceived reality, a new door was opened and allowed us to capture a set of new possible futures. Given that it progressively became feasible to occupy a larger portion of reality than what we could originally imagine, such as the notion that human flight was achievable. To attain this, we followed two paths. And here lies the most interesting part of our self-aware consciousness. First, through art and *mythos*, the exploration and interpretation of the world was unlocked. As an example, since antiquity we´ve had mythical tales of flight such as the Daedalus and Icarus fable, where people explored the desire and longing of human beings to fly like birds. Through millennia, those tales kept alive the idea of human flight.

Second, through trial and error, reason and *logos*, we came to identify and understand some of the boundaries of reality, which we organized, systematized and turned into science and new technologies. The Wright brothers, frustrated by the lack of progress in building an airplane, questioned Otto Lilienthal's aerodynamic data. They built their own wind tunnel; carried out thousands of experiments; deciphered the principles of aerodynamic thrust, and designed the first functional airplane wings, which led to the development of the first airplane in history(16). To supplement this example, one only must look at the large number of instruments and sensors through which we have expanded our perception and interaction with reality: electron microscopes, particle accelerators, space telescopes, X-ray and magnetic resonance equipment, radio telescopes, radars and sonars. These make that which lies beyond our senses visible and translate different phenomena to render them accessible to our limited sensory and perceptive capabilities.

Insofar as we currently understand reality's boundaries such as the second law of thermodynamics, there are no more meaningful and adequately funded projects attempting to build perpetual motion machines. Nevertheless, any patent office can confirm that every year thousands of people continue trying to register this type of devices as they persist in the *mythos* and artistic imagination of many individuals, even though they cannot exist in the reality of physical laws. The concrete boundary imposed by reality in creating perpetual motion and the awareness of this absolute, thanks to scientific endeavors, lets us know, for example, that investing in finding new ways to build better gas turbines to generate electricity is indeed useful. Hence, distinguishing between fantasy and reality helps us invest society's time and resources in productive concerns or in making attainable dreams come true, such as flying like the birds.

Just as patent offices have come to reject, *a priori*, any requests to register perpetual motion machines, the time has come to unshackle traditional philosophy from the restrictions that attempt to turn it into a pseudoscience, so that it may develop as the art of philosophical fiction (Daedalus and Icarus) and the philosophy of the fantastic (perpetual motion), which may or may not lead to new ideas or pathways to help us discover unidentified aspects of reality. Just as when cosmology broke away from theology, it is high time to approach social sciences' boundaries, precepts, and procedures in a rigorous and demanding manner at their most fundamental level.

Other scholars have already forewarned us about fragmentation and deficiencies of the epistemological framework of social sciences. Shiping Tang's(17) analysis indicates that it is possible to organize the various schools of social sciences into eleven foundational paradigms, in turn subdivided into two categories. The first one comprises nine bedrock paradigms stemming from intuitive assumptions developed through the art of traditional philosophy, in which Tang fails to identify a common denominator or articulating guiding principle (Table 1). The second one entails two possible integrative paradigms, whose main function is turning the first category into an organic whole.

The proposed integrative paradigms are the Social System Paradigm (SSP) and the Social Evolution Paradigm (SEP). According to Tang, SEP is the "...most interesting, the ultimate or definitive..." paradigm. He establishes three guiding principles for its development: 1) Human society may be studied in a productive manner from an evolutionary approach; 2) The application of evolutionary thought is not just metaphorical or biological; and 3) The mechanisms to explain social change are the artificial selection of variation, selection, and heredity, which may be interpreted as the agent's volitional or self-guided behavior.

	First Dimension: Material vs. Ideational	Second Dimension: Individual vs. Collective	Third Dimension: Human nature as Drivers of Behavior, Three Levels	Fourth Dimension: Harmony vs. Conflict
Paradigms with less ontological priority	Ideationalism	Collectivism	Antisocialization Socialization	The harmony paradigm
Paradigms with ontological priority	Materialism	Individualism	Deterministic biological evolution	The conflict paradigm

Table 1: The nine bedrock paradigms of social sciences according to Tang.

As part of the analysis of foundational paradigms of social sciences, Tang also compares the imprint of the main sociological schools against the eleven foundational paradigms, (Table 2) and thus illustrates more clearly the analytical deficiencies of the main tenets of social thought.

	Functionalism	Marxism	Weberianism
Materialism vs. Ideationalism	Mostly ideationalism	More on materialism, but also emphasizing class consciousness, ideology	Both, but more on ideationalism, emphasizing ideology, legitimation and rationalization
Individualism vs. collectivism	Collectivism (i.e., society as organism)	Collectivism (i.e., class as the basic agent)	Both
Human nature: A) Biological evolution B) Socialization C) Anti-socialization	Only socialization	Mostly anti-socialization (e.g., alienation, contradiction, conflict); implicitly admitting biological evolution	Both socialization and anti-socialization; implicitly admitting biological evolution
Conflict vs. Harmony	Mostly harmony	Mostly conflict, but harmony within classes	Mostly conflict, although harmony also exists
SSP: How systemic	Very limited because it ignores too many bedrock paradigms	Quite limited because it too ignores many bedrock paradigms	The best among the three because it contains most bedrock paradigms
SEP: How evolutionary	Antievolutionary: the system cannot be changed	Quasi-evolutionary: conflict drives changes	Quasi-evolutionary: conflict drives changes

Table 2: Imprint of the schools of sociology versus the bedrock paradigms of the social sciences.

Therefore, the cultural evolution model I propose coincides with Tang's two main conclusions: 1) The fragmentation of the epistemological framework of social sciences, and 2) The need to address the problem through a paradigm such as the social evolution paradigm (SEP). So, only by increasing our social knowledge within the sphere of tangible reality will we be able to focus our efforts in a productive manner.

Cultural evolution

To escape the problem of epistemological biases in social sciences, it is of the utmost importance to find a way in which we can create foundational categories and taxonomies that are linked somehow to reality's hard data. There are three scientific references that are suitable to build more up-to-date and formal social taxonomies. For many years, these have been used by biologists and ethologists in the comprehensive study of animal species except the human one.

It is important to underscore the notion of comprehensiveness currently employed in these fields of knowledge. Just as veterinarians make fun of the fact that physicians are just veterinarians that tend to a single animal species, biologists and ethologists may well say that social scientists — economists, sociologists, psychologists, and demographers — are the only ones (biologists and ethologists) that study a limited and disconnected aspect of the animal species that concerns us. Therefore, applying the systemic and integrating capacity of complexity science in social sciences is essential.

The scientific references used as a framework to formulate research models in biology and ethology include:

1. **The laws of thermodynamics.** First presented by William Rankine, Rudolf Clausius, and William Thomson (Lord Kelvin) in the 1850s, these laws study heat and energy variables and their relationship to work. They define macroscopic variables, such as internal energy, entropy, and pressure, and establish that their behavior is subject to restrictions(18). All systems that consume energy and generate work (value or results) — from the metabolism of bacteria to the behavior of galaxies — are governed and limited by these laws.

    At present, a substantial part of biological research encompasses thermodynamic exchanges between organisms. For example, calories produced versus calories consumed, trophic chains, anatomical and physiological characteristics, heat dissipation in organisms, and load capacity of ecosystems. Complexity science uses thermodynamics as the main restriction benchmark in the systems it studies. Currently, converting energy into results and the difficulties associated with the earth's energy flow are at the heart of crucial economic, ecological, and social problems such as climate change, economic development, and social and political instability in the Middle East.

2. **The laws of biological evolution.** Since *The Origin of Species*(19) was published more than 150 years ago, the theory of evolution has been the most significant scientific reference in biological science. It has been validated by vast empirical and scientific evidence throughout the years. All the issues and concerns of biological science derive from and are related to the laws of biological evolution. Therefore, we need to learn more about the relationship between biological evolution rules and human social behavior.

    Charles Darwin's genius resides in the fact that, from its inception, the theory was formulated on a basis that, we can say today, perfectly conforms to the approach of complex systems: few interaction rules, exemplified in the description of random mutations and the survival of the fittest individuals, and room for the emergence of the properties that are not explicitly defined by the interaction rules, such as the autonomous evolution of species and the diversity of behaviors such species, including humans, manifest in nature.

3. **Information theory.** This is the branch of applied mathematics devoted to the discovery and exploration of the laws that govern the behavior of information. It has applications and overlaps with several branches of science such as biology, genetics, physics, neurology, and cryptography(20). In the field of biological science, information theory became essential for the advancement of molecular biology, genetics, and the study of communication and signaling systems of social animals. It also enabled the development of artificial life forms(21).

Addressing social sciences through complexity science charts a totally different course if we consider that social disciplines such as economics were founded by pioneers like Adam Smith and David Ricardo based on the epistemology of Newtonian or deterministic linear systems. Ever since the 18th century, we have been — and still are — searching for static and linear cause-and-effect relationships to achieve equilibrium (i.e., incentive-based or reward and punishment systems). This, together with the previously analyzed problem of cognitive prejudice in modeling the principles of social sciences, represents one of the main obstacles that render them useless.

In fact, Adam Smith found it hard to explain the evolving and emergent nature of social systems based on the Newtonian approach. In *The Wealth of Nations* (1776), Smith acknowledged the evolution and emergence of market configuration in metaphysical terms through the existence of an "invisible hand" that maximizes benefits when agents pursue their own interests in the market: "...he intends only his own gain, and he is in this, as in many other cases, led by an invisible hand to promote an end which was no part of his intention...".

In epistemological terms, this was one of the most important turning points in the history of economic thought. Despite Smith's intuition regarding the market's evolutionary complexity, at that point in history and in methodological terms, he had no way of going beyond deterministic systems. In his time, the most solid ideas for a systemic approach were Newton's laws of motion, formulated during the 1690s, while Darwin's ideas on evolutionary systems surfaced only in 1859, that is, 83 years after Smith's work was published. This temporal accident in the emergence of economics as a discipline came when the Newtonian worldview was already consolidated. But the possibility of observing society from the standpoint of evolutionary thought was still far away. Still, Smith's work allowed for the linear and deterministic vision and ambition of social sciences to solidify over almost a century from 1776 to 1859. It was impossible to backtrack and, as no further explanation was given to Smith's "invisible hand," economists adopted it as a persistent metaphysical entity. The important point is that currently and bolstered by complexity science, it is possible to revisit the origin of economics and clearly understand that said "invisible hand" refers to the market's emerging and evolving configuration. Smith's representation of competition and self-interest is just one of the configurations that social systems can acquire, given the interaction rules that define it.

To illustrate the problem of studying society within the framework of linear systems and the opportunities awarded by complex systems, one only must imagine what contemporary biology would be like without the adaptive approach contributed by Charles Darwin. Imagine for a moment that biology was founded based on deterministic linear systems. If that were the case, today we would have countless biological theories attempting to explain the emerging, diverse, and shifting properties of living beings through linear relationships. It would be easy for bird specialists to have a general theory on life based on the physical characteristics of the beaks of toucans and cranes, which would fail to relate to other discoveries such as DNA chains and

microbiology. Nothing would fit together. There would be no first principles on which to incorporate every new discovery to help improve
the scientific understanding of reality. Fortunately, the framework on
which evolutionary theory was formulated (nomothetic approach) has
already proven its robustness over one and a half centuries, so much
so that the daily discoveries made in molecular biology and genomics supplement and validate it. Meanwhile, the desire to explain human complexity through specific case studies and deterministic linear
models (idiographic model) only contribute to a continuing and vast
intellectual confusion.

The proposed approach to link the study of human culture to natural
laws through social sciences is nothing new. Its first occurrence in modern
times in a serious and conceptually supported way, was the postulation
of the cultural evolution idea by Pierre Teilhard de Chardin, a Jesuit priest
and naturalist, in his posthumous work *The Phenomenon of Man*(22).
Sadly, his statement was limited and lacked subsequent development
due to the absence of progress in information theory.

Without delving deeper into Teilhard's hermeneutics, the idea behind
cultural evolution is that human culture is an additional manifestation
of biological evolution, which is subject to evolutionary rules such as
reproduction, heredity, and adaptation. The latter occurs faster in culture than in genes and, just as in biological evolution, includes energy,
information, complexity, and entropy exchanges.

My introduction to this complex, dry, and abstract corner of science
can be traced to a practical need. In 2009, I joined the climate change
global negotiations in the United Nations (UN) in my capacity as representative of Mexico's Energy Ministry. At that time, the climate change
summit, scheduled for the end of that year in Copenhagen, was expected
to achieve a far-reaching international agreement. Members of a small
group of individuals and specialists (including myself) scattered around
the globe, were under pressure from their respective governments to formulate public policy proposals that could lead to produce a substantial
change in humankinds' future. The planning horizon imposed on us was
the year 2050. Evidently, the magnitude of the assigned task completely
surpassed any existing public policy, economic analysis, and even ethical or philosophical framework, since the ramifications of an agreement
to decarbonize the global economy are so vast and complex that even
today we are unable to fathom them.

The outcome of this hopeless quest to find solutions to "save the world" was the discovery that existing social science and public policy tools were downright obsolete for this purpose. Even when the idea of stopping pollution seems to be a simple matter of reaching an agreement, the absence of a way to implement any of the agreed-to solutions thwarted our efforts. In addition to the prejudice and behavior of the representatives of the nations of the world, civil society organizations and big business made it very clear, even before the summit, that the endeavor would fail to reach a final solution as it has failed to do so for more than 20 years and continues to do so to date. The solution of the problem entails abandoning the established policy and discussion frameworks to discover and accept that the taxonomy employed to discuss this problem — based on the concepts of mitigation, adaptation, finance, and technology — has kept us from looking beyond what our eyes and mind allow us to currently grasp about a complex and fast-changing reality.

The climate change summit was held in December 2009. Negotiations failed miserably. The last conversation I had in Copenhagen took place in the early morning of the last day and involved a crest-fallen and respected architect of the negotiation process. He had devoted most of his professional life to reach this moment and for months had sworn that it was all a diplomatic game of "chicken" that would be resolved at the end at a table around which the masters of the world would sit to amend the situation. After the summit failed, and the table of the masters of the world had adjourned, and Barack Obama and Hilary Clinton had abandoned the conference center, this man, slouching over the handrail of a staircase, simply said, "...I really don't understand; this was a beautiful baby that we had nurtured for years and then, after such a long time, it turned out to be a horrible adult...."

From that moment on, I was convinced to dig deeper and do research on these topics to better understand the forces and variables that shape our perception of the world and which support the way in which our actions are modeled. This effort was supported and encouraged by two prominent scholars from Duke University in North Carolina in the United States of America and Toulouse in France: Adrian Bejan and Sylvie Lorente, who work with complexity science in the field of engineering and have used it to formulate a theory that contributed to the design and optimization of complex thermodynamic systems. This theory, known as the Constructal Law(23), states that:

> *For a finite-size flow system to persist in time (to survive), its configuration must evolve in such a way that it provides easier access to the currents that flow through it.*

and

> *All systems are destined to remain imperfect (with restrictions); therefore, the system's design must be based on the homogeneous distribution of the restriction.*

The findings of my research were published in an international article that was peer-reviewed in 2011 after having been presented at an international conference held in the city of Pisa, Italy. This work, titled "Cultural Evolution, Design and Philosophy: For the Change of Era"(24), constitutes the conceptual bedrock of this book; thus, its main elements are summarized below.

Cultural evolution model summary

In life sciences, the use of thermodynamics, evolutionary theory, and information theory as the framework to develop new knowledge is customary and compulsory. This boils down to the fact that any new discovery must agree with these foundational paradigms of science. Hence, even if the discoveries and developments that define the cultural evolution model, are well established, it is necessary to take yet another step toward some knowledge integration and interpretation to understand the evolutionary survival strategies available to living beings. The foregoing is always in accordance with the three bedrock paradigms of biology.

By combining thermodynamic restrictions, biological evolutionary laws, and information theory, one may say that the evolutionary strategies of living beings shift according to two directives:

1. Despite being circumscribed to universal laws and physical restrictions, life uses everything within its reach to endure through time. This is achieved through survival instinct, reproduction, and heredity.

2. Life works through changes in its complexity levels to widen its possibilities of information exchange or order accumulation (negentropy).

As greater complexity entails risk and requires larger amounts of energy, either due to a population increase or to an increase in the complexity of living beings and their interactions, at the limit, life will achieve as much order as the available energy and entropy level of the universe will allow. Therefore, despite the irrevocable calling to survive and expand, the speed at which life adapts to generate as much order as possible will vary and change its complexity levels over time.

On the other hand, dependence on the environment and changes in its carrying capacity, generate exchanges or trade-offs between Directive One, survival over everything else, and against Directive Two, searching for new opportunities to increase order or negentropy. This dependence prevents the speed at which life expands in the environment from being constant, since whenever the restriction level of the environment changes, it is necessary to change the strategy through adaptation to achieve, above all, permanence over time. When facing more restrictive environments, surviving is more important than increasing the ability to generate negentropy, although the changes in the capacities of living beings, like creating new metabolic strategies, many times allow the living beings that take on the risk of creating a new strategy during difficult times, to prevail over long-standing environmental restrictions.

Thus, the two interaction forces, vectors or rules that impact the phenomenon of life in terms of survival strategies include:

1. The complexity or negentropic capacity of living beings (Table 3); and
2. The response to restriction (scarcity/abundance) of the environment (Table 4).

Schematically, the model's possible configurations or strategies based on these two vectors are shown in Figure 3:

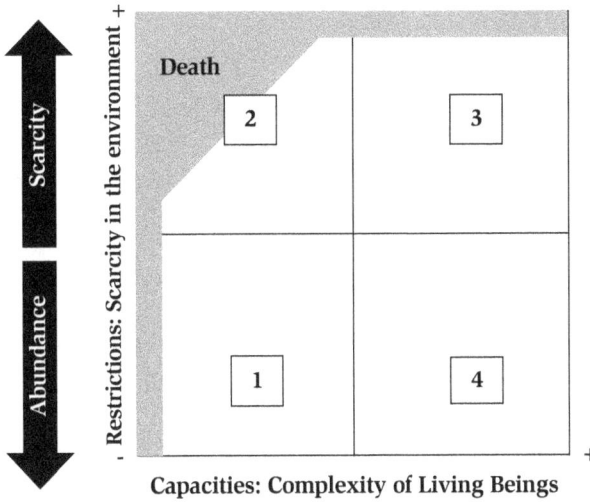

Figure 3: Schematic representation of the cultural evolution model.

Vertical and horizontal cut lines in the diagram (Figure 3) are defined in Table 3 & Table 4:

← Vertical Cut →	
Submission (left): low complexity and capacity; environmental conditions overcome life's long-term evolutionary dynamics and the options are limited. Negentropy generation is low.	**Freedom (right):** high complexity and capacity; the long-term dynamic for order increase works unbounded by environmental conditions. Negentropy generation grows, as well as energy use and the entropy exchanged with the environment.

Table 3: Rule #1. Submission and Freedom.

↑ **Horizontal Cut** ↓	**Optimization (top):** there is little waste of energy and cooperation prevails over competition. The challenge imposed by the environment is more important than rivalry. Metabolism is optimized, and the efficiency levels used to incorporate energy to the life process are increased. There is a low rivalry level.
	Maximization (bottom): energy use is maximized, and competition prevails over cooperation. Evolutionary competition is more important than the environment's challenge. Efficiency is not important, but final metabolic throughput is. There is instability due to environmental factors and/or because of a high degree of rivalry.

Table 4: Rule #2. Optimization and maximization.

By combining the characteristics of each quadrant, it is possible to define four survival strategies:

	Low complexity	High complexity
High restriction	Submission + Optimization = **2. Survival**	Freedom + Optimization = **3. Transformation**
Low restriction	Submission + Maximization = **1. Status quo**	Freedom + Maximization = **4. Growth**

Table 5: The four cultural evolution strategies.

The ecological niches held by living beings within the model are explained as follows (Figure 4):

1. **Autotrophs.** They populate the different restriction levels through species differentiation. Each species is a point. There is no locomotion or behavior, but the whole forms a negentropic capacity line (e.g., photosynthesis). They evolve through adaptation of physical features or "hardware." (1.1, 1.2 and 1.3 in Figure 4).

2. **Non-human Heterotrophs.** They acquire capacity so that each species populates a vertical line, and through locomotion, they generate a new adaptation strategy: migration, which means capacity to run away from danger, attack, and pursue pleasure (instinct). Species manage to settle on new capacity spaces by differentiating their energy strategy: herbivorous, carnivorous, and omnivorous. Behavior emerges and is always closely related to hardware, and consequently, species also evolve through adaptation of physical features. Locomotion accelerates their evolutionary competition. (2.1, 2.2 and 2.3 in Figure 4).

3. **Human Heterotrophs.** They abandon evolution through hardware and develop a new strategy for life: evolution through software (knowledge). They can choose any quadrant, be it through migration, aversion to pain, attraction to pleasure, or cultural development. They also can choose their behavior, which adds extra capacity mechanisms and information to the ones granted by genetic inheritance. They manage to change their resource usage pattern very fast through a new mechanism: cultural evolution(22) that is passed to their descendants through knowledge transmission (cultural reproduction), which means the accumulation of information and negentropy in culture (3.0 in Figure 4).

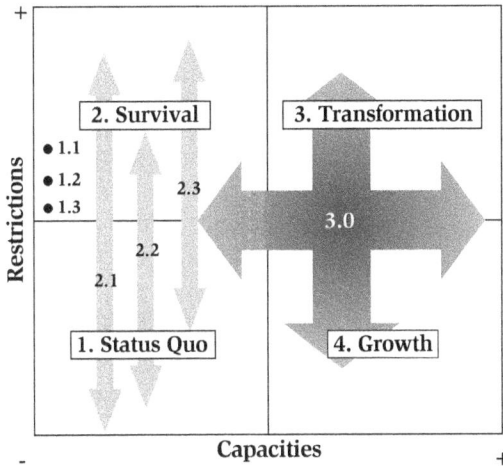

Figure 4: Ecological niches.

Having established the biological configuration possibilities that define the model's overall framework and the correlation between biological evolution and cultural evolution, the cultural evolution model may be summarized as follows:

1. Changes in the complexity level of societies, the efficiency with which they transform resources (i.e., energy into information [culture]) and the cooperation and competition relationships, allow us to classify human societies into groups that correspond to the four basic survival strategies: Status quo, survival, transformation and growth.

2. Human culture, from the perspective of economic transformation of resources such as energy, the generation of human development, the cooperation and competition conditions, the changes in the stages of information of societies and the restrictions to which all these phenomena are subjected, allow us to state that cultural evolution is comparable to biological evolution and both are part of the overall evolutionary phenomenon.

3. The model's theoretical classification is consistent with the empirical observations and concepts taken from reality. Graph 5 shows the semi-log relationship between the human development index and the use of energy by the world's nations.

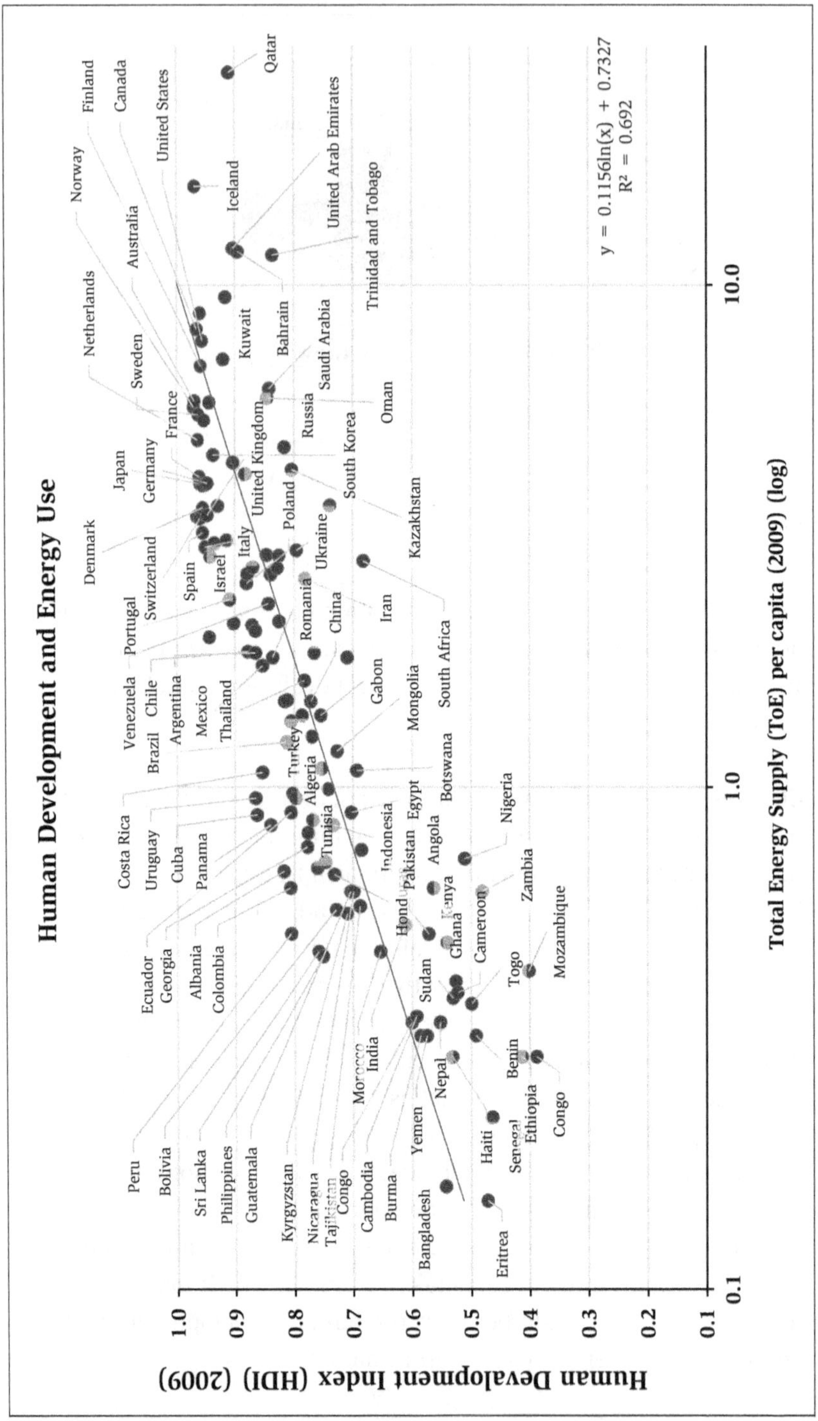

Graph 5: Semi-log relationship between total energy supply and human development index.

4. The long-term trend of human societies is toward greater complexity levels and resource consumption. Therefore, system efficiency and configuration changes are essential to attain higher degrees of efficiency that avoid crises and collapses, which is consistent with assumptions made by the Constructal Law. Graph 6 shows several years of the log/log relationship between patents produced per million inhabitants as a measure of cultural complexity and energy use as a measure of efficiency. The cloud of dots represents all values for the 1978-2007 period, except for South Korea, the best performer over past decades and which follows the regression model with an $R^2 = 0.98$, which is extremely high. The diachronic analysis (regarding a specific time period) for the selected countries represented in Graph 7 shows those countries with trajectories above the regression model. Labeled "Rest of the World" in Graph 6, they have low efficiency concerning utilization of resources. Those nations that are below it, or whose economies are too small, have oscillatory and regressive trajectories that indicate situations of crisis and/or collapse.

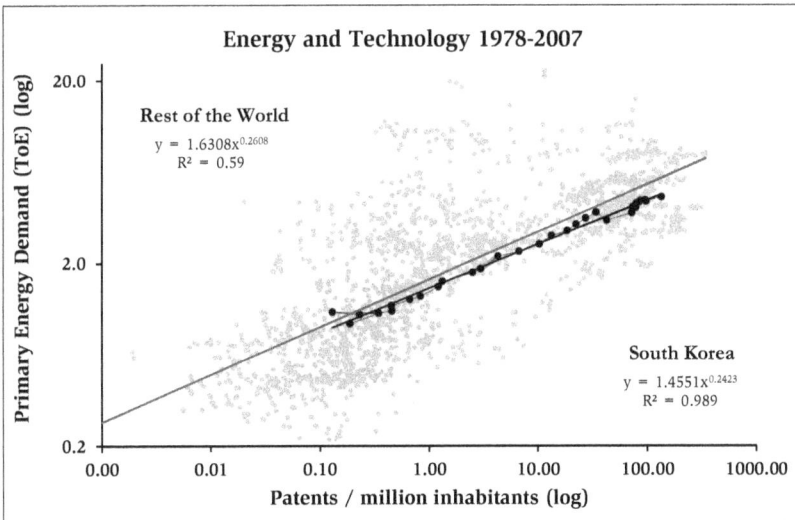

Energy and Technology 1978-2007

Rest of the World
$y = 1.6308x^{0.2608}$
$R^2 = 0.59$

South Korea
$y = 1.4551x^{0.2423}$
$R^2 = 0.989$

Primary Energy Demand (ToE) (log)

Patents / million inhabitants (log)

Graph 6: Log/log relationship between patents/million inhabitants (complexity) and energy use.

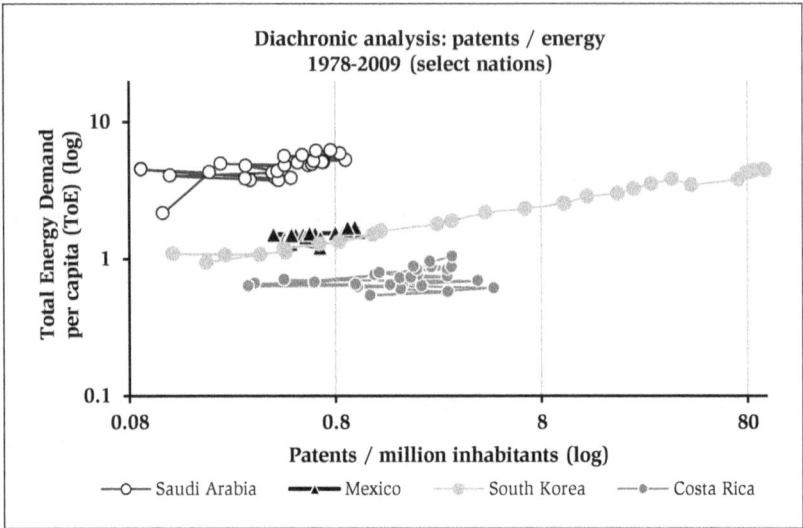

Graph 7: Diachronic analysis of the relationship between patent/energy use and GDP (bubble diameter) selected countries.

5.   Cultural evolution liberated human beings from instinctive deter-
     minism. Self-realized awareness allows them to choose and adopt
     any one of the four survival strategies, which may also be defined
     as their design philosophies. This illustrates the different ways in
     which human beings build and set the course of their own existence.
6.   Individuals and groups may be classified according to cultural
     complexity levels and resource transformation efficiency:

   i. **Complexity**
       a. **Low complexity.** Equals closed and authoritarian systems.
          They tend to resist change and greater freedom.
       b. **High complexity.** Equals open and free systems. They tend
          towards greater freedom.

These differences are compared in Figure 5:

- Ignorance, no logos
- Sickness
- Reduction time / life
- Less energy use
- Insecurity
- Being guilty
- Aversion to change & risk
- Closedness
- Limitations

- Knowledge, logos
- Health
- Increment time / life
- More energy use
- Security
- Being responsible
- Acceptance of change & risk
- Openness
- Aspirations

Capacities: Complexity

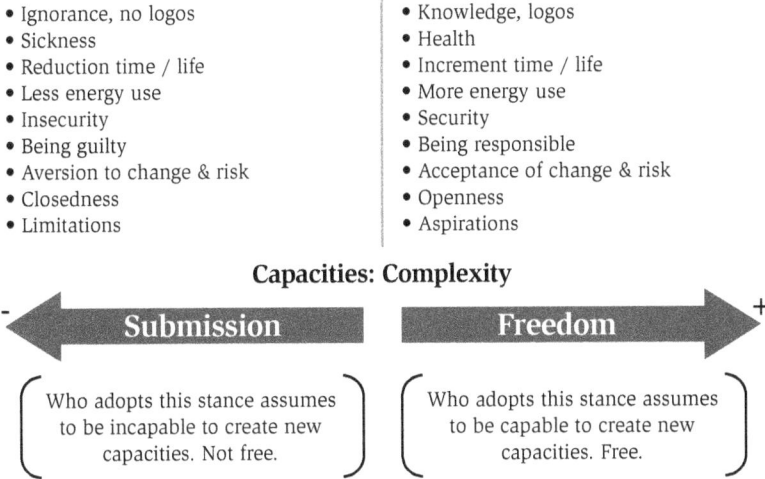

Who adopts this stance assumes to be incapable to create new capacities. Not free.

Who adopts this stance assumes to be capable to create new capacities. Free.

Figure 5: Closed vs. open systems.

ii. Efficiency

1. **Low efficiency**. Competitive systems that require abundant resources so as not to collapse.
2. **High efficiency**. Collaborative systems resilient to scarcity.

Similarly, these differences are compared in Figure 6:

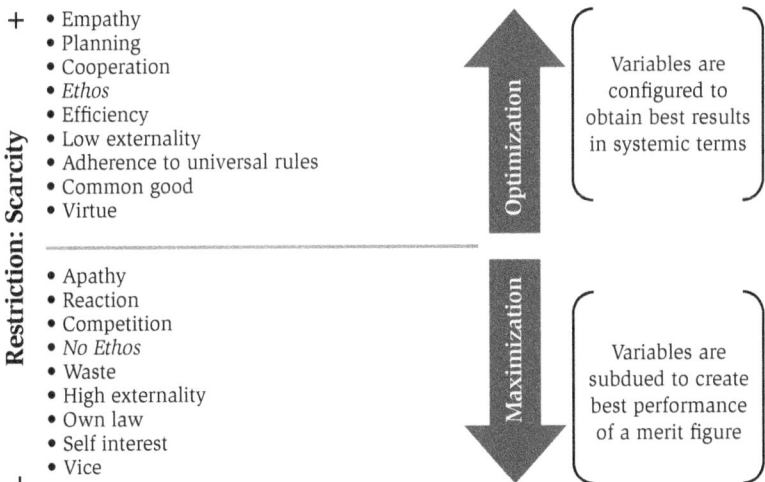

+
- Empathy
- Planning
- Cooperation
- *Ethos*
- Efficiency
- Low externality
- Adherence to universal rules
- Common good
- Virtue

- Apathy
- Reaction
- Competition
- *No Ethos*
- Waste
- High externality
- Own law
- Self interest
- Vice

Restriction: Scarcity

Optimization — Variables are configured to obtain best results in systemic terms

Maximization — Variables are subdued to create best performance of a merit figure

Figure 6: Collaboration vs. competition.

51

Considering the intersection of complexity and efficiency variables, the model's overall visual diagram is shown in Figure 7:

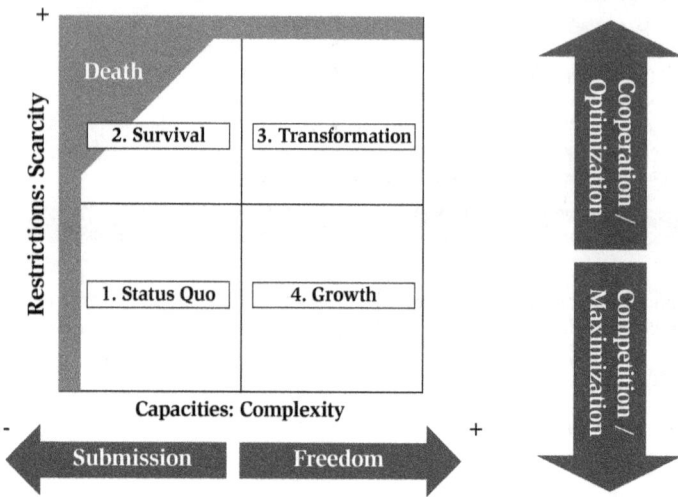

Figure 7: Overall scheme of the cultural evolution model.

In summary, complexity and efficiency categories define two interaction rules in the system, the combination of which generates the four survival strategies of cultural evolution:

	Submission		Freedom
	2. Survival		**3. Transformation**
Optimization	• Ignorance, no *logos* • Disease • Life/time reduction • Less use of energy • Insecurity • Guilt • Aversion to change and risk • Narrow-mindedness Limitations	• Empathy • Planning • Cooperation • *Ethos* • Efficiency • No externality • External law: compliance with universal rules • Common good • Virtue	• Knowledge, *logos* • Health • Time/life increase • Greater use of energy • Security • Responsibility • Change and risk acceptance • Openness • Aspirations
Maximization		• Apathy • Reaction • Competition • No *ethos* • Waste • Externality • Individual law • Self-interest • Vice	
	1. Status Quo		**4. Growth**

Table 6: Characteristics of the four survival strategies of cultural evolution.

Thus, some emergent properties arise from each strategy. Said properties are linked to foundational concepts of social sciences such as ontology, motivation, ethics, epistemology, and politics. Table 7 shows the global system and the characteristics of the four cultural evolution strategies.

	Cultural Evolution Strategies			
Category	1. Status Quo	2. Survival	3.Transformation	4. Growth
Ontology	Materialism	Determinism	Transcendence	Objectivism
Motivation	Have	Give up	Be	Do
Restriction Vector	Maximization	Optimization		Maximization
Ethics	Self-interest	Common good		Self-interest
Capacity Vector	Submission		Freedom	
Epistemology	Superstition		Reason	
Politics	Closed		Open	
Configuration	"Top-Down"		"Bottom-Up"	

Table 7: Cultural evolution strategies and foundational concepts of social sciences.

Given the significance of the two interaction rules in the design of the cultural evolution model, they are exposed in greater detail here:

Interaction rule #1: Complexity (freedom or submission)	
Submission (low complexity). Deters any increase in complexity and avoids the risks and costs that generate an increase in capacities. More value is assigned to what one has than to what one can gain, explore, or invent.	**Freedom (high complexity)**. Allows an increase in complexity, greater information exchange and use of energy, as well as additional entropy exchange with the environment. The risk of energy investments destined to explore new possibilities is assumed with ease. It means freedom to evolve.

Table 8: Submission and freedom.

Interaction rule #2: Cooperation and competition
Optimization (cooperation). Cooperation prevails over competition; an efficient metabolic configuration is more important than metabolic capacity, and the system's variables are harmonized to obtain the best possible result in terms of systemic balance. The outcome and balance of several variables, such as amount of money, sales, profits, stakeholder value, and reduction of externalities, are considered simultaneously. This is consistent with the attainment of empathy, planning, *ethos*, compliance with external rules, efficiency, low externality, cooperation, virtue, and common good.
Maximization (competition). Competition prevails over cooperation; reproductive competition and metabolic capacity are more important. The system's variables become subsumed to a single variable considered the systems' merit figure *performance* variable. The system is configured to obtain the best result out of a single variable — the money made, or the power achieved — despite having poor performance in the rest of the variables and high levels of negative externalities. Those are consistent with the realization of apathy, reaction, competition, no ethos, waste, externality, individual law, self-interest, and vice.

Table 9: Cooperation and competition

More clearly in the cultural evolution model, human beings within our own individuality and freedom of action, make two major decisions that steer the course of our personal belief system toward one of the four survival strategies:

- We may pursue or reject the increase in complexity, which is akin to changing to evolve, seeking more freedom, increasing our capacities, pursuing new opportunities, and the other characteristics outlined in Figure 5 and
- We may seek cooperation or competition with our peers, which is also akin to the characteristics outlined in Figure 6.

In other words, an increase in complexity, just as with cooperation and competition, are phenomena that have always been observed with different names, but up until now they had not been classified nor identified as foundational interaction rules that are different from the emergent properties of the system.

So far, the best description of the complexity phenomenon is: *the greater the evolution or complexity level, the greater the number of possible behaviors*. According to this definition, human beings are at the apex of evolution because of our still undepleted capacity to create new behaviors through culture. However, this means that we also have a greater need for resources and, even if this opens possibilities to find new resources such as new energy technologies, it also increases risk. Ultimately, the increase in complexity is a gamble, a risk that we take to discover new possibilities and acquire new behaviors with no guarantee they will allow our survival.

Human beings, within our complexity, do more things than cockroaches, and yet cockroaches are more likely to survive an ecological or nuclear catastrophe than we are. This would happen because, in evolutionary terms, the cockroaches' lower complexity makes them better adapted to survive catastrophes, but poorly adapted to create and find new opportunities. Having said this, it is also necessary to consider that in the long run, life as a general phenomenon, tends to evolve toward higher degrees of complexity. A day-to-day example of this is the risk and cost incurred by young people in attending university and delaying their entry into the job market in hopes of doing so later with a better occupation thanks to the capacities acquired and cultivated throughout several years of study. In a burgeoning and wealthy economy, this wager would probably pay off, while in a recessive economy it would not. That is why there are young people who, when the time comes to decide what to do, decide to go to university and others who don't. Some will opt for more freedom, complexity, and cultural evolution, while others won't. Those who venture to reach new complexity levels may succeed in doing so in certain environments; in others, they will fail. And as contemporary history proves, the long-term global or macroscopic trend is toward an increase in the average number of years of education, which equals greater systemic complexity, albeit, at the individual or microscopic level. Success and failure stories are written everyday linked to the decision and possibility of attending universities.

Regarding cooperation, competition and its homologous terms, such as common good and self-interest, what is interesting about the stance people may take is that cooperation generates higher efficiency levels in the long term and increases the system's resilience. Competition is more effective in the short term but increases the system's fragility. In environments lacking resources, cooperation is more successful because it accomplishes more efficient arrangements. In environments with plenty of resources, success in competition and a high rate of resource consumption in the short term are more important than long-term efficiency.

Thus, a complex system's capacity to adapt to the physical conditions imposed by the environment through the interaction rules that define it indicates that persistence or homeostasis (i.e., the uninterrupted operation of a complex system for millions of years), is attained in those systems whose configuration evolves within a delicate and narrow balance between efficiency (cooperation and competition) and changes in complexity levels (freedom and submission).

An interesting example of this kind of fine-tuned systemic optimization was discovered by means of the complexity science approach. Graph 8 shows the scaling relationship between velocity and mass for flying animals and airplanes against a highly correlated forecast that includes insects and large passenger airliners. Regardless of their origin (biological or artificial), the propulsion method or structural materials, all these objects are linked to the same mathematical efficiency relationship. According to Bejan and Lorente(23), the **Aérospatiale/BAC** Concorde, no longer produced, was an airplane whose design characteristics were far from the constructal optimum, and that explains the lack of commercial success for supersonic airline passenger services.

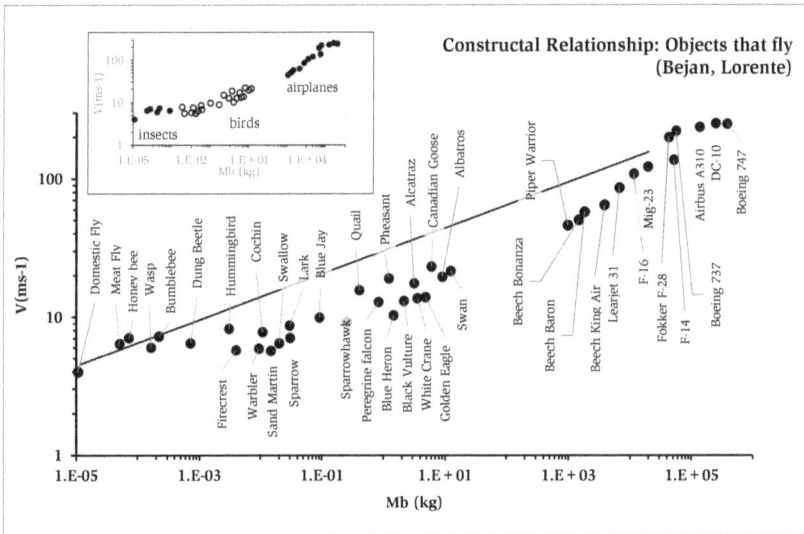

Graph 8: Correlation between a constructal optimization model and the velocity/weight relationship of flying animals and airplanes.

This analysis shows that the optimum constructal pathway is like the diachronic study illustrated in Graph 7. Upon analyzing the case of more than one hundred nations, few were found to have a stable development route as well as a high complexity, efficiency, and energy consumption levels, which in the long term tend to converge in their coefficients; these are the open society nations. On the other hand, there is a large group located far from the stable route, with oscillatory trajectories that indicate rises and falls and that tend to diverge in their coefficients. That's where the rest of the nations, configured in an authoritarian or closed manner, are grouped. The coefficient convergence and divergence phenomenon shown by both groups (Graph 3, Graph 4 and Graph 15), points to the existence of an optimization route with narrow development margins and indicates that the long-term increase in social complexity is hard to attain and does not happen in many ways. Establishing an analogy with Leo Tolstoy's Anna Karenina: "All happy families are alike; each unhappy family is unhappy in its own way." The analogy would be: "open societies look alike; closed ones are closed in its own way."

Thus, the taxonomy and the methodological approach, based on the two interaction rules (complexity and efficiency) from which the four survival strategies of cultural evolution derive (status quo, survival, transformation, and growth), are the means that allow us to transcend our limited and biased perception of social reality. This is in an effort bent on finding and explaining the main levers that move societies to the bright side of the coin, that of greater complexity and freedom, that of the open society.

Resistance against the nomothetic approach

Years ago, a scientific society in Mexico City invited me to attend one of its meetings. On that occasion, new members were inducted and, as part of the process, one of the candidates, a transportation systems researcher, presented an obsolete paper on the merits and importance of roadway engineering, with a bibliography that dated back to the seventies.

Days before, I had taken part in a European congress on biomimetics (the study of nature's design characteristics and rules that can be applied to the design of man-made objects). For centuries, this scientific and technological approach has led to the development of well-known designs such as Velcro, Radar, and the Sagrada Familia basilica in Barcelona, just to mention a few. And as I saw at the biomimetics congress, there is a multitude of research groups and institutions exclusively devoted to this field. Those groups participated in the event and presented a series of innovative projects, such as a robot that emulated the creeping movements of a caterpillar that was used to provide maintenance to elevator cables.

With this experience in mind, my question to the candidate was: "Has your research group considered incorporating biomimetic concepts into the design of transportation systems and into the study of traffic problems in cities?" The answer, which could have been succinct or as simple as "no," turned out to be ambiguous and convoluted, but ended with the candidate asserting that he didn't think that nature's designs had anything important to contribute to the engineering of transportation systems because, in his view, nature creates without restrictions, while engineers are limited by numerous restrictions.

This is false. The interesting thing about biomimetics is that nature, over millions of years of experiments and trial and error efforts (evolutionary and adaptive), has optimized a myriad of systems. For example, ant columns are always in motion and never experience traffic jams(25). Transportation engineers might find this feature especially useful and worth studying. Biological optimization occurs because every tiny change in the design of a natural structure inevitably feeds back to other variables that are kept in check by the system's restrictions such as thermodynamics. For example, if an animal suddenly became bigger and heavier, its weight increases, given system restrictions such as metabolic laws, would bring about, among many other things, new food requirements, a thicker skeleton and a larger contact surface for heat dissipation. Likewise, this would have an impact on the local ecology and the chain of consequences would go on until all the surrounding elements adapted to this change and became stabilized in a homeostatic state of dynamic equilibrium, which, in terms of complex adaptive systems, is known as a regime. It could also be that said animal and its offspring failed in biological terms and became extinct, as it happened with the Concorde in aviation. This, by analogy, applies to a wide variety of contemporary social problems that need to be solved.

The anecdote exemplifies the resistance with which the adoption of the proposed biomimetic and nomothetic approaches may be met or, in other words, the opposition to accept and use the taxonomy and interaction rules from the cultural evolution model or a similar complex adaptive systems approach. The way the study of social sciences is structured today indicates that it is more comfortable to have a wide variety of frames of reference at hand whose taxonomic origins are unknown, developed based on vague concepts, because this supposedly grants leeway to intellectual freedom. However, it has become evident that biological, cultural, thermodynamic, and astronomical systems that persist over time follow interaction, efficiency, and design rules that systemically optimize them. In the meantime, most of the social science designs (or models) that are not formulated based on complex adaptive systems (idiographic) remain in the artistic realm of the philosophy of the fantastic and philosophical fiction. These designs are based on the obsolete epistemology of deterministic linear systems, which is ill equipped to explore our complex and problematic reality.

3. Complexity, authoritarianism, democracy, and power

The rule that divides society

In the proposed model, human societies develop according to four strategies based on a dominant interaction logic, namely, the one followed by the greatest number of agents that results in the emergent properties of each type of system. As we discuss this model, let's first focus on the separation established by interaction rule number one (difference between freedom and submission) since, historically, the schism between authoritarian (or closed) and democratic (open) systems is dominant in describing "the world as it is." In the first part of the book, the discussion of interaction rule number two is limited to the description of the serfs and establishing the difference between the two types of democratic systems. However, in the second and third parts of the book, the distinction resulting from interaction rule number two (difference between cooperation and competition) will become crucial in understanding the challenges and changes brought forth by the 21st century.

As several outcomes re-examine the ideas and intuitions of authors from the past, a "best effort" approach complements this with an independent review by an extensive group of experts giving credit to whom credit is due. However, given the uniqueness of complexity science to explain countless interactions and emergent phenomena in any given system, some still unidentified coincidences can persist, and they will be solved in future versions. We must not forget that the goal is to arrive at an explanation that is well-integrated, accessible, and easy to communicate. That can help pave the way to the future, and not demand an encompassing review of the philosophy, anthropology, and history behind every issue. This would be the realm of hyper objects, which defeat us from the start and would be contrary to the transdisciplinary integration and synthesis we wish to accomplish.

Some aspects of both interaction rules have been previously identified in the social sciences, either in philosophy, sociology, history, or economics and, therefore, have synonyms (Figure 5 and Figure 6). In regard to interaction rule number one, it relates to the differences between low or high complexity.

As the concept of complexity is still distant and far removed from the orthodoxy of the social sciences, we shall begin by describing what it means to follow interaction rule number one from the perspective of the agent's behavior: choosing between freedom and submission. In any complex system, the agents' various degrees of freedom following the interaction rules alter the emergent properties and outcomes of the system. The degrees of freedom for human beings are so vast while, at the same time, also extremely personal. It is essential in this process to describe the agent's behavioral possibilities at different layers from the inner self and the decisions that create the individual's behavior all the way to the aggregated collective behaviors. In each analysis layer, there's a corresponding characteristic that we shall analyze below: locus of control, human dignity versus prostitution, responsibility versus irresponsibility, and democratic legality versus *raison d'état*.

Locus of control

Mind sciences lack a unified body of knowledge and abound in personality and behavioral theories that overlap and contradict each other. However, some concepts are widely disseminated and internationally accepted. One such concept, transcribed below from a specialized site(26), is the locus of control or place of control that can be internal or external, and defines a general direction that agents take in their decision-making process.

People with an external locus of control:

> *...will tend to blame external causes for everything that happens to them. For example, if a student gets a poor grade on an exam, he may attribute his failure to bad luck, the excessive difficulty of the test, or the teacher's extreme strictness. These people perceive effort as not contingent on their actions, but as the result of chance, fate, luck or a supernatural power. Thus, the external locus of control is the perception that events are unrelated to one's own conduct and cannot be controlled, in such a way that effort and dedication are not deemed important.*

People with an internal locus of control:

> *...will tend to attribute everything that happens to them to internal causes. For example, a student that gets a good grade in an exam will attribute the outcome to his effort and hours of study. These people perceive the positive or negative events that come about as resulting from their own actions and believe them to be under their personal control. Consequently, these people attribute a positive value to individual effort and skills.*

Human dignity and prostitution

From the formal perspective of complexity science, human societies struggle with coordination. Unlike other social animals, whose rules are fixed — for example, the same coordination model always emerges in groups of chimpanzees and lions — what makes us special as human beings is that we can choose between centralized (authoritarian) and decentralized (democratic) coordination structures. In centralized or closed coordination arrangements, most of the agent's freedom of action is limited by those agents that exert centralized control. In historical terms, this has been established as the higher dignity of monarchs and emperors over their subjects and slaves. For centuries, this configuration inhibited cultural evolution and generated terrible inefficiencies and costs. Such was the culture of the Middle Ages.

Yet, and despite regressions, the long-term cultural evolution continued to move toward higher degrees of complexity. The system's configuration had to become more efficient and, as described in constructal law, this resulted in the homogenous distribution of the system's imperfection. Quite simply, things shifted toward a less centralized coordination model founded on the abolishment of the sovereign's special dignity and the acknowledgement of an equal and universal form of human dignity. Hence, the idea of human dignity is not just a philosophical stance, but the basis of a social evolutionary reconfiguration and redesign that enabled the birth and expansion of open societies. Thus, the foundational idea of the contemporary Western world is that there's an intrinsic and inalienable dignity to which every person is naturally entitled. The centricity of this idea in our civilization is ascertained in the first lines of the preamble and in the first article of the Universal Declaration of Human Rights(27):

*Whereas recognition of the inherent dignity and of the equal
and inalienable rights of all members of the human family
is the foundation of freedom, justice and peace in the world;*
***Article 1.**- All human beings are born free and equal in digni-
ty and rights. They are endowed with reason and conscience
and should act toward one another in a spirit of brotherhood...*

Just like a building, a person's dignity constitutes the foundations on which human rights — the principles of equality before the law, justice, democracy, and citizenship — are erected. Without it, the whole building surely collapses. However, the existence of the Universal Declaration of Human Rights, founded on human dignity, is one thing, and the existence of dignity, as a general interaction rule, is another.

This distinction shows there is always a huge difference between open and democratic societies, which manage to make citizens the center of things, and closed authoritarian societies that suppress them. In authoritarian societies, the concept of human dignity is largely unknown; it is not experienced and is not disseminated at street level. In these societies, despite the universal acceptance of the inalienability of human dignity, it is trampled daily.

On the other hand, any exchange in which individuals consent to the infringement of his/her dignity or when a person acts against his/her own dignity, usually in a monetary exchange, an act of prostitution occurs. Contrasting with what is commonly understood as prostitution, it does not take place only in sexual trade. It is a much broader concept that encompasses any activity in which, in exchange for something, one acts against one's own dignity or that of other individuals. As examples, the doctor who accepts a beach trip as a perk from a laboratory for prescribing unnecessary drugs to his patients; the man or woman who consents to inhumane working conditions without raising any objections; the politician who incurs in conflict of interests, are not more clever, realistic, or pragmatic than others. They simply prostitute themselves and fail to recognize that, by infringing the boundaries of their own dignity, they forego the possibility of exerting their citizenship. For, in the submission engendered by prostitution, citizens become lackeys or serfs by becoming submissive to the whims of the highest bidder.

Lackeys are those who prostitute themselves consciously, and even gladly, as a way of furthering their interests above those of others. Their motto: better to be a proper lackey than a measly serf. Serfs are people who simply submit without knowing, recognizing, or asserting their inherent dignity.

Once prostitution spreads and takes root as something normal, the notion of inalienability of human dignity vanishes and is transformed into daily currency. In these conditions, the goal of lackeys and serfs will be to prostitute themselves at the highest possible price. By so doing, they create and normalize many of the toxic processes that uphold contemporary authoritarian regimes, such as buying votes and the complicity of professional associations in corrupt government spending.

Responsibility and irresponsibility (problem ownership)

Responsibility is an imperative condition, both for the existence of citizens as well as for that of an effective rights and obligations regime. However, with an external locus of control and a wide spreading of prostitution, responsible individuals cannot exist. That is why authoritarian systems fall short on a culture of responsibility and justice, which is only simulated through the designation of wrongdoers and the use of "scapegoats" every time it suits this type of model. This situation is the basis of the high level of impunity over which many authoritarian systems are built.

Without a sense of responsibility, people won't take ownership of problems, not even the immediate ones and whose solution is within their reach unless there is an external influence that triggers an action. Each person, according to their situation, will use as an excuse the absence of or the need for triggers such as foreign investment, need of technology transfer and technical assistance, orders from above, journalistic criticism, institutional assistance, or support from the rich and powerful. The fact is that in these systems, without external pressure or incentives, solutions are not created *ex officio*: this hinders the existence of permanent institutions. The latter, according to North(10), is an essential condition for the transition from a limited access to an open-access order.

A common example that illustrates the relationship between responsibility, problem ownership, and behavior is the resident of an authoritarian nation who throws trash on the sidewalk in his own city but does not do so when he travels to a country inhabited by citizens and institutions. This action is due to the sense of ownership derived from responsibility.

In authoritarian nations, lackeys and serfs behave as tenants and not as owners of their surroundings. Because of their trampled dignity, they resent their abusive landlords — the masters — and that is why they have no problem with vandalizing their homes (countries, cities) because they do not perceive them as their own. Outside this environment, in fully democratic countries, lackeys and serfs immediately realize that they must obey the civic rules under penalty of being scorned by any of the many owners that roam the streets of nations made by citizens.

Democratic legality and *raison d'état*

Political science literature maintains that Niccolò Machiavelli (1469-1527) was the first theoretician to surmise that there are certain conditions in which preserving the State is more important than preserving the rights of individuals. Today, this notion is identified as *raison d'état* (justification for a policy on the basis that the State's own interests are primary)(28). Shortly after this premise was published, the concept was employed by Cardinal Richelieu (1585-1642) when France moved from a fragmented feudal structure to a consolidated nation State. According to Henry Kissinger(29), Richelieu tried to justify *raison d'état* in metaphysical terms when he declared: "Man is immortal; his salvation is hereafter. The State has no immortality, its salvation is now or never."

Despite having been used for more than five centuries, this idea, to date, has not been systematically developed. In the global context, there is no widely accepted definition that clarifies its meaning. Yet, aside from its theoretical limitations, it is commonly used in contemporary political practice as the foundation of countless important decisions. A well-known and recent example was the United States' authorization to use its military base in Guantanamo on the island of Cuba as an extra-territorial prison and placed war prisoners there in a legal limbo. Combatants captured during the war on terrorism(30) were concentrated there, where protection of human rights, the due legal process, the presumption of innocence, and the safeguard of the physical and emotional integrity of the prisoners, which are guaranteed to any defendant by that country's judicial system, evaporated into thin air.

Consequently, it is not surprising that in other parts of the world *raison d'état* is used to justify a series of measures which are as diverse and contrasting as waging war or making peace. In fact, over the past decade, tension between the ideas of democratic legality and *raison d'état* has significantly increased, especially after the terrorist attacks on New York City and Washington, D.C. in 2001. Western governments decided to alter the balance that had existed on this subject ever since the founding of the United Nations (UN) in 1945 and up until the date of the attacks.

On the other hand, democratic legality is rooted in the protection of the human dignity of all individuals that make up society. Human rights are derived from it, and their realization constitutes the main source for the rule of law to exist in a democracy.

Human rights must be the guiding principle in State action, since together with the generation of public goods such as public security, the rule of law, and public health, they enable the attainment of democratic legality. The latter means that the State must, first and foremost, protect human dignity, human rights, and public goods and, subsequently, the State itself. When State defense supersedes democratic legality, as in the case of Guantanamo, then, *raison d'état* prevails.

Over the past few years, the controversy between human rights and *raison d'état* has been thoroughly discussed with ever more complicated examples. The important point is that within *raison d'état* it is possible to identify the masters.

The submission of lackeys and serfs may lead us to think that the masters of the authoritarian model operate pursuant to an internal locus of control since they are forced to determine the system's general direction. But they also share the external locus and prostitution as the acquiring parties. The difference is that masters gain their perceived operational independence by using *raison d'état* as a source of inspiration and guidance. Along these lines, *raison d'état* acts as the supreme master that sets the course of the authoritarian system. Contemporary authoritarian masters still resort to supernatural explanations, as monarchs did in the past, because, in all cases, authoritarianism requires external motivators who encourage and give meaning to the implementation of the actions.

This explains why the language of authoritarian masters necessarily abounds in references to the interests of the nation, the institutions, the enemies of the State, divine callings or some truth that they may deem to be absolute and is consistently devoid of authentic references to individuals, their dignity, responsibility, democratic legality, and human rights.

Authoritarianism and democracy

Having laid down the main characteristics created by interaction rule number one, it is now possible to explain how authoritarian societies are established and develop through positive feedback loops that originate in people's consciousness, pervade the decisions they make, and are incorporated to the world through their actions.

Erica Chenoweth and Maria J. Stephan(31) demonstrated that the violent deposition of an authoritarian regime usually brings about new authoritarian systems. And this changes only when the system's inherent logic is altered. This links to Eric Liu's Citizen University(32) and Gary Slutkin's Cure Violence projects(33) that are some of the next-generation solutions showing how positive change is possible when the authoritarian logic, at the base of society, is moved toward the internal locus of control, responsibility, human dignity, and democratic legality ideas. Likewise, analyzing authoritarianism and democracy as the emergent properties of a complex system helps ascertain the importance of changes in bottom-up interaction logic of agents as an essential precondition to move away from authoritarianism.

In the traditional top-down view, it's always been pointlessly said that the process of change consists of establishing democracy (by seizing power or making the revolution), developing a state of democratic legality, building a culture of responsibility, defending human dignity and, gradually in the last stage, changing people's authoritarian culture.

However, in Mexico, along with many other examples around the world, 200 years of independent history confirm that any attempt to bring about democratic openness is soon immunized and decays if the authoritarian interaction logic remains intact at the base of society. Even with fair and free elections, and alternation between different political forces, the authoritarian interaction rules people use in their daily lives are the ones that, ultimately, encourage and allow authoritarianism to persist.

For example, a candidate running for mayor in the community of San Blas in the Mexican State of Nayarit admitted to stealing while holding public office. Despite his confession, he continued to win the election in a democratic way(34). How can this be explained? Exposing a corrupt politician had no significant impact on the population because there is no clear democratic responsibility model among the citizens in this community; therefore, the corrupt candidate still got more votes. Cases such as this one provides insights into how important it is, as a first requirement, to restore citizenship from the periphery to change the emergent properties of the center. From complexity's perspective, this is the way to build a happier future in which nations that are immersed in an authoritarian and corrupt culture may become communities with thriving citizens who manage to move away from the hardships that result from being part of authoritarian coexistence.

		Authoritarianism	Democracy
External Realm	Collective Action	Raison d'état	Democratic Legality
	Personal Action	Irresponsibility	Responsibility
Internal Realm	Conscious	Prostitution	Human Dignity
	Subconscious	External Locus	Internal Locus

Table 10: Interaction rules and emergent properties of the authoritarian and democratic models.

Table 10 illustrates in blocks and layers the main characteristics that branch out from interaction rule one according to the authoritarian or democratic parts of the model.

Power

From the perspective of complex systems, authoritarianism and democracy are the ultimate consequences of a process that stems from the interaction of agents and the system's initial conditions. They are built from the inner world of individuals by means of the locus of control and dignity and become manifest in the personal and the social behaviors driven by responsibility and democratic legality. Within this train of thought, the perception of power as something tangible changes. Power is classically defined as a metaphysical entity that can be taken; the causal origin that facilitates or hinders social change; that habilitates or corrupts people.

But power, be it authoritarian or democratic, is in fact, a consequence that indicates the causal origin of the interaction rules that are most commonly used by people. It is the background radiation leftover from the Big Bang and not the Big Bang itself. The latter does not counter the contemporary notion of power, defined as the capacity to influence the behavior of others, either through submission or conviction. Given that within this definition, the individual's will and freedom of choice are conserved.

The proposed shift in how we focus things entails looking at power as an emergent outcome and not as a foundational element of the system. People with an external locus of control easily submit to power because they have a psychological need to obtain external references that help them make sense of their actions and satisfy the external locus with which they chose to face life. These people consider power to be a true force of nature, i.e., they perceive power as something tangible, and this perception turns into a self-fulfilling prophecy. Many people with an external locus of control create conditions in which submitting to the will of others is easy; consequently, their perception of power as something tangible is reinforced.

To consider power as a superior force coming from above — as an inherent characteristic of the system or as a result or emergent property of the system coming from below — would appear to be the same thing. Eventually, the outcome is the same: either way, a few people have power or influence over the actions of others and many others don't. It is, nonetheless, important to have a better understanding of the mechanism of power. This opens a different perspective on the subject, especially in today's world, when most of the formative and transformative mechanisms of influence in contemporary society are changing due to the digital revolution. The idea of power as an emergent characteristic of social systems allows us to propose that there is no generic and interchangeable power for all types of systems. Every social coexistence model, which stems from the use of the interaction rules, creates a distinctive mechanism of influence or power that has its own operational logic.

Therefore, being a democrat and gaining power within an authoritarian system to promote a democratic and reform agenda is not enough. Most of the times, in this kind of situation, instability, chaos, disappointment, and deadlocks are more likely to ensue. There are also cases where, when the interaction process at the base of society changes overall, making it impossible to maintain the same influence or power mechanisms; these become outdated in the new way of doing things. In other words, power is built, not taken.

That is why revolutions and regime changes are not the beginning but the end of a process, which, for the most part, has already taken place at the core of society. Though they may often seem to come out of nowhere, and no one can foresee them, revolutions are not spontaneously generated. It is always possible to analyze and explain them *ex post* as historical phenomena that originate in logical cause-and-effect relationships. On the other hand, the takeovers, coups d'état, overthrows, and political transitions in the historical record, which may be regarded as examples of the fact that power is taken and not built, show us that, when the configuration of power (authoritarian or democratic) is firmly established it is possible to transfer the system's management from one individual to another. However, changing the individuals at the top of the configuration can only succeed when the desired goal is to protect the established order. Conversely, this fails when a change in course is attempted without altering the system's logic.

To further clarify this, two recent historical examples are worth mentioning. In Iraq, Saddam Hussein was the apex of a system that maintained stability in a society with a millenary authoritarian tradition. After the United States invaded the country in 2003, and the artificial establishment of a democratic parliamentary regime was made, the country plunged into a state of disarray that sank into a condition of chaos that persists to date. In Mexico, electoral alternation did not imply that the internal democracy of the political party that achieved the transition was transferred to the Mexican society through a new governance model. The need to be relevant within the system itself led the members of the PAN to abandon their democratic tradition, so much so that today they have blended into the very same authoritarian system they set out to defeat.

This illustrates the emergent quality of power. In Iraq, the unruliness and adamant resistance of the Iraqi people against moving toward stability and democracy — despite the takeover and violent dismemberment of authoritarian power that included the imprisonment and execution of its leaders such as Saddam Hussein, who was hanged — demonstrate that the emergent authoritarian interaction logic is even stronger that an invasion by the most powerful army in the world.

In Mexico, democracy-building without enough citizens and without a method for building citizenship, made the PAN leaders choose between either becoming electorally irrelevant — by eliminating authoritarian, corporatist, and populist government practices — or attempting to maintain their electoral relevance by preserving these practices. That ultimately happened when the political and electoral partnership agreed with the corrupt National Education Workers' Union (SNTE), an organization that had managed to forestall the educational system's reform in exchange for prerogatives. By so doing, the new PAN governments gave up the construction of democratic power and lost credibility as crusaders of democracy. But even if they forsook building democracy, in fact, they failed in becoming authoritarian enough as to stay in power. In 2012, discredited and having lost their course, they gave back the country's presidency to the same authoritarian party they had defeated in 2000. For want of results, disenchanted citizens went back to consuming the original brand of Mexican authoritarianism under the PRI. Thus, we can see that in Mexico the emergent bottom-up construction of authoritarian power remained intact. It permeated and transformed an originally democratic political party into an authoritarian government. The examples illustrate why it is said that power corrupts. Whoever wishes to change the functioning of a social system without building a base of power that follows a different interaction logic faces two alternatives: conform to the established configuration (corrupt) or die.

Naturally, our communities simultaneously entertain various operating modes and individualities. We all live and coexist, regardless of the location, with authoritarians and democrats. No matter how authoritarian a system may be, there will always be autonomous and dignified individuals who will not be broken, at least in their inner world. What is important to underscore is that without a sufficient quantity of citizens (internal locus, dignity, responsibility, democratic legality) devoted, and determined to build citizenship daily, it is impossible to create and sustain an authentic democratic coexistence. All that is needed to build democratic power is to start at the core of individuals, in their close and personal surroundings, and then move on to society at large.

Are you a part of the authoritarian system?

Look around and listen to what people are saying. That burnt out light bulb that infuriates you and has been ruining you night-time reading for months, is it working or are you expecting it to spontaneously repair itself? Are you mad because co-workers brought a cake to the office and "you were forced" to eat it? When you scold your children, do you tell them: "Don't do that because the policeman is watching you! What will people think? What will they think of me?" instead of telling them that what's not right is simply wrong! Do you send your children to school so that they can be taught or for them to have more opportunities to learn? Do you accept incorrect situations to avoid trouble? When you are in a restaurant, do you prefer to ask what your friends are going to order because you fear you will make the wrong choice? Are you driven by guilt, but not by responsibility? With what social organization are you affiliated? Do you take part in philanthropic activities? Do you spend part of your free time helping others? When you leave home, do you pick up the piece of trash in front of your doorstep or do you just keep on walking?

You might be surprised to find out that all these apparently harmless situations, together with the antisocial behaviors that may be witnessed each day in the streets of authoritarian nations, are but a small sample of how persistent characteristics such as external locus of control are in an authoritarian society. However, this is not a common, let alone normal, occurrence in communities primarily made up by citizens.

These small deeds, which reveal the social health of a community, are linked to issues connected with the lack of understanding of human dignity, responsibility and attainment of democratic legality. Although it may not seem evident at first, citizenship building, at present, does not begin, nor is it possible, in institutions such as the Mexican Congress of the Union or the Presidency of the Republic.

Suffice it to recall one of the recent political scandals, which, as many others, went unpunished, in which several legislators were filmed at a party in the company of prostitutes during a business trip funded by Congress(35).

In traditional logic, which considers power as an element of the system, many people — probably the relatives and friends of the representatives in question — would say that they were corrupted by power. Therefore, it would be necessary to reform power (Congress) so that people's behavior could change (outside-in). This mindset is precisely the one that sustains the social analysis models such as that of rational choice, from which extrinsic incentive (reward and punishment) systems derive.

Now, from the perspective of complexity and emergence of power, such an event is not due to a flaw in the institutional configuration of Congress or to the corrupting potential of power. It originates within the family structure that shaped these people's character, and throughout the years forged their external locus of control and their penchant for prostitution, irresponsibility, and *raison d'état*. Hence, curtailing similar phenomena, associated with corruption and authoritarianism, depends on propagating and using the interaction logic of the democratic model: internal locus of control, dignity, responsibility, and democratic legality.

4. Masters, lackeys, serfs, heroes, and bandits

The banality of evil

W e have already established that the authoritarian world is meant for three characters: the masters, the lackeys, and the serfs. We have also mentioned that in the outer fringes of authoritarianism there are also heroes and bandits. Let us remember that once authoritarianism has been firmly established, only heroes and bandits constitute a clear opposition to the continuity of the authoritarian model, as Anthony Bourdain rightly pointed out in the case of Mexico. The existence of heroes and bandits does not guarantee the reconstruction of society or citizenship if the rest of the conditions do not change, but their emergence and proliferation indicate that the authoritarian system's thriving stage is over.

Nowadays, the first obstacle in facing authoritarianism is our inability to portray authoritarians in their true human measure. Authoritarianism is simply the outcome of the actions done by thousands, even millions, of ordinary living and breathing individuals. Throughout history, we have overrated the authoritarian's image in an attempt to create symmetry between the magnitude of those who act in an authoritarian manner and the damage and aversion they induce. This happens because we want correspondence between the high costs produced by authoritarianism and the Machiavellian character of authoritarian figures. But, in fact, in authoritarianism there is often a great disparity between small acts of incompetence, corruption, pettiness, negligence, selfishness, and injustice, and the enormous damages caused by the perpetrators.

One of the few voices that understood this paradox in her analysis and description of authoritarianism, especially the totalitarian and tyrannical kind, was the German-born American philosopher Hannah Arendt (1906-1975). As a German Jew, she personally experienced the tragedy of World War II in a French labor camp and coined the concept of the banality of evil after covering the trial against Nazi war criminal Adolf Eichmann for *The New Yorker* magazine in 1961(36). In one of her controversial articles, she stated that true evil — the origin of which history's great atrocities may be traced and attributed — was not only found in psychotic monsters like Hitler, but that large-scale brutalities were necessarily designed, constructed, and operated by apparently normal individuals, occasionally "petty bureaucrats like Eichmann," the small man or *keliner Mann*, who carries out "thoughtless and senseless acts." For this philosopher, understanding, discovering, and unmasking those "who in renouncing thought presume to be free from any responsibility, abandoned to the currents of time" became an essential task. Especially since "in renouncing reflective thinking, all traces of humanity are lost and thus evil becomes absolute."

Disparaging all authoritarians as monsters is pointless when fighting against them. They only become legendary in our imagination and, seen through this lens, they are harder to confront and contend with, especially when these descriptions find no echo among the operators of the authoritarian world.

For the *kleiner Mann* or small man, reading that an authoritarian is a giant monster, entitles him to follow the same path, since that cartoon monster has nothing to do with the simple duty, in the case of a lackey, of following the master. Seeking personal gain and transferring the risks and costs to others is justified if one obeys and thoughtlessly submits to a bureaucratic process, system, or boss. This results in the justification to behave with incompetence when providing a service at a counter, delaying the delivery of medicines to patients at a hospital, relabeling expired products in a supermarket or, in the case of Eichmann, developing the transportation logistics that delivered tens of thousands of Jews to Nazi concentration camps.

For Hannah Arendt, Adolf Eichmann was precisely that petty man, abandoned to the banality of evil. Even when he was sentenced to hang, he could not be brought around to grasp the magnitude and significance of his responsibility in the atrocities of the Holocaust. This was largely because he was able to psychologically distance himself from the monster portrayed by the prosecutors during the trial. This is also true of contemporary authoritarians, who do not see themselves as unworthy, petty, submissive, prostituted, or harmful because they — and others — fail to associate their selfish and trivial motivations with the enormous consequences and damages caused by their actions. Therefore, we must urgently break away from our need to establish psychological symmetry, linked to our sense of justice, between the petty causal origin of authoritarian acts and the high costs and damages they create.

A single Mexican example, among many others, will suffice to illustrate this relationship. Elba Esther Gordillo headed the National Education Workers Union from 1988 to 2013(37). During those 25 years, the national education system was deadlocked due to the union's adamancy against improving or reforming the educational model. So firm was the union's position that, during said period, the international instruments for measuring educational quality, efficiency, and effectiveness consistently exhibited the deterioration of the Mexican education system(38), a situation with enormous economic and social implications.

This persisted until 2013, when *Forbes* magazine ranked Elba Esther Gordillo among the 10 most corrupt people in Mexico(39). That same year, she was charged and convicted for several corruption charges(40). Many journalists tried, to no avail, to assess the fortune she had amassed as leader of the teachers' union. For years, the luxuriousness and excessiveness of her daily expenses were publicized, verging on tackiness, but she always maintained that she earned the same salary as any other teacher in the country.

Regardless of the exact amount of Gordillo's fortune — estimated by some at between 1 to 100 billion pesos(41), the ratio between the probable size of her fortune and the damage wrought upon society may be compared in orders of magnitude.

In 2014, Mexico's nominal gross domestic product (GDP) was 17.8 trillion pesos, and for many years, the country has invested 6% of it in education. This represents more than 1.068 trillion pesos per year. On the other hand, it is estimated that the poor quality of education represents a loss of several percentage points of annual economic growth. Each GDP percentage point in 2014 is equivalent to 178 billion pesos. Therefore, in an extremely conservative estimate, if one percentage point of annual expenditure or investment in education is wasted due to corruption in the educational system (10.68 billion pesos) and one percentage point of the GDP is lost every year (178 billion pesos), the minimum loss for the country would amount to 188.68 billion pesos per year. Said figure, multiplied by the 25 years that Gordillo was the union's leader — without considering compound adjustments for inflation — tells us that the minimum damage accrued by her and her collaborators equals 4.71 trillion pesos, between 47 and 4,710 times greater than her alleged fortune of 1 to 100 billion pesos.

This gets worse as the value of the lost annual GDP and the budget wasted due to corruption changes. If the calculation is repeated using an estimate of 10% of the education budget wasted due to inefficiency and corruption, and 2 % of the GDP lost per year — both figures still quite conservative — the damage amounts to 11.57 trillion pesos. This enables us to say with some certainty that the ratio of losses for Mexico/profits for Gordillo, reaches a factor between 115 and 11,500 times. Most probably, therefore, for every dollar that the union leader added to her personal fortune, the damage to society was increased thousand-fold. So, every $10,000 designer handbag that Elba Esther Gordillo flaunted in public over decades implied $10 million in damage, or more, to Mexican society (10,000 x 1,000 = 10,000,000). This demonstrates the great asymmetry that exists between the petty motivations of an authoritarian act — showing off a designer handbag — and the extent of the negative economic consequences, even if we overlook other impacts such as development and employment opportunities for several generations of Mexican children, which, translated into monetary sums, are probably much greater.

This also indicates that we need to initiate a debate on the domain of justice. Our feeling that the extent of the fault must be equal to the magnitude of the punishment is highly developed. Therefore, we instinctively try to magnify authoritarians upon analyzing the damages they cause, or fail to see said damages deliberately, once we discover the trivial source of the shortcomings that bring them about. This situation produces a discordance that appears to be hard to solve. In terms of justice, it is hard to distinguish between the assignment of responsibilities and the quantification of guilt. Gordillo is in jail and, even if she is held legally liable, remains in jail for several years and all her assets are seized. The damages she caused will be impossible to amend due to the substantial difference that exists between the direct responsibility of the acts committed and the guiltiness of the damages inflicted.

The main purpose of depicting the authoritarian system's characters is to change the terms of the discussion, to reveal and expose the pillars of the authoritarian system's structure: The behavior and acts of the *kleiner Mann* or *Frau*. They have become dehumanized by forsaking the conscious consideration of their motives, and strive day after day to justify and expand a creed that renders impossible the well-being of the great human community. It is unreasonable to think that we can be more civilized and humane when we allow everyday life to be shaped by those who, as Arendt declared, have renounced their own humanity.

In view of this, maybe our first reaction would be to say that there is no way authoritarians can see or acknowledge themselves as such. No matter how perfect a picture of themselves we may show them, that it is a wasted effort. Nonetheless, there are various examples in which discussions that seemed initially lost, may, over time, be approached from a different perspective, supported by new evidence and, before long, transform culture and entrenched social behaviors.

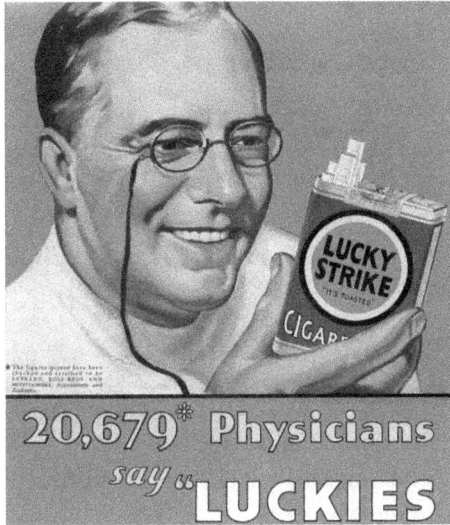

Figure 8: Cigarette ad from 1960: A physician recommends smoking.

For example, during the 1960s, smokers were praised as symbols of social sophistication and admiration to the point of using the image of physicians to promote tobacco consumption as something healthy (Figure 8). This advertising campaign — like many others — was public and privately sponsored by the tobacco industry and political interest groups linked to them. However, this image has totally changed. Today smokers are viewed as addicts and/or sick people victimized by tobacco companies (Figure 9). In recent years, smoking in public places has become a socially frowned-upon, restricted, prosecuted, and penalized activity around the world. Many countries have been able to reduce tobacco consumption, even against economic and political interests that only a few years ago seemed impossible to oppose.

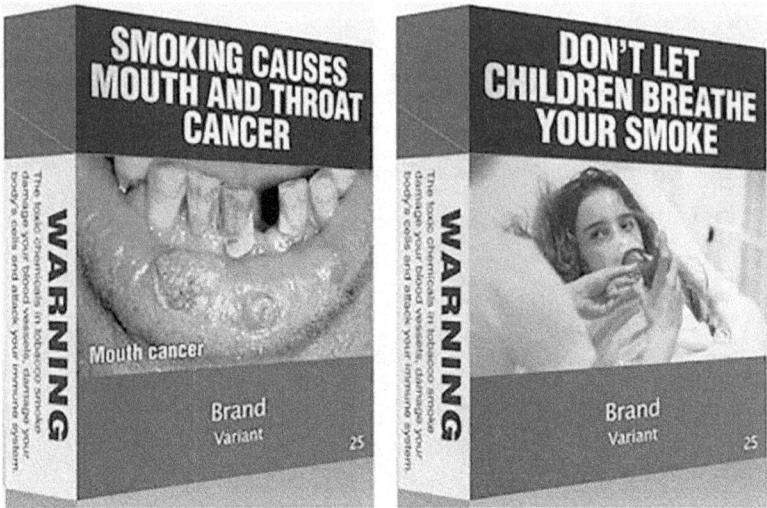

Figure 9: Current cigarette pack health warnings.

Likewise, I maintain that changing the terms of the discussion allows us to open new routes for building citizenship. Let us start by raising awareness about the fact that acts of corruption and authoritarianism must be multiplied a thousand-fold to discover the real damage they create. If we just spread the word that "every dollar a corrupt individual pockets is worth $1,000 or more in damages to society," the social cost of flaunting handbags, cars, houses, and dirty dealings will rise. This is the first step toward transforming the ambition to become a master, a lackey, or a serf into a negative social stigma. Renouncing what it is to be human cannot be a valid aspiration. It is up to us, as members of the human family, to avoid this from happening, especially when everything that is truly dear and significant to all of us is at stake.

Violence

Before describing the authoritarian characters and to provide a context for the behavior of bandits, we must summarize the state of the art on understanding violence and crime. In academic literature, violence and crime are subjects that are abundantly discussed from every imaginable angle, but there is insufficient knowledge based on sound empirical analysis about them. This means that, although we have plenty of theories regarding the origin and causes of violence and its solutions, most of them come about from philosophical conjecture instead of from a solid scientific approach.

One point of agreement is that homicidal violence has decreased over the past centuries. Steven Pinker, a Harvard University professor, is part of a group of scholars who systematically analyzed the decrease in violence, mainly related to homicides and armed conflicts. *Better Angels of Our Nature*(42) is the work in which he documented, organized, and analyzed the existing data on this topic.

According to Pinker, statistics show that deaths associated with armed conflicts and crime have decreased in most parts of the world, except in regions like Mexico and Central America, where violence has lately escalated. For ordinary citizens, this conclusion is counterintuitive, since along with the decrease in homicidal violence, violence perceived through the media has increased. While the average number of murders declined in both streets and battlefields, the number of murders that people witnessed on television increased exponentially. There are studies that indicate that an average child in the U.S. will witness on the media around 200,000 violent acts and 16,000 murders by the age of 18(43).

At present, experts agree that a nation may be regarded as peaceful and safe when the annual homicide rate per 100,000 inhabitants is less than 10. On the other hand, as this rate increases, it will be regarded as progressively violent and uncivilized. It is believed that 50 violent deaths a year per 100,000 inhabitants is the threshold of a failed state or a severe internal conflict. Even if in the long-term, downward trend of homicides and armed conflicts is accepted, there is still no agreement on the causal explanation for said reduction.

Another driver of violence — where there's also agreement — is that most of the violence is caused by men between ages 15 and 29. The charts (Graph 9 and Graph 10) show the age and gender of the people who were arrested in the U.S. for violent crimes in 2012(44). This is the same for data reported in other parts of the world, and clearly support the link of violence, gender, and age of most criminals. We can, therefore, assert that crime and violence is primarily a young male phenomenon.

Another similar hypothesis, or one that can be derived from the one previously mentioned, is that violence should fluctuate together with changes in cohorts or age groups of the population. But, in many parts of the world, the possibility of ratifying it is limited by the low granularity and unavailability of sufficient demographic data.

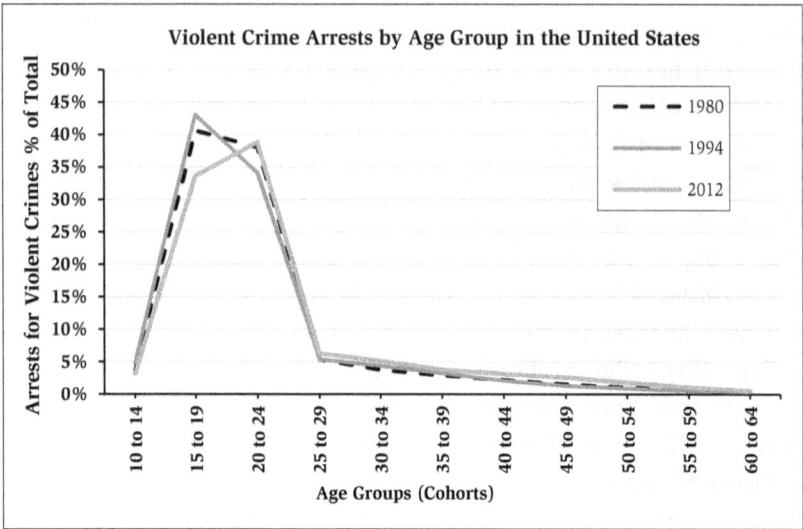

Graph 9: Violent crimes by age group.

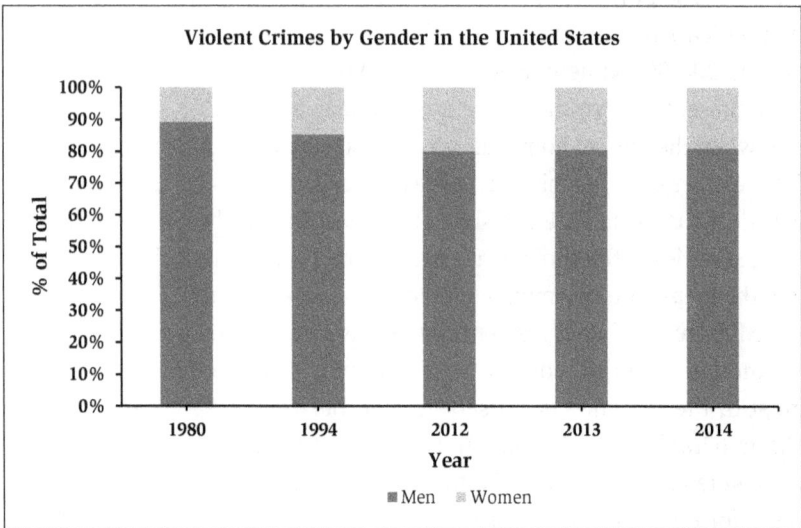

Graph 10: Gender of detainees.

Fortunately, there are exceptions, as in the case of the U.S. where, for over a century, population age cohorts have been estimated annually. The hypothesis that suggests that fluctuation in youth-cohort size may be related to changes in a country's levels of violence and may be put to the test thanks to these records. The population dynamics of the U.S. shows a sharp reduction in parts of the population composition. For example, during of the pre-Depression period of 1928-1929 there was a "baby bust" of low birth rate, and an accelerated growth between 1945 and 1965, the Baby Boom. To a large extent, this huge demographic shift defined the U.S.'s economic, social, and political development over the past century.

The data also reveals that once the Baby Boom got to its highest point during the mid-1960s, a steep birth-rate decline developed. This is consistent with the market availability and widespread use of the birth control pill, which marked the beginning of the sexual revolution in 1965.

Graph 11 shows the evolution of male cohorts in the U.S. (ages 15-19, 20-24, 25-29, and 30-34)(45) compared with the annual homicide rate per 100,000 inhabitants from 1920 to 2012, as well as the predictive values of a multiple correlation model that uses population composition as an input variable(46).

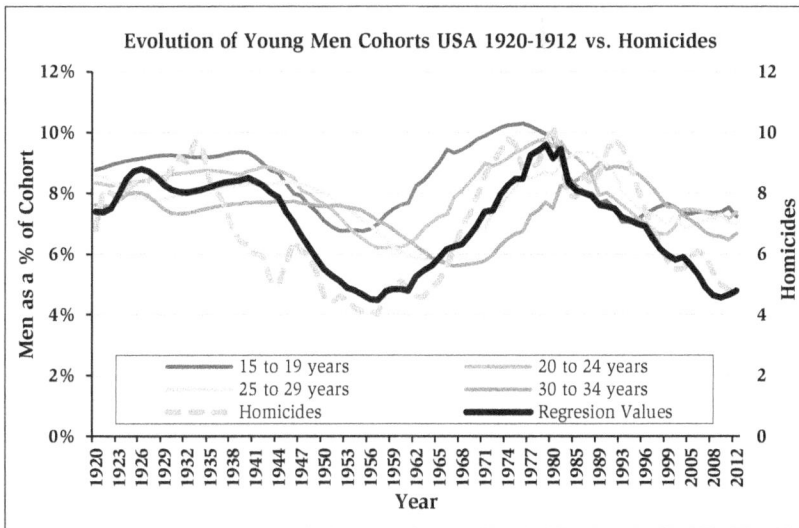

Graph 11: Evolution of male cohorts, homicides, and regression values.

The regression curve presented in Graph 11 (with an R^2 of 0.81) indicates that the variation in the rate of homicides in the U.S. over the past century can be explained, for the most part, by the share of young males within the total population.

Even if the U.S. case provides an ideal scenario to analyze the relationship between violence and population composition, the data collected by the United Nations on more than 200 nations and regions(47) shows that population dynamics are more complicated than we usually believe because it entails complex short, medium, and long-term changes and cycles whose effects are not taken into consideration or are not regarded in most social science studies (Table 11). This happens because we are used to considering population dynamics on an average basis.

Cohort Men 15-24: Percentage of change compared with the previous period (Select nations or specific regions)												
Area, region or country	1955	1960	1965	1970	1975	1980	1985	1990	1995	2000	2005	2010
Africa	8.8	9.9	12.5	16.0	15.9	15.2	15.6	15.3	16.5	16.1	13.4	10.7
Central America	11.1	15.9	18.2	21.8	20.5	15.5	12.4	16.3	9.3	3.9	2.3	6.7
Egypt	6.2	6.0	21.6	22.9	13.4	13.8	11.9	5.6	9.6	17.0	13.9	1.8
Latin America	10.5	12.1	15.5	20.0	18.3	15.0	10.5	7.8	8.0	7.4	3.7	2.0
Mexico	11.0	17.2	18.4	22.0	21.2	16.1	12.6	17.8	8.7	1.4	-0.6	5.4
Rwanda	1.6	2.5	13.6	33.0	19.5	12.5	10.7	19.8	-5.3	39.6	17.4	0.3

Table 11: International analysis of male population percentages.

One of the examples highlighted in Table 11 is that, since 1995, the growth rate of the cohort 15-to-24 years old in Central America is lower than in previous years. That should imply a reduction in the homicide rate, but one of the most important growth trends of violence in the world, according to the UN, is precisely the increase of the homicide rate in this region, which reached 24 per 100,000 inhabitants(48) and as high as 60-per-100,000 in El Salvador. However, upon comparing the homicide rate in Mexico against the data in Table 11, the relationship between the demographic changes and the decrease in homicides for the 1995-2005 period is maintained, although there is an increase as of 2005.

The disparity in data quality may be the reason why the specific analysis of Mexico does not point in the same direction as that of the U.S. The same is true of Rwanda, which in the 1965-1990 period registered high population growth rates — like those of Mexico — but which ended in the 1994 genocide when more than 700,000 people were gruesomely killed in just a few weeks. Egypt is another example where there seems to be a mismatch in the relationship between youth, violence, and population composition. In 2005, the youth growth rate was lower than in previous periods. However, the Arab Spring, an uprising mainly led by young people, took place only until 2011.

This situation, in which some nations evidence a stronger correlation between violence levels and demographic composition than others, is due to additional factors that depend on contextual conditions that inhibit or enable violence-rate fluctuations. That's why the global study was extended to the usual suspects: availability of weapons, levels of inequality, unemployment levels, economic growth, and human development rates. However, in a wide range of countries, none of these variables are significantly correlated with the homicide rate. This confirms why the debate on the causal factors that affect homicide rates is more in line with the realm of philosophy and narrative than with that of data and statistics.

To steer clear of a conventional philosophical statement about violence based on the lack of hard causal ideas, we reviewed the research on cooperation and punishment. Fehr and Gächter(49), in a series of experiments using cooperation and punishment games, discovered that cooperation declines and anti-social behaviors increase when a social system lacks consequences (punishments) against anti-social behaviors. On the other hand, cooperation gradually improves when there's consistent use of a consequence or punishment mechanism.

Just as the age and gender of criminals led us to correlate demographic composition and violence, it is possible to link Fehr and Gächter's experimental results with the consequence system's effectiveness against negative social behaviors (e.g., the quality of its justice system, the extent to which people experience the rule of law). The previous must illustrate a relationship between the quality of the justice system and violence levels. Hence, to examine this assumption, we used the data from The World Justice Project (WJP) Rule of Law Index(50), which comprises eight elements or factors:

- **Factor 1:** Constraints on Government Powers
- **Factor 2:** Absence of Corruption
- **Factor 3:** Open Government
- **Factor 4:** Fundamental Rights
- **Factor 5:** Order and Security

- **Factor 6:** Regulatory Enforcement
- **Factor 7:** Civil Justice
- **Factor 8:** Criminal Justice

Based on these factors, we performed different multiple regression analyses and found that the criminal justice factor is the one with the greatest explanatory power vis-à-vis the homicide rate in the nations examined by WJP. Although the correlation coefficient of a potential model is 0.57, it exhibits a geometrical phenomenon linked to systems analysis, the envelope (Graph 12), which is not very well known within the field of social sciences and is, therefore, generally overlooked. The envelope of a family of curves refers to the curve that is tangent to each member of the family at some point.

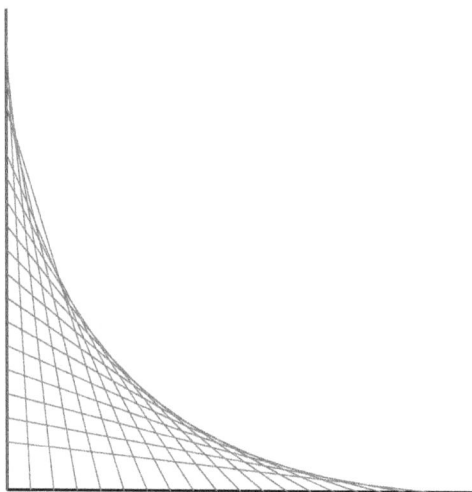

Graph 12: Envelope.

Graph 13 shows an envelope that may be interpreted as follows: a more mature criminal justice system imposes a maximum limit to the violence in each country. Thus, a nation with an incompetent criminal justice system, where there are no consequences for antisocial behaviors, will have such degrees of freedom that both the possibility of high violence exists — as in Venezuela, El Salvador, Guatemala, and Mexico — and low violence, as in Bolivia, Cameroon, and Cambodia. These systems are more sensitive to other factors that influence violence, such as the political, cultural, and the economic environment.

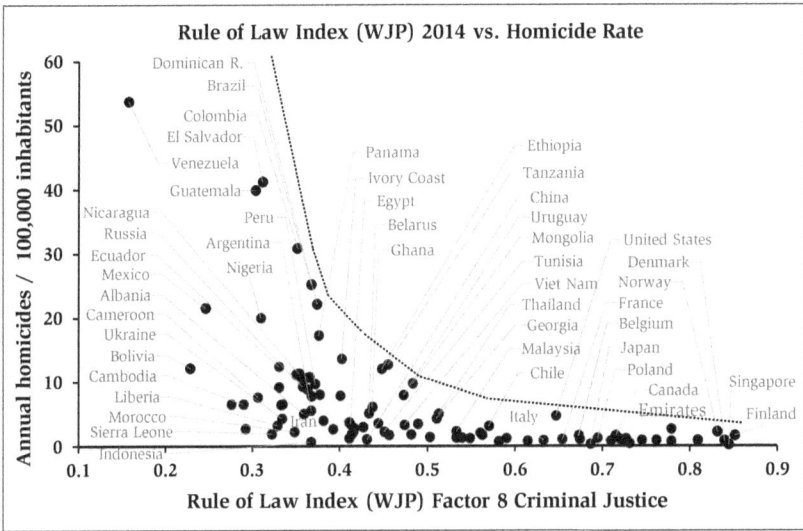

Graph 13: Envelope of the Rule of Law vs. the homicide rate.

On the other hand, the more mature a criminal justice system becomes, the fewer the degrees of freedom for violence.

Another finding between the criminal justice system and violence is the greater maturity of the system, measured by WJP, through the following subfactors:

8.1 Criminal investigation system is effective.

8.2 Criminal adjudication system is timely and effective.

8.3 Correctional system is effective in reducing criminal behavior.

8.4 Criminal justice system is impartial.

8.5 Criminal justice system is free of corruption.

8.6 Criminal justice system is free of improper government influence.

8.7 Due process of the law and rights of the accused.

These mean that a high rating in the criminal justice system and a low level of violence are not the exclusive of advanced and democratic nations. Several nations considered to be authoritarian (e.g., China, the United Arab Emirates, and Singapore) exhibit acceptable degrees of maturity for their criminal justice system and low homicide levels. This means there is no one-size-fits-all solution to reduce violence. Both some of the authoritarian and democratic systems have found ways to restrain, control, and reduce violence by means of punishment and consequence mechanisms. These solutions may be as diverse and different as the criminal justice systems of China, the U.S., and the United Arab Emirates. This is consistent with the inverted U concept cited by Pinker regarding the work of LaFree and Patterson(42):

> *...Established democracies are relatively safe places, as are established autocracies, but emerging democracies and semi-democracies (also called anocracies) are often plagued by violent crime and vulnerable to civil war...*

This is also in line with the practical experience of the International Justice Mission (IJM) and, with Gary A. Haugen and Victor Boutros's proposal, summed up in *The Locust Effect: Why the End of Poverty Requires the End of Violence*(51) regarding the endemic situation of violence and injustice that billions of predominantly poor people endure around the world as a result of the dysfunctional criminal justice systems. A dysfunctional criminal justice system is the same as the absence of a system of consequences. The latter is an essential element of many political systems with a thriving authoritarian model.

In sum, the global homicidal violence that we experience today is less than before, but this positive change and the existing divide between less violent nations such as Japan, with 0.3 annual homicides per 100,000 inhabitants, and the more violent ones like Venezuela and Honduras, with 53.7 and 90.4 homicides per 100,000 inhabitants, respectively, illustrate the magnitude of what still needs to be addressed(48).

In nations with efficient and stable criminal justice systems, the downward homicidal trend will probably run its natural course as the population growth rate stabilizes and the average age of the population increases. But in weak democracies, anocracies, and in nations and cities with a fast-growing young male population, that trend will remain unpredictable and volatile. In Mexico, the INEGI (National Institute of Statistics and Geography) census data(52) and the youth population growth long-term projection, formulated by CONAPO (National Population Council)(53), show a declining trend in the percentage of young population as of 1990 (Graph 14).

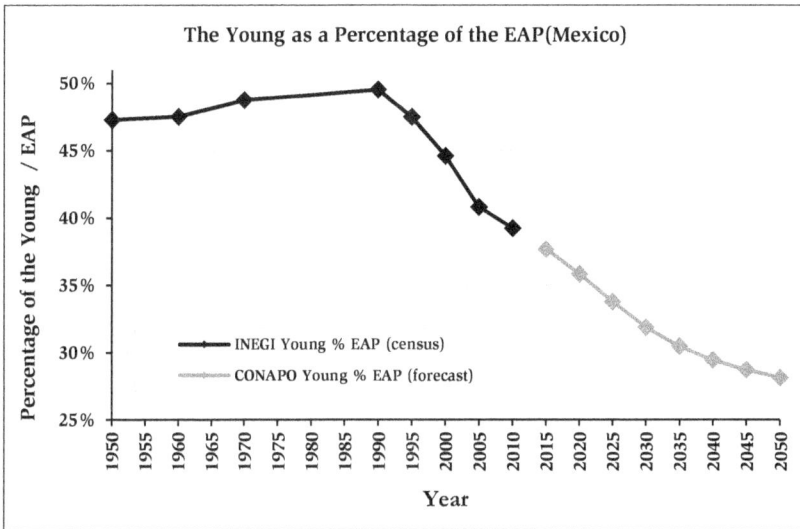

Graph 14: Youth evolution as a percentage of the Economically Active Population (EAP) in Mexico.

According to the graph, a declining homicide rate starting in 1990 would be consistent, as occurred from 1995 to 2005, due to a slower incorporation of young people into the economically active population. This, however, was not due to an improvement in the criminal justice system. Hence, it might be possible that the decline in homicides does not correspond to the abatement of everyday injustice, which limits the population's development possibilities nor to the country's long-term social stability. We must also consider that, should the weakness of the criminal justice system persist (Graph 14), there's no reason why the annual homicide rate could not vary unpredictably up to 50 or more per 100,000 inhabitants.

An example of this paradox may be found in Mexico's National Survey on Victimization and Perception of Public Security (ENVIPE)(54), which constitutes a specific analytical instrument for the Mexican context. In many parts of the world, crime is measured through the reports produced by the criminal justice system. At present, this is impossible to do in Mexico since the system's incompetence has driven citizens to almost completely abstain from reporting crimes to the authorities. The ENVIPE is an alternative method that estimates the country's criminal incidence through a survey. Within a short time, the instrument conclusively demonstrated that there is a huge difference between violence and crime experienced by citizens in their homes and the government's statistics that fuel political discourse. Table 12 shows some of the relevant results from ENVIPE 2014.

Question	Total number of households	Affected households	%
Households that were victims of crime.		10,741 139	33.9
Households with some protective measures against crime.		13,554,128	42.8
Households that changed their place of residence due to a crime (internal displacement).	31,683,869	390,209	1.2
Households that experienced vandalism.		2,407,919	7.6

Table 12: Relevant data from the 2014 ENVIPE.

In conclusion, this section's review offers three elements that explain violence:

1. Violence is predominantly a young male phenomenon.
2. Limits to violence are imposed by the criminal justice system's maturity and effectiveness.
3. Violence, like power, is one of the system's emergent properties that are not defined by the interaction rules. It occurs and grows under certain operating conditions.

This implies that solutions to the problem of crime and violence are linked to opportunity and protection mechanisms for the young as well as to those that guarantee the existence of justice as a standard practice for peaceful coexistence. Simply stated, as Haugen and Boutros mention in *The Locust Effect*(51), "…building such systems is admittedly costly, difficult, dangerous and unlikely. History does not make the struggle seem easier, cheaper or safer — but it does make it seem possible."

The Masters

THE CULTURAL EVOLUTION CAST

Donald J. Trump The point is, you can't be too greedy

Locus of control: External
Self worth: Prostitution
Personal action: Irresponsibility
Collective action: *Raison d'état*
Ethics: Self Interest

MASTER OF NEW YORK

A recurring feature in many tragedies is that the rise and success of the characters, who wouldn't go far under normal or commonsensical circumstances, is made possible thanks to the conditions generated by the plot itself. This is precisely the case of the masters.

Their psychological profile is the least complex of all. They are one-dimensional characters whose main feature is their unwavering determination to attain a single objective. Their extraordinary motivation to do so is supported by some type of *raison d'état* or supernatural belief, and, hence, they believe themselves to be enlightened by the magnificence of their fate and their mission in life. They see life in black and white and are not bogged down by complicated explanations about the world. So, they divide mankind into two categories: followers — all those who help them reach their goal — and enemies — those who are not subject to their designs.

Their audacity and determination to achieve their goals make them seem courageous and indomitable, and so they become the protagonists and antagonists of the authoritarian world. But despite their popularity, they are not familiar with true friendship or love for others. Their personal relationships are exclusively transactional.

Real masters don´t acknowledge having peers, but the most intelligent ones can accept the existence of rivals with equal or greater power and can also establish coexistence relationships in situations where these are more advantageous than confrontation. Nonetheless, they do not hesitate to fiercely attack seemingly feeble opponents, and therefore, showing strength is of the utmost importance. They know that any other masters will react similarly upon perceiving any weakness in them.

Masters are scarce, percentage wise, against the total population. They either thrive or wither. They are maximalists and are incapable of living in middle-of-the-road conditions. Unlike lackeys and serfs, they are born, not raised(55), where there's no contention mechanisms against them. Pushed forward by their supernatural enlightenment, they will create some intense tragedy in which they will be the pivotal character of the story.

These types of characters put their heart and soul in every transaction. Although not all of them are driven by the same appetites, their apparent set of motivations is rather limited. Most of the time they focus on obtaining some absolute: money, control, power, fame. Deep down, the true nature of their reason to be is their incapability to accept defeat. The wealthiest millionaire or the most celebrated conqueror who operates under the master model will agonize over losing a coin flip or a tug-of-war contest with the same intensity as losing a big contract or the most significant battle in history.

Their amount of money, fame, or admiration symbolizes, to them, the number of times they have overcome defeat. This is what they are really accumulating, and they can't stop doing it. They go to any length for the sake of winning. And this unstoppable urge constitutes the main source of attraction for the lackeys, who depend on the master's compulsion to win so they can perform.

Many masters are unsuccessful in societies that endured and learned in the past from the destructive consequences of an authoritarian master. In such places, when the lesson has been learned, contention mechanisms against masters (e.g., hate speech prohibition) are usually incorporated to the social norms. There, masters are segregated and perceived as misfits with delusions of grandeur who must get help for the sake of their dignity.

Fortunately, the non-authoritarian, contemporary world also offers them paths for development. There are some fields, regarded as high-risk for ordinary people, in which the success of masters can generate social benefits or become harmless. These are in the forefront of technological innovation where success can only be attained by contributing tangible value within the open and challenging setting of high competitiveness. It includes fields like show business and sports, and the unyielding defense of the territory against invasion by a more powerful enemy.

Masters may prove to be flamboyant when they are rising, mainly because of their penchant for building monumental projects and their ability in making spectacular promises. However, except for the entertainment industry, sports, high risk, extreme or desperate endeavors. Masters always leave higher costs than the benefits they produce.

Even in environments that do not curtail the free progress of masters, few of them ever succeed in fulfilling their ambitions. This does not prevent a single, glorified master from turning a children's fairy tale into the darkest and most twisted tragedy.

Most masters end their ascent to enlightenment, and their lives, in spectacular bonfires of scandal, war, fraud, or violence that leaves behind a long-term aftermath. Their own beliefs usually lead them to think that natural and social rules don't apply to them and are different from those that must be followed by ordinary mortals. Furthermore, they are never willing to concede or compromise on their central purpose. They only stop when they are contained, exposed, or defeated.

Any indication of success reinforces the master's sense of enlightenment and strengthens his impulse to stay the course. On the other hand, signs of failure are quickly interpreted as actions concerted by enemies, so they redouble their efforts to overcome them. They live locked up in a circular operating logic from which they cannot escape and in which all roads always lead to repeat the same behaviors.

An important characteristic of the masters' closed logic is that they see themselves as the nourishing source of society, as the flowing spring of power, money, ideas, decisions, and justice they impart to others. This may be corroborated every time someone says: "This project — law or social change — was made by..." followed by the position or name of a single individual. Citizens, as the shareholders that make up society, are nonexistent in the master's authoritarian model. Normally, masters view themselves and act as the owners of everything within their reach, whereas lackeys and serfs undertake the role of tenants and beneficiaries of their masters' favor. Thus, the landlord/tenant dynamics of the authoritarian model come full circle.

The Lackeys

Just as in the dramatic arts, lead characters cannot exist without the supporting actors. In the authoritarian world, this role is performed by the lackeys. These individuals are more complex and have greater psychological depth than masters, with whom they share the transactional relationship with others, as well as an exacerbated sense of self-interest. They also operate with a one-dimensional vision of the world: to obtain a profit/avoid personal losses in every decision they make, regardless of the consequences their actions have for others.

They are characterized by the intense selfishness that guides them through life. Unlike masters, they do not have an ultimate belief about their own fates and are pragmatic about the personal gains and losses brought about by every decision they make.

THE CULTURAL EVOLUTION CAST

Adolf Eichmann I never had the power and responsibility to give orders

Locus of control:	External
Self worth:	Prostitution
Personal action:	Irresponsibility
Collective action:	*Raison d'état*
Ethics:	Self Interest

LACKEYS OF THE REICH

The flexibility of not being bound by ultimate beliefs and obsessions, together with their characteristic selfishness, allows them to evade the master's black and white vision by incorporating shades of gray that make it easier for them to develop more varied and complex relationships with others. This makes them adaptable and, in many cases, pleasant. However, the common denominator of the relationship circle created by lackeys is that they must give back some type of gain or advantage. These characters continuously modify their relationship circle to get closer to whomever may be able to secure them with benefits. Therefore, lackeys will be seldom found at the foot of a hospital bed, unless it is their ailing masters' bed. For lackeys, personal relationships are mostly of a collusive or confrontational nature.

When lackeys team up with masters, the limitations imposed by the external locus as a barrier that impairs their success are defeated since masters overcome the external locus hurdle by means of *raison d'état*, through the realization of an enlightened design that drives them to achieve victory. No matter how absurd the conquest may be, lackeys without a master shall join it. Lackeys, without their masters' motivation, will be stranded and have little chance of making headway to attain their personal interests.

Lackeys lack the courage and confidence to initiate and lead a movement, be it political or commercial. Masters, with their simplistic and monochromatic view, are incapable of creating the complex elements of an authoritarian system (ideology, control systems, political, commercial, and social organizations). That is why they depend on the greater range of action, complexity, and intelligence of lackeys, who undertake the architecture, construction, and operation of the authoritarian world. Such is the case of Adolf Eichmann in World War II.

Masters and lackeys constitute a co-dependent binomial without which the authoritarian world could not exist. Lackeys need the masters' motivation, drive, and concessions to function, while masters require the flexibility, commitment, and work of lackeys to develop their vision. What is paradoxical about this partnership is that, far from being supplementary or mutually reinforcing, it, in fact, generates a weak, contradictory, and even pathological relationship based on the psychological shortcomings of both characters.

Irrational masters can only be followed by undeserving and prostituted lackeys. This also reveals how weak this relationship is. Deep down, masters are only interested in achieving the goals that guide them. They are not concerned with the well-being of lackeys. Lackeys are only interested in their personal gain, not their masters' ultimate goal. So, if they both move forward in their agendas, the relationship will be strong, and lackeys won't hesitate to stand by their ailing masters' bedside, just in case he might pull through. The moment either one of them reckons there is no chance for further gains, masters won't think twice about sacrificing their lackeys, and lackeys will have no qualms about abandoning their masters. This explains the large number of betrayals, intrigues, and crimes that have taken place over the master/lackey relationships throughout history. Even today, in an authoritarian system's crisis, it is not uncommon for masters to separate themselves from their lackeys by saying things like: "I was wrongly advised." "I trusted the technicians." "We were betrayed." Meanwhile, lackeys have no compunction about saying: "I followed orders from above." "He wouldn't listen." "It wasn't my call." "I followed the rules." Collaboration between masters and lackeys is as hypocritically affectionate as that experienced between prostitutes and their clients: If there's a profit, the illusion of a profound and affectionate relationship will persist.

We must not forget that lackeys are the ones who exploit the psychological weakness of the masters. The latter's personality is the result of a pathology from which it is hard to escape, while lackeys do have freedom of choice regarding their course of action. Therefore, upon analyzing the consequences of authoritarianism, we must assign most of the responsibility to the lackeys. Various studies on the epidemiology of mental illness have found an incidence of sociopathic, narcissistic, and psychotic disorders that is several times higher among the top echelons of political and corporate leadership(55). Which leads us to wonder if what goes on in authoritarian systems is not, in fact, the criminal exploitation and manipulation of masters at the hands of lackeys.

Viewed from the human rights perspective, sociopathic masters are a vulnerable group that should be protected so that it may not be used as a weapon or unlawful instrument. In fact, this is what currently happens in many professional environments that implement preventative measures to avoid the combination of a sociopathic condition with a high-responsibility situation. An example of this is the disaster of the Germanwings plane that crashed with 150 passengers and crew in March of 2015 and that stirred international public opinion(56). The analysis performed by the experts in forensic psychology indicate that Andreas Lubitz, the copilot who deliberately caused the plane to crash, had, among other things, a sociopathic disorder(57). The question that remained unanswered was: How could someone with compromised mental health be made responsible for a plane full of passengers? Zero tolerance is expected from commercial aviation authorities and airlines when it comes to keeping mentally unstable individuals from obtaining operational command of an airplane. The same may be asked about the authoritarian world, which, to exist, requires the combination of the sociopathic delusions of illuminated masters and the criminal intentions of the lackeys who follow them.

The master/lackey alliance can also help explain the centrality of corruption in authoritarian systems because it is the source of the compensation that lackeys expect in return for their submission and loss of dignity. Without corruption, the lackeys' loyalty may not be secured nor can the absurdities of authoritarian masters be financed.

Relationships among lackeys are complicated. Each one strives to maximize his own personal gain, and given their inherent psychological structure, minimizing risk exposure is regarded as vital. This results in a toxic combination: 1) aversion to risk; 2) hopes of high profits; 3) the need for an ever-growing flow of resources that avoids internal conflicts among lackeys, and 4) a scheming and competitive atmosphere that hinders genuine cooperation and the generation of value for others. The best possible outcome in this set-up is a zero-sum game: each lackey works for himself, and his gain is another one's loss. The worst possible outcome is a negative-sum game, where everyone loses. This happens to be one of the historical sources of crises in authoritarian systems.

Chinese emperors knew that when the court's eunuchs started fighting each other, the stability of the empire was uncertain. Likewise, the internal problems of the Pretorian Guard fractured more than once the stability of the Roman Empire. Hence, two essential measures are frequently established in authoritarian systems for the sake of stability. First, discipline is a lackey's main virtue or "value" because it implies total submission to the master's command. More important than disagreements among lackeys, it prevents the lackeys' unrestrained self-interest to overflow and crash the system. Second, there is the generation of gains for lackeys and masters despite the losses sustained by society, which, in the long run, constitutes the authoritarian model's main weakness.

The long-term pillaging or destruction of a natural resource, which generates short-term benefits for those who perpetrate it, is a good example of this, as in the logging described in the Zempoala lagoons postcard. In colloquial terms, we may say that an imperative requirement for the stability of an authoritarian system is the generation of benefits for lackeys, even with zero-sum or negative-sum games for society. As they say in the world of gambling, the house always wins and must always win, otherwise the relationship between masters and lackeys grows weaker, and the system's stability is lost. Douglas North also identified and underscored this situation when he said that the main thing that makes limited access orders stable is the appropriation and distribution of economic rents among the members of the elite(10).

In percentage terms, lackeys are more numerous than masters, which implies greater diversity when attempting to classify them. But, so as not to dwell further on the taxonomy of this character susceptible to subdivisions, we shall only discuss the general characteristics of lackeys.

One of their most interesting features is their capacity to adapt, changing to blend with the environment and apparent way of thinking. In the face of adversity, a lackey is usually shrewd enough to show ideological, religious, philosophical, and mindset changes. For a lackey, hard referents such as an ideology or a philosophy of life are but mere accessories that can be used and interchanged according to the prevailing needs.

Because of this, they can occupy many different places in society, provided a receptive master and the opportunity to gain something. Lackeys can get on board their master's program but are incapable of believing in it. That is why they are the only ones who truly do well under an authoritarian regime.

Unlike their masters, lackeys are stealthy and have high tolerance for frustration. Most likely, lackeys will not burn at the stake for being heroic or defending their interests, as is frequently the case with masters. In fact, lackeys provide authoritarian systems with resilience. Through selective acts of resistance and sabotage, they constitute an effective anchor and almost always succeed in undermining the change and reform initiatives aimed at diminishing or taming some element of the authoritarian system.

Although the construction of the authoritarian world is the work of lackeys, they find it easier to remain in a situation of plausible deniability vis-à-vis decisions and their consequences. After all, in the master/lackey society, the deal is that success and recognition belong to the masters. But the difficulty for masters and lackeys lies in the fact that they run the risk of blaming each other for problems and losses whenever it is impossible to pin them on someone or something else, such as society or the market. Authoritarian masters expect submissive lackeys to accept the negative consequences of the acts in which they participate. Lackeys, shielded from public scrutiny, expect the admonishing fingers to point at the disgraced masters. Thus, one of the many perversions of the authoritarian world is that masters or lackeys who err on the side of naiveté may end up being framed by their own accomplices.

Adaptability, tolerance to frustration, discretion, tenacity in defending personal interests, and plausible deniability are the building blocks in the art of being a lackey. In the authoritarian political domain, these are known as good political practices. In the shady business realm, they are known as entrepreneurial guile.

In the non-authoritarian world, lackeys can be functional. They are usually embedded in the government and corporate bureaucratic systems and enjoy acquiring some sort of technical expertise. They try to substitute their codependent relationship with their authoritarian masters by getting close to the top-management levels of the organization in question. In environments that seek to create value for clients and citizens, lackeys don't usually fare well. They feel frustrated by not having the creative and innovative capacity to stand out in meritocratic environments, which they are bitterly opposed to, even if they have the operational expertise regarding the methods. Transparency and the result-oriented approach exposes them. They are thwarted by the constraints imposed on parasitism or free riding. Bureaucratization and instigating dissention by exercising the small power, often brings them satisfaction and solace.

In cognitive terms, lackeys who are immersed in a non-authoritarian environment sublimate their need for a master through submission to the system, processes, and rules. They will continually try to find ways of taking advantage of these mechanisms, regardless of whether their personal use and interpretation of them conform to the purpose or spirit with which they were created. This way of operating and undermining the rules of coexistence from within for the sake of satisfying their self-interest is precisely one of the stability challenges that exist in contemporary democratic systems. Here are some examples: using loopholes and gray areas in the law to secure unlawful electoral funding, tax evasion, or selling harmful products in the market.

By analogy with an iceberg, in the authoritarian world, the masters' actions are the part exposed above the water line. But the largest part of it is the lackeys' daily efforts to sustain the system. They remain unseen and protected below the surface. Just like masters, lackeys have a circular operating logic that allows them to transfer the authoritarian model's responsibility to the master and the losses of authoritarianism to society and the markets while they secure the profits for themselves. At the same time, they shun any responsibility, along with the weight of complicity and manipulation of the masters.

For lackeys, losing their dignity under the yoke of the masters is a necessary and sufficient excuse to dodge the responsibility for their actions. However, as in street prostitution among consenting adults, the master/lackey relationship entails a joint responsibility partnership in which lackeys definitely have a share.

The Serfs

Serfs fulfill the role of giving life and color to the plot as supporting actors. Serfs, like most supporting characters, are static, i.e., they remain unchanged throughout the storyline. They exemplify the lack of mobility, social mobility in the case at hand. Through a wide variety of roles, serfs

THE CULTURAL EVOLUTION CAST

Mineros de Serra Pelada — Everything in this life is for sale (Coronel Carvalho)

Locus of control:	External
Self worth:	Prostitution
Personal action:	Irresponsibility
Collective action:	*Raison d'état*
Ethics:	Common Good

SERFS OF SERRA PELADA

are ubiquitous, despite having little individual influence (power) in the overall development of the plot. Both masters and lackeys expect serfs to play a passive role, though they use them as the main participants in the dilemmas to overcome, such as: "saving the good-natured and kind folk from the clutches of the oppressor."

Most masters and lackeys are born in the world of serfs, which is more extensive. And just as the dynamic characters in a play, they rise from among the serfs, start out as minor supporting characters and, along with the plot, undergo changes and transformations to become protagonists or antagonists. According to interaction rule number two (collaboration or competition), for this to happen either of these two conditions must be met: 1) giving free rein to a master's sociopathy, or 2) foregoing the serf's sense of community to walk the selfish path of the lackey.

Even though masters, lackeys, and even serfs, themselves, fail to appreciate their merits, we must acknowledge that the submission and disempowerment conditions in which they live make them experience all sorts of difficulties that force them to be resourceful, to improvise, and face everyday life with limited resources. This exchange renders them colorful in terms of their behaviors, expressions, and outlook on life. Something that differentiates serfs from masters and lackeys is that, aside from following rule two in the collaborative but not competitive configuration, is that they have a low motivation level to change the situation in which they live, despite their best efforts to survive.

According to Pérez López's(58) anthropological motivation theory, there are three ways human beings may be motivated: by having (fame, fortune, power), by doing (discovering, knowing, creating), and by being (service, dedication, fulfillment in doing good for others). Furthermore, in accordance with the survival strategies (status quo, surviving, growing, and transforming), one of the effects of submission associated with an external locus of control is that actors in the authoritarian world lack the creativity and innovation required to transcend the existing ideas and concepts, as they are dependent on external factors to act (refer to Table 7).

This means that masters, lackeys. and serfs cannot be motivated by being or doing. These motivation modalities require the ability to go beyond what already exists. Consequently, there are two possibilities left: 1) lacking the motivation to change the situation (the case of serfs that corresponds to the survival strategy), or 2) to pursue the status-quo strategy. Serfs are not bent on changing their living conditions because, aside from having strong incentives to maintain their customs and traditions intact, the situation of poverty, violence, and hardship experienced in an authoritarian society forces them to invest most of their efforts in sorting out their short-term survival needs.

Another difference is that the difficulty to survive in an adverse environment drives serfs to create solidarity and mutual-help bonds with their peers, bonds that are not based on the intrinsic value of individuals nor on considering individuals and their needs important since they are not aligned with the concept of human dignity. This, together with the external locus of control, leads them to establish as the paramount value the idea that the people — the community, the collectivity, the hive — constitute the goal that must be preserved by all serfs, regardless of the negative cost for the individuals. This characteristic constitutes, simultaneously, the main strength and the fatal flaw of serfs. It is a strength because the serfs' ability to collaborate and coalesce as a group allows them to craft the tools for tradition, defense, and aggression that they use to preserve their community. Traditions, conventions, and customs codify the practices that have ensured survival throughout history. Various anthropological studies, which analyzed the cultural traits of traditional societies regarding the distribution of food and the performance of rituals and celebrations, revealed that many traditions result in an equitable distribution of sustenance(59), thereby abating hunger and redistributing income. The serfs' collective solidarity and uncompromising defense of tradition are features that intend to project the external locus of control into the notion of the group as an impersonal metaphysical entity that allows them to unite into a community, which becomes strong, improves the possibilities of survival for the group, and produces stability provided it becomes the barrier to bring about change in the social rules that are important for survival.

Second, the well-being of the community or the people, seen from the perspective of *raison d'état*, is a fatal disadvantage when such a concept is seized and manipulated by masters and lackeys to influence the collective force of serfs in favor of their own interests. George Orwell's *Animal Farm*(60) is a classic allegory on this subject since it describes the animals' rebellion against a cruel and alcoholic farmer. Little by little, the pigs, who lead the rebellion, take over and create a new, repressive situation for the other animals. In the real world, through *raison d'état*, a systematic alignment between masters, lackeys, and serfs — identical to that described by Orwell at the beginning of the animal's rebellion — takes place. Serfs will see in *raison d'état* the legitimate defense of community and tradition, while masters and lackeys will manage to obtain the necessary influence over serfs to fulfill their personal desires. This is the ideal state that an authoritarian system tries to attain.

The serf's allegiance and mobilization capacity may prove to be both powerful and fragile. It will be powerful when it relates to subsistence and the collective values that bind them, but it will be fragile insofar as the goals are less related to the group's traditions. The foregoing indicates that, upon trying to change a tradition that is important to the group or one that is considered as vital for subsistence, the effort invested in the initiative will be futile vis-à-vis the resistance to change by the serfs, which will be decisive, frontal, and carried to the bitter end.

When changes do not affect tradition, like modernizing initiatives — and have less tangible short-term objectives that do not entail a cultural change — the serfs' mobilization will lose its momentum and will be easily stopped by masters and lackeys through some prostitution mechanism. Therefore, in the authoritarian world, the social mobilization of serfs is often easily neutralized through shameful negotiations.

In fact, in countries like Mexico, intermediation or management of social movements are the backbone of the political process. They allow serfs to derive small, short-term profits without changing their long-term condition of submission and serfdom and allow masters and lackeys to maintain a long-term influence over the system despite the costs incurred by paying the short-term serfdom fee. The use of this mechanism is facilitated by irresponsibility.

In sufficiently large and complex societies, the negative costs of the interaction between masters, lackeys, and organized groups of serfs can be transferred to some other segment of society. For example, Mexico City and the nation's busiest highways are a usual venue for this dynamic. Here, different social groups of an authoritarian ilk frequently take over and block some important avenue or highway precisely when traffic is at its heaviest, like at the start of a holiday or school term.

This situation soon turns into an act of extortion for the population(61). Most of the time, roadblocks end up with some shady negotiation in which money, political favors, private concessions of public goods, or the curbing of some reform or modernization initiative are exchanged. History is full of democratic advocates who got derailed because they tried to seize authoritarian power without previously building democratic power. In the authoritarian world, unexpected twists in serfs' social movements are not uncommon.

Extreme mobilization of serfs occurs when a desperate situation, fueled by heroes and bandits, overflows and brings about the collapse of the authoritarian regime from its head, top-down, but without there being a bottom-up change in society's interaction rules. This kind of revolution ends up substituting an old and depleted authoritarian regime with a new one in which the serfs' mobilization capacity is quickly renewed to strengthen *raison d'état* and consolidate the authority of the new group of masters and lackeys that will restore the authoritarian configuration.

The most convincing example of this in Mexico is the 1910 revolution instigated by Francisco I. Madero, who managed to fragment the dictatorial control that Porfirio Diaz held for more than three decades. That revolution unleashed a violent, factional civil war that took 10 years to die out, leaving a legacy of more than 1,000,000 deaths, economic ruin, and the birth of a new authoritarian system that prevails today as the center of Mexican political life.

The present situation in Iraq constitutes a recent and iconic example, where the dictatorial control of Saddam Hussein and the Iraqi Republican Guard were defeated by the U.S. military invasion in 2003. Nonetheless, that invasion did not lead to a change in the social logic despite the establishment of a democratic parliamentary system. It has produced widespread chaos and violence, fueled by international funding by various economic, political, and religious groups vying for control of the oil-rich territory.

Another contemporary example is Egypt. In 2011, there were huge social mobilizations as part of a regional phenomenon known as the Arab Spring, which led to the simultaneous fall of several governments, including that of Hosni Mubarak, who ruled Egypt for 30 years (1981-2011). This case is the first revolution in which the effects of a change in network topology resulting from digital technology can be observed. Despite the new element of turbulence generated by the digital world, the end of Mubarak's government did not disrupt the interaction logic at the base of society nor did it culminate in the transformation of the country into an open and democratic society. So far, Egypt's main challenge is achieving short-term social and political stability, which after everything that has happened, is more dependent on the actions of the military — still holding power — than on the actions of an internet-empowered society.

In all cases, it seems clear that despite the initial major social mobilization, the end results were different from the originally stated intentions. Francisco I. Madero ended up murdered in a *coup d'état*. The U.S. — despite having militarily defeated the Hussein regime and invested more than a trillion dollars and more than a decade in attempting to stabilize the region — is still caught up in an ongoing chaotic regional conflict that is supported by new stakeholders such as the Islamic State (IS). The Arab Spring revolutionaries witnessed Mubarak's fall from power but did not achieve any other strategic goals. The Supreme Council of the Armed forces in Egypt agreed to celebrate free elections in 2012, but then staged a coup and imprisoned Mohamed Morsi in 2013, suspended the constitution, and to this day, maintains the political control of the country with high approval ratings from the population(62).

Unlike masters and lackeys, serfs do establish friendship and affection bonds with relatives and members of their community, but beyond the inner circle in which they grow up, they tend to be sectarian, tribal, and wary of the unknown and of outsiders. This, together with a temporal short-term vision, produces unstable and volatile interactions with the people who do not belong to the community with which every serf identifies.

On the other hand, it is possible to belong to the inner circle of serfs by investing a significant amount of time and effort to overcome the initial resistance. This is because — based on resistance and mistrust of the external world — several cultural codes that give rise to the stratification and compartmentalization of the authoritarian world emerge among serfs. Each group tends to create an identity that differentiates it from other groups, and that relates to some cohesive element such as the geographical area or some commercial, artisanal, professional, religious, or sports activity. Each group has representatives or leaders, who, most of the time, are masters or lackeys responsible for preserving the traditions designed to guarantee the survival of the community.

According to these rules (group identity and leader's responsibility to preserve the community), authoritarian world communities are fragmented into groups, fiefdoms, phalanxes, guilds, and rival localities that require complicated and costly vertically articulated relational networks to coordinate with one another. This fragmentation, whose foundation is the basic and consistent logic used by serfs, limits the assimilation and dissemination of modern concepts that promote systemic integration, such as dignity, liberty, democracy, and the rule of law.

The foregoing may lead to a discussion about the difference between the fragmenting traditional values and the integrating modern values of societies. This is an issue that must, undoubtedly, be carefully reviewed in the future. But for present purposes, it is sufficient to underscore two points: 1) the backwardness concerning gender issues and violence against women in most traditional societies, despite community solidarity values, and 2) the constant complaint voiced by academia regarding the abandonment of traditions due to urbanization and modernization processes. This confirms that neither the collectivizing solidarity nor the authoritarian traditions of serfs manage to survive the shift from a closed society to an open one, which strengthens the notion that each interaction logic — authoritarian or democratic — generates emergent outcomes that are not interchangeable or mutually compatible.

Communities of serfs require representatives — Sherpas or stewards — whose main virtue is coming from the same group or having paid the price of overcoming vetting. They must concentrate in achieving narrow goals and short-term tradeoffs that provide specific benefits for the community, regardless of the improvement of the system at large.

One of the paradoxes of the authoritarian system is that, even if it is a simpler and easier model to establish to reduce violence in the short term, it stagnates its reduction in the long term. Once traditions are established, they become resistant to change. The community authoritarianism of the serfs can have less violent rules than the cause that originated them, e.g., mutilating those who infringe social rules after a trial instead of killing them through blood feuds. But as time goes by, the permanent rules in traditionalist serf societies become obsolete versus the moral changes in society.

In the same train of thought, Steven Pinker, in *Better Angels of Our Nature* (2011), points out that one of the "better angels" is our moral sense. He explains that it "sanctifies a set of norms and taboos that govern the interactions among people in a culture, sometimes in ways that decrease violence, though often (when the norms are tribal, authoritarian, or puritanical) in ways that increase it."(41)

So, even if the serfs' collective solidarity acts to improve the probabilities of survival — and if community-building initially allows a decrease in feral violence — a significant number of serf-serf interactions are most probably regulated by inflexible and outmoded cultural codes in relation to humanist values founded on human dignity. In contemporary authoritarian societies, this results in endemic violence, like gender-based and domestic violence, which are presently frowned upon.

Two examples of this situation are associated with religious traditions that have not changed for centuries due to their taboo nature and that draw the attention of international public opinion. First is female genital mutilation (FGM), sustained by between 100 and 140 million women around the world(63). Second are the unequal legal rights of women compared to men's that exist in nations governed by Islamic law(64).

Once people choose to settle into the serf mode, having a leader who interprets, articulates, and embodies that which the community (non-existent metaphysical entity) wants and needs becomes a natural necessity. This makes it easier for masters and lackeys to occupy a leadership position that is there and naturally available. They only need to transmit — in the case of masters or build, in the case of lackeys — the *raison d'état* that best suits their interests camouflaged as the voice of the community preached by the prophets. If serfs consider that their spokespersons — the masters and lackeys who represent them — are credible, they will meekly submit and will not be judgmental of the incongruities, injustices, and faults their leaders might incur. Some platitudes and clichés that illustrate the condition of serfdom in Mexico show up whenever an authoritarian leader is caught in an act of corruption: "He's a thief, but he shares." "He steals but is effective." "That's the way things work."

Notwithstanding the above, the relationship between serfs and masters and lackeys may overturn if the identity between the community and its leaders is lost. Again, we may resort to Egypt's recent history as an example. Hosni Mubarak was a war hero who became president. He remained the country's main figure — its pharaoh — for 30 years despite several corruption scandals during his administration, but those scandals did not mobilize Egyptian society. Prior to the Arab Spring, nothing predicted the end of Mubarak's rule given that his tenure was free of any major social hiccups. However, he was overthrown during massive protests that even mobilized international public opinion.

It appears that a complex combination of factors shattered Mubarak's credibility as Father of the Nation. This is a case in point because, in the aftermath of his resignation, the military managed to separate the people's repudiation of Mubarak from the credibility of the armed forces as the ultimate guarantors of social leadership. This flipping of public opinion was so great that the military — long an integral part of Mubarak's government — overthrew the first elected government in the country's history in 2013 without a reprise of the massive repudiation protests and without undermining the trust and popularity which the officers and soldiers continue to enjoy in Egyptian society(27).

Much like lackeys, who shrug off the responsibility of their actions by brandishing their masters' dominance as an exonerating shield, serfs do not internalize the responsibility of their actions either, least of all when these are collective actions. A powerless serf, who is only part of the herd led by the master — or by the lackey on behalf of the master — and who is in favor of the community's necessary welfare, has every opportunity to disengage from taking any responsibility. Fame or defeat belong to the masters, who are the fount from which the community's *raison d'être* flows. Therefore, lackeys and serfs are but mere tenants. They are unworthy of a commemorative bronze statue, and therefore, do not assume responsibility for problems resulting from mob violence.

On the other hand, serfs who are in the unfortunate situation of facing life away from their community in an unsafe and unpredictable environment are under such stress that they may betray or forget their traditions. This has already been the case for millions of individuals who abandoned their rural customs and became modernized through urbanization. But they may also try to recreate traditional ways of life in the new environments where they settle. An example of this is the reintroduction of cockfighting in the U.S. by some immigrant groups(65). This illegal activity, which according to this country's moral perception constitutes an abominable and unlawful practice of animal cruelty, takes place even if the organizers, breeders, and spectators run the risk of ending up in jail.

In less extreme cases, serfs outside the authoritarian world — who do not assume the autonomy and liberty that personal dignity affords — will find it difficult to function without the guidelines that a traditional community offers. They will be easy prey for the many situations that the contemporary world presents to all who choose to put the course of their lives in somebody else's hands, like the round-the-clock offerings available in all the media of junk psychology, esotericism, miracle products, get-rich-quick schemes, televangelists, and, of course, populist politicians, who are currently part of a subtler form of serfdom. Modern-day serfdom no longer puts shackles on people and require them to build a pharaoh's temple, but it does subject them to bondage through credit card debts, addictions, destructive consumption patterns, or devotion to an irrelevant or harmful cause that prevent them from realizing their full human potential.

The Heroes

We have already mentioned that authoritarian interaction rules essentially involve masters, lackeys, and serfs. However, reality is more complex. Even if an authoritarian system can be stable and functional for a long time, more often than not, some people will always be excluded from the three previously mentioned authoritarian roles. These individuals can only occupy the periphery of the system, where they are marginalized and forced to choose between one of the following options:

THE CULTURAL EVOLUTION CAST

Hugo Chávez Either we take the path of socialism or the world will end

Locus of control: External
Self worth: Prostitution
Personal action: Irresponsibility
Collective action: *Raison d'état*
Ethics: Self Interest

BOLIVARIAN HEROES

1. **To convert to authoritarianism.** In *The Devil*(66), Giovanni Papini suggests that if one lives in hell, there are only two ways of escaping suffering: by becoming a demon to be part of hell, or by turning a small piece of hell into heaven. Similarly, the first route to

escape authoritarian marginalization (hell) implies becoming an authoritarian to escape the hardships it generates, even if it means prostituting oneself and losing ones' dignity (being a demon).

2. **To migrate.** Migration due to political, economic, social, and environmental reasons is one of the main concerns facing the world. The driving factors of migration, including the environmental ones, often originate in the negative consequences of authoritarian systems, which force millions of people to abandon their communities to try to build a better future elsewhere. For example, over the past century, direct immigrants from Mexico and their children are believed to have created in the U.S. a Mexican-American nation of approximately 34.6 million people(67), equivalent to 28% of Mexico's current population. Similar situations involving millions of migrants each year — people who leave authoritarian nations bound for democratic ones — exist in other parts of the world, from Northern Africa to Europe, from Southeast Asia to Australia and New Zealand.

3. **To rebel.** Rebellion is an act that gives rise to the authoritarian system's heroes. Heroes are those who, dissatisfied with the state of affairs, rebel and embark on a path toward changing the situation.

Some might propose a fourth way of subsisting in an authoritarian system without being part of it: doing nothing. However, this is tantamount to converting to authoritarianism. Although these days, non-involvement — doing no wrong but doing no good, either — is a generalized practice regarded as an intelligent strategy that reduces risk exposure. The spectator stance is tantamount to being a tenant in the world in which one lives. It's a type of self-delusion to pretend one is neither a lackey nor a serf.

Along the same lines of what has been stated about dignity, citizenship, and the banality of evil, the non-involvement strategy is the same as active participation in authoritarianism, since, according to Western ethical concepts regarding the supremacy of human dignity, not doing good is doing wrong!

However, several characters may be classified under the rubric of rebels, and we shall analyze them separately. In this section, we will describe heroes, and later and within the portrayal of the democratic world's characters, the other types of rebels known as superstars and paladins to differentiate them from the authoritarian heroes and from the legitimate individuals who, through their daily actions, manage to allow a small part of the world to stop being part of the authoritarian hell.

The description of authoritarian heroes is simple. Heroes are powerless masters. They are the ones who, from a powerless situation and through authoritarian interaction rules, forge a path that allows them to expand their influence within the system. The road or recipe used by the authoritarian hero is:

1. **To identify the most serious flaws in a mature or unstable authoritarian system.** The main flaw of any authoritarian system is its inability to curb violence. According to various classic authors such as Max Weber(68) and contemporary ones such as Douglass North(10), the containment and control of violence is the State's ultimate purpose. As an authoritarian system matures, the most deeply felt flaws are the ones that are most intensely withstood by the serf communities, those that undermine traditions, endanger the community, and imply imminent threats to survival such as hunger, or that represent the need to redress an offense or injustice directed against community values.

2. **To drum up rhetoric that binds negative feelings to a clearly identified enemy.** This is essential to channel and capture, through the external locus of control, the serfs' and lackeys' willingness and energy to act. Authoritarian heroes do not build responsibility and citizenship but are adept at assigning the blame for the problems to the ruling masters. The essence of their revolutionary message always has slogans such as: "What we need and deserve has been taken away from us." "We have to take power to recover what belongs to us." "We don't need a bigger cake, we just need to recover the slice that was taken away from us." "The resources are there, but they are poorly distributed," etc.

3. **To stir the pot until the goal is achieved (making a revolution).** This is accomplished when the idea of a revolution is sufficiently distilled, and it becomes a *raison d'état* that organizes the authoritarian logic of masters, lackeys, and serfs into a system. This is the most sensitive part of the process as it can be solved through a velvet revolution that does not engender more violence or it can imply the beginning of a lengthy, chaotic, and violent conflict.

4. **To establish and construct a new authoritarian system.** The new system must solve, at the lowest possible cost, the pending grievances of the previous regime, but also benefit masters and

lackeys, even at the expense of serfs and the rest of the population. It must also marginalize and prosecute those who do not accept the rules of the game until the system matures and a new authoritarian hero takes advantage of the flaws to renew the life cycle of the authoritarian system. That is, to restart the process from its starting point.

One thing that must be pointed out about heroes is that, when the authoritarian system starts to decay, the people may easily see them as the solution to all their problems and even consider that "it couldn't be worse," because they are sick and tired of that which hurts them the most. But the fact is that one can always dig a deeper hole, as when criminal violence overflows into a civil war or when the reduction of freedoms and the hardening of an authoritarian regime are accepted in favor of the reduction of violence. Therefore, it is crucial to understand that, as far as rebels seeking to change the authoritarian system are concerned, authoritarian heroes are not the answer.

The Bandits

Aside from the three ways to escape authoritarianism that we mentioned above (converting, migrating or rebelling), there is another solution: the excising role of bandits. Though this road may resemble that of rebellion, it is in fact a different one since it does not seek to change or take control of the system. What it aims to do is to narrow and fragment the control of a part of the system. In legal terms, to excise, or cut out, is to breakdown an entity, which constitutes a whole, into two or more independent entities

THE CULTURAL EVOLUTION CAST

Chapo Guzmán Friends are plentiful when you have cash

Locus of control:	External
Self worth:	Prostitution
Personal action:	Irresponsibility
Collective action:	*Raison d'état*
Ethics:	Self Interest

CAPOS FROM SINALOA

created from the components of the original one.

Bandits, not unlike legal excising, wish to take control of one or several areas through violence so they may fulfill, in functional and operational terms, their yearnings and desires. Gabriel Zaid(69) states that when crime escalates to organized levels, controls a territory, charges for protection (taxes), and administers punishment, the State disappears because it has been replaced by crime. This means that part of the country has been excised and falls under the control of the bandits. From a different perspective, when bandits thrive, and the people are submitted to a daily state of violence, the meaning and significance of "Nation" fade away despite the persistence of a national iconography, a flag, and an anthem. In places where people are mugged and harassed everyday due to the criminal fragmentation of their neighborhoods, the "Nation" ceases to exist. Whenever nations coexist with bandits, it is impossible to uphold a country's identity, understood as a shared history and culture that allow those who participate in it to achieve a better life.

One description that clearly illustrates the bandits' purpose may be found in Thomas L. Friedman's *From Beirut to Jerusalem*(70). In it, he explains that of all the complex phenomena he experienced and observed in the 1980s as a correspondent for the *New York Times* in Beirut during the Lebanese civil war, the one that upset him the most was the persistence of violence and conflict as the staple of a dysfunctional way of life that affected many and benefitted a few:

> ...During the first decade of Lebanon's civil war, the various Christian and Muslim militias became not only private armies representing the interests of different religious communities but also vehicles for the social and economic advancement of members of the Lebanese underclasses. The longer the civil war continued, the more the members of this underclass were able to take over Lebanese society from the traditional aristocracy, capitalists, and industrialists. Small-time crooks like Muslim militia leader Ibrahim Koleilat, frustrated middle-class lawyers like Shiite militia leader Nabih Berri, government schoolteachers like Shiite extremist Hussein Musawi, and medical students like Phalangist boss Samir Geagea (who became known as "Dr. Samir" only after his appointment as a Phalangist militia chief retroactively made him a medical school graduate)

became big men around town overnight. The civil war pro-
vided them with a route to the top that would otherwise
not have been available to them....

Bandits, like heroes, are masters and lackeys, generally young, who lack the aspiration, capacity, and possibility to do well within the system. They resort to violence as their main tool, possibly the only one, and consider that their reason for living is taking control of a space that enables them to carve a niche for themselves in society.

To say that criminals are only opportunistic individuals going after easy money is the most commonly used, meaningless platitude to explain criminality as a way of life. However, this explanation, which describes only part of reality, does not delve into the more profound reasons that motivate bandits to commit a crime or to use violence and force of arms to resist any attempt to integrate them to society.

This is not trivial. None of the many rights listed in the Universal Declaration of Human Rights explicitly state that people, including bandits, have the fundamental need to be somebody and have a place in society. Although, in fact, this idea is the basis of many human rights, such as having legal standing, the right to have a family and to own property. It is also pivotal to the customs, rituals, traditions, rights, and obligations that give meaning to people's aspirations and that sustain society. Some examples of that which confers us a place and recognition as members of society are parenthood, a professional degree, marriage, personal wealth, profession, business, artistic and scientific achievements, sports victories, initiation rituals (christenings, and the like), among other possibilities that are often unattainable by marginalized people no matter how ordinary and conventional they may be for most of society.

Considering that violence and crime are phenomena mainly carried out by young people — and that youth is when a person must move from dependence to independence — "youth" should be understood as a natural stage when there's an impulse to find a role and be acknowledged as part of society, however asocial the individual. Those societies where access to public goods that promote capacity building such as health and education are inadequate; where opportunities for economic development and employment are scarce and disgraceful; where social mobility is low; where the young population is large; where the criminal justice system is weak; and the social interaction logic is dominated by the authoritarian model (external locus of control, prostitution, irrespon-sibility, and *raison d'état*) — those societies constitute the ideal breeding ground that facilitates the transformation of numerous groups of young masters and lackeys into gangs of authoritarian bandits.

Mexico's social, economic, and demographic process in the last few decades illustrates how bandits and their way of life have proliferated. For more than 40 years, Mexico's net economic growth was low, its young population increasing, the education and health systems inadequate, and the criminal justice system unacceptable. The Global Impunity Index(71) ranked Mexico as the second worst in the world. Economic disparity in-creased, unemployment and sub-employment rose, and social mobility stagnated(72). There's very little chance that the son of a blue-collar worker will ever become the owner of a manufacturing plant, so much so that those of us who live in Mexico have never heard of such a thing happening nor have we seen it reported in the media. Instead of providing meritocratic social mobility routes, the country only offers poor young people, who do not submit or migrate, two alternatives to go from rags to riches: the road of bandits (drug trafficking and organized crime) and the road of masters and lackeys in shady businesses and corrupt politics. Upon asking several officials, who at some point worked in specialized organized crime task forces, about the motivation that persuades cap-tured bandits to pursue a life of crime, they stated that the oft-repeated phrase used by bandits was: "Better to live a month like a prince than a lifetime as pauper."

According to *Skills Outlook*(73), published by the Organization for Economic Co-operation and Development (OECD), whose members are the advanced and rich economies in the world, one out of every four people in the member countries in the 16-29 age group are currently neither employed nor in education or training. This situation does not represent an impending threat of an increase in crime and bandits to nations that have mature criminal justice systems, populations with a higher average age, and that are geared toward the democratic model. However, this shows that the new and widespread phenomenon of total youth idleness will continue swelling the ranks of bandits and multiply-ing violence-related problems in other parts of the world.

The bacchanal in the authoritarian brothel

In 2003, I was invited to a meeting that was unprecedented in the political life of Mexico City, but consistent with the prevailing times. This was after the presidential electoral alternation that ended the same political party's rule (the PRI) of more than 70 years. It was the first formal visit of the city's chief of police to an opposition political party's headquarters.

The main point of the meeting — an open dialogue without a script — was a topic dominating the city's public opinion surveys at the time: whether the police were controlled by a criminal organization known as "La Hermandad." Various authorities debated the existence of this police mafia. On the one hand, some officials downright denied it, while on the other, evidence to the contrary was being leaked to the media, which presented it to an audience that had been long appalled by the escalating crime rates and by the journalistic reports about "La Hermandad."(74)

In response to this situation, the head of government of Mexico City — the second in history to hold this position by citizen election — hired the services of Rudolph Giuliani, the former mayor of New York, to: 1) diagnose the city's crime-related issues, 2) review the internal situation of the police force, and 3) make recommendations and support their implementation.

On this setting, those of us who attended the meeting asked the chief of police three questions: Does "La Hermandad" really exists? What does Giuliani's report say about the internal corruption of the police? How will the police force be cleaned? His answers revealed, probably unwillingly, the profound knowledge he had about the twisted inner-working logic of these organizations, which allow the emergence and permanence of systematic corruption. Ever since then, his words became a powerful example of the origin and emergence of bad institutional habits.

The chief answered that "La Hermandad" did not exist as an actual criminal organization with a permanent structure, leaders, and processes, but that, from his perspective, "It was a *modus operandi*, a set of agreed upon values and behaviors, a culture that articulated the chronic and legendary criminal reputation of Mexico City's police. Hence, finding the visible bosses, prosecuting them, and putting them in jail was not enough to change the situation because, if the city did purge the culture of "La Hermandad," there would always be replacements for the mob bosses, thus perpetuating the model of corruption and abuse against the citizens."

This issue is relevant to wind up the explanation of authoritarian dynamics. Having described all the roles (masters, lackeys, serfs, heroes, and bandits), it is worth delving a little bit deeper into the plot dynamics, the interactions between the characters, which we shall call the authoritarian bacchanal.

The daily stories published by newspapers and read by those of us who live in these environments often resemble or surpass any episode of the most controversial and popular TV series of recent years, which, given the crudeness of their stories, have shocked their global viewers. Following are some examples that confront actual, recent news with television fiction.

April 12, 2012. "El Pozolero"/"Breaking Bad."

Fact: Police captured a criminal gang member known as "El Pozolero." This man specialized in dissolving the bodies of the group's enemies in lye. The detainee declared he had dissolved 300 corpses through the years(75).

Fiction: Several web pages claim the writers of the U.S. television series "Breaking Bad" were inspired by "El Pozolero" when they incorporated the dissolution of bodies in acid as the most sordid part of the series. According to its fans, only six bodies were dissolved throughout the five "Breaking Bad" seasons(76).

September 26, 2014. Ayotzinapa/"Sons of Anarchy."

Fact: As per instructions of the mayor of the municipality of Iguala in Mexico's State of Guerrero, the police apprehended a group of 43 students considered to be inconvenient and handed them over to a group of drug traffickers who executed and incinerated them(77).

Fiction: The overall plot of "Sons of Anarchy" takes place in a small, fictional town called Charming, which is dominated by an outlaw motorcycle gang engaged in arms trafficking. The outlaws have struck a deal with the police to maintain peace and control of the town in exchange for the free flow of arms and payment of dues. As the series unfolds, it is normal for criminals and authorities to sit around a table to determine the course of action to be followed. Verging on the absurd, the gang usually has trouble concealing or disposing of the large number of corpses generated by their criminal activity.

June 2012. Monex case/"House of Cards."

Fact: The winning candidate of the 2012 presidential election is accused of receiving illegal funds through a complicated triangulation scheme operated by the Monex firm. The investigation takes several years and finally concludes in 2015 with the acquittal of the party that nominated the candidate, who has been in office as president for more than two years(78).

Fiction: As the plot of "House of Cards" unfolds, we discover that, during the presidential election, a businessman, whose interests in China are favored by the incumbent administration, carried out a complex triangulation to illegally fund the campaign. In the series, the president does not fare well and is forced to resign once the scandal is uncovered.

June 30, 2014. Tlatlaya case/"Scandal."

Fact: Members of the armed forces kill 22 people in a warehouse in the municipality of Tlatlaya, State of Mexico. The initial report by the army states that the deaths were due to a shoot-out between soldiers and criminals. Further forensic analyses and witness accounts indicate that it was a mass execution(79).

Fiction: In "Scandal," there is an organization called B613 that operates above the law and institutions. It is designed to safeguard the republic at all costs. Its black operations include murder, enforced disappearances, and torture.

November 9, 2014. The "White House"/ "House of Cards."

Fact: A team of journalists discovered that the president's wife owned a house — white — valued at $7,000,000, which she bought from an entrepreneur who was part of the Chinese consortium that had been awarded a $7 billion contract to build a high-speed train in Mexico(80). The scandal led to the cancellation of the project on the eve of a Mexican state visit to China, whose government expressed its discontent over the situation. In the media and political circles, rumor has it that the information about the existence of the house was leaked to the media by a former head of government of Mexico City who aspired to become a presidential candidate in 2018. Ever since that time, this politician has experienced a series of incidents that have prevented him from becoming a member of Congress. Another rumor going around is that those affected by the "White House" scandal have engaged in revenge politics. On the other hand, the journalists that revealed the information were fired, months later, from the company where they worked.

Fiction: In "House of Cards," the presidential campaign's illegal funding source is a Chinese citizen. But, after an intricate storyline, he ends up being extradited and presumably executed in China because of the scandal.

2013-2015. Pedro Ferriz de Con(81), Ciro Gómez Leyva, Carmen Aristegui(82) and Terecer Grado/"House of Cards."

Fact: Over the 2013-2015 period, four popular newscasts in Mexico, whose common denominator was showcasing political discussion forums, critical postures against the government, and the dissemination of the findings of journalistic investigations, were cancelled amidst polemical and controversial circumstances.

Fiction: In "House of Cards," reporter Zoe Barnes, who maintains a complicated love-hate relationship of convenience with Senator Frank Underwood, is pushed in front of a train by the senator himself. On the other hand, Lucas, another journalist who helps Barnes, is arrested for cyberterrorism and sentenced to 10 years in prison. Thus, Underwood has a clear path to become vice-president of the U.S.

August 11, 2014. Representatives' party/"Sons of Anarchy."

Fact: Several conservative party representatives are filmed at a party with prostitutes during a working meeting held at a holiday destination. The trip was financed with public funds(83).

Fiction: Every time the members of Samcro, the outlaw motorcycle club in "Sons of Anarchy," manage to defeat an enemy, save one of its members from jail, or carry out some kind of business, they organize a party that invariably ends up in a wild orgy.

July 12, 2015. El Chapo's escape/"Prison Break."

Fact: Mexico's most wanted drug trafficker is recaptured and imprisoned in one of the country's maximum-security jails. After spending one year and five months in prison, the criminal made a spectacular breakout through a 1,500-meter-long tunnel built by his henchmen from outside the compound. He had already escaped from a high-security prison once before.

Fiction: "Prison Break's" main plot is based on an escape plan that a man, thanks to his exceptional technical knowledge, implements to free his brother, who is imprisoned in a high-security jail.

The most shocking aspect of these real and fictitious stories is the travesty of masters, lackeys, heroes, and bandits, and the banality of the rewards they achieve. One day, a political candidate may be a hero; on another, a master and then a bandit. Likewise, a bandit may go from being a hero to a master, or fall from grace, as have many former Latin-American guerrilla fighters who ended their days as lackeys, sheltered in the bureaucracy of the systems they once pledged to destroy. Deep down, the system of values needed to fill any of these roles is the same.

As an Italian friend, whose European friends could not understand her fascination for visiting Mexico City, once told me: *"So che la città è un bordello, ma è un bordello interessante"* ("I know the city is a brothel, but it's an interesting brothel"). From a democratic, moral-sense approach, these twisted tales and partnerships between masters, lackeys, heroes, and bandits, look like a brothel. However, this is a common situation in authoritarian systems. As the chief of police told us back in that 2003 meeting, mafia-like organizations are the result of the mafia-like way of doing things, just as an authoritarian system is the result of an authoritarian way of doing things. To play an authoritarian role, all you need is to commit to the authoritarian world interaction logic as a principle of life. To support this idea, we may resort to a controversial statement on corruption that Mexico's president made during a press conference on August 20, 2014, when he said that he considered corruption to be a cultural trait(84).

The chief of police referred to in the anecdote was Marcelo Ebrard, who ironically best exemplifies the authoritarian politician's chameleon-like ability to perform all the roles of a closed model. Ebrard was an active member of most of the country's political parties: a prominent member of the authoritarian political system (lackey), and a revolutionary chief of police and member of the opposition (hero). In 2006, he managed to become the third democratically elected head of government of Mexico City, and, thus, a presidential hopeful (master).

As head of the city's government, he commissioned, among many projects, the construction of a subway line that, only a few months after opening, proved to have multiple serious basic engineering flaws that led to the closure of approximately half its route from March 2014 to November 2015(85). This is one of the most significant engineering and public work disasters in Mexico's history. Investigations by supervision bodies, like the local legislative branch and the judiciary, indicate there were several cases of technical and administrative corruption involved in the construction of the subway line. However, the inquiries to establish the criminal responsibility of the former head of government (bandit) are still pending(86). Much of the information regarding the responsibility of those involved in this case was made public in the media by the contractors themselves, in a comedy of the absurd in which the technicians (lackeys) claim to have acted against good engineering practices under Ebrard's full knowledge and authority(87), and Ebrard himself claims to have been deceived by the technicians that he entrusted with the project(88).

Ebrard was also the head of government that some of the media identified as responsible for having leaked information about the president's wife's White House(89). During the 2015 electoral process, despite all his efforts and the help of two different political parties, he failed to become a candidate to the federal congress, a position that, according to the Mexican legislation, would have given him judicial immunity for three years. Ebrard stated that the president's authoritarian influence on the electoral authorities was the way he retaliated against him(90). In the meantime, the White House case did not instigate any legal or fiscal responsibility, not even the start of an independent investigation. It did, however, inspire the president of Mexico to suggest the creation of a national public ethics committee(91) to be chaired by the president himself and comprised of the state governors. Said proposal went no further, given the unanimous social reaction against the absurdity of having the very same politicians accused of acts of corruption monitoring themselves.

As scandals build up in an abundant stream of news that make it impossible to separate facts from conspiracy theories, on the flip side of the coin — that of all the authoritarian characters' profits — we once again discover that these are but a tiny fraction of society's losses, as in Elba Esther Gordillo's case. We only need to look at the ratio between the White House's $7,000,000 appraisal (the profit) and the $7-billion loss to the Chinese contractor resulting from the cancellation of the project linked to the scandal. As in "Sons of Anarchy," this hefty collection of anecdotes and stories proves that the only goal of criminal activities is to stay alive until the bacchanal at the end of the episode. Without imagination, knowledge, or creativity, the money obtained by these characters serves no other purpose.

In fact, that orgy is tantamount to the public flaunting of $10,000-worth of watches by those in charge of the poverty reduction programs(92), the million-dollar houses of unknown origin, the political vendettas, the catastrophic engineering flaws, the cancellation of necessary projects, the indiscriminate disclosure of unlawfully obtained telephone calls and videos, the disappearance of newscasts that expose corruption(93) and, of course, the vast excesses of politicians paid with public funds and captured on video in an economically stagnant country, one devastated by crime, violence, injustice, and poverty. Under these circumstances, a nation's scene turns into a brothel, where reality — that of Mexico, and surely that of other similar nations around the world — is more adept at contriving situations. There are true tales of far-fetched crime, corruption, injustice, and violence that surpass any work of fiction by the most renowned scriptwriters in Hollywood.

Hence, based on the analysis of the complexity level that differentiates authoritarian and democratic societies, it is possible to define an authoritarian disposition according to the agent's or individual's behavioral model. Through this model, we may establish analogies, identify and explain the system's emergent phenomena, provide empirical support to causal explanations and perceive — through the intricate state of reality — the main structures and forces that articulate and shape this world, which, unfortunately, persist and thrive in the 21st century. After reconstructing the social complexity that results from the roles, behaviors and relationships between the authoritarian characters, we may now forge new paths that will allow us to figure out how to face, sort out, and reduce the problems they create.

5. Why authoritarianism?

Violence reduction

So far, authoritarianism looks bleak: violence, corruption, and injustice in an unyielding and endless cycle that is renewed thanks to the despair and desperation of those who endure it. However, it is no accident that approximately 88 % of the world's population currently lives under the shadow of one of the three types of closed systems: the consolidated authoritarian regimes, the hybrid systems, and the dysfunctional democracies. If we consider the data presented so far, leaving our democratic prejudices aside, we can see that the global popularity of authoritarianism is brought about by a concrete value proposition.

There are positive aspects to authoritarian systems. For example, the most authoritarian side of the spectrum does a better job at containing poverty than dysfunctional democracies. On the other hand, 59 % (30/51) of the nations considered as consolidated authoritarian regimes by *The Economist* have homicide levels of less than 10-per-100,000 inhabitants (Table 13). Furthermore, the consensus is that the creation of nation-states is based on the consolidation of the monopoly, on the use of physical force, and violence specialists. Hence, the reduction of violence is the main benefit that both democratic and authoritarian systems may offer the population.

#	Country	Homicide Rate	#	Country	Homicide Rate
1	Kuwait	0.4	16	Iran	3.9
2	Bahrain	0.5	17	Cuba	4.2
3	Algeria	0.7	18	Yemen	4.8
4	Saudi Arabia	0.8	19	Belarus	5.1
5	China	1.0	20	Laos	5.9
6	Oman	1.1	21	Afghanistan	6.5
7	Qatar	1.1	22	Eritrea	7.1
8	Tajikistan	1.6	23	Chad	7.3
9	Jordan	2.0	24	Cameroon	7.6
10	Azerbaijan	2.1	25	Kazakhstan	7.8
11	Morocco	2.2	26	Burundi	8.0
12	United Arab Emirates	2.6	27	Guinea-Bissau	8.4
13	Vietnam	3.3	28	Guinea	8.9
14	Egypt	3.4	29	Gabon	9.1
15	Uzbekistan	3.7	30	Russia	9.2

Table 13: Authoritarian regimes with homicide rates of less than 10/100,000 inhabitants.

Cheap to implement, costly to maintain

One important difference between implementing an authoritarian solution or a democratic one is the contrast between efficacy and efficiency within each system. This, in turn, relates to two socio-biological systems' problems: 1) the coordination cost of agents; and 2) the risk and cost of making a mistake in choosing the survival strategy. Because of these problems, we have:

- **Authoritarian efficacy.** It has a centralized coordination model with a low coordination cost and high risk of error regarding the choice of strategy. It is effective in the short term, but inefficient in the long run, since it has less flexibility to adapt to the changing conditions of the environment and is more likely to make more mistakes upon choosing a strategy.

- **Democratic efficiency.** It has a more decentralized coordination model that reduces the risks of error when choosing a strategy. The system is more responsive to feedback, but incurs higher coordination costs. It is, therefore, efficient in the long term, but expensive in the short run.

This means that authoritarian systems are cheap to implement, but costly to maintain. In a society burdened by violence and desperate to solve it, effective short-term political proposals will probably be the ones favored by society, but they will not be efficient in the long term. The problem is that, in terms of complex adaptive systems, origin is destiny. Once the choice of embarking on authoritarianism has been made, the opportunity costs incurred will be the long-term democratic efficiency.

Let us recall that successful authoritarian nations, with annual per capita incomes exceeding $10,000, are oil-producing countries (Graph 3). Therefore, if we incorporate the data on proven oil reserves per capita into the graphical representation of income, democracy, and countries by type of regime (Graph 15), we can see that, given the size of the bubbles, those that represent the magnitude of proven oil reserves in barrels per inhabitant, the possibility of living off the exploitation of natural resources, and being authoritarian go together as much as peanut butter and jelly. The exceptions are Canada and Norway, which began large-scale oil exploitation after having reached a high level of democracy.

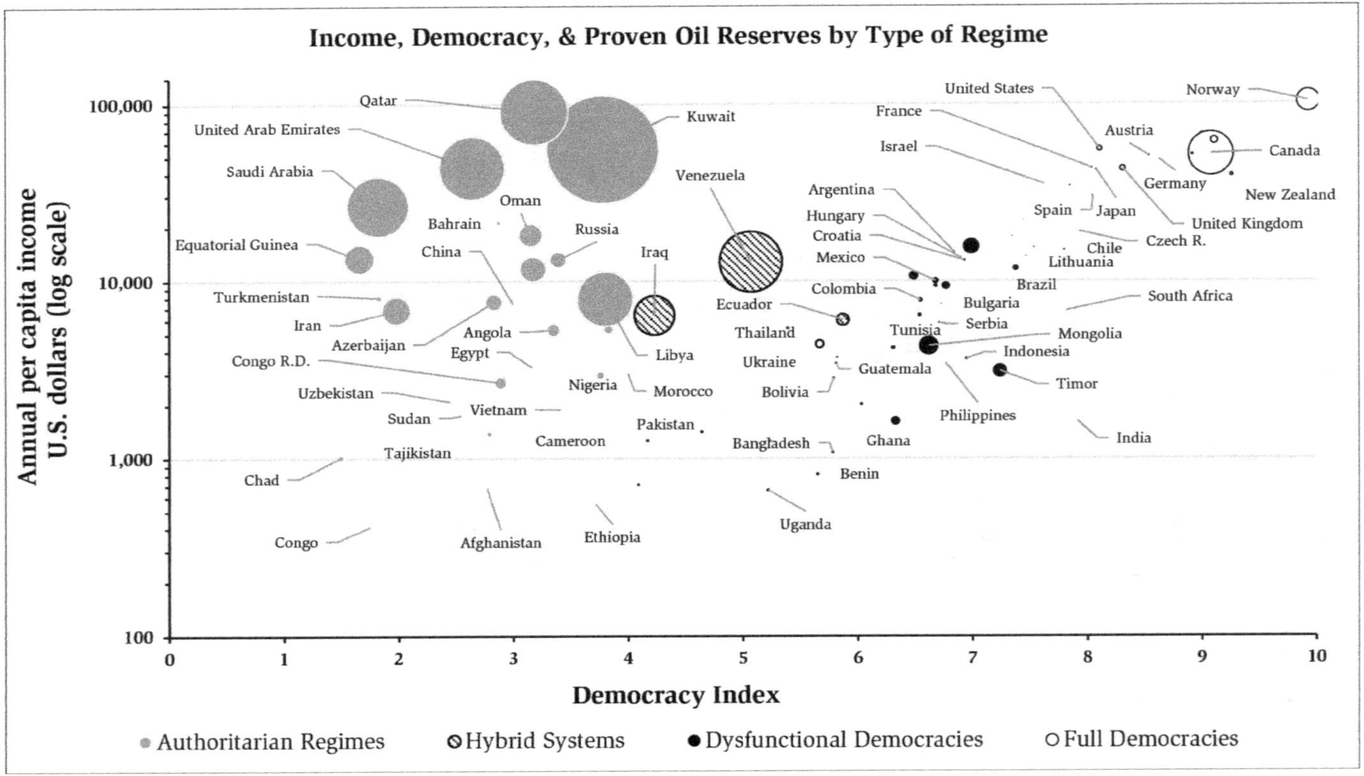

Graph 15: Income, democracy, proven oil reserves per capita and countries by type of regime.

To illustrate the magnitude of the differences, look at the figures in Table 14:

Country	Barrels per inhabitant	Value of annual production per capita ($90 x barrel)	2014 GNI (WB Atlas)	Production value / GNI	Reserves in Years
Kuwait	29,890	$24,727.46	$55,470	44.58%	108.79
Mexico	84	$682.31	$9,980	6.84%	11.08
China	19	$102.21	$7,380	1.38%	16.73
United States	96	$968.61	$55,200	1.75%	8.92

Table 14: Reserves per capita, value of production, and oil as % of GNI.

Graph 15 shows the U-type phenomenon when comparing authoritarian vs. democratic nations, which strengthens the premise that authoritarianism is not a primitive nor embryonic stage of the so-called advanced nations, but rather a different type of system that emerges and is configured with its own set of rules. This phenomenon, which has been observed many times before, is known by different names: the paradox of plenty, the curse of natural resources, or rentier states. The counterpoint is that full democracies, for the most part, are nations with limited natural resources that face marked seasonal cycles. That has led to the emergence of a North/South geography made by the difference between "northern" developed nations and "southern" or tropical developing nations.

To function and survive, northern nations are forced to have permanent mechanisms of efficiency, planning, and long-term cooperation because the population knows that long-term efficiency is more important than short-term efficacy. This awareness stems from having endured food shortages and the need for large amounts of energy every winter throughout their history, which has been marred by major famines due to systemic errors. This does not mean that only countries with adverse climates allow for the dominant logic of democratic interaction. Australia and New Zealand are examples of how an open society can function in different latitudes of the world, other than those in which it normally emerges.

Graph 16 shows, on a logarithmic scale, the estimated duration of oil reserves, at current production rates, compared with the production value of oil as a percentage of national income. Except for Canada, most of the authoritarian ecosystem is located in oil producing countries that have reserves for more than 20 years (separated by the dotted line on the chart), or in which oil revenues are equal to or greater than 10% of their national income. This means that Mexico is a nation that no longer has the necessary wealth to return to the authoritarian path it followed during the 20th century; that Venezuela has the necessary resources to turn into an autocracy that may last a century; and that limited access to oil resources in China and India make it impossible for them to take on the costs and risks of long-term authoritarianism. The rest of the nations that don't have the necessary natural resources to be truly authoritarian nor the civic orientation to become democratic, live in the worst of all possible worlds. As the data confirms, incompetence in being authoritarian is worse than authoritarianism itself.

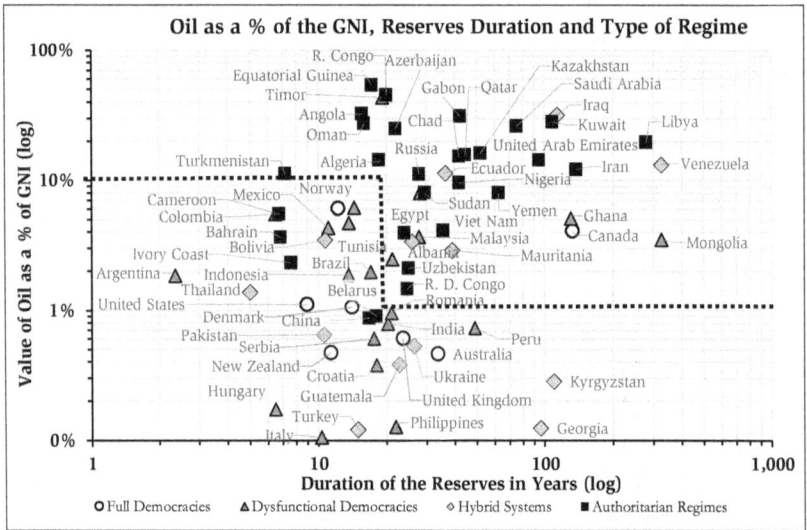

Graph 16: Value of oil as % of GNI, Duration of Reserves (in years) and Type of Regime.

Where there are no people, there´s no value
Anonymous

6. The value of the open society

A framework to study democracy

E ver since the Cold War, propaganda clashes between authoritarian and democratic regimes have been characterized by two negative stereotypes. The authoritarian stereotype is the world of power, State violence, lack of human rights, economic stagnation, control, corruption, and institutions above individuals and dogma. The democratic stereotype is the materialistic world of money, vanity, superficiality, the absence of community bonds, inequality, consumerism, and an empty individual freedom.

Basing the analysis of the two systems on these stereotypes is, evidently, not objective nor useful. Doing so would imply getting caught up in the taxonomy created by postwar biases, which already have their own conclusions and to which nothing new can be added. On the contrary, the taxonomy of the cultural evolution model allows us to tear apart both stereotypes and discover, for example, that several authoritarian systems add value to those who live in them by reducing violence. On the other hand, it also makes it easier to delve on the causes that substantiate the stereotype, such as the persistence of poverty and lack of opportunities for women.

The description of authoritarian systems led to the analysis of power, violence, and the behavior and motivations of authoritarian characters. We have concluded that authoritarian systems follow a logic based on ease of implementation, low coordination costs, and a concrete value offer represented by the reduction of violence and short-term efficacy, but all of this at the expense of dignity, liberty, efficiency, diversity, sustainability, and long-term stability.

However, according to the beforementioned data, the democratic world offers less poverty and higher education and health levels than the authoritarian world. But it is worth examining the democratic world from the perspective of its most controversial elements: the sustainability and inequality issues that cast doubts on its long-term viability.

What is value?

In today's world, market freedom seems to guide and justify the existence of democracies. Their most visible outcome is money, since GDP is regarded as the main indicator of wellbeing and success, despite efforts to create and use other indicators such as the happiness or the human development indexes.

At the individual level, money also plays a leading role. In democratic societies, in absence of other references, an individual's net monetary value (or net worth) is often regarded as a measure of success. The paradox of open systems is that there has never been so much money as today. But after a certain level, more money and satisfiers seem to go hand in hand with greater levels of dissatisfaction and social inequality. Furthermore, after every economic crisis, like the one in 2008-2009, larger movements emerge, such as Occupy Wall Street in the U.S. and the "indignados" (outraged) movement in Spain, that challenge the meaning of money as the ultimate outcome and measure of the value democracies create. Because of this and many other reasons, we need to review the deeper meaning of value without any prejudice or pre-acceptance regarding whether money and value may be considered as equivalent concepts.

Value as a concept has been the nightmare of countless social thinkers, as it acquires different meanings depending on the context in which it is used. In Wall Street, it is understood as the net worth of a company, which results from multiplying the stock price by the number of shares available in the market. For Marxist economists, it implies the gain in utility the raw materials acquire by the addition of labor by means of the production process. In philosophy, it is linked to values and to what is right or good. In all cases, however, value is an outcome that one craves, and therefore, it is something one wishes to attain, and that is important, because it drives the system's evolutionary direction.

It was explained in Chapter 2 that a system is a set of interrelated components that consume energy and produce work and results. Said results are the value produced by a system. In terms of physics, the universe is an inhospitable place for order. It follows an overall trend toward the net increase of entropy, but comprises phenomena such as life and culture that, without violating the physical laws, manage to increase order or negentropy wherever they arise, by means of gains in their information levels. This increase of order is the value or outcomes biological and cultural systems produce.

130

So, energy use, entropy, negentropy, information, evolution, and complexity are inextricably bound by the laws of physics. As César A. Hidalgo from MIT explains(94), there are formulas, like Seth Lloyd's, that help us estimate the theoretical amount of information that may be stored in the universe (10^{90} bits), and the maximum amount of information that our planet may hold (10^{56} bits). The same formula is used to estimate the theoretical information storage capacity of any physical system. In 2007, Martin Hilbert and Priscilla López concluded that information stored in culture — texts, pictures, sounds, and videos — was 10^{22} bits. César Hidalgo himself, estimated that the amount of information stored in the Earth's biological and cultural systems is 10^{44} bits. Putting these figures into perspective, the cultural information created up to 2007 (10^{22} bits) represented only 0.0000 000000000000000000000000002 % of the theoretical storage potential of the planet, and 10^{44} bits — the sum of the information stored in both biological and cultural systems — barely represents 0.000000000001 % of that same potential. It may well be that, despite the fast increase of information produced by the digital age, that percentage will probably decrease as biodiversity and ecosystems are lost.

Another interesting aspect of these theoretical calculations, as the author suggests, is that:

> ... although Earth has an enormous capacity to store information, order is still rare. [...] That insight, tells us a lot about how information is created and processed by the planet and the hurdles that could limit its growth in the future. [...] The first thing the informational emptiness of our planet reveals is that information is hard to grow, difficult to make, tough to preserve and challenging to combine into new configurations.

Thus, the long-term outcome, or the value that human culture creates, is the increase in information levels, order, or negentropy as the complexity levels of human societies increase.

This conclusion may seem cold and dehumanized, but upon observing the value of cultural phenomena from a complexity perspective, it turns out that we naturally and intuitively understand it, since we give greater value to that which contains more order and information. There are countless examples. We marvel at the majesty of a pristine jungle and the diversity of species that inhabit it and are horrified by the images of its destruction. Similarly, we show greater appreciation for a Renaissance work of art than for a stick figure drawing or appreciate more a piece of classical music than the monotonous music of a TV commercial; a great literary work more than a gossip magazine; and a great meal made by a chef instead of a serving of boiled cabbage.

Brave new world

Even though the laws of physics allow us to establish generalized rules to measure the value created by biological and cultural evolution, human beings frequently disagree with a universal perception of value, and therefore, follow different paths to achieve it, unlike other complex systems where agents consistently tend to the optimum and seek the same value objective or result. For example, river basins are complex systems whose vascular design evolves over time to the mathematical optimum because of physical laws, since water and sediments are passive agents that inevitably flow toward (or choose by default) the paths of least resistance.

Conversely, the agents of human culture, given our individuality and freedom of action, are active agents with the option to assign more value to any of the possibilities within the cultural evolution decision space. Hence, those who opt for the survival strategy assign value to community and traditions. Those who choose the status quo strategy favor the satisfaction of their selfish appetites and authoritarian order. Those who practice the growth strategy strive to compete, innovate, and gain personal achievements. And those who decide on the transformation strategy are motivated by discovery and connectedness with others. This diversity in the perception of value is what simultaneously: 1) allows us to be highly adaptable as a species; 2) makes it hard for us to understand each other; and 3) enables us to make mistakes that produce adverse results. In other words, our ability to take risks and run counter to the optimum is part of what makes us human. In the words of Saint Augustine: *errare humanum est*.

i.   Adaptability is the capacity to respond to the challenges of our environment in a differentiated manner. Throughout history, humanity has faced situations in which fleeing was the best alternative for survival. Others included fighting when it was necessary to defend what we had (status quo) or conquering (growth), which brought about benefits. Additional ploys included doing something new (transformation), and that could turn out to be the right choice.

ii. Given the importance of our perception of value, whenever it is challenged we usually react in a visceral and violent manner. Therefore, all that is needed for conflict to arise is for two individuals with different value perceptions to meet.

iii. Errors occur when we choose a strategy and a definition of value that doesn't agree with the prevailing environmental conditions, such as deciding to get into a fight when it's better to do something else.

To cope with the complex interactions created by the adaptability, conflict, and the error issues created by our flexible ideas in value, there are two possibilities:

1. **Situational determinism**
   From a deterministic perspective, human beings have four response models to face the challenges of our surroundings, and success will be dependent on matching the environment with the chosen strategy despite our complexity and sophistication. With this approach, we only have the capacity to adapt to the environment and no actual freedom of action. Thus, determinism puts an end to the illusion of free will. Let us remember that the evolutionary precept states that only the best adapted survive, i.e., those who choose the right strategy imposed by the environment. Therefore, in this view, free will and the illusion of value are only a sophisticated adaptation mechanism of subordination to the environment.
   Accordingly, nations with abundant natural resources will always tend to be authoritarian and closed, extremely restricted nations will be backward and primitive. Those nations with seasonal restrictions are forced to plan and cooperate, albeit allowing accumulation; They will be the only ones that succeed in making headway to complexity and openness. So, in every case, the use of a strategy relates to the type of environment and the open society only evolves in a particular one. This is what cosmologists define as the Goldilocks Zone: to make life and evolution possible, several average conditions need to come together, like the planet not being too far away or too close to the star, or a star not being too old or

too young, or the atmosphere not being too thin or too dense, or the planetary mass not being too small nor too big, among others. Therefore, as part of the necessary conditions for the sustained cultural evolution of life toward complexity, it would be necessary to add a not too rich and not too poor environment.

This coincides with the dystopian vision of the future described in Aldous Huxley's *Brave New World*(95). In the novel, mankind reaches a point at which it identifies the different ways human beings operate and the development possibilities of each geographical zone. Therefore, to attain global happiness, the human race becomes stratified and organizes a system with castes and regions in which each caste is genetically modified and conditioned from birth to strike a balance between what they want and what they have. Meanwhile, regions that are inhospitable for development are abandoned and are only inhabited by "savages," who are not considered to be members of society.

Other general audience texts, such as Jared Diamond's *Guns, Germs and Steel*(96) and *Collapse*(97), analyze the macroscopic environmental effects on human culture's evolution based on the availability of resources and geographical characteristics. Both books convincingly illustrate that these two factors explain most of humankind's history. One tacit thing that this approach poses is that the challenge of the social sciences can no longer be that of gauging humankind's progress toward overall complexity and openness. Diamond's conclusion suggests that environmental and geographical conditions won't allow it. If so, we could come to think that it might be better — more rational — to find a way to balance what we want and what we have at hand to build Huxley's brave new world.

Taking this deterministic case to the point of absurdity would imply furthering better democracies in places that meet the Goldilocks Zone conditions as well as better organized and more professional autocracies wherever it would be more practical to have them. This would result in the reduction of violence in semi-democracies, anocracies, and hybrid regimes, as well as in the isolation and abandonment of regions that are inhospitable for development. This, which in black and white may seem unreasonable, is not far from contemporary reality. For decades, and paradoxically, wealthy and open nations have extensively supported and taken part in establishing and overthrowing authoritarian and democratic regimes. They have also ignored humanitarian crises, such as the Rwanda genocide of 1994, based on what their national interests dictate, and with disregard for the continued construction of an open society outside of the places where it has already been established.

2. **Intelligence, awareness, and creative will**

Based on the premise that human intelligence is sufficiently powerful and aware to acknowledge and overcome strong genetic, cultural, and environmental influences, we may opt to refine our perception of value and find better paths to define success. An example of this is the biological and cultural evolution of our sense of taste and its relationship with contemporary public health challenges.

For millions of years, the main problem faced by our ancestors was access to food. Hence, our sense of taste and smell in conjunction with the hunger and satiety mechanisms evolved to privilege and assign a high sensory value to foods with a high caloric content, such as those having a high content of fat and sugar. Likewise, to make the most of the times of plenty — and against seasonal conditions of rain and drought in the tropics and cold and hot weather in temperate zones — primitive human beings were forced to follow a pattern of feasting during the times of plenty and fasting during the times of want.

This, which in natural terms represents genetic and social adaptations that protect us from starvation, becomes in our present world the source of different public health issues. There are few foods in nature that contain both high levels of sugar and fat. But humans are ingenious. Encouraged by the high value that our senses assign to carbohydrates and fat, we have developed food manufacturing and preparation methods. We produce cheap and ubiquitous foods that combine these properties together with aromatic substances (e.g., cacao beans) into a powerful mixture that stimulates our satiety and brain pleasure centers, much like the effect produced by psychotropic drugs. This is especially so with foods like pizza that has a fat and carbohydrate energy ratio of 50:50(98). Ice cream and cheese cake fall into the same category. So, today a person living above the food poverty line is not likely to experience long fasting periods during the winter or the drought season, thanks to inventions such as refrigeration and food processing science. Therefore, the permanent availability of foods with characteristics that exceed the individual's energy requirements and that encourage their consumption leads to the so-called global obesity epidemic.

From a deterministic perspective, the situation seems insurmountable. We are caught between genetic predisposition, which assigns a high value to energy-dense foods, and our capacity and ingenuity that allows unrestricted consumption of this type of foods in the present-day markets. But this does not mean we are destined to become hostages of our environment and circumstances.

In fact, public health efforts in several nations indicate that, once we identify the source of a problem, it is possible to develop solutions to tackle it. According to the World Health Organization (WHO)(99), between 1950 and 2002 there was a decrease in the incidence of deaths due to cardiovascular diseases in four developed nations (U.S., Australia, the United Kingdom, and Canada). This happened after deliberate public health measures were implemented to improve the diagnosis and treatment techniques of these diseases. When behavior changes in the population were observed, such as a decrease in tobacco consumption, changes in dietary patterns and increased physical activity followed.

Another example that substantiates the possibility of escaping environmental circumstances by using different value parameters than those established by default by our appetites is the case of Norway when it became an important oil-producing nation.

In 1971, the discovery of the first oil field in the North Sea led to a stream of oil revenues for the Nordic nation. In 1974, the Norwegian government authorities began discussing the role of oil and oil revenues in Parliament. The debate lasted until 1983, when it was proposed that the nation should create a sovereign fund to sterilize oil revenues and isolate Norway's economy from the effects of oil price variations. In 1990, the fund was established; since then, Norway follows an oil revenue management model and a development path unlike that of any of the other authoritarian oil-exporting nation(100).

In 2015, the fund was worth approximately USD $1 trillion ($10^{12}$), which guarantees all the pensions of the fast-aging Norwegian population and allows the country to have a diversified investment portfolio, which is estimated to reach up to $3.3 trillion by 2030.

Thus, Norway maintains its position as an advanced economy and an open democracy. It is a country with high social standards that does not wax and wane every time the price of oil changes.

Masters of our destiny or victims of circumstance?

It is easy to think that our psychological configuration, appetites, genetics, and the environment inevitably conditions us to adapt our sense of value and behavior to environmental circumstances, just as it is easier to prefer a diet based on processed foods and soft drinks, smoking, and violent behavior. In fact, these predispositions and our responses to them are part of an age-old philosophical debate on human nature between those who think it is mostly predetermined and those who believe that, restrictions withstanding, human beings can change and forge their own destiny through discovery and reason. This issue was adroitly addressed by Plato.

The allegory of the cave describes a man (the philosopher) and a group of his companions confined in a cave, who have lived all their lives chained to a wall and can only see the shadows projected on the back of the cave, shadows which are created by the events that take place behind them.

Hence, the prisoners' knowledge of reality only entails the incomprehensible shadows cast on the wall. In the story, the philosopher manages to break free from his chains and first explores the cave and then the outside world. Then he understands that the shadows are only the rough reflection of a fuller and more pleasant reality that lies beyond the cave. After the philosopher raves and rejoices about what he discovers beyond, he feels compelled to return and free his companions. There is, however, a caveat: If the philosopher returns to liberate his comrades and shows them the grim and miserable reality in which they live, he might probably get killed, for he would brutally confront the reality of the outside world with the grim reality within the cave.

One interpretation of this allegory would be that by breaking the chains — ignorance and irrationality — individuals attain greater liberty and new potentials that render them more human. Therefore, Plato's approach is that human nature is a potential that is developed, is realized, or attained through reason and discovery.

On the other hand, Hannah Arendt also believed that the ability to establish a conscious and rational relationship with the world was the mainstay of human nature and censured irrationality as a trivial and dehumanizing possibility within the decision spectrum of human beings, but one that has no value.

What this discussion tells us is that both situational determinism and creative consciousness are possible. The answer to this conundrum is that these are self-fulfilling prophecies. We fall victims to situational determinism when we believe that is the way things work (external locus). But when we dare to seek-out possible solutions through reason, imagination, and creative consciousness, we are liberated (internal locus). This is consistent with the characteristics of complex adaptive systems since different emergent characteristics become manifest through the changes in the behavior of agents. And so, the definition of value that people use is paramount; it defines the system's configuration and emergent properties, which are equal to saying that our ideas about value, literally, shape the world.

Don't eat the marshmallow!

It is worth taking a look at the world of cognitive sciences to find out whether individuals who break free from ignorance and step out of the cave (democratic value) fare better than those who remain alienated in the shadows (authoritarian value). To do so, three discoveries must be considered.

1. **Connection/Intimacy.** Researchers studied children who were institutionalized from birth in Romanian orphanages. Those institutions are sadly notorious because there the newborn's human contact is limited only to feeding and diapering times. Research revealed that the lack of close and continuous contact during the first months of life produces irreversible degradation of the brain's electrical activity, which was observed through encephalography and imaging studies(101). Two of the implications of this physiological change, observed during the long-term follow up of the cases, were a low average intelligence and a higher incidence of behavioral and socialization issues. The outcome indicates that connectivity and interaction at an intimate and close level with other members

of our species is vital from the moment we are born, so much so that it affects the brain's physical development, mental health, and the individual's development and social integration capabilities.

2.   **Self-control.** In the 1960s, Walter Mischel(102) conducted the marshmallow experiment to study children's capacity to delay gratification. The experiment consisted of offering four-year-old children, who were left alone in a room, a marshmallow that they could eat immediately or until the researcher returned to the place where the experiment was being carried out, which delayed gratification a few minutes. If the children could refrain from eating the marshmallow while the adult was away, they got a second marshmallow as a reward, i.e., they got a 100% return in exchange for waiting a few minutes. Long-term follow-up of the cases showed, with a high level of correlation, that those who delayed gratification at age four attained higher levels of social and economic wellbeing as adults. The same experiment was replicated around the world and obtained similar results: one third of the four-year-old children in the studied cultures could delay immediate gratification to obtain a bigger reward later. This self-control capacity turned out to be very useful in predicting the children's future success, as well as problems and less possibilities of success in children who gobbled up the marshmallow as soon as they were left alone in the room.

3.   **An appetite for learning.** There are two experiments that demonstrate the innate intellectual curiosity of humans. The first one is Sugata Mitra's Hole in the Wall(103), a famous experiment carried out in India where computers with online access were set up in the walls of public buildings so that poor children — with no access to a good education, computers, or the Internet — could use them without adult supervision or instruction. The results were an emergence of an efficient collaborative learning scheme among the children. The second example is the spaghetti tower, a challenge in which participating teams have a short period of time to build a tower made from spaghetti sticks, adhesive tape, and one marshmallow. The winner is the team that builds the highest tower with the marshmallow on top of the structure. According to the data published by Tom Wujec(104), pre-school children's teams consistently get better results than most adults because they collaborate without fighting over the group's control, build prototypes, and experiment

in short time cycles. This outcome has been corroborated by the research of Stanford and MIT scientists(105), which shows that preschool children are inherently inquisitive and curious in a sophisticated manner that resembles scientists' behavior in formulating hypotheses, designing experiments, and isolating variables to test them later. But this characteristic tends to fade as children grow up and adopt the various cultural models to which they are exposed. On the other hand, in positive psychology — a branch devoted to analyzing happiness and the state of wellbeing in humans, unlike traditional psychology, which studies individuals from the mental pathology perspective — Scott Barry Kaufman(106) concluded, after reviewing various studies on tens of personality traits and how they relate to wellbeing, that the two traits that best predict a state of satisfaction and wellbeing are love of learning and gratitude.

All of the above results tell us several things. First, that many of the social science theories are based on the premise that the behavior of adult individuals reflects the natural behavior of humans, failing to acknowledge that adult behavior has already been molded and biased, and is, therefore, an emergent result that encompasses the sum of influences and decisions each person has assimilated and made throughout their life. So, what is interesting about exploring the characteristics and trends of individuals during the first part of their lives is gathering information on the probable default state that helps us develop as individuals and become part of society. Hence, human beings with higher levels of intimacy and closeness with their social group, self-control, curiosity, and creativity tend to be healthier, create more value, and, generally, to have better lives.

Should we need to choose value categories consistent with the realization of human nature, the current neuroscientific and psychological evidence would point to collaboration (connectivity/intimacy) and a higher cultural complexity level (curiosity, love of learning, and self-control). But we are not strictly meant to pursue that course since we have the capacity to choose any one of the four strategies of cultural evolution, as proven by the social and economic evidence of the first chapters.

So, we are free to choose a value scale that justifies eating ice cream, pizza, and cheese cake three times a day, and to stay inside the cave, watching the shadows in the company of Plato's murderous friends, as does a high percentage of the world population (masters, lackeys, serfs, heroes, and bandits) who experience, endure, and build closed societies. More than 2,000 years have elapsed since Plato wrote the allegory of the cave. However, based on data and empirical evidence — and through an analysis based on values and not on money or influence — we may currently claim that the people who abandon the cave through discovery and reason, and who come together to build and become part of society, are more likely to lead better and more meaningful lives. And this conclusion gives more weight to the value that the growth and development of democratic societies has.

How do value, money, and prices relate?

The end of World War II brought about the schism between economics and the rest of the social sciences. Economics, which originally addressed questions such as What is value? and What is the agents' behavioral model? reached a conclusion regarding these questions and turned into the discipline that took over the problems of the real world, such as money, markets, and meeting the needs of the economic agents. The rest of the social disciplines, such as sociology and psychology, which failed to reach a definitive solution regarding these topics, were left out of the market-related issues and charged with the behavioral problems forsaken by economics.

The clearest example of this schism was the postulation of *homo economicus* as a human behavior model, one based on the rationality of agents in seeking the maximization of utility through the market's price system. The final solution of *homo economicus* to the problem of value and its exchange in the market simplified the study of economic problems, allowed the formulation of rational and scientific public policies and gave rise to international institutions such as the International Monetary Fund and the World Bank. However, from the systems theory perspective, it failed to consider that utility maximization ended up turning into a linear interaction rule that unequivocally bound economic science to deterministic linear systems. The prevailing problem is that — while the economic consensus became stagnant with *homo economicus*, psychology, and sociology like the rest of cognitive sciences — it moved forward in the study of value-related issues and people's behavior, and concluded that, even if *homo economicus* made the economists' task easier, this model is not consistent with the experimental results showing that human behavior is more complex and irrational. According to these results, the interaction rules followed by agents in the market allow multiple solutions to the same problems. This change means that to understand the market, it is necessary to revisit the relationships between money, value, and prices through complexity science and human behavior.

The relationship between value, money, and prices constitutes the main difficulty regarding value because there are interactions between these three concepts that are hard to separate.

For engineers and scientists who study complex systems, the performance or value produced by a system relates to variables like movement, volume of flow, and information. Therefore, the "value" created by a river basin is measured in tons/kilometer of water and displaced sediments. In human culture, value metrics are varied and may arise in cases like that of authoritarian masters, who value power to such an extent that they are willing to exchange a nation's entire wealth to attain it. Or there is the case of the Norwegians, who assigned value to money derived from their oil revenues but decided that the long-term economic and social harmony of their country was more important.

Therefore, the main thing to consider when talking about value and how to create it is having a clear idea of the merit figure (performance variables), which is the expected ultimate result of a system. Public goods are a good example of important merit figures. These are measured in variables like national security, public security, public health, and food security and not in monetary units. Even though value and money are related, as in the link between public expenditure and public goods creation, the generation and measurement of value may be independent from money and prices. To delve deeper into this, the following divides the discussion into two topics:

1. **Prices and the market.**

   Throughout most of humankind's economic history, money has not been the universal means of exchange. Nonetheless, ever since human beings have engaged in commercial exchanges — and apparently this has been happening since before we were even the *homo sapiens* species — prices have existed. Simply stated, a price is the amount for a good that one is willing to exchange for another good. This means that prices are dependent on the idiosyncrasy and needs of those who carry out the transaction at any given time.

The first commercial exchange mechanism was barter, in which it is difficult to establish prices and equivalences between different types of goods. The accomplishment of every exchange will depend on the existence of a correspondence between the need and the goods offered by each party. In a bartering system, goods may have prices as varied as the agents and assortment of merchandise found in a bazaar; a camel may be exchanged for different amounts of rugs, fabrics, grain, sheep, and vegetables and/or combinations thereof. The invention of money simplified trade by creating a new commodity with special characteristics that made it possible to link all prices to a same reference. This allowed, among many other things, comparison of the prices assigned to items as different as camels and rugs against the same unit of exchange.

In economics, it has been empirically demonstrated that once the price of a commodity has been set, it may behave in a predictable manner. For example, if the supply of a product increases in the market, but its demand remains unchanged, its price will tend to decrease. This is the basis of the economic law of supply and demand as well as of the economic theories based on the rationality of economic agents that maximize utility, or *homo economicus*. But over the past few decades, linear and deterministic models of the agents' behavior, such as rational choice, have been surpassed by the demonstration that the decision mechanism of economic agents is more complex. That complexity is shown mainly by the prospect theory of Daniel Kahneman (2002 Nobel Prize laureate in economics) and Amos Tversky(107), who postulated and proved that the decisions of agents are not focused on the transaction's final benefit, but on the assessment of potential gains and losses that lead to "good enough" decisions through heuristic mechanisms where the risk of experiencing losses has greater weight than the possibility of obtaining gains. Heuristic mechanisms are problem-solving, learning, and discovery techniques that do not guarantee finding the best solution (maximizing profit), but that are efficient in reducing the response time and may be as ordinary as a rule of thumb, an educated guess, or an intuitive judgment(108).

Basically, the shift from rational choice to prospect theory implies forsaking deterministic linear models for the analytic approach of complex adaptive systems and indicates that price formation in the market is a complex idiosyncratic matter that may not be linked to value. This helps to better explain several examples of price phenomena, such as the three bottles of 1869 Château Lafite Rothschild, 146 years old, that cost $232,256 each(109) at an auction in 2010, and whose contents, according to experts, most probably turned into vinegar decades ago. Or there is the Open Source movement, in which software developers contribute their knowledge and time free of charge to create programs that many companies use to create profits and build the platforms that support the digital society.

An additional experiment that supports the results of prospect theory, and that combines its postulates with biology, is the one carried out by the behavioral economists at Yale University's Comparative Cognition Laboratory. Over the past decade, they taught a troop of capuchin monkeys how to exchange money for products such as grapes, apples, and cucumbers. These tests yielded a broad and increasing body of knowledge(110) that shows that when monkeys face simple decisions in the *monkey market*, such as buying a piece of apple for one coin versus another buying offer of two grapes for one coin, the decrease in price, in the case of grapes, increased the demand of that product, although we must consider that the initial price — one grape or one apple for one coin — was arbitrarily defined by the researchers. On the other hand, when the monkeys face more complex decisions, the same cognitive flaws regarding losses and gains that Kahneman discovered in humans are validated. An interesting point is that the economists cannot differentiate the data derived from transactions with monkeys from those obtained in similar studies involving humans.

However, as the head of the laboratory Laurie Santos explains in an interview published by *The Wall Street Journal*(111), a significant difference between the economic behavior of capuchin monkeys and that of humans is that monkeys have no self-control, without exception, they spend all the money they are given and take advantage of any oversight in the laboratory to steal from the researchers. During one of such oversights, one of the monkeys stole the box that held all the tokens and threw it into the communal area of the troop, which led to chaos and some unintended experiments. One of the researchers reported that on this chaotic day he observed a male monkey trading one coin with a female in exchange for sex. Later, the female went to the market to exchange the coin for a grape, which indicated to researchers that the monkeys had attained a sophisticated understanding of the possibilities of exchange generated by money. Santos also explained that a discrepancy in the comparison of monkeys with humans is that in an experiment designed to induce payment of a higher price for a luxury product, monkeys remained indifferent.

If these results are confirmed, the capacity to have a flexible and dynamic perception of value, influenced by concepts such as luxury, could be construed as an advanced capacity of the human brain which allows us to choose new and different strategies. Those results would prove that capuchin monkeys, having a lower level of consciousness, are the victims of a program that induces them to maximize the satisfaction of their more immediate appetites.

Therefore, the maximization of profit in the market is not an advanced characteristic of *homo sapiens*, who through culture evolved into *homo economicus*, but rather an archaic trait that continues within the behavioral possibilities of *homo sapiens*, and which is more persistent in the Yale research of capuchin monkeys, something that could come to be known as *cebus economicus yalensis*.

Another outlook that supports the existence of complex behavioral mechanisms in agents is that of Dan Pink. In *Drive*(112), the author analyzes the knowledge accrued since 1950 regarding the extrinsic (external locus) and intrinsic (internal locus) motivation models based on Harry F. Harlow's groundbreaking experimental work with Rhesus monkeys(113). This theory states that human beings have two motivational mechanisms: the extrinsic that relates to reward and punishment stimuli (carrot and stick), and the intrinsic that relates to the desire to seek innovation, practice an activity, learning, discovering, and mastering an occupation. One of the salient points raised by Pink's research is that, in the presence of extrinsic motivational stimuli, intrinsic motivation decreases, and high-level cognitive functions are dulled. Several experiments proved that extrinsic motivators generate better results only when they are related to mechanical and repetitive tasks. On the other hand, when tasks require the use of basic cognitive functions, extrinsic motivators produce worse results than in the cases where these types of motivators simply do not exist. In other words, they appeal to the archaic side of animal behavior — which is the same as saying that these incentives are linked to instinct — while the intrinsic ones allow the activation and operation of the high-level cognitive functions of the prefrontal cortex. That's is the same as saying they are linked to reason and more evolved motives.

For many decades, academia, politics, and the entrepreneurial world dismissed the significance of these discoveries, which date back to 1950, because the results challenge the entrenched interests of social researchers who believe in *homo economicus*, challenge politicians who have a simplified interpretation (carrot and stick) of reality to be able to relate to electoral constituencies, and challenge entrepreneurs who believe companies only have the social purpose of generating money, not value, in the market. So, several of the most transcendental contemporary problems, like the 2008-2009 economic crisis, can no longer be explained by the rational choice theory, the flaws in incentive systems (rewards and punishment), or the savage nature of the market. "Too big to fail" companies constitute the perfect example to illustrate that this mindset is the problem and not the solution. These companies were poorly managed by executives that were extrinsically motivated to an obsessive degree by million-dollar performance bonuses. This facilitated a long series of poor judgment calls and bad decisions, which ultimately led the companies they managed to the brink of bankruptcy. The State's bailout prevented this catastrophe through the investment of public funds and without changing the extrinsic motivational system, which still operates in the companies that survived the crisis.

Furthermore, at the time these words are being written, what appears to be the biggest commercial and industrial scandal in Germany's history is in full swing. In September 2015, carmaker Volkswagen® Group admitted to having incorporated a piece of software called "defeat device" into 11 million vehicles equipped with diesel engines that do not comply with environmental regulations. The function of the "defeat device" is to cheat the emissions testing systems. As far as anyone knows, the executives tied to the scandal were extrinsically motivated, and determined at any cost to turn Volkswagen into the most important automotive company in the world, above Toyota® Motor Corporation. That is why they made the decisions that, according to the initial assessments, led to an initial 35% decrease in their stock prices and which, during the first remediation phase, will imply a direct cost of close to $19 billion, as well as losses regarding legal and reputational damages, future sales, and share value, which will add up over time and cannot be estimated at present(114).

Another illustration of the problems that human cognitive boundaries — the need of heuristic decision-making methods and trade-offs between extrinsic motivation and prefrontal cortex — produce upon linking value and price was the proliferation of subprime mortgages in the U.S., which caused the huge economic crisis in 2008. An important element in the unbridled proliferation of this type of mortgage had to do with the design and marketing of complex, obscure, and predatory financial instruments for a segment of financially illiterate customers(115). But despite the huge damage to the global economy, the discoveries of cognitive sciences are still being negatively used in the *modus operandi* of many current commercial practices that put consumers in situations where they find it hard to differentiate between the changes in the value proposition and the prices accompanying them.

Dan Ariely(116) provides an example of this through the subscription options for *The Economist*. This journal offered the consumer three choices: a digital subscription for $59, a printed subscription for $125, or both for the same last-mentioned price. The first two options represent some sort of loss for the consumer, which make the third option seem like a good bargain. But in fact, what *The Economist* wanted to accomplish with this marketing proposal to induce the consumers' aversion to the simpler or cheaper subscription. Other Ariely experiments(117) on the same subject illustrate that the capacity to relate value with price depends on the options or context that make up the offer. For example, a $5 cup of coffee is too expensive if you compare it against a $2 cup. But if the coffee shop's chalkboard advertises a $10 coffee cup next to a $5 one, the consumer will consider the $5 option a cheap and sensible choice. This is the reason why there are more and more products sold as bargains and packages that are difficult to compare, as in the case of telecommunications, software, travel, and financial products.

Yet another mechanism that seems to be inspired by Ariely's investigation — and which reveals how cognitive science's discoveries influence the market — is the use of the so-called guerrilla marketing techniques, such as upselling, which raise the price tag without increasing consumer value, i.e., when the consumer is presented with confusing options that indicate possible losses and gains. For example, some hotels offer low rates online to attract customers but compensate for these low invoicing prices with alternative upselling mechanisms. Upon checking in, the receptionist will inform the guests that they have "earned" a special bonus for an upgrade, which would ordinarily cost $30 per day, but with the preferential bonus it is only worth $15-a-day per person, which means a "benefit" of $420 that they may lose out on if they don't take advantage of the promotion. For a family of four and separate rooms over a seven-day stay, the bonus represents a $420 increase in the bill (15x4x7), which hotels generate effortlessly and at no cost by pressing and exploiting the cognitive buttons that make it difficult for the client to associate and compare losses and gains. According to prospect theory, the transaction is framed between the "loss" of $420 "gained" and the idea of a better view for "only" $15-a-day per person. And the lack of transparency in this type of transactions prevents us from finding out if customers who accept the offer obtain something qualitatively better, since the characteristics of a better view are intangible and hard to evaluate in a hotel that the client is not familiar with and that has hundreds of rooms. In fact, even after paying, the client may well get the same room he might have been originally assigned.

In sum, the subject of prices, that appeared to have been overcome ever since the postulation of the law of supply and demand, and the theory of rational choice, which related value to money through profit maximization, helped perpetuate deterministic behavioral models, such as *homo economicus*, as the preferred means to explain human conduct. But developments such as prospect theory, the theory of extrinsic and intrinsic motivation, and the *monkey market* experiments indicate that price is a problem in itself. As price may be dissociated from the generation of value, it significantly affects the way markets and society operate since the relationship between value, price, and money is a dynamic and complex one. The way these three concepts interlink modifies the configuration of economic relationships, which are essential elements of the social pact.

2. **Money and its boundaries.**

Money is one of the most peculiar human inventions and has a long and winding history of successes and failures. Contemporary money, called fiduciary money, is an abstraction that has no concrete reference in reality and whose special characteristics illustrate important aspects of how we organize socially. Therefore, the following analysis of money and its relationship with value and prices is approached from three different angles: exchange, value, and stability.

i. **Exchange**. Contrary to what is still commonly believed today, a country's fiduciary money is not linked to tangible or actual goods such as gold and silver. It is called fiduciary because the value of money depends on the confidence that the agents in an economy have in the value and stability of said money. To explain this, which sounds like madness, we must revisit the shift from barter economy to monetary economy.

   Money was originally created on the basis of goods whose value was widely accepted. During Roman times in Europe, the salt centurions received as payment was so important that it gave rise to the term "salary." Later, gold and silver were so scarce and universally relevant that they became the commodity against which a wide variety of goods were benchmarked. Thus, exchanging a horse for a given amount of gold, which in turn was easy to exchange for other goods, became a better alternative than barter. In Mesoamerica, gold and silver had architectural and artistic value, but were not useful enough to improve the exchange of goods, unlike cocoa beans which were more widely accepted and became the commodity of reference and a primitive version of money.

   Over the centuries, the concept of money evolved into bank notes, documents that initially represented fixed amounts of gold or silver issued by the goldsmiths who usually stored the precious metals because handling paper notes was found easier than handling the cumbersome metals. Goldsmiths, in turn, found that the agents' confidence in the notes they issued allowed them to issue notes without backing them with metal reserves. This led to the emergence of bankers and the financial crises of fiduciary money. This situation continued until the relationship between money and tangible goods such as gold and silver ceased to be practical. As economies flourished and became more sophisticated, the variety of goods and the number of transactions increased, as did the need to maintain a money supply commensurate with the dynamics of individual economies. It became impossible to maintain sufficient precious metal reserves to back up the amount of money required by the economy.

Economies were monetized, and the spread of money achieved universal proportions. Exchange markets between the various nations' currencies were established and the development of international trade became easier. As it was possible to assign a monetary price to many value exchanges, ideas such as "everything has a price" and "everyone has a price" also spread across the world and were strengthened by Europe's colonial expansion when the global slave trade was a common and legal practice that gave a price to people.

The interesting thing about the rise of money is that it stumbled against two domains that are impossible to monetize. First, the series of relationships and exchanges that are closest and most dear to humans: family and friendship. These intimate domains turned out to be refractory and impervious to monetization. Dan Ariely cites the work of Margaret Clark and Judson Mills(118), who describe this phenomenon as the division between an individual's social and economic worlds. Sustaining that the intersection between these two worlds is one of the most important and rigid taboos in society, which prevents these exchanges from becoming monetized. No one in their right mind invites friends to their home for lunch and then asks the friends to pay for the meal, even when a great deal of value is produced and transferred through these non-monetized exchanges. Other values can be in the form of goods, services, and intangible satisfiers, such as the nurturing of newborn babies by their parents, which contributes to the mental health of society at large, as proven by the study of babies in Romanian orphanages.

Some economists have developed estimates of the economic (monetary) impact of these social exchanges like housework.

They concluded that without the "free" provision of these social transactions, the economy could not function in the same way it does now, mainly due to the high impact and cost that monetizing these activities would imply(119). An example of the clash between non-monetized value exchanges and the market is the potlatch, a tradition observed by indigenous peoples of the Pacific Northwest Coast of the United States and Canada, which entails the redistribution of income through lavish feasts and gifts — sometimes bringing a family to the brink of ruin. The impact was so great that potlatches were legally banned and prosecuted by the governments of these countries(120).

The second barrier against the complete monetization of society are the restrictions established after human rights were acknowledged and the reach of the market limited through the prohibition of slavery, human trafficking, organ trade, child abuse, and all other evil practices that seek to profit from misery and harm to human dignity. These two barriers illustrate that, even though money and the monetization of the economy have reached extremely high levels and that a great number of people may be convinced that "everything has a price" and that "everyone has a price," a substantial part of the value generated by humankind does not have nor has it ever had, a price. Therefore, money is constrained only to a part of the value exchanges created by human beings.

ii. **The value of money.** Among the unexpected consequences that *homo economicus* incorporated to human culture is the establishment of utility maximization as an interaction rule of agents. In analytical terms, this simplified the problem of value and rendered the issue of prices insignificant, a simple gear that connected in a linear way the law of supply and demand with the value-money relationship. Admittedly, to explain problems like the unpalatable wine with an exorbitant price, other elements were added to economic theory, such as the asymmetry of information and market flaws, which provided a rational way out to the irrationality of *homo economicus*. All this happened without upsetting the value-money correspondence.

The foregoing shows that the death of *homo economicus* at the hands of prospect theory is not a trivial matter because it tears down the neat world of economic theory and calls into question decades of economic research. Increasing the flexibility of the concept of value, as a choice related to the use of heuristic mechanisms by economic agents, turns us back to the problem of value, price formation mechanisms, and the measurement and quantification of the economy. As if this weren't enough, this change subordinates money to the level of a platform that participates and influences exchanges of value but does not define them. Thus, economics, through this lens, is no longer a discipline that sees everything through the flow of money. This brings us back to the complicated world of the study of human nature, which requires the use of tools that are developed in other branches of science.

Furthermore, the example that proves that the death of *homo economicus* is a fact and not a rumor are initiatives like the Commission on the Measurement of Economic Performance and Social Progress, created by former French President Nicolas Sarkozy and directed by Joseph Stiglitz (2001 winner of the Nobel Prize in Economics) to investigate and suggest economic and social progress indicators that exceed the measurement limitations of GDP.

Some of the conclusions that the Commission's report(121) reached are:

Quality of life includes the full range of factors that make life worth living, including those that are not traded in markets and not captured by monetary measures.

...recent research has shown that it is possible to collect meaningful and reliable data on subjective well-being. Subjective well-being encompasses three different aspects: cognitive evaluations of one's life, positive emotions (joy, pride), and negative ones (pain, worry, anger)...

iii. **The stability of money.** Once the transition to the fiduciary money system was achieved, and after inordinate trial and error tests that resulted in severe economic and financial crises involving banking system collapses, recession, and inflation (stagflation), such as the ones endured by Latin America during the

1970s and 1980s, it was discovered that even if fiduciary money is an abstraction minted into a currency, printed in paper, or stored as bytes and bits in an electronic system, there needs to be balance and control between the supply and the demand of money. This is because the value of money decreases and prices increase and generate inflation when governments overdraw and print money in excess to pay their bills. When there is not enough money in the economy to cover the number of transactions that agents are willing to perform, money becomes more expensive and the economy stagnates.

After analyzing money from the exchange, value, and stability perspectives, the conclusion regarding its role in society is simple: money is just a platform that enables and facilitates the exchange process of a part of the value created by human beings, and therefore, it is not the definition of the value of democracy.

Platforms

Cultural evolution is enabled by several platforms or systems that simplify and solve in a permanent way some network function. For example, in barter economies, the lack of a currency implies that every exchange is built slowly and costly on a case-by-case fashion because it is hard to determine if the price of a camel should be five rugs, four cabbages, and a sheep or three sheep, a bale of hay, and two flintstones. Hence, money has become an exchange platform that enabled a permanent function of exchange to exist, which everyone can use and replicate as many times as they like.

Examples of other platforms that promoted cultural evolution by cheap and reusable functions are spoken and written language, laws, the Internet, traditions, and religions. The latter are included because they standardized belief and behavior systems that for centuries cheapened and facilitated the functioning of society. Suffice it to consider that in subsistence agricultural societies, with a life expectancy of less than 40 years, it was unacceptable that a significant percentage of the economically active population endured extended existential crises up until adulthood, as is now the case with a considerable fraction of the young population.

Some of mankind's biggest problems have involved platforms like religion and money, but this does not mean that platforms are inherently negative, but that issues related to them result from the manner and intent with which they are used, as happens with any kind of technology. At present, the Internet is used for positive things such as art and education, just as it is used for criminal purposes.

Having separated the concept of value as an outcome from the concept of money as a platform and the complex and many times irrational relationship existing between both concepts through the price system, the following chapters deal with the problems of democracy and how it's associated with platforms that are used to make it work.

7. The Democrats

Democratic diversity

A tacit premise in the discussion on authoritarianism/democracy is that democratic societies are more diverse or complex than authoritarian ones. Nevertheless, it's worth examining beforehand some data and indicators regarding this topic: those, for example, that indicate the cultural development of nations. One of these indicators is the annual register of patents. Graph 17 includes the average number of patents produced per million inhabitants from a sample of 167 nations divided into type of regime.

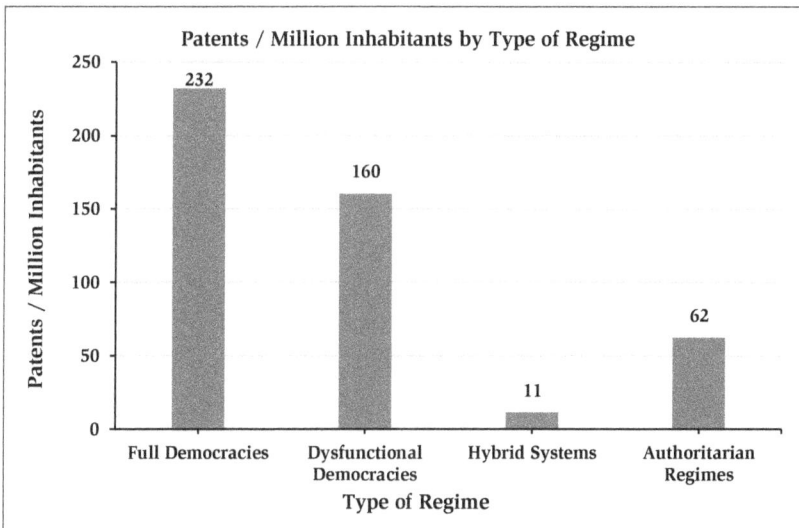

Graph 17: Patents/Million inhabitants by type or regime. Source: WB (2013).

The study shows the decreasing relationship between the level of democracy and the innovation indicator. Once again, we observe an inferior level of achievement in hybrid systems when compared to authoritarian systems. On the other hand, except for China, the high volume of registered patents in 2013 by the 10 most innovative authoritarian nations does not coincide with their economic competitiveness on the international market. Table 15 shows the 10 democratic and the 10 authoritarian nations with the greatest number of patents per million inhabitants. It's clear by the position they maintain in the innovation index, the authoritarian nations with the greatest production of patents (more than 100 registered patents per one million inhabitants), such as Russia, Belarus, and Iran, are not an international reference of economic and innovative competitiveness.

Country	Patents Requested 2013	Population 2013	Patents/millions of Inhabitants	Democracy Ranking	Democracy Index (2015)	Innovations index Ranking (2015)	Category
United States	287,831	316,497,531	909	20	8.05	5	Full Democracies
Germany	47,353	80,645,605	587	13	8.64	15	Full Democracies
New Zealand	1,614	4,442,100	363	4	9.26	17	Full Democracies
Finland	1,596	5,438,972	293	8	9.03	6	Full Democracies
Austria	2,162	8,479,375	255	14	8.54	23	Full Democracies
Sweden	2,332	9,600,379	243	3	9.45	2	Full Democracies
Denmark	1,341	5,614,932	239	5	9.11	9	Full Democracies
United Kingdom	14,972	64,106,779	234	16	8.31	3	Full Democracies
Norway	1,101	5,079,623	217	1	9.93	16	Full Democracies
Luxemburg	113	543,360	208	11	8.88	12	Full Democracies
China	704,936	1,357,380,000	519	136	3.14	35	Authoritarian
Russia	28,765	143,506,911	200	132	3.31	62	Authoritarian
Belarus	1,489	9,466,000	157	127	3.62	77	Authoritarian
Iran	11,305	77,152,445	147	156	2.16	113	Authoritarian
Kazakhstan	1,824	17,035,275	107	140	3.06	84	Authoritarian
Armenia	125	2,992,192	42	116	4.00	59	Authoritarian
Azerbaijan	156	9,416,801	17	149	2.71	105	Authoritarian
Saudi Arabia	491	30,201,051	16	160	1.93	42	Authoritarian
Uzbekistan	299	30,243,200	10	158	1.95	133	Authoritarian
Egypt	641	87,613,909	7	134	3.18	108	Authoritarian

Table 15: The 10 democratic and authoritarian nations with more registered patents per one million inhabitants (2013) and innovation index (2015).

Regarding the atypical case of China, it's possible to point out that this nation finds itself in an accelerated process of social, economic, and technological modernization after having lost two centuries of development that corresponded to the wave of Victorian industrialization in the 19th century and the wave of manufacturing industrialization in the 20th century. Thus, since the opening imposed by Deng Xiaoping in 1978, China has gone from being a feudal agrarian economy to an industrialized economy in a few short years. In the second place, the technological launch in China in the last decades, while significant in volume, still does not find itself on par with post-industrial economies. China is a manufacturing giant, and little by little, it is growing due to the value-added margins incorporated into exports. The greater part, however, of the value added to the goods produced is still captured by Western technology companies. Because of this, the high volume of patents does not correspond to the value added, which is taken in locally(122).

These distinct development conditions, referred to as "State capitalism," are the result of low labor costs, the enormous unsatisfied local market potential, and overlaid with an enormous international appetite for low-priced products, a consequence of the process of globalization. But these conditions have begun to show signs of adjustment. On one hand, the principal advantage of low manufacturing wages has disappeared since this type of wage is currently matched with those that are paid in other regions like Latin America(123). China's economic growth rate began to drop, the international markets are saturated, and the internal markets have begun to mature, and, as the population ages at an accelerated rate, the effects of four decades of the one-child policy are felt.

Several questions linger with respect to long-term State capitalism in China. While the economy has grown at rates of 10% annually, and while there was widespread social mobility, the new and complex Chinese society was tolerant of the old communist authoritarianism. The following, however, remains to be seen. Upon facing a significant and prolonged recession along with the existing and elevated levels of inequality in a society where several hundred million people are outside of the economic miracle — and, at the same time, a new and vast middle class that aspires to being cosmopolitan and global — will the dynamic tension carry China toward a democratic opening? It is, thus, that development in China in the upcoming decades will be an important test for the idea that links complexity to an open society. The hypothesis is that once the Chinese miracle diminishes or stagnates, growth, stability, and authoritarian control will become disjunctive. No one knows today what a serious recession in China would mean to the world. It is the world's second largest economy, and no one can guarantee how the economy of State capitalism would manage a crisis of such magnitude. Based on the history of past centuries, the great fear of neighboring countries like Japan, Taiwan, India, Korea, and Russia is that the age-old authoritarian reflexes of China would lead them to international aggression (*raison d'état*) and not to a new phase of internal reforms toward openness (democratic legality).

To sum things up, the data tell us that the greatest freedom of democratic systems is related to a greater cultural diversity measured by patented novelties and discoveries; that fully authoritarian systems are better organized than hybrid systems, and that, in spite of having significant innovation efforts, the end productivity of authoritarian systems with regard to innovation — generally achieved through State directed supply mechanisms — reaches neither the productivity nor the results in economic competitiveness of democratic or demand-based innovation systems. This last factor reinforces the point about the true high cost and low productivity of authoritarian systems.

When taking diversity as the first emerging quality of democratic systems, it is possible to move forward with its definition. In formal systems-theory terms, the degrees of freedom that democracy provides through a decentralized coordination model allows for faster exploration and discovery of new, potential futures (e.g., patents that generate new products and services in the economy). These degrees of freedom stem from the concept of dignity, from which liberty and individuality emerge, allowing human beings to learn, explore, discover, create, and generate value. New models of optimization such as Bejan and Lorente's constructal(23) or A.D. Wissner-Gross and C.E. Freer's causal entropic forces(124) indicate that the evolution or rise in complexity, including the growth in intelligence and knowledge, are the result of an optimization between the capture of the greatest number of possible futures (entropy) and the available resources.

On the other hand, it is more difficult to represent characters in the democratic world by means of discrete categories, such as masters, lackeys, and serfs, since, by definition and the internal locus of control through which they operate, these characters define and redefine themselves over time in countless ways within the mechanism of cultural evolution and re-evolution.

Re-evolution

For centuries, the philosophical, sociological, and anthropological position with respect to human culture emerged from the premise that the expression of culture was unique and exclusive to human beings. During the past 50 years, however, a body of knowledge has accumulated suggesting that within the animal kingdom, a wide range of cultural archetypes exist. The teaching-learning between parents and descendants is seen, for example, in the hunting techniques that big cats transmit to their cubs. The use of tools such as branches and sticks to obtain food, widely documented in the case of the great apes, is another along with the evolution and transmission of abstract cultural artifacts that generate trends or tendencies. Those are seen in the case of humpback whales, who adopt, adapt, and transmit their songs throughout the oceans of the world(125).

The most fascinating cultural manifestation, due to it being so distant from the reality of humans, is that of the humble and primitive octopus (*Octopus vulgaris*), which can learn from observation. The experiment, which brought ethologists to this conclusion, consisted of presenting different octopuses with the problem of unscrewing the top of a clear jar containing an oyster, one of the octopus's favorite foods(126). The investigators found that several the octopuses captured from the wild can solve the problem of opening the bottle to remove the oyster, while the remainder are never able to open it on their own. Despite the limitation of the octopuses that can't open the container, when they observe from an adjoining tank an octopus that has found the solution to the problem, they quickly learn how to extract the oyster from the jar. All these examples indicate that the evolution of knowledge and learning is a common optimization strategy in nature. Without having to pass through the slow and erratic process of genetic evolution, it allows the capture of new, possible futures, as seen with the octopuses that learned a new technique to obtain food.

In terms analogous to the digital revolution, it's possible to say that cultural evolution is the increment of possible futures, and complexity or possibilities of survival by means of a software upgrade, without the need of a costly hardware modernization (upgrade). Thus, the development and transmission of culture introduces a multiplier to the general process of evolution, which allows individuals and multifaceted populations to evolve and re-evolve in short periods of time.

Social animals with the ability to learn, ones that became flexible through their modest abilities to learn and update their software, but that conserved the evolutionary advantages of specialized hardware like claws and sharpened fangs, were different from human beings whose commitment to the strategy of software evolution became absolute. This can be seen with the loss of claws, jaws, muscles, and instincts in favor of an enormous and energy-hungry brain, a self-realized conscience, and two free hands with prehensile thumbs.

This is important because in genetic evolution the change in a gene is a high-cost, risky experiment whose reversal is difficult. Cultural evolution, however, allows one single individual to search with low cost and risk new possibilities through the invention and utilization of cultural artifacts. These are taken advantage of and reused when they generate value (cultural evolution) and are eliminated when they generate loss and unnecessary high risks (cultural re-evolution). It goes without saying that analogous genetic mechanisms exist. They have only been seen to date in simple organisms such as bacteria, which serve as accelerators in the evolutionary process. The most well-known is the recombination of genetic material, which, in the past century, facilitated the rapid evolution of antibiotic-resistant bacteria. This produced the swift dissemination, on a hardware level, of sophisticated mechanisms of defense such as antibiotic pumps and biofilms, which point out the ironic example of the rivalry between the cultural evolution of complex living beings (the development of antibiotics) and the accelerated genetic evolution of simple living beings (bacterial resistance).

Along with the advantages and flexibility of cultural evolution, disadvantages appear as well. There is, for example, the possibility to make mistakes, which is unthinkable in the instinctive behavioral model. In that model, lack of wide-ranging cognitive flexibility diminishes mistakes. Consider taking stock of senseless deaths among humans such as recent deaths related to the so-called "selfie death" phenomena that have reached significant numbers. Selfie death refers to deaths that occur when people in a dangerous location become distracted and suffer a mortal accident while trying to take a selfie with the camera on their cell phone. Something similar happened to the first person that ate a poisonous mushroom in search of a new experience and climbed and fell from the highest mountain in the region.

From the point of view of the proposed model, the issue of risk mitigation has two different strategies. In authoritarian systems, the initial cost of implementation and coordination of the system was reduced, yet it fell into a larger probability of systemic risk because the group follows the path established by the master. The historic solution to mitigate risk was to codify culture into rigid traditions and customs; in other words, you do what you know already works so as not to run the risk of a systemic risk to materialize. We see this during the Middle Ages, when change, knowledge, and innovation were outlawed and persecuted, including by the penalty of death. For this reason, authoritarianism and innovation don´t combine well. These systems follow relatively undiversified strategies that take them to glory or catastrophe with no intermediate points for risk mitigation. This situation repeats itself over and over in authoritarian nations that rise and fall when they gamble on raw materials such as oil, soybeans, and copper for their development. This is referred to as the resource curse. Authoritarian systems that achieve stability generally flee from innovation and change, to maintain the synergy between the status quo, which benefits masters and lackeys, and exposure to systemic risk.

On the other hand, democratic systems count more on feedback channels and adaptation, mitigating the risk of systemic error yet incur the increase of individual risk. By allowing the exercise of free will — which reduces the cost of coordination of the system and increases the paths to innovation — changes and innovations in small, individual experiments of lower risk to the system are allowed. When these experiments prove to be successful, they can be extended and become contagious through re-evolution. This occurs in waves of cultural changes that express themselves through what is in fashion, much like the octopuses when they imitate and utilize techniques that allow them to obtain oysters confined in bottles. But when these experiments fail, the cost of error is paid by the individual who carried out the experiment and not by the entire group, which, contrary to the spread of fashion, learns from negative experiences to avoid them. We hope this will occur in the future with the spread of risk involved in becoming distracted and taking a selfie in a dangerous location.

In the economy, this phenomenon is observed in the foundation, development, success, and failure of small businesses that represent more than 98 % of total business in all economies worldwide. These generate the greatest proportion of employment and have a high death rate during the first five years of existence. For big businesses within competitive societies, it is also normal, and one could even say organic, that each year several companies this size will grow and fail. For this reason, the existence of businesses "too big to fail," those capable of operating in an insolvent or harmful way within the remainder of the economy, are symptomatic of the failures in the functioning of open systems.

Access and membership in society, such as the possibility to open small businesses, indicate another great innovation of democracy: participation (being someone and having a place to create value in society). This mechanism opens new paths of development and accelerates cultural evolution while reducing systemic risk when most people truly participate in the process of cultural construction in the broadest sense that one can give to this phrase.

By comparison, if individuals cannot gain permanent access to the possibility of success or failure (work, education, health, credit, security), democracy will not work. Thus, the large number of young people who currently neither study nor work (the "neither nors") are one of the main challenges to democratic societies and to those societies hoping to become democratic. This last conclusion is important because the decisive point of the contemporary economic debate has to do with the balance between the large components (corporations) and the small ones (small business and entrepreneurs). Linked to this, we find problems of access to the economy, inequality, and economic growth.

From the point of view of the systemic architecture developed up to this point, the large-scale strangulation and pillaging of the small actors by the big actors increases systemic risk and inhibits the possibilities of generating value and innovation. In the same way that change and innovation jeopardize stability in authoritarianism, in democracy, the lack of access and fair play and economic and social paralysis end up being corrosive and unnatural. This should break the myth linked to the epistemology of deterministic linear systems in that in an economy, conditions of stability exist and should be reached. This often justifies sacrifice of the small in favor of the large. Complex adaptive systems follow roles of performance that lead to homeostasis and operating regimes that, when they function well, are evolutionary and dynamic. When the flows that feed them are limited, like the access of individuals to the economic network, homeostasis and operating regimens are disorganized.

The great financial crisis of 2008-2009 — the way it was addressed and the repercussions it left behind — reflect the poor understanding we still have regarding the needs and limits which an open and complex system require to function. Strictly speaking, the containment of the crisis required the protection of deposits and assets of savers and those in debt, and the reorganization and continued operation of credit and payment systems in the real sector of the economy — productive businesses — since all those objectives are related to maintaining the connection of flows within the system. The main criticism made about the management of the crisis is that there wasn't a balance between measures protecting the small components of the system — home owners whose homes were foreclosed and auctioned off — and those destined for the large components — the bankers, whose assets, salaries, and bonuses were protected even during the bankruptcy. The system was neither fixed nor reorganized. The "too big to fail" banks were merged and made into even bigger banks. Despite the large losses and the suffering of millions of people, the largest financial crisis in the last century is anonymous. Responsibilities were not delineated nor were responsible people named. This eroded the confidence of the agents (voters) in the operation of the system. Due to its magnitude, it's quite probable that this trauma has formed an important part of the fierce and irrational anti-establishment movement seen in the United Kingdom with Brexit and in the U.S. with Donald Trump. Here, the negative part of the mechanism of re-evolution could end up as a process of cultural regression, from democracy to authoritarianism, which has its origin in the base of the system and reinforced with the generalized change of the interaction rules agents use.

Conservatives and liberals

Throughout the 44 years of the Cold War, the factual and ideological confrontation between the Western bloc and communism polarized the world. After the fall of the Berlin Wall and the resulting dismantlement of the Soviet bloc in 1989, after multiple economic crises and the stagnation of the economy in the West, after the start of a new ideological war between Muslim extremists and Western civilization, along with the controversial wars in Iraq and Afghanistan, the world today finds itself in a state of confusion, exhaustion, and rejection of traditional Western ideologies.

This rejection stems from different transgressions against the logic of the democratic system, such as the amalgamation of contradictory political and ideological stances. For example, while in the U.S. the conservative movement promotes the right to life and the criminalization of abortion, it simultaneously promotes the death penalty. The Tea Party gained strength within this same movement. It was driven by libertarian values that promote anarchistic and individualistic initiatives to eliminate interference of government and institutions from the lives of citizens. It demands, however, an interventionist foreign policy like the one that facilitated the wars in Iraq and Afghanistan. As far as the liberal movement is concerned, civil and human rights agendas are promoted, but attacks and the use of lethal force from unmanned aircraft is defended. On the electoral politics stage, the persistent meddling of private funds in the selection and election of candidates lays the foundation for rejection, just like the growing obedience of government officials to this type of backer and not to the electorate.

In Mexico, for reasons previously described, the anti-political party movement is in vogue. This movement permitted Cuauhtémoc Blanco, a retired soccer player with no political experience, to become municipal president of Cuernavaca in the 2015 elections. Cuernavaca is the most important municipality in the state of Morelos, which at this moment in time finds itself in the most serious public security crisis it has ever faced. In Guatemala, also in 2015, President Otto Pérez Molina resigned after being accused of corruption. Then the voters elected Jimmy Morales as president, a man whose most significant public precedent was his successful career as a television comedian. That same year, the candidacy of Donald Trump for president of the U.S. emerged and grew. At first glance, he was considered a light-hearted joke, but as time went by the campaign captured the resolve and sympathy of voters through a political proposal full of nonsense and contradictions. In addition to these cases, the success of State capitalism in China and the economic stagnation of the Western bloc questioned the need to maintain a market economy and democracy as an indivisible identity.

It is within this context that it becomes difficult and complicated to make an ideological or psychographic segmentation of the democratic actors. In fact, it's possible to state that the Zeitgeist or the spirit of the moment we are living in is pessimistic, which leads to the desperate thinking that this type of classification is useless or irrelevant. But it is, indeed, the state of things that compels us to identify or re-identify and articulate ideas and principles that increase the viability of democratic systems in the 21st century. The assessment that can be constructed based on cultural evolution is that the emerging anomalous phenomena that are observed today in various democratic and semi-democratic systems, originate in the transgressions of the operating principles of open systems, in the loss of influence and possibility of participation on the part of common citizens as opposed to political backers, in the exaggerated exposure to risk and the cost of error to small businesses compared to those of large corporations, and in the adamant insistence of politicians to construct, through consensus or central rhetoric, dissonant and confusing postures — proposals that, at the same time, are white and black for a citizen who only has one moral identity with which to face life.

Based on the model of the four strategies of the cultural evolution, the response to this democratic confusion is, in the first place, phenomena such as lack of access, opportunities, high risk, and low personal benefits that are signs of a process of authoritarian degradation. This situation begins to facilitate the existence and functioning of the dynamics of master, lackey, and serf as it limits the diversity and participation that are foundational characteristics of the open society.

In the second place, according to interaction rule number two (cooperation and competition), open systems are divided into two large spectrums: the conservative, where the dominant idea is that the construction and capture of value are competitive and individual endeavors; and second, the liberal, where collaborative creation of shared value is the dominant posture. Even though these spectra share characteristics related to the achievement of freedom or the interaction rule number one (internal locus, dignity, responsibility, and democratic legality) — which unify them as the force that opposes authoritarianism — they are deeply divided by the ideas of common good and self-interest.

To understand these differences, it is worth developing profiles of the characters who share the use of rule of interaction number one on the side of freedom, but who, at the same time, are divided by interaction rule number two, that is between the construction of liberal common good and the protection of conservative self-interest. The four characters of the democratic world are conservatives, liberals, superstars, and champions.

The conservatives

The birth of open society has its origin in the transformation from a centralized control network to a decentralized control one. Sociologically, this is referred to as the transfer from the sovereignty of a monarch through divine endowment to a positivist sovereignty of self-law through the acknowledgement of human dignity. In the West, this rupture with obedience to a sovereign and to divine law, was pendular in nature and emphasized the positivist nature of self-law among human beings. Nevertheless, although this marked the beginning of the development of open societies during the 18th and 19th centuries, it did not prevent the expansionist and colonialist projection from Europe toward the rest of the world. The expansion that Western technology generated, from the interoceanic voyages of Christopher Columbus in the 15th century to the generalized use of the steam engine in the 19th century, did not moderate the decline of the absolutist monarchs and the appearance of the first democratic regimes.

Ultimately, the new democratic reasoning of modernity, while different in aspects such as the innovation and development of mercantile and industrial economies made possible by newly emerging phenomena, found, within the ethical framework of self-interest, a bridge and common language with the old imperial interests of the monarchs. Ideologically, there are many examples of this adaptation. The primary one is the continued application of the idea of the superior dignity of the European male above all other human beings. Among other things, this idea sustained the segregation of European women through the end of the 19th century into the first half of the 20th century, when they finally won the right to vote, among other legal rights.

In terms of the cultural evolution model, this explains why conservative democrats, masters, and lackeys, while different in the vision they have of freedom, share self-interest regarding interaction rule number two. The absolutist monarchs and the thieving barons of the 19th century sought domination and capture of the world for themselves, even though each one of them carried this out in a different fashion. Monarchs used violence. Conservative democrats used new forms of expansion, such as fierce and often unfair industrial, mercantile, and commercial competition.

Over time, and thanks to the plasticity of human culture — which in the long run responds to social upheavals by means of a cultural re-evolution — the most extreme part of the conservative model remained tempered in different ways. First, the old colonies of the Victorian monarchic period rebelled. They opposed control of the metropolis and formed new nations with independent aspirations. Second, it was impossible to maintain the idea of the supremacy of European male dignity above the rest of humanity, and slavery in the West was abolished. Additionally, segregation of women and the brutal exploitation of workers in the first industrial era diminished. Third, the process of expansion was no longer possible once all the territories of the planet were discovered, colonized, and conquered. In ecological terms, humans encountered the limit of their own ecosystem. This continued to be defined in a configuration that was profoundly unequal, unjust, and conservative.

Despite the problems it created, the interesting or positive aspect of conservative expansion is that it achieved things that had never been achieved in the history of mankind: public works, platforms, institutions, science, technology, and Victorian infrastructure all represent one of the most vibrant eras of progress and change in the history of humanity. In the 20th century, after colonial expansion ended, there arose a new authoritarian momentum, which, when faced with the new democracies, culminated in the First and Second World Wars. The conservative competitive model was one that, due to its economic, technological, and military organization, allowed for the salvation of Western democracies. To illustrate the strength and benefit conservatives achieved in the face of authoritarian expansion, it's worthwhile reviewing an excerpt of Winston Churchill's inaugural speech as Prime Minister, delivered to the British Parliament on May 13, 1940(127):

...We have before us an ordeal of the most grievous kind. We have before us many, many long months of struggle and of suffering. You ask, what is our policy? I will say: It is to wage war, by sea, land and air, with all our might and with all the strength that God can give us; to wage war against a monstrous tyranny, never surpassed in the dark and lamentable catalogue of human crime. That is our policy. You ask, what is our aim? I can answer in one word: victory. Victory at all costs, victory in spite of all terror, victory, however long and hard the road may be; for without victory, there is no survival. Let that be realised; no survival for the British Empire, no survival for all that the British Empire has stood for, no survival for the urge and impulse of the ages, that mankind will move forward towards its goal. But I take up my task with buouyancy and hope. I feel sure that our cause will not be suffered to fail among men. At this time, I feel entitled to claim the aid of all, and I say, "Come, then, let us go forward together with our united strength."

After the defeat of the authoritarian fascist axis in 1945, the confrontation during the Cold War continued between Western democratic nations and the conglomerate of communist authoritarian nations. In the final phase, in the decade of the 1980s, it was clear the inefficiency of communist economies could not sustain the economic and military competition coming from the Western bloc. During this period, under the conservative impulse of U.S. President Ronald Reagan and Britain's Prime Minister Margaret Thatcher, the commitment to military spending intensified with programs such as Star Wars. The communist bloc, in turn, sought a symmetrical response. This last and desperate endeavor ended exacerbating the socialist economic fatigue and the system collapsed. Indeed, another example, which illustrates the competitive capability of democratic conservatives against authoritarianism, is the conservative speech that President Ronald Reagan delivered at the Berlin Wall on June 12, 1987(128):

...Where four decades ago there was rubble, today in West Berlin there is the greatest industrial output of any city in Germany — busy office blocks, fine homes and apartments,

proud avenues, and the spreading lawns of parkland. Where a city's culture seemed to have been destroyed, today there are two great universities, orchestras and an opera, countless theaters, and museums. Where there was want, today there's abundance — food, clothing, automobiles — the wonderful goods of the Ku'damm. From devastation, from utter ruin, you Berliners have, in freedom, rebuilt a city that once again ranks as one of the greatest on earth. The Soviets may have had other plans. But my friends, there were a few things the Soviets didn't count on — Berliner Herz, Berliner Humor, ja, und Berliner Schnauze. [Berliner heart, Berliner humor, yes, and a Berliner Schnauze.] In the 1950s, Khrushchev predicted: "We will bury you." But in the West today, we see a free world that has achieved a level of prosperity and well-being unprecedented in all of human history. In the Communist world, we see failure, technological backwardness, declining standards of health, even want of the most basic kind — too little food. Even today, the Soviet Union still cannot feed itself. After these four decades, then, there stands before the entire world one great and inescapable conclusion: Freedom leads to prosperity. Freedom replaces the ancient hatreds among the nations with comity and peace. Freedom is the victor.

To round out the characterization of the conservative way of being from a sociological perspective, let's look at how George Lakoff's description of the moral model of the strict father balances it out(129):

In this view, the world is a dangerous and difficult place, there is tangible evil in the world and children have to be made good. To stand up to evil, one must be morally strong – disciplined. The father's job is to protect and support the family. His moral duty is to teach his children right from wrong. Physical discipline in childhood will develop the internal discipline adults need to be moral people and to succeed. The child's duty is to obey. Punishment is required to balance the moral books. If you do wrong, there must be a consequence. The strict father, as moral authority, is responsible for controlling the women of the family, especially in matters of sexuality and reproduction.

Children are to become self-reliant through discipline and the pursuit of self-interest. Pursuit of self-interest is moral: If everybody pursues his own self-interest, the self-interest of all will be maximized. Without competition, people would not have to develop discipline and so would not become moral beings. Worldly success is an indicator of sufficient moral strength; lack of success suggests lack of sufficient discipline. Those who are not successful should not be coddled; they should be forced to acquire self-discipline. When this view is translated into politics, the government becomes the strict father whose job for the country is to support (maximize overall wealth) and protect (maximize military and political strength). The citizens are children of two kinds: the mature, disciplined, self-reliant ones who should not be meddling with the whining, undisciplined, dependent ones who should never be coddled. This means (among other things) favoring those who control corporate wealth and power (those seen as the best people) over those who are victims (those seen as morally weak). It means removing government regulations, which get in the way of those who are disciplined. Nature is seen as a resource to be exploited. One-way communication translates into government secrecy. The highest moral value is to preserve and extend the domain of strict morality itself, which translates into bringing the values of strict father morality into every aspect of life, public and private, domestic and foreign.

It should be added that a substantial part of the history of democracy was defined by the expansionist push in industry, weapons, economy, and commerce, which proved to be more efficient and effective than the authoritarian fascists and communists who were defeated. Despite this, the conservatives face two challenges that have them up against the wall.

The first is that the attainment of the competitive model of self-interest, which also implies adherence to self-law. That produced a vision of the world where environmental restrictions — representing the materialization of an external law, and therefore, contradicting one of the fundamentals of the conservative model — were relegated or eliminated from the social sciences that had lent support to the conservative model. For this reason, the frames of reference on the conservative side, such as law and economics, are poor and insufficient when tackling present-day problems such as climate change and its allocation of costs to negative externalities created by the economic process like water pollution and the destruction of biodiversity. The second problem is that when the conservatives share the ethical focus of self-interest (interaction rule number two) with the authoritarians, they are susceptible to succumbing to the temptation of following the authoritarian paths when their democratic convictions weaken.

In fact, the geopolitical configuration of the post-war world created a very important pivot point for the general prosperity of conservatives in the 20th century. In the axis of freedom, the conservatives coincided with the liberals in the defense of democracy and against the threat of communism. In the axis of self-interest, it was the conservatives who related better to authoritarian regimes such as the oil-rich countries in the Middle East, with whom it was necessary to conduct business. Following the Cold War, however, the conservatives have had difficulties finding their place. First, because the need to incorporate natural law — understood as the limits of sustainability — into the economic, political and social process violates the foundation of the conservative system of beliefs and places it in confrontation with the liberals, who, from the point of view of the common good, have embraced the environmental agenda. Furthermore, after the fall of the Berlin Wall in 1989, a common enemy that united conservatives and liberals, in defense of democracy, no longer exists. And the emergence of the chaotic and ungovernable digital world, breaks with the ability to maintain corporate and institutional order and discipline, through which the conservative understands and structures the world around him.

At present, there is a very clear example of the confusion that reigns on the conservative side. Despite international scientific consensus, the conservative movement in the United States maintains a rigid posture negating the anthropogenic origin of climate change; it cannot find common ground with the liberals on which to build a new agenda; and it promotes, by granting extraordinary powers to institutions of security and espionage, the development of all-out digital communications surveillance programs. These are detrimental to the rights to free speech, due process, and privacy of citizens. This tells us that the lack of a new conservative program for the 21st century, along with the degradation of the democratic spirit in those who hold this worldview, is beginning to increase the probabilities of an authoritarian involution in the largest democracy on the planet. An example of this new authoritarian-conservative spirit it the quote obtained by journalist Ron Suskind of the *New York Times*(130) from an important advisor to President George W. Bush, which indicated a new authoritarian vision of the world:

> *"That's not the way the world really works anymore," he continued. "We're an empire now, and when we act, we create our own reality. And while you're studying that reality – judiciously, as you will – we'll act again, creating other new realities, which you can study too, and that's how things will sort out. We're history's actors...and you, all of you, will be left to just study what we do."*

The liberals

In the same way that conservatives find themselves disorganized and confused in the postmodern context, liberals, from the birth of modern democracies on, found it difficult to define the path to follow in the open society. The architects that opened the way to dismantling monarchies and defined the open society, were liberal thinkers such as John Locke(131), who established the philosophical staging that allowed for the justification of the break with the divine origin of the sovereign's dignity. Montesquieu defined the need for a constitutional regime founded in civil liberties(132). Even the redaction commission of the Constitution of the United States, headed by Thomas Jefferson, channeled the spirit of liberal ideas in the preamble to The Constitution, which is considered one of the gems of liberal democratic thought:

THE CULTURAL EVOLUTION CAST

Joseph Stiglitz It is trust, more than money, that makes the world go around

Locus of control:	Internal
Self worth:	Dignity
Personal action:	Responsibility
Collective action:	Democratic legality
Ethics:	Common Good

LIBERALS OF COLUMBIA

"WE the People of the United States, in Order to form a more perfect Union, establish Justice, insure domestic Tranquility, provide for the common defense, promote the general Welfare, and secure the Blessings of Liberty to ourselves and our Posterity, do ordain and establish this Constitution for the United States of America..."

As the Industrial Revolution unfolded in the 18th and 19th centuries, mounting negative externalities, which the conservatism of self-interest incorporated into modern societies, gained a presence. Such externalities arose from new phenomena: the polluting of the River Thames, for example, which triggered several cholera epidemics as well as the Great Plague of 1858. This paralyzed the city of London and caused Parliament to consider changing the location of its headquarters(133). They included, as well, labor atrocities against children, women, and men in textile and metalworking factories. As a response to these phenomena, politicians and reformers like Robert Owen (1771-1858) introduced into the legal design of new democratic nations the first norms for labor advocacy. Nevertheless, outside of the domain of great ideas inscribed in stone or of the specific cases of legal reform, liberal democrats were left in the corner in an ideological space that became a dead-end road when the 19th century ended.

The first part of the liberal problem can be found in the very origin of modernity. To leave behind the monarchic era, it was necessary to break with the adherence to natural law with which the monarchs had legitimized themselves. The core modern philosophies defined themselves based on the positivist foundation of self-law, which anchored them to the ethical focus of self-interest. The conservatives will most likely endorse this argument with no opposition, while the old communists and socialists will find the point to be contentious. Some will say that the focus of their ideologies was to reach the general good for society rather than self-interest. However, Marxist socialism did not change the anchoring of modernity to the foundation of self-interest.

In fact, the class struggle between the bourgeoisie and the proletariat, with which the conceptual frame of historic materialism was defined, ultimately endorsed the idea that the historic process is expressed through a struggle of self-interests that is resolved in a confrontation which leads the proletariat to dictatorship. It's not surprising that once socialism and communism were defined by the modern axis of self-interest and the revolution of the proletariat as a form of establishing a closed system, we see that their premises coincide with the interaction rules of the status quo in the cultural evolution model. Socialism became popular as a vehicle to modernize and bring to the 20th century the authoritarianism that was lying dormant in the foundation of many societies. Perhaps it was not the original motivation of Marx and Engels, but the underlying interaction rules that defined the Marxist model resonated in earnest in the spirit of the people because, even though they appeared modern, deep down they overlapped with the ancestral authoritarian social system of masters, lackeys, and serfs.

For liberals, the impossibility to see options outside the modern principle of self-interest put them in a position where the economic liberalism of laissez faire clashed with the attempt to resolve the growing negative externalities of the conservative hegemony. With the tools of the period, it was not possible to produce a useful synthesis between individual liberty and the common good. Consequently, they entered a dilemma between economic liberalism and the construction of shared value of the common good, which requires the concurrent construction of public goods and governmental norms, as well as the preservation of democratic freedom.

The second part of the problem was the rapid growth of socialism as a reaction and counterbalance to conservative control. The harsh clash between socialists and conservatives polarized the modern world. That prevented the existence of a space for the development of democratic liberalism as an integrated system with actionable ideas. In this conflictive and incoherent situation, democratic liberalism and the common good did not strengthen and remained defined, most likely by the conservatives, as a form of light and benevolent socialism that irritated socialists and conservatives alike. When they were diluted by the confusing linear political spectrum of the left and the right, where they played the role of pivot and buffer between conservatives and socialists, the liberals were able to introduce significant changes in the legal and institutional design of democratic nations.

The paradigmatic example of a liberal, successful in solving a great crisis, can be found in the U.S. in the administration of President Franklin D. Roosevelt. When the Great Depression followed the crash of 1929, the government had to cope with the collapse of the conservative model and eventually face authoritarian fascism in the grand theater of World War II. Apart from the exceptional character of historic conditions to which any president must respond, the Roosevelt case shows two facets of the potential that an idiosyncratic liberal democrat must have to shape history despite the partisan opposition which came from the Republican Party, and at times, from the Democratic Party as well.

When Roosevelt took the office of president in 1932, the Great Depression was in its third year. Under the old conservative dogma of non-intervention of the State in the economy, the potential for solving the crisis was not good. In this context, President Roosevelt shifted the role of the State and introduced the New Deal. This defined a new and more active role of government in the economy and was the basis of emerging work programs and new institutions, some of which continue to operate today.

Later, in the 1940s, according to the memoirs of Prime Minister Winston Churchill himself(134), the United Kingdom found itself in a desperate situation: France had fallen, the Soviet Union maintained a pact of non-aggression with Germany, and Japan was about to join the Axis. Meanwhile, a strong isolationist sentiment persisted in the U.S. and translated into elevated costs for those politicians who proposed getting involved in the conflict. From the presidential elections in 1940 to the attack on Pearl Harbor in 1941 in which the U.S. officially entered WWII, President Roosevelt discovered a way to supply war materials to England at no cost. This kept the British war effort alive during that very critical year in history. Convinced of his responsibility and the need to stop the Nazis, he later expanded the scope of the program and implemented the financial leasing program called "Lend-Lease Act," which lasted until the end of WWII maintaining open supply lines for the Allies.

With an earlier process, in the 19th century, the Catholic Church took on the development of the concept of common good in the new industrial society in the encyclical Rerum Novarum(135). This document established the Church's social doctrine and the action principles for the Christian democracy movement with which it sought to address the un-evangelization of the worker, as much due to the marginalization created by the conservatives as to the efforts of socialist indoctrination. The emergence of Christian democracy is interesting because, as part of the reformation of the Church in the modern era, the change to democratic freedom was accepted as irreversible, and achieving the common good from the point of view of Christian ethics was emphasized. This proposal, however, ran counter to the process of modernization, which intended to escape, at all costs, the influences of natural law that prevailed during the authoritarian monarchic era when the Church played an important role. Perhaps for that reason it also took some work for Christian democracy to find a voice and a program, in the same way that liberal democrats remained trapped in the logic of the left and the right. The slowness with which the social doctrine of the Church has adapted to the world is confirmed by the fact that it took more than a century to take up a clear position on caring for the environment. This occurred with Pope Francis's encyclical *Laudato Si'*(136).

That said, from the point of view of Lakoff's model of moral identity(129), the description of liberal democrats coincides with the identity of the nurturant father:

> *It is assumed that the world should be a nurturant place. The job of parents is to nurture their children and raise the children to be nurturers. To be a nurturer you have to be empathetic and responsible (for yourself and others). Empathy and responsibility have many implications: Responsibility implies protection, competence, education, hard work and social connectedness; empathy requires freedom, fairness and honesty, two-way communication, a fulfilled life (unhappy unfulfilled people are less likely to want others to be happy) and restitution rather than retribution to balance the moral books. Social responsibility requires cooperation and community building over competition. In the place of specific rules, there is a general "ethics of care" that says, "Help, don't harm." To be of good character is to be empathetic and responsible, in all of the above ways. Empathy and responsibility are the central values, implying other values: freedom, protection, fairness, cooperation, open communication, competence, happiness, mutual respect and restitution as opposed to retribution. In this view, the job of government is to care for, serve and protect the population (especially those who are helpless), to guarantee democracy (the equal sharing of political power), to promote the well-being of all and to ensure fairness for all. The economy should be a*

means to these moral ends. There should be openness in gov-
ernment. Nature is seen as a source of nurture to be respected
and preserved. Empathy and responsibility are to be promoted
in every area of life, public and private. Art and education
are parts of self-fulfillment and therefore moral necessities...

To conclude the description of liberals, it is necessary to discuss the situation in which they find themselves today and the obstacles they face
in the 21st century. And for that, it is time to recount a meeting with an
interesting and dynamic liberal of the new era. In the summer of 2010, I
went to Montreal as the head of a delegation of Mexican civil servants to
participate in North America Day, an annual trilateral meeting on electronic government. In that encounter, the participants met Todd Park,
a dynamic and vibrant technologist from the U.S. National Institutes of
Health (NIH) and a recognized entrepreneurial technologist from Silicon Valley who joined Barack Obama's campaign in 2008. Later, consistent with his interest in generating a positive change in society, he sold
his stock in the business he had founded, at a huge opportunity cost, to
join the Obama administration with the objective of pushing the transformation of the government through technology and the culture of entrepreneurship. That night, Todd and I connected at the hotel's rooftop
bar, where we spoke until the early hours of the morning. Todd shared
his campaign experiences with me, the spirit and objectives — liberal,
without a doubt — held by the still-new Obama administration. As for
me, I talked about the cultural evolution model, which was in its final
stages of development. I explained the main obstacle, visible from this
model's point of view, to advance the construction of the solutions that
President Obama and his team wanted to implement. That same spirit was
transmitted in an excerpt of the speech known as "A New Beginning,"
which President Obama delivered at the University of Cairo, Egypt(137):

I have come here to seek a new beginning between the United
States and Muslims around the world; one based upon mutu-
al interest and mutual respect; and one based upon the truth
that America and Islam are not exclusive and need not be in
competition. Instead, they overlap, and share common prin-
ciples – principles of justice and progress; tolerance and the
dignity of all human beings.

The personal reflection shared with Todd was that the modern era started with the break with natural law and was founded on the grounding of self-interest. But the problems of the 21st century, such as climate change, impose upon us the reincorporation of natural law to the design of social sciences. This represents a non-trivial change because that one fact marks the end of the modern era and forces us to define a postmodern era where present social technologies such as politics, law, and economy don't exist or are not in place. This hinders the implementation of new postmodern solutions. By the same token, my opinion was that the system of ideas with which the great social spirit of the Obama campaign could be transformed into a stable democratic force didn't exist. Consequently, if the obstacles to construct the postmodern social technologies were not soon defeated, the recycling of modern tools in the implementation of postmodern solutions would hinder the advancement of Obama's liberal agenda.

Even though the concept was interesting to Todd, he showed himself to be a skeptic regarding the difficulty they would encounter in building Obama's transformational world. He remained optimistic that they would achieve this because there was a great spirit of change, renovation, and hope for the U.S. surrounding the figure of his presidency.

In 2012, in addition to being personal advisor to the president, Todd Park was named the first Chief Technology Officer in the history of the U.S. In this office, he emphasized the emerging role he played in reshaping and salvaging the collapse of the website healthcare.gov, which put the implementation of the "Affordable Care Act," sometimes known as "Obama Care," and with it the very Obama administration, on tenterhooks. The administration suffered a severe attack from the conservative sector of Congress, which took advantage of the failures in the system to reverse the reform of health care. After Todd and his team made healthcare.gov viable — and after a long political stalemate in Congress, out of which the Obama administration never managed to emerge — Todd abandoned public service in Washington and migrated back to Silicon Valley to dedicate his time, talent, and liberal energy to objectives related to the private sector. Meanwhile, the Obama administration was unable to realize the goals of a new beginning with the Muslim world, in part because he didn't abandon the violence of drone attacks and because — outside of the traditional methods of U.S. foreign policy — the path delineated in the Cairo speech lacked channels and political technologies for its implementation. Thus, at the dusk of the modern era and the dawn of the postmodern era, liberals continue to be unclear and confused as they wander through the remnants of the era of competition, which is foreign to them, and they don't dare give form and clarity to a project that will unveil the new era, one founded on collaboration and shared value.

The most authentic thing about us is our capacity
to create, to overcome, to endure, to transform,
to love and to be greater than our suffering.
Ben Okri

Leadership, paladins, and superstars

The principle divergence between power (or influence) in the authoritarian world and the democratic world is found in the relationship that each system has with value. In the authoritarian world, subjugation, lack of diversity, and the curbing of innovation limit the construction of new value. Consequently, the power and value play is circumscribed to the capture of value, which already exists, such as ownership and rent extraction of natural resources or the monopolistic and oligarchic exploitation of captive markets. This situation allows the dynamics of master, lackey, and serf to function and endure. On the other hand, we have the democratic world, where the construction of new value or the capture of new, possible futures is through innovation, curiosity, diversity, freedom, and the characteristics that define open societies (Chapters Three and Seven). The relationship this system has with value is founded on its expansion, discovery, and dissemination.

Regarding the distribution of value, despite the considerable contemporary challenges about inequality, the economic and technological model of the industrial and postindustrial economies is founded on the dissemination and massification of new technologies. The examples abound: from the cheapening and mass production of automobiles by Henry

Ford, and the massification of sanitation and public health — such as washing of hands with soap and making use of drinking water and sanitation networks — to the almost universal use of the mobile telephone. (There are 6.8 billion mobile phones in use in a population of 7 billion people(138)when only just 30 years ago there were practically none.) Seen in another light, in the open society a detergent mogul is not possible without the existence of the adequate technological diffusion that makes possible the mass market for cleaning accessories.

Thus, the relationship of influence and power on open societies is diametrically opposed to that which exists in authoritarian societies, especially when the articulation of the process to elect leaders in the democratic system facilitates the construction of power with an emphasis on the generation and distribution of value. It is from this difference that one can analyze the influence of open societies from the perspective of leadership.

Despite the importance that the word "leadership" has in our time — the term is frequently used and abused in political and corporate discourse — a precise or widely accepted definition of this concept does not exist. Proof of this is that a search of the Internet results in headlines like "33 ways to define leadership."(139)

Based on the definition of power employed in Chapter Three (the ability to influence the behavior of others through submission or persuasion), we can state that leadership, is the influence gained by free concurrence on others when in pursuit of the construction and dissemination of value. The authoritarian counterpart to leadership is the influence, which is exerted by subduing others in pursuit of the capture and appropriation of value.

To illustrate the difference between the two definitions, let's return to the example of the humble, yet-skilled octopus. To the dismay of political scientists who study power, we find a cultural archetype of leadership in the experiment where one octopus figured out how to open the jar and the other learned and copied this behavior. In animals that have some level of cognitive flexibility to learn and evolve through software, the ability to identify new and better solutions in the software of their neighbor — and to assimilate through observation and learning — reveals the natural transmission of the discovery of value and influence. Another aspect that the results of the experiment reveal is that the octopus that fails to open the jar remains open to the possibility of a different solution and has the patience to analyze the movements of his tank mate. He concurs with the possibility of leadership, he learns, and in the end, he obtains as a reward the knowledge of a new technique to acquire food. If we apply this example to an absurd mental experiment, such as an ocean inhabited strictly by octopuses and oysters trapped in all kinds of jars, it's easy to think that the octopuses most capable at deciphering all manner of ways to open bottles would be the most closely followed and influential octopuses in the sea.

It is necessary to judge this example within its corresponding dimension so as not to spark its use in other fields where anthropomorphism is not pertinent. As far as we know, the case of the octopus is not common in the animal kingdom, and therefore, the existence of a leadership archetype stands out. On the other hand, it is more normal to observe examples of the opposite behavior in nature, those that coincide more with the cultural archetypes that define authoritarian power, as is the case of the opportunistic behavior of the African hyena. More complex and social than the octopus, hyenas closely observe the movements and hunting techniques of other predators of the savannah to later attack with the strength of the group and steal the prey. Nor do we know how octopuses interact outside of the laboratory conditions. Without the transparent division between the compartments in the tank, the observed behavior might very well change.

In open societies, the emergent properties of power develop into forms of leadership, which are based on a consensus aimed at the construction of value. Conservative leadership gives origin to superstars and liberal leadership to paladins.

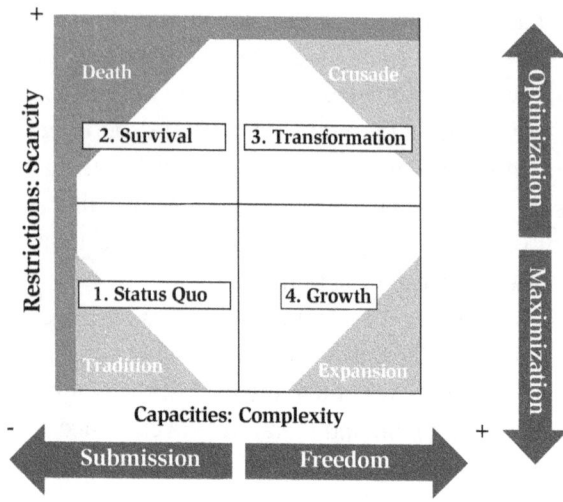

Figure 10: Quadrants and sectors of the cultural evolution model.

It is necessary to bring back the graphic representation of the cultural evolution model (Figure 10) to explain that, based on the definition published in 2011, there are two states for each proposed strategy. One is stable, where the use of interaction rules is dominant and consistent and corresponds to each quadrant. The other is unstable, where the strength and consistency with which agents apply one of the other models of decision is more uncertain. In the model, this difference is expressed in the following fashion (Table 16):

Strategy	Consolidated State	Description	Characters
1. Status quo	Stagnation	There is neither change nor evolution; there are no external threats that drive change. A stable state of stagnation has been reached.	Hero, master and bandit
2. Survival	Death	In an environment of high restriction and low capability, the thresholds of survival are surpassed. The stable sector of this strategy is death.	Fanatic[1]
3. Transformation	Crusade	Evolution is maintained despite the environmental restrictions, which are achieved thanks to a sense of common purpose.	Paladin
4. Growth	Expansion	It is the scene of unlimited growth. The environment is colonized while new ways of utilizing it are discovered.	Superstar

Table 16: Consolidated states.

In the case of the paladins and the superstars, we refer to the characters that use the strictest stance of the interaction rules. In other words, the paladins are found in "crusade," the stable subsector of the strategy "transformation." The superstars are found in "expansion," the stable subsector of the strategy "growth."

Before continuing, it's worthwhile tackling the discussion about the number of states that can exist for each interaction rule. The analysis stems from two possible states for each interaction rule: a binary framework, which in combination produces four strategies. Each strategy is divided in two sectors, one stable (shaded sectors) and another dynamic (transparent sectors). In total, these produce eight subsectors defined in Figure 10, within which the cast of characters of cultural evolution are spread out and dwell (Figure 11).

---

1 The fanatic is the character that leads movement to the stable sector of the survival strategy (death). A classic example is the religious group Heaven's Gate lead by Marshall Applewhite. He took 39 of his followers to their death in 1997. The description of this character wasn´t developed because it was deemed marginal to the main objective

It turns out that complex scales such as values and the locus of control are measured as analogue gradients, which are interpreted through discrete categories because of methodological economy. These discrete categories can be as simple as binary states (e.g., submission, freedom) — the method used in the model — or they can be broader, as in Richard Dawkins's theistic possibility spectrum(140). He divided the gradient of believers and atheists into seven categories. A possible, and probably impractical, analogy of the cultural model of evolution drawn from the seven discrete categories like those Dawkins proposes, is presented in the following matrix (Table 17):

#		A Absolute Subject	B De facto subject	C Technically not a subject, but a subject	D Neither subject nor free	E Technically not free, but free	F De facto free	G Absolute Free
1	Strong empathetic	1	2	3	4	5	6	7
2	De facto empathetic	8	9	10	11	12	13	14
3	Technically not empathetic, but leaning toward empathetic	15	16	17	18	19	20	21
4	Neither empathetic nor egotistic	22	23	24	25	26	27	28
5	Technically not egotistic, but leaning toward egotistic	29	30	31	32	33	34	35
6	De facto egotistic	36	37	38	39	40	41	42
7	Severe egotistic	43	44	45	46	47	48	49

Table 17: Expanded interaction rules spectrum.

In this expanded model, in lieu of describing nine characters (masters, lackeys, vassals, heroes, bandits, liberals, conservatives, superstars, and paladins), it would be necessary to record 49 different idiosyncrasies. Characters such as masters, heroes, and bandits would occupy the sectors 6A, 7A, 6B, and 7B (cells 36, 37, 43 and 44). Nevertheless, the multiplication of categories beyond the original binary system is not regarded as useful to this discussion.

The problems of optimizing complex adaptive systems are another aspect that reinforces the argument regarding the emergence of leadership and the use of a few discrete categories. To operate inside a regime or reach a state of homeostasis, these types of systems need to find a balance between efficiency and the change to a new state of complexity (flow or capture of possible futures), and the time in which to resolve the problems of optimization. The element of time of optimization or decision is of great importance since, in mathematical terms, the location of a good solution in the short term is preferable to the best solution in the long term. This is consistent with prospect theory, which explains the heuristic behavior of the agents. Evolutionary psychologists explain this with the premise that in human beings as well as in animals, fleeing from an uncertain danger is a better response than waiting for a specific answer. The animal that always flees survives, but the animal that always waits for absolute certainty at some point will encounter a danger from which it cannot flee.

In this manner, as variables and states are added to a system, the problems of optimization easily grow in the amount of time and computing power for them to be solved. In fact, complex adaptive systems must not have many interaction rules because it is easy for systems with too many configuration possibilities to exceed the trans-computational barrier, which is defined in absolute terms by all those problems that require processing of information greater than 10^{93} bits(141). In local terms, a problem exceeds the trans-computational barrier when the information processing is greater than the computing capabilities of the system. So, the trans-computational barrier of a cockroach, measured by the computing power of its nervous system, is far smaller than that of a chimpanzee.

That's why human societies require and have convergence mechanisms, such as leadership, that simplify in a heuristic manner the possible states of the social system. In other words, societies have the approaches to life or points of view that reduce the cost in time and effort to optimize the system. Because of this, individuals learn and develop heuristic methods through knowledge and practice just like an expert hunter who learns to identify hidden dangers in the brush. They become influential and exert leadership in society. In the words of Sir Francis Bacon: "Knowledge is power."(142)

In recent years, those who study the components of success and leadership have found that many of the figures who stand out in democratic societies have similar traits. The most well-known is the rule of the 10,000 hours, discovered by Anders Ericsson(143) and popularized by Malcolm Gladwell. It proves that people with international mastery in one field of activity or another (culture, sports, academics, or business) are those who achieve 10,000 hours or more of deliberate practice before adulthood. By deliberate practice, the tacit model is one in which the person attempts to better his abilities in a conscious and decisive fashion for each hour of practice.

But, even in large populations, few people can count on the resources, the interest, and the will to accumulate 10,000 hours of deliberate practice (or approximately 20 hours a week during 10 years of life) between infancy and adulthood. What is more, this phenomenon of the accumulation of hours, according to what Ericsson said in a recent interview(144), also depends on:

- the presence and example of mentors to follow;
- the diversity of practice experiences because the point is not to have the same experience repeatedly, but to enrich the practice through diversity;
- the recognition of the difference between knowing and doing because it's about doing and not knowing; and
- the ability to understand past experience to drive a better future experience.

This is an important aspect to consider when the path a group follows is one of the construction of value. In our time, the possibility of advancing the boundary of cultural evolution and capture new possible futures requires a great effort of cultural assimilation, meaning thousands of hours of deliberate practice. Moreover, it makes sense to multiply the results and experiences of those who discover those futures, which are difficult to reach via the leadership of liberal paladins or conservative superstars. The difference between one and the other — easy to understand but not to digest — is that the superstar creates value for himself while the paladin develops value to share it with others.

In our times, it is easy to find, any day of the week, examples of superstars in the newspapers. It's normal to see a superstar who one day achieves a sports feat and the next day becomes a product of the egotism that defines him or is involved in some scandal of abuse or family neglect. The political superstar of the 20th century, without a doubt, was

THE CULTURAL EVOLUTION CAST

Winston S. Churchill We will never surrender

Locus of control:	Internal
Self worth:	Dignity
Personal action:	Responsibility
Collective action:	Democratic legality
Ethics:	Self Interest

SUPERSTARS OF THE EMPIRE

British Prime Minister Winston Churchill. By contrast, paladins are more difficult to find. As the modern confusion between the left and the right has persisted so long, with no real possibility of proposing a map with an alternate route founded in the common good, paladins are obscure and poorly classified in the history of the 19th and 20th centuries. The obligatory references in the U.S. are President Franklin D. Roosevelt and The Reverend Martin Luther King, Jr., the latter assassinated. This occurs frequently when paladins come up against authoritarians with whom they have nothing in common, neither in the aspect of freedom nor in that of the common good. President Abraham Lincoln is another figure from the U.S. whose actions and discourse show a disposition toward being a liberal paladin, even though he was a member of the conservative party and the true meaning of his political positions is today still being discussed, plus he is certainly another key figure in the history of assassinations. In the second half of the 20th century, an interesting example of the paladin is President Nelson Mandela because of the democratic transformation he led in South Africa. The process of truth and reconciliation championed by him, despite bearing and surviving decades of authoritarian aggression, stands out.

For the first decades of the 21st century, as the first African-American president of the U.S., Barack Obama is a model in rhetorical and historical terms that meets the standard of the paladin. In praxis, however, there was discordance. President Obama appears to be the liberal paladin who, facing a breaking point in history, was not able to achieve the clarity of vision to transform it. On the other hand, there is the sad case of Malala Yousafzai (Noble Peace Prize 2014), a young Pakistani paladin who on becoming the only voice from her country in favor of educating women, was seriously shot and exiled.

Bill Gates is another interesting character with a mixed history. His infancy is cited by Gladwell as the example of the accumulation of 10,000 hours of practice, in this case, in software programming. In adulthood, he became the owner of one of the largest technology companies in the world, Microsoft Corporation, which was accused and sanctioned for anti-competitive practices under his control. Up to this point, the history of Gates is the history of a superstar in the world of technology. But, in 2000, Gates decided to leave the management of the Microsoft Corporation and dedicate the greater part of his fortune — the biggest and most consistent in the world during two decades — to philanthropic work such as fighting poverty, malaria, and climate change. In 2010, along with Warren Buffet, he formalized the The Living Pledge foundation, which looks for other millionaires with fortunes greater than $1,000 million, to commit to leaving in life 50% or more of their personal fortunes to philanthropy. In 2016, he announced, along with other figures of his caliber, the Breakthrough Energy Commission (BEC), which looks to invest $1,000 million to break the barrier of energy technology, which today impedes the continuation of the process of conservative economic expansion.

The history of Gates is atypical because it possesses characteristics of the paladin and the superstar. Furthermore, it should be evaluated in light of the participation of Belinda Gates as his equal in the foundation that carries his last name and that is a vehicle through which the philanthropic initiatives of the couple are implemented. It seems that between the two, there exists a well-balanced collaboration (yin-yang), which provides this history with a mixed character. A similar collaboration existed between Preseident Franklin D. Roosevelt and First Lady Eleanor Roosevelt. President Roosevelt was the seasoned and ambitious

THE CULTURAL EVOLUTION CAST

Franklin D. Roosevelt Self Interest is the enemy of all true affection

Leon A Perskie

Locus of control:	Internal
Self worth:	Dignity
Personal action:	Responsibility
Collective action:	Democratic legality
Ethics:	Common Good

PALADINS OF THE REPUBLIC

politician, while his wife pushed the more liberal agenda of the couple. This culminated in 1948 when the first lady, after the death of Roosevelt, coordinated the wording and negotiating of the Universal Declaration of Human Rights, the foundational pillar of the United Nations.

To sum things up, the cultural evolution of humanity will depend in part on conditions that allow for the formation of paladins and super-stars. Today they exist in very low numbers because they depend on the conditions that allow these type of leaderships to emerge.

In the case of the conservative path led by superstars like Bill Gates and his friends from the Breakthrough Energy Commission, the princi-ple limitation is energy. Overcoming this restriction — still improbable today — would bring a Victorian postmodernity of reconquest and dom-inance of nature. One can only imagine that if Gates' initiative is able to develop an abundant, practical, continuous, and easily disseminated source of energy, an order of magnitude less expensive than hydrocar-bons and non—polluting, from one day to the next, unimaginable things will be possible. Consider the creation of a vast interior fresh-water sea in the middle of the Sahara that will convert the desert into an orchard, or the large-scale filtering of the atmosphere to recover and capture CO_2 and the greenhouse gases. They can be transformed through a chemi-cal synthesis into stable solids such as plastics, carbonates or even new hydrocarbons. Today this seems like science fiction, but the technology exists. The high cost and the pollution it would produce to implement it; however, render its materialization impossible. Equally, and in spite of the strong organization of conservative superstars, at the knowledge and technology level that is available today, the future continuity of the con-servative model is not seen as the most viable or probable to implement.

In the case of the liberal model, it is still undefined and lacking suf-ficient paladins. A good number of the possible solutions to address the current environmental and energy constraints, are: 1) the deployment of distributed and variable sources of energy; 2) the development of market solutions that incorporate the cost of externalities to the pricing system; 3) the development of thousands of open source technological solutions; 4) the reduction of waste and the development of the shared economy. However these solutions first require clarity of a design philosophy that helps identify the open and collaborative proposals and segregates those that look to shut down the open society. Some proposals of an author-itarian nature are also on the table to impose energy restrictions and establish a world government that allocates and monitors, by decree, the emissions quotas through a CO_2 mitigation mechanism known as Cap & Trade.

Thus, with the level of knowledge and technology we have on hand, there exists the need for a new, liberal model to thrive so we can face the new reality. The irony, however, is that even though this approach to postmodernity seems to be the one which has the best chances of bearing fruit to sustain the development of the open society, the need and requirements for this endeavor are still not well-identified, organized, or articulated. It will be interesting, then, to analyze this model in the following chapters in light of the challenges and opportunities of postmodernity.

8. The Malaise of the Open Society

Pleonexia

After going over the open society characters, the question remains: If the technological barrier is defeated, will it be possible to restart the conservative expansion process without regressing to authoritarianism? If the technological barrier is defeated without destroying the planet. *A priori*, no difficulty appears to exist to propel a new era of expansion and affluence. However, other restrictions or conditions exist that are worth considering.

The first of these is knowing if people in open societies still have spare capacity to absorb the services and products that a new phase of economic expansion would produce. This problem, which seems to be modern, is an ancient preoccupation that dates to Plato and Aristotle, who also wondered about the limits of wealth. How much is enough? According to Carlos Llano, several philosophers have attempted to solve that question, customarily with lists of necessary and superfluous goods, and whose excesses and oversights have always proved controversial. The best answer we have is that of Llano himself, given in his lectures at the IPADE Business School (*Instituto Panamericano de Alta Dirección de Empresas*). The method he used to identify the superfluous from the necessary was to examine the necessity of the good in terms of the satiety effect it produced. When the possession or consumption of a good — be what it may — generates satiety at any given consumption level, then it is possible to say that we are talking about a necessary good. Thus, superfluous goods are those that can´t generate satiety at any consumption level.

In this manner, the issue of the necessary or the superfluous is no longer addressed with the definition of a list that is external to the person. With this approach, the necessity or satiety is internalized according to the personal, material, and psychological needs of every individual. The ancient Greeks identified the inability to achieve a state of satiety as an illness, which they called pleonexia. Nevertheless, the insatiable appetite that generates pleonexia is paradoxically considered a virtue of the successful individual in the contemporary society(145).

In fact, the issue of consumption for consumption's sake is so important nowadays that President George W. Bush, after the attacks of September 11, 2001, asked the American people on repeated occasions to show their patriotism by continuing to shop(146). This brought massive criticism when in 2008 the economic crisis erupted, in the sense that the time had arrived to pay for those unnecessary purchases(147). Once again, behavioral economists who conducted interesting social experiments to review the patterns of consumption and the satisfaction produced to the individual give us interesting clues linked to this matter. The results collected from around the world by researchers in the Harvard Business School show that consumerism is overrated, people obtain more satisfaction when they buy for others (pro-social purchases) and not so much when the purchases are for themselves(148).

Among the social phenomena linked to modern day pleonexia, there also is a new category of service providers: professional organizers, people dedicated to reducing problems of saturation and accumulation that exist in the homes of those overwhelmed by material abundance. Among them, Marie Kondo stands out(149). This Japanese woman, and many others like her, offers clear and direct methods for organizing one's home. They also propose what can be deemed as a therapeutic path for the treatment of pleonexia. Kondo asks her clients, as they progress category by category in the organization of their belongings, to take the time and put each object in their hands and consider if it gives them joy. The philosophical premise of this method is that people should be surrounded by and keep only those objects that create joy. Kondo's customers who have followed the simple but laborious process of the Konmari affirm that they discovered that few objects gave them satisfaction and happiness, and few were the objects they needed to keep.

On the other hand, as digital communication and technology have made the lifestyles of all strata of society more porous and transparent, especially that of the rich and famous who entered *en masse* into fashionable reality shows and social networks, opulence has begun to lose the mystery and glamour of yesteryear. This makes it apparent that beyond a certain level of income, extreme wealth becomes immaterial. This is, first, because a substantial part of the great fortunes is invested in stocks from which investors can´t easily divest themselves. The stocks of many investors simply cannot be liquidated from one day to the next because this type of movement destabilizes the markets.

It took Bill Gates 10 years to carry out a programmed strategy, explained in advance to the financial markets(150), and divest from his Microsoft stock. At the end of the day, most of the money obtained from Microsoft essentially ended up being reinvested in diversified stocks of other companies, which points out the difficulty in transforming financial assets into tangible things. Second, the immateriality of financial super fortunes comes about because they represent the existence of more money than the capacity large investors have to create value in the economy. This ends up driving philanthropic schemes such as the The Living Pledge as one of the few paths that exist to convert those speculative assets into something real and tangible.

Furthermore, at levels of wealth exceeding billions of dollars, no matter how much money you have to spend, except for a reduced number of exclusive products, even the most affluent oil sheikh cannot have a more advanced version of a mobile phone, computer, film or television series than that of many middle-class homes. The rapid diffusion of value and technology has made generic a significant part of the goods and services to which anyone can have access in the contemporary economy. Even in cases where people resort to extravagance to escape mediocrity, the uselessness of extravagance is more apparent today. Two examples come to mind: during the 2008 crisis, Dubai suffered the collapse of the real-estate sector. Overnight, the real-estate magnates who went bankrupt drove to the airport to leave the country, trying to avoid the consequences of strict Muslim laws regarding debt. They just abandoned some of the most expensive and exclusive cars in streets and parking garages. A few days later, photographs showing the cars ruined by the harshness of exposure to the desert weather went viral on the internet(151). The photos were taken by onlookers who were openly making fun of the situation. The other example is that of Prince Jefri of Brunei, who squandered $14.8 billion from the national treasury. To build, among other things, the biggest and most luxurious exotic car collection in the world, and which was kept in an airconditioned garage. In 1997, he was exiled by his own family and his assets were seized. Since it made no sense, even to his wealthy relatives, to take charge of the collection and maintain the expensive garage. The automobiles were left to the mercy of Brunei's climate. Soon they got ruined and it became impossible to recover any of the lost treasure. Today, the 5,000 cars remain in the shell of the palace as a symbol of shame for the royal family of Brunei(152).

Additionally, in recent years, due to the interminable broadcast of reality shows, some behavioral disorders — once hidden and unknown to the mainstream audience — have become part of conversations in everyday life. These are linked to anxiety and obsessive-compulsive disorders such as hoarding, compulsive buying, and addiction to the internet, video games, and promotions, which likely make many viewers think about the role that consumerism plays in their lives. Further proof that a different reflection process exists can be seen in the millennial generation that is showing different attitudes compared to preceding generations. According to the data collected by market research companies, their attitudes toward consumerism, money, and work are a sign of worry. The millennials are less interested in owning a television, a car or a house. They are more interested in cheap and simple pleasures that enhance quality of life(153). All the above indicate that at the base of society the modern dream of material affluence is beginning to change. Because of this, it is no longer possible to ensure that there is capacity to relaunch a new period of conservative affluence and accumulation, even if it becomes technologically possible.

Inequality and fairness

In the modern age, inequality — an old topic— had two poles. On one pole we find the ideas of the British economist Joseph Alois Schumpeter (1883-1950). When he delved into the efficiencies and the economies of scale created by large enterprises, he concluded that it was more efficient to promote economic centralization through the existence of large corporations, even at the expense of small businesses. At the other extreme we find the German economist Ernst F. Schumacher (1911-1977), who coined the expression "small is beautiful" to refer to the need to create decentralized economic systems on a human scale. It goes without saying that thus far this discussion hasn't been settled. Perhaps the reason is that both economists were lacking an inclusive framework that would have allowed them to see that their observations are not disjunctive but different and concurrent aspects of a complex system.

Without elaborating too much here on the science behind networks and complex systems, it must be said that, given that many complex systems are structured like vascular networks, in recent years, important advances have been made understanding the relationships between system structure, symmetry, and scale. So today we know that many vascular systems share configuration functions and algorithms, which, in turn, explain the characteristics of their structure. Some general findings on this type of systems are:

- Vascular systems solve two types of problems: transportation and distribution. To do so, they have large components, like the heart and the aorta, which, by taking advantages of the economies of scale, solve the transportation problem, and small components that, even though are less energy efficient, solve distribution problems by taking advantage of higher diffusion capacity.
- Vascular systems are scaled and balanced based on the system's diffusion limits. Thus, the size of the large components, such as the heart and the aorta, coincides with the sum of the diffusion limits of all the capillaries in the body. The lack of network symmetry between the different scale levels disrupts the continuity of flow in the system.
- In terms of energy consumption, the large components consume more, but they do so with better efficiency than the small components. Gram for gram, the aorta is more energy efficient than the capillaries, even though, being the largest vessel in the system, it consumes more energy.

Based on the above, in collaboration with my father(154), we found that in the Schumpeter vs. Schumacher discussion, both are right: it's just that they erred when proposing the dominance of one type of business over the other. Our conclusions indicate that:

- No matter what type of economy you analyze, small businesses pervade worldwide — greater than 98% of the total — which indicates the existence of a vascular network made up of many small components and only a few large ones.
- In advanced economies, large corporations comply with two types of functions. First, they create economies of scale that bring down the prices of strategic products that feed the economy (energy, credit, telecommunications, raw materials, etc.). Second, they invest to drive forward the most advanced and difficult technological barriers, in such industries as pharmaceuticals, semiconductors, aerospace, and energy. On the other hand, it is characteristic in

dysfunctional and authoritarian economies for large corporations to drive prices of strategic goods and services upward and use them to exploit internal markets. In addition, no large innovative corporations exist in dysfunctional and authoritarian economies.
- Different types of economies reveal different patterns of network symmetry in the distribution of GDP in which large and small enterprises participate.

Thus, equality neither exists nor is it possible for it to exist, in the vascular structure of human economies. Inequality is a condition inherent to the vascular network's form or topology. Within this condition different problems at each scale level are solved. Thus, both large and small components with a specialized purpose are required. Conversely, for this type of system to establish a homeostatic regime, certain conditions of symmetry, scaling, and flow must be met. The large components should carry out their scaling function at a high level of efficiency. While the small ones, though less efficient, should maximize the diffusion capacity of the system. This means that the rules of play should be made so the system scales from the restriction, which means the capacity for the small business to exist and function. Therefore, it is not surprising to see that dysfunctional authoritarian economies always show high rates of poverty and informality, as well as a high access cost to formality.

According to our data, economies are healthiest and most dynamic when the relationship between the GDP invoiced by small businesses (> 98% of the total) and by large enterprises (< 2% of the total) approaches a 50:50 ratio. This deteriorates when the relationship changes in favor of the large enterprise. This proportion is analogous to a mammal's vascular system, where the volume of blood that flows through the aorta is equal to the sum of the volume that flows through all the capillaries in the body(155).

From a more traditional economic analysis, Thomas Piketty concludes — in a similar fashion — that symmetry conditions in the economic network flow are important. According to him, the problem of income inequality has its origin in the inequality $r > g$, where r is the capital return rate and g is the economic growth rate. This means that inequality grows when the capital return rate is greater than the economic growth rate. Piketty's proposal has polarized economists in advanced economies. He tells us that we must review the conditions that allow the growth of the profits of big business beyond the economic growth rate of the economy.

Said in a different way, to prevent large agents from preying on the small ones, particularly when the economy is not growing.

Regarding inequality and the balance of flows, complexity science can contribute a very important discovery to the study of economics: scaling laws, which indicate the mathematical relationships of growth in complex adaptive systems. One of them is Kleiber's metabolic law. Discovered in 1932, it describes the relationship between the metabolic rate of an animal (q_0) and its mass(M): $q_0 \sim M^{3/4}$. In recent years, it was discovered that this law predicts, at a macroscopic level, a stable ecological relationship between the quantities of prey and predators(156).

That said, no matter the type of complex system in question, and because of universal thermodynamic restrictions, many scaling laws show trade-offs. For example, Kleiber's law $(q_0 \sim M^{3/4})$ indicates that, as an animal's mass increases, energy consumption by unit of mass diminishes. So, a 25-gram mouse, that consumes 3.14 kcal/day and a three-ton elephant that consumes 20,268 kcal/day, do not maintain a continuous relationship of energy consumption. A population of 120,000 mice, which all together weigh three tons (0.025 kg x 120,000 = 3,000), equivalent to the weight of a single elephant, consumes 376,800 kcal/day. But the metabolic rate of the mice per unit of mass is 18 times higher than that of elephants (377,230/20,268 = 18.61). This highlights the trade-off between the metabolic rate and the size of the animal as the scale changes.

This type of relationship and trade-off also exist in the economy. For example, Mexican SMEs (Small and Medium Enterprises) sell, on average, $40,540 of products or services a year and average three employees ($13,513 in sales per employee). Pemex, the largest enterprise (LE) in the country, sells $106 billion in products and has 150,000 employees ($706,666 in sales per employee). In this scale relationship, Pemex sells 52 times more per employee than the smaller businesses in the economy, but, in terms of employment, a modest growth in the GDP at the SME level has a larger effect. If the scale relationship remains constant, a growth in sales of $13.5 billion in the SME sector, equal to 0.63% of the GDP, would produce a growth of one million jobs while the same level of growth in sales at the Pemex scale would only produce 19,122 new jobs. (Pemex is not an international reference of productivity because it is said to have two or three times more staff than it needs.) Similarly, when as pointed out by Piketty $r > g$, the economy does not reflect the trade-offs that should exist with the increase of scale.

If the economy is confined to the general operation rules of complex systems, as enterprises change scale, and grow, the earnings should grow as the volume of sales increase, while the profit margins decrease as they create new economic efficiencies. Those, for the most part, should be transferred as new value to the rest of the system. An example of this is the personal computer market.

For many years, the diversity of personal computer manufacturers on the international market allowed competition to lower the margins, increase the volume, and keep prices low for the consumer. Over time, the market consolidated and matured with larger enterprises, which were sufficient to supply the worlds market. Meanwhile, the profit margins remained low, in a range of 3%, with peak sales at 352.8 million units in 2011 at an average cost of $500 per unit. Using these numbers, we can estimate that this market generated sales of $176.4 billion and profits of $5.2 billion, which appears to be not such a bad business. It's better to have a profit of 3% on sales of $176 billion than a profit of 99% on sales of $10 million. But in the eyes and financial sensibility of present day investors, companies that manufacture and sell computers are not a good business. The slim return rate of 3% ($r < g$, where g is the growth of computer sales) is not enough to feed the return rate expected by financial capital. This example of growth in volume and reduction of the profit margin by transfer of efficiencies to the market coincides with microeconomists' classic marginal analysis of the conditions that create perfect competition, as with the Marxist analysis of the non-viability of capitalism to maintain the capitalists' rate of return. And this is at the heart of the question of inequality.

It isn't important if the matter is viewed from the Marxist or the marginalist analytic perspective. There's consensus on the growth of enterprises, competition, costs, prices, and margins. When markets are strong, industry grows until it reaches the size that the economies of scale allow. The problem is that at the limit, an inversion of roles becomes apparent. In the mental model of financial capitalists, the system only works well when the relationship between size of the capital and the rate of return increase at the same time. In other words, when there's no trade-off between the change of scale and profit margins. That's why the computer equipment market seems like a bad deal to them. The only way to achieve greater rates of return as the scale grows is to establish barriers that prevent competition and the transfer of efficiencies to the economy.

This is a paradox because then the capitalist looks to go against scaling logic and economic freedom. By the same token, communists want capitalist market efficiencies to materialize at a level which impedes the reproduction of capital with the hope of seeing the collapse of the system. It's clear that none of these twisted expectations are wise.

Now, it's worthwhile taking note of some of the arrangements that currently operate to protect the inequality $r > g$. Thus, limiting competition and efficiencies transfer to the economy fuel growth of economic inequality. According to Joseph Stiglitz(157), the first is the capture of government and politics through electoral financing, which leads to the issuance of regulatory frameworks that protect special interests with concessions, exclusive permits for the exploitation of natural resources, excessive protections on industrial and intellectual property, government purchasing contracts, and above all, fiscal subsidies and tax exemptions. Altogether these practices were identified in a scathing and caustic fashion by Gore Vidal as a change in the democratic rule book. Those changes produced a *"corporate welfare"*(158) system that privatized earnings, but socialized the losses, creating a benevolent socialism for the rich and a predatory capitalism for the poor.

What calls our attention to this topic is that many economists still hold Schumpeter's point of view to be valid. The consulting firm McKinsey & Company recently released an analysis of the Mexican economy titled, "A tale of two Mexico's: Growth and prosperity in a two-speed economy."(159) Once again, the firm found that when comparing changes in productivity, there is disparity between small businesses (SME's), grouped under the name of the "traditional sector," and the large exporting enterprises (LE's) named the "modern sector" of the economy. According to the authors, the problem of economic stagnation in the Mexican economy lies in lack of modernization of the traditional sector. In their opinion, the later needs to be more like the modern sector. As such, they attribute an independent causality to each sector's problems. Therefore, the recommendations they made are tangential to the plundering and lack of access to the economic network which small businesses experience. They didn't notice that in an economy like Mexico's, a substantial part of the prosperity of large enterprises originates in the exploitation of consumers and of small businesses. To highlight this situation of economic depredation, the intelligence unit of *The Economist* investigates and publishes the Crony-Capitalism Index(160), with which they measure the weight and growth in the rentier sector in various world economies. According to *The Economist*, in 2014, Mexico found itself in seventh place out of the 10 most predatory economies in the world. Contrary examples are the Asian tigers, countries where synergy, integration, innovation, and growth exist. In those nations, explicit networked and collaboration models were established between large and small enterprises (*chaebol* in South Korea and *keiretsu* in Japan). For decades, these created stable and fast growth of the economy.

Ultimately, in the Schumpeter versus Schumacher's debate between the big and the small, we see the inversion of roles among capitalists, who became averse to competition, and the socialists who became attuned to capitalist efficiency. Complexity science and network theory can provide us with new diagnostic tools to break the impasse. By understanding the rules, the scaling coefficients, and the limits within which the system can be functional, it will be easier to locate and understand the failures and the asymmetries, and to later imagine solutions that escape the binary logic of Schumpeter vs. Schumacher, which impede us from seeing that the big and the small will always exist and that both scales must coexist and prosper as they are part of a synergetic ensemble.

In support of this last point, Stiglitz has pointed out that the importance agents give to the concepts of fairness and equality(161), declaring that, for the individual, the idea of fairness is more important than the need to achieve equality:

> In a society in which inequality is widening, fairness is not just about wages and income, or wealth. It's a far more generalized perception. Do I seem to have a stake in the direction society is going or not? If the answer is a loud "no," then brace for a decline in motivation whose repercussions will be felt economically in all aspects of civic life...

Alienation and *acedia*

Our world is a complex collection of networks formed by large and small communities that are woven and linked together. A family, a small business, a sports club, a national political party are networks in which any of the cultural evolution strategies dominates. And in the combination of things, all these small networks converge in a quorum that frames society's general path. But this does not mean that an unanimity of points of view exists. As was mentioned earlier, within authoritarian societies dissatisfied democrats will always exist, just as in democracies latent authoritarians will always remain. In both cases, people must coexist in a reality, which, at its heart, is alien to them. In the contemporary democratic world, problems like pleonexia, inequality, the growing dysfunctional "unfairness" of the economy — together with authoritarian regression traits — force millions of citizens, liberal and conservative, to live and try to adjust to this new reality that overwhelms them and is perceived as immutable and irreversible.

Given that the construction of the quorum arises from the aggregation of millions of personal decisions that follow the interaction rules, change itself, or as is colloquially referred to as "changing the culture," seems to many citizens — except for the paladins and the superstars — an impossible mission to achieve. For that reason, most people frequently resort to alienation and *acedia* as a means of coping with the situation.

Before expanding on both concepts, we need to remember the three main strategies for escaping authoritarianism (Chapter Four): 1) become an authoritarian; 2) migrate; and 3) rebel (heroes and paladins). The last one is also a choice, of liberal and conservative citizens, who refuse to authoritarian conversion in the close and personal space. But now we will discuss a fourth option: the path to alienation and *acedia*, the "do nothing," strategy neither good nor bad.

In classical political literature, alienation is addressed as a spell that the powerful cast upon the populace to co-opt or eliminate the will of the masses. But this type of explanation, beyond providing support to a myriad of conspiracy theories, is not useful in analytical terms. Nevertheless, under the influence of emerging, bottom-up phenomena, it could be said that, given that mankind has a tendency toward value generation in any of the spaces that the cultural evolution strategies define, alienation is the process, the activities and the behaviors that, even though they require human effort, don't result in the pursuit of value anyone aims to reach. In a nutshell, the citizen who opts to "do nothing," upon abandoning the pursuit of value, faces the problem of filling that void in one way or another. The clearest and most universal example of alienation is pleonexia: Hundreds of millions of people dedicating their lives to purchasing and accumulating objects without achieving satiety or satisfying their needs. This also shows the weight and scale that alienation has in our time.

We can examine other concrete examples. The amount of time that the 1,590 million active Facebook users(162) set aside to check the site, on average 20 minutes a day(163), 40 in the U.S., adds up in time to the equivalent of the daily work shift of 66.25 million people. That's equal to the total work force of a country like Japan(164). Facebook's annual earnings in 2015 were $18 billion(165), equivalent to $49.3 million-a-day, which means that the income earned by Facebook for each 8-hour day invested by the users of the site is $0.74 (49.3 million/66.25 million), an amount similar to the minimum daily wage of a worker in Bangladesh(166). The enormous amount of time that the 1,590 million of the most connected and educated people on the planet spend or waste on this social network is as big as the total labor force of a country that generates $4.21 trillion a year in GDP(167), equivalent to 234 times the daily earnings of Facebook. Is obvious that this produces a negative global economic impact and provides support to the idea that a large portion of the world's population lives alienated in activities that probably give them back little value in exchange for their immensely more valuable time. But, for someone looking to spend their time not doing anything, or not thinking about anything, or escaping from a reality they don't understand or like, having something sterile to do for 20 or 40 minutes a day, and for free, seems like a bargain.

In fact, looking for and finding the way to produce consumer stimulus without generating the feeling of satiety is inherent to the business model of the new entertainment industry, which invests heavily in cognitive science to discover and press the switches and levers that capture consumers' attention. For that reason, we now live immersed in a sphere of sounds, icons, reminders, and vibrations that feed an irrational collective anxiety that demand our constant attention: social networks, email, TV on demand, videogames, music, and in general, all digital content. The paradox of this new world, which promises the immediate satisfaction of our desires, is that the user is the product. In cases like Facebook, the product that the company sells on the market is the information and the attention that users give to the platform. Here the user's satiety is contrary to the business model but fits perfectly with the desire to find distractions that allow an individual to fulfill the personal and collective objectives of "doing nothing" to escape a challenging reality.

Unfortunately, Facebook is only a small part of the contemporary distraction diet (13% for the U.S. adolescent). According to Common Sense Media(168), on any given day of the week, U.S. adolescents between the ages of 13 and 18 average eight hours and 56 minutes with different media sources. This excludes time spent at school and doing homework. According to this organization, the breakdown of use by type of media is as follows (Table 18):

Adolescents (13 to 18 years old)	Time
Television, DVD, videos	2:38
Listening to music	1:54
Videogames	1:21
Social media	1:11
Other activities on the computer or cell phone	0:32
Navigating websites	0:36
Reading	0:28
Video chat	0:13
Going to the movies	0:03
Total on screen media	6:40
Total on media	8:56

Table 18: Use of media in U.S. adolescents between 13 and 18 years of age.

In addition to the above-referenced data, Common Sense Media indicates that the same group of consumers engages in passive use 39% of the total time, interactive use (videogames and surfing the net) 25% of the time, communicates with others 26% of the time, and engages in creative activities (art, music, writing) only 3% of the time.

Based on a growing body of empirical knowledge regarding the effects that multitasking activities have(169), we can be sure that the new forms of distraction cause a reduction in the quality of human cognition, which is neither futile nor insignificant, since in recent years car accidents caused by a distracted drivers, mainly due to cell phone use, have become the Number One cause of death among young people(170). With such a high rate of media use, the possibility of an adolescent accumulating 10,000 hours of deliberate practice in any other type of activity is very slim. If the 8 hours and 56 minutes number is annualized, we find that the average adolescent spends 3,260 hours a year using media. Hence, if they allocated the same amount of time to the deliberate practice of any other activity they would achieve mastery and command of said activity in just over three years.

Ray Bradbury imagined this situation in *Fahrenheit 451* (171), a futuristic and dystopic novel in which people live completely alienated, constantly distracted by an incessant festive activity and by devices such as walls made of screens that speak to them and project images all day long while books and critical thinking are outlawed. In a key moment in the story, when the main characters are talking about a plan to escape alienation, Professor Faber says to the fireman Montag that there are three things needed to achieve doing something of importance: 1) quality of information, 2) time to reflect, and 3) freedom of action. In our time, for those who are convinced that the route to escape authoritarianism is "doing nothing," Bradbury's dystopia comes true in an inverted sequence. From the start, self-censorship exists about the freedom to do something. One choses the incessant activity and distraction to avoid reflecting on things that gives rise to poor quality of information and in the end to erroneous decisions.

Unlike what traditional political science proscribes, escape from alienation will not arrive as a gift from the enlightened one that breaks the chains of the superstructure. Nor does it require a Messiah. One simply must resume the construction and enjoyment of value as a way of life. Seen in this light, the solutions in the open society are not complex, unlike what occurs in closed societies. On the level of our material lives, the cure to alienation linked to pleonexia can be as simple as what Marie Kondo proposes. In social, political, and personal aspects, it's enough to put distractions aside and generate intimate and significant connections with people close to us and reconnect ourselves with the value which the human experience holds.

Despite all the forms of distraction that we have and can imagine, they are soon to be reinforced with new technologies such as the explosion in the market for virtual reality devices. Those forms will be together with other aspects of alienation (e.g. the use and abuse of legal and illegal psychotropic substances) along with the ease with which it is now possible to surrender to pleonexia. The weak point in the strategy of alienation or "doing nothing" is that human nature has not changed. For many people today, dignity has no merit and meaning because they perceive themselves as islands, isolated from this fundamental need.

They see existence as useless to create value or have closeness, connection, and intimacy with other persons. However, the inability to fill the void that leads to pleonexia indicates that "doing nothing" is a self-destructive transgression that attempts to bypass or unsuccessfully replace our deepest human needs. For that reason, we can conclude that doing nothing is equal to self-inflicted harm.

The final component of the problems that afflict contemporary democratic societies is *acedia* (spiritual or mental sloth; apathy). In a diverse and open society, the existence of alienated groups, while serious, should not close off the possibility to build and rebuild the open society by dedicated groups of citizens. Nevertheless, as the allegory of the cave illustrates, alienated people not only stay inside the cave admiring the shadows, but turn into the passive agents (serfs) or the active agents (lackeys) of authoritarianism. They become violent against anyone who invites them to come out. In the contemporary world, the phenomenon of depression, sadness, or even resentment toward the construction of value, is referred to as *acedia*, and without a doubt, that is the great mass of the iceberg hidden beneath the surface that can sink the democratic spirit. Those who are alienated constantly proselytize the democrats, trying to infect them with *acedia* and convince them to acquiesce and remain inside the cave in contemplation of the shadows.

9. Cast of Characters and Dynamics of Cultural Evolution

The Cast of Characters of Cultural Evolution

The cultural evolution framework draws from first principles in the field of philosophy of science. It is anchored on the boundary conditions of thermodynamics, biology, and information theory and developed on the epistemology of complex adaptive systems. As a result, two interaction rules have been described along with four behavioral models or survival strategies that human beings use to face existence. Based on these strategies, as well as on concepts and findings from ethology, psychology, economics, and sociology, we have been able to expand the model's description to represent and describe nine characters that enable us to study society's evolutionary dynamics from a new point of view.

In comparison with other social science models, the nine cultural evolution characters represent a much richer and diverse analytical ecosystem. For example, much of the development in economic sciences in the 20th century is based on the description of a single identity: *homo economicus*. Contemporary society's most important institutions and laws were based on this limited framework, that tried to explain, with little success, all the different human behavioral possibilities. In a similar fashion, various sociological and philosophical approaches — grounded in the epistemology of deterministic linear systems — fell under the assumption that human behavior has one single configuration possibility, and hence, the different behaviors that are observed result from external environmental factors such as incentives and institutions, and not from the individual's will and decisions. Thus, traditional approaches to social sciences cannot explain phenomena that haven't been explicitly described beforehand as the system's rules and components. Meanwhile, the cultural evolution model, by means of emergence, is in fact able to describe and explain the most complicated social categories such as power and the relationship that the construction of power has with each cultural evolution strategy, without the need to define them from the starting point.

Even though the model has a greater analytical capability than other approaches, it is possible to summarize it — the interaction rules, the four strategies, and the nine characters — in a simple diagram (Figure 11):

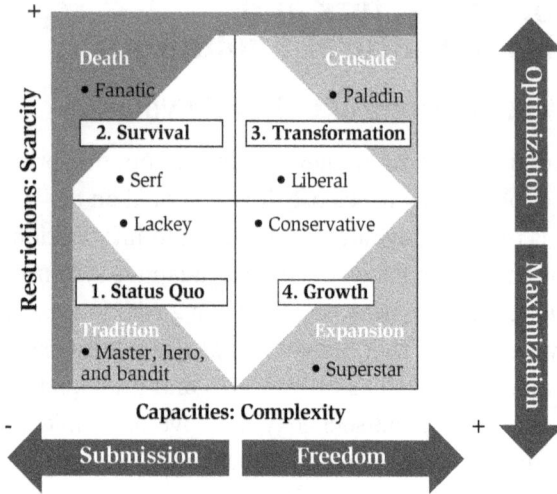

Figure 11: The cultural evolution model.

The dynamics of cultural evolution

There's a relationship of agreement between the interaction rules and the environment, or as biologists would say, "fitness" of the agent with the environment (e.g., the case of well-functioning authoritarianism and oil-rich nations). In this way, for each cultural evolution strategy, it is necessary to take into account the environmental conditions, scarcity, or abundance. The status quo and growth strategies are possible and effective in low-restriction environments, while survival and transformation strategies are better for high-restriction environments. On the other hand, human beings, because they are endowed with heuristic capabilities and the will to act, can change their strategy, which represents both a problem as well as an advantage. We can successfully adapt when the environment changes, or we can also fail when our judgment is mistaken. These moves or changes, which indicate cultural evolution dynamics, are explained below (Figure 12):

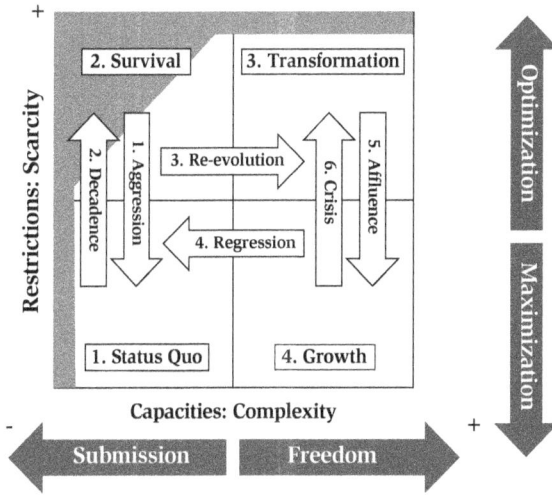

Figure 12: Cultural evolution dynamics.

1. **Aggression.** This is the movement that reduces shortages by means of violence and depredation; there is no growth in capacity or complexity. What cannot be obtained by one's own means is taken from someone else.

2. **Decadence.** When it is no longer possible to sustain the status quo by intensive resource use, the system declines, generally accompanied by disorder and with violence.

3. **Re-evolution.** It aims toward growth in capacity and complexity to discover and take advantage of new opportunities (e.g., the green revolution, the Enlightenment, the digital revolution). It should not be confused with the violent connotation of "revolution" as an aggression synonym.

4. **Regression.** It means the rise of obscurantism, ignorance, and alienation.

5. **Affluence.** This is the movement of the golden ages of expansion, where complexity grows, and new abundance boundaries open (e.g., the Victorian era, the Gold Rush, and the Silicon Valley tech boom in the past decades).

6. **Crisis.** When the age of abundance and expansion dries up, periods of instability and turbulence occur. These have become recurring and normal in contemporary society. Reducing their occurrence is the great unsolvable problem in contemporary democracies.

Something else that complexity science's analytic framework contributes to social sciences is the concept of dynamic equilibrium, or homeostasis, which is essential to the explanation of movements in cultural evolution dynamics. Without the epistemology of deterministic linear systems, the concept and pretense to find static equilibrium is also relinquished. For human society to be persistent in the long term, it needs to function within constant adjustments and change pointed toward a general evolutionary direction bringing it to a condition of homeostasis.

From a cynical perspective, a small part of each of the six movements from the cultural evolution model, by trial and error, would lead to a natural selection of the human groups with better fitness to the environment and the disappearance or death of those who get it wrong. Nevertheless, setting aside fundamental ethical considerations, the cynical position is not possible because we find ourselves at a point in history where errors and economic, political, and social crises can be absolute. The food production and/or the environmental collapse, and even a bacteriological or nuclear war, could destroy humanity.

Since the late 1940s, the *Bulletin of the Atomic Scientists* has estimated and published the risk of a great catastrophe(172), such as a nuclear war, in the form of a clock that approaches midnight (zero hour). As the clock's hands get closer to midnight, the risk of an apocalyptic event occurring is greater. Since the publication of the first Doomsday Clock, 1991 was the year of least risk (the clock marked 23:43), and from that point on, the hour has moved forward until it reached 23:57 in 2015 (Graph 18).

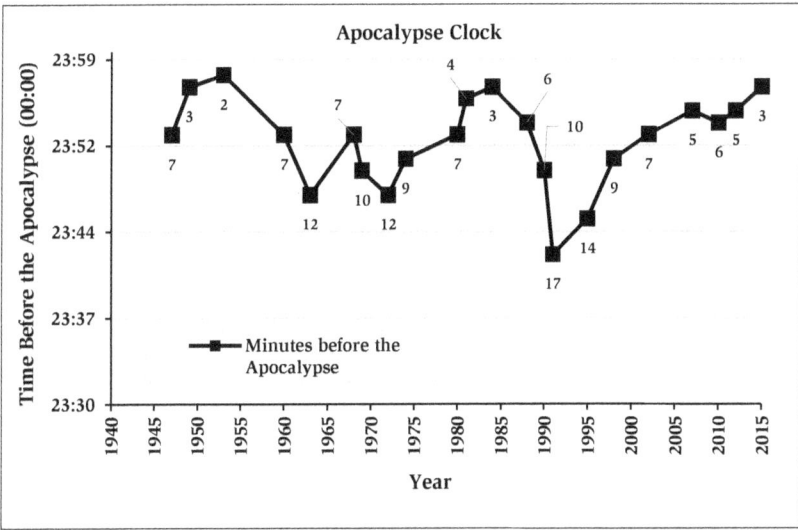

Graph 18: Doomsday Clock for the years 1947-2015.

The clues that indicate the most sensible strategy for reaching homeostasis in our time are:

1. **Prehistoric vulnerability.** The genetic register of our species indicates that our lineage lived completely exposed and vulnerable to environmental conditions (survival strategy) since before the existence of *homo sapiens*. Geneticists such as Spencer Wells, director of The Genographic Project, traced various genetic bottlenecks, which gave rise to the human species. These indicate that several times in the history of the evolution of our species, cataclysmic events took place where hardly any of our ancestors survived. It is estimated that the last of these took place 70,000 years ago. These indications reveal that humanity's first great achievement was to escape from the providential natural state. Presently, there are few human populations left in a homeostatic state within the survival strategy, examples being the Yanomami in the Amazon and the San people from the Kalahari in Africa — are very threatened in our time. Today, it would be impossible for millions of people to adopt such a natural life style. It's sufficient to estimate the per capita consumption of wood of these tribal groups and project them on a population of 7.6 billion people to clearly see that with this type of economic and

social organization, humanity would quickly obliterate the meager natural resources that are left and would ultimately collapse. Furthermore, the serfs, forced to live in the harsh conditions of the unstable survival subsector (Figure 11), find themselves in a situation they want to leave, and in the clear majority of cases, they don't want to follow the fanatic's suicidal leadership. Hence, it is neither materially nor culturally possible to bring back the homeostasis of the natural state; it's been a long time since we escaped from it.

2. **Authoritarian instability.** The cultural and cognitive launch of our species accelerated 8,500 years ago with the invention of agriculture in the fertile crescent of the Middle East. From that point on, egalitarian tribal societies began to decrease and little by little were substituted with vertical rule societies such as empires. The development of more complex societies led to the start of the historic register in Sumeria and Mesopotamia around 3500 BCE. With it, countless rises and falls, conquests, and defeats have been described for all posterity. Together with the exploration of all the possible forms of authoritarian systems that our species has experienced over thousands of years, we have not proved the long-term functionality or stability of the status quo strategy. The main problems that this strategy faces are the interminable conflicts linked to aggression and economic discontinuity derived from the incapability to solve plagues, epidemics, and meteorological events, and in general, the inefficiencies that cannot be fixed with the *mythos* and the superstition associated with the *raison d'état*. Furthermore, the status quo strategy was never able to completely halt the increase in either the complexity of human culture nor the new advances and ideas, which, long term, always destabilize closed systems. Today, only a few nations, such as the oil-rich countries of the Middle East, can pay for the luxury of using this strategy to achieve stability. It is very probable that in the next decades, it will be more and more difficult to maintain it. On the other hand, nations that today find themselves outside of true authoritarianism and authentic democracy — where poverty, violence, corruption, injustice, and lack of respect for human dignity and human rights prevail — are the clearest evidence that status quo is exhausted. Erosion of stability in the world, which makes the Doomsday clock tick toward midnight, stems in large part from the instability of those societies that live

under the status quo model, and which can no longer be preserved due to the lack of resources. Unfortunately, as it happens with societies in decline, the majority resists abandoning the strategy, even when they find themselves in the middle of chaos.

3. **Conservative uncertainty.** Modern democracies, whose success appeared to grow and be safeguarded after the conservative victory over communism and the fall of the Berlin wall in 1989 — even with the political and economic hegemony they hold — can't solve the conundrums of their own malaise, the environmental degradation and the digital revolution. As was previously stated, contemporary social sciences are better equipped to support the conservative expansion than the liberal transformational strategy. Nevertheless, it will be possible to reach a path from expansion toward homeostasis only if the conservative drive is able to break the energy and environmental barrier, while at the same time expand the limits of pleonexia. But this scenario is unlikely. Particularly if we consider that, in every historical period, it was always possible to deplete abundance. For example, evidence shows that the end of the hunter-gatherer period was linked to the depletion of the mega fauna due to excessive hunting, that our vast planet was entirely colonized with the Victorian expansion, and that the modern hydrocarbon energy boom will one day end.

4. **Liberal opportunity.** To act, we now find ourselves before slim margins, and according to the cultural evolution model, the best bet we have to implement a more robust, predictable, and stable process of homeostasis is to construct a liberal democracy based on the principles of the internal locus of control, human dignity, responsibility, and democratic legality. This tells us that we should opt for a liberal democracy that answers to environmental and social challenges that require integration of the common good to social sciences. Fortunately, there are examples of societies that have pushed cultural evolution to the transformation strategy because of harsh ordeals in their history. Such examples are the Scandinavian countries, where it is possible to trace their collaboration traits to cultural artifacts such as Jante's Law and the concept of *lagom*, which means "just the right amount" or "perfect and simple," and Japanese Shinto syncretism, which encourages balance, an equilibrium with nature, and collaboration among people.

Thus, we can now introduce some examples of political and social systems for each cultural evolution strategy (Table 19):

Survival	Transformation
Ancestral survival cultures such as the Kenyan bushmen and the Amazonian Yanomami. Theological social design.	An explicit political design for this system does not exist, the post-industrial market economy designs are close, which maintain a balance between the market and social cohesion systems such as "Lagom," "The Law of Jante," and "Shinto," which exist as the axis of contemporary culture in the Scandinavian nations and Japan. Collaborative social design.
Status Quo	**Growth**
Authoritarian systems such as: empires, fiefdoms, dictatorships, absolute monarchies and nations rich in natural resources and poor in human development. Institutionalist social design.	Several of the western capitalist economies known as developed, more recently the BRIC countries. Competitive social design.

Table 19: Examples of social and political systems for each cultural evolution strategy.

Design Philosophy

Another way of synthesizing the cultural evolution model is through the design category, even though design is intuitively linked to the liberal arts. Every creative act, whether it is philosophical, artistic, or industrial, is designed, and any design attempt brings together capabilities — ideas, techniques, and aspirations — around restrictions — physical laws, availability of resources, space, and energy. This can be seen in the significance and form a designer gives to each element. And in this sense, design is also the substrate of creativity and the compass that directs motivation in a specific direction.

Restriction, capability, and philosophy coordinate within the design concept. Even today this remains an intuitive process that emanates more from the subconscious than from reason and science. In fact, our first design approach rises from the conscious and unconscious answers we give to the following questions (Table 20):

Type of question	Internal world	External world
1. Origin questions	What are my capabilities?	What restrictions do I face?
2. Destination questions	Can I increase my capabilities?	Can I overcome the restrictions?

Table 20: Questions of origin and destiny.

Regarding the internal world questions, we find the central epistemological problem: daring to discover the world. As was mentioned earlier, knowledge requires an increase in complexity, a costly process in terms of resources, lifespan, and effort. Because of this motive, people may have various reasons to give it up.

In accordance with the possible answers to the questions in Table 20, a design objective is chosen: to leave or stay in any of the four strategies (status quo, survival, transformation, or growth). The selection of the design objective involves adopting a design philosophy (Table 21) that complements the strategies table and the social science concepts seen before (Table 7).

Category	Cultural Evolution Strategies			
	1. Status Quo	2. Survival	3. Transformation	4. Growth
Ontology	Materialism	Determinism	Transcendence	Objectivism
Motivation	To Have	To Renounce	To Be	To Do
Restriction Vector	Maximization	Optimization		Maximization
Ethics	Self Interest	Common Good		Self Interest
Capability Vector	Submission		Freedom	
Epistemology	Superstition		Reason	
Politics	Closed		Open	
Configuration	«Top Down»		«Bottom Up»	
Design	Institutional	Theological	Collaborative	Competitive

Table 21: Design Philosophies.

It is worth explaining the characteristics that give shape to each design philosophy:

1. **Institutional.** It creates rules and structures that place people in their pertinent place according to a pre-established order. It also gives importance to the structure and not to the person. It leans to rigidity and bureaucracy, toward the extensive use of natural resources without giving importance to the system's efficiency or productivity. In addition, it creates centralist structures that concentrate decision-making and establishes rigid chains of command that transmit top-down instructions.
2. **Theological.** It draws from a divine origin that explains the world and through which all aspects of people's lives are regulated. Its goal is to place the efforts of society at the service of the deity, and thus, it evolves in a top-down fashion. It doesn't strive for innovation, solution of problems, or prosperity. Its only goal is to gain divine favor and grace.
3. **Cooperative.** While it moves the boundaries of innovation, it also takes into consideration their effects on the world. It looks to empower and provide value to the individual while it considers and minimizes the possible negative externalities. Within this philosophy, a new design becomes valuable when the contributed value is greater than the negative externalities it creates. Global systemic value is more important than the achievement of a single merit figure or performance variable.
4. **Competitive.** This is the individualist design philosophy where the design of the whole is subordinated to a merit figure or performance variable, such as money. Based on this premise, one looks for the transference of externalities outside of the accounts of the transaction and away from the final measurement of contributed value.

In a metaphorical way, but with a close relationship to contemporary societies' problems and achievements, the four design philosophies can be illustrated using different vehicle models that show the diversity of personal preference. Those designs respond to the societal needs and the effect those decisions have on the environment (Table 22):

Characteristics	Theological: Amish Carriage (Cars are taboo)	Cooperative: Toyota Prius
Weight:	ND	1,380 kg
Power:	1 or 2 horses	98 hp
Fuel economy:	ND	25 km/L
Maximum speed:	12.8 km/hr	180 km/hr
Production:	1800-present	1998-present

Characteristics	Institutionalist: Hummer H1	Competitive: Bugatti Chiron
Weight:	3,272 kg	2,036 kg
Power:	298 hp	1,500 hp
Fuel economy:	3 km/L	4 km/L
Maximum speed:	128 km/hr	419 km/hr
Production:	1998-2006 (extinct)	Began in 2017

Table 22: Design examples.

In conclusion, the way in which we consume and design goods and services, architecture, art, ideas, politics, and in general, technology and culture, is intimately linked to heuristic decisions that lead us to adopt one of the cultural evolution strategies. The latter is a positive note that should help renew our optimism because it shows us that the capability to imagine and design, which is also the capability to reflect and act, makes us free and able to transform the world.

Page intentionally left blank.

II

The world that will cease to be

Small is beautiful, but big is powerful.
Ken Thompson

10. Networks

The hidden structure of complex systems

In the first part of the book, the discussion focused on explaining the possibilities of action that the agents have through the two interaction rules, the four strategies of cultural evolution, and the system's emergent and adaptive phenomena such as power and violence. The agents' widespread and consistent behavior coupled with the emergent properties create stable and predictable relationships that, over time, consolidate and create pathways or structures that sustain the cyclical operation of the system (or regime) and provide it with feedback. Examples of this are the rivers, where cycle after cycle the flow of water erodes the soil, increasing the likelihood that the liquid will flow down the same path. Over time, the water's constant flow through the same terrain produces a structure called a riverbed that, millions of years later, may well become as impressive as the Grand Canyon in Colorado. In the same way, the structure of the invisible paths through which ants move and with which they efficiently reach their food sources is created by the ants' successive passage through the same pathways while they release pheromones(173); the more the number of ants pass through the same spot, the more intense is the pheromones' scent and, consequently, more ants tend to follow the same route.

The topic of the system's structure is vital, especially in the social systems' arena, given that at times it is easy to confuse the causal relation between the agents' behavior and the structure that emerges due to its repetition. From a simplistic point of view, such as that of Marxism that refers to the superstructure, water flows within the river because the riverbed confines it to follow that path. However, the water's behavior is determined by the structure, which, in turn, is established by the water's erosive capacity and the sediments it drags (agents). In causal terms, the system's form comes from the water's physical properties, but once the regime (the riverbed) is well established, the evolved structure created over time influences and provides feedback to the agents' behavior. Basically said, it is easier for water to flow within the riverbed than out of it. This feedback between the agents' causal behavior and the emergent results that produce the structure has been the catalyst for countless philosophical debates on the behavior of human beings, freedom, and determinism in society. From the viewpoint of complex adaptive systems, these relationships that emerge and become consolidated and provide positive and negative feedback to the agents are called networks.

Networks are the complex systems' hidden structure. They have been studied for decades in the different areas of knowledge such as mathematics, neurology, and electronics. Yet, after many years of study, we still don´t have a general network theory for all disciplines. Nonetheless, the results obtained in various areas can provide us with concepts and tools to better understand the relationship between the agents' behavior and the bottom-up emergent properties as well as the top-down feedback processes coming from evolved network structures. Hence, with the knowledge we currently have about networks, we can still have a comprehensive theoretical framework that will allow us to dig into "the world that will cease to be" and "the world as it can be."

Fundamentals

Every technological era, besides introducing technological developments, also transforms the lenses through which we interpret reality. The technological area of mechanization let us build a systemic vision of causes and effects founded on the machine's linear model, one with which we are now at odds. The new paradigm that is linked to dynamic systems and that transforms our perspective is that of networks. The concept of networks and the flows they create is already widely and intuitively used to explain all types of social, cultural, and economic phenomena, but our empirical understanding of them remains limited, although scientific development of these networks in all the aforementioned areas is moving ahead at a fast pace.

The first mainstream concept emerging from the study of networks is the use of their graphic representation through diagrams of nodes (agents) and connections (or edges) as shown in Figure 13.

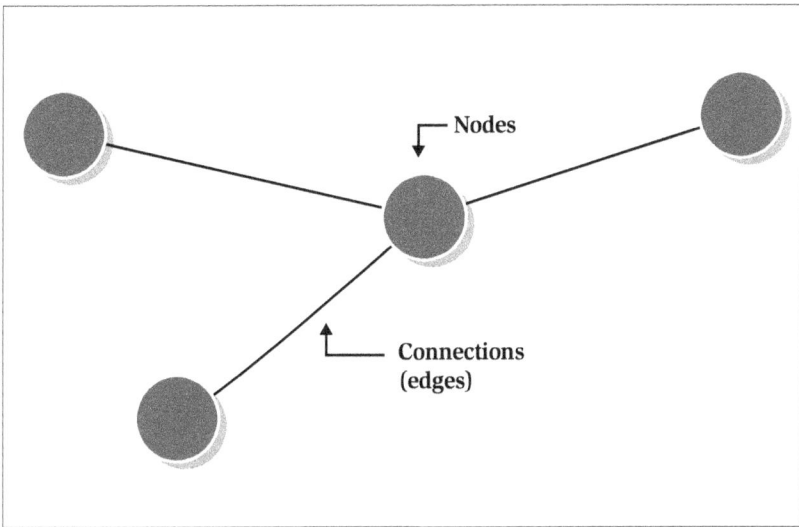

Figure 13: Nodes and connections.

Even though network diagrams are widely used today, underlying the general idea of a network, there are diverse phenomena and concepts that go beyond the diagrams. Some of these concepts are already understood, while others are still a mystery. The first concept that is usually lost in diagrams is the substrate. Networks don't exist in a vacuum nor are they isolated from their environment; they exist within a substrate or environment with which they have a two-way relationship, and the substrate's conditions affect the network just like the network affects the substrate (Figure 14). Thus, there are consumption relationships of the substrate's resources that stem from energy sources or reserves and transfer relationships of by-products and wastes that go toward the sinks.

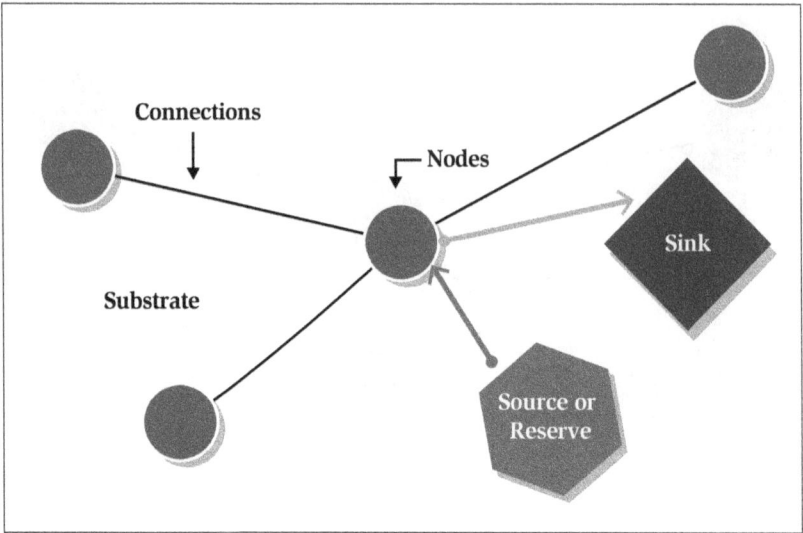

Figure 14: Network and substrate.

The connection between the nodes and the substrate links in thermo-dynamic terms the node's microscopic operation with the networks' macroscopic behavior. To clarify this, we first have to explain the usual architecture of most thermodynamic systems (Figure 15).

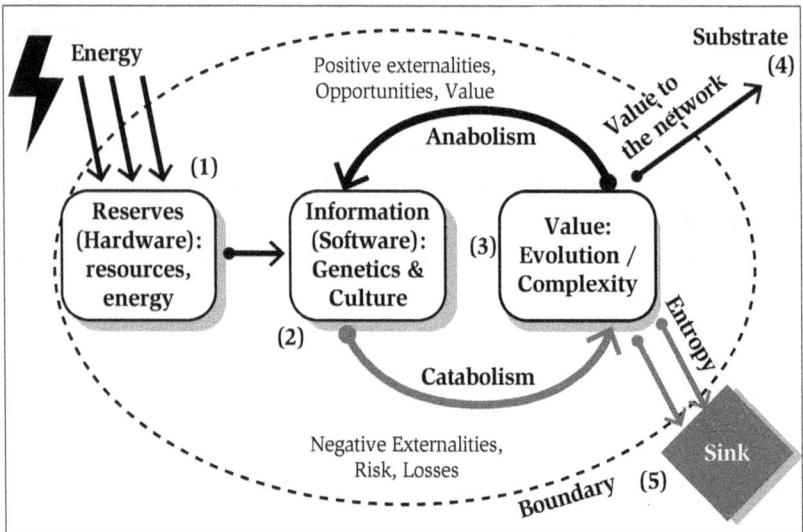

Figure 15: General scheme of a thermodynamic system.

In simple terms, Figure 15 shows that the node or the agent assimilates from the substrate and through its boundary[1] resources such as energy and materials, and accumulates them in an internal reserve, assimilates them in its structure (hardware) or uses them in its own processes. The node then uses the resources through the hardware and modifies them according to what is established in the software (genetics, information, or cultural evolution strategy). Energy usage is known as the catabolic phase of the thermodynamic cycle where some form of order is produced (negentropy, useful work, or value)[3], although with the production of a higher amount of disorder and entropy[5]. The two results, order and disorder, have effects inside and outside the node. One part of the negentropy recirculates in the anabolic phase of the cycle as a value increase toward the node's interior such as a greater level of information, while another part is transferred to the network as a gain that other nodes in the network can benefit from[4]. Conversely, entropy creates a negative effect on the node's internal functioning — as it happens with aging — whereas most of it is transferred outside the node's boundary to a sink located in the substrate, or as a loss transferred to other network nodes[5].

Although it may not seem obvious, this pattern lets us explain and understand countless numbers of physical, natural, and social processes. Thus, it is well worth it to present some specific examples:

1. **Any other morning**. It is night before dawn; someone is sleeping. Several hours have gone by since the last meal; the individual is consuming part of his internal energy reserves[2]. When he wakes up, he's hungry, and heads for the kitchen to look for something to eat[1]. Little by little, the coffee with sugar and his morning toast give him a boost, and he feels more alert[2]. They help him pay attention as he begins to take in the morning news. While he finishes breakfast, he feels better informed and ready to begin his workday[4]. The coffee machine and the fridge slowly dissipate the heat into the atmosphere [5]. The breakfast leftovers and wrappings are stored away in the garbage bin (sink) to be processed later when they'll be taken to a dumpsite[5]. This individual is fortunate to live in a network economy where it's easy to get the power he needs via the electric grid, the gas station, and the food store. He does not need to worry too much about being well fed

or disposing of the garbage and wastes, which allows him to be more productive at work than many other people on the planet.

2.   **Climate regulation**. The physical, biological, and cultural processes supported by our planet depend almost entirely on the sun's energy[1]. Whether they are the air currents or the fuel used by our vehicles[3], all that energy comes from our star[1]. In fact, the amount of energy that reaches earth is overwhelming, and most of it has to be reflected toward space (entropy). When that energy is dissipated at a great speed, the earth cools down and the glacial eras begin. But when that energy remains for a longer time, it heats up the planet. Thus, the thermal resistance of the atmosphere (boundary) is the valve that regulates the planet's relationship with space (the sink)[5], making it possible for life to exist.

3.   **The energy footprint of elephants and humans**. In another chapter, we mentioned the relationship between the average energy consumption and the human development index, as well as the estimate of a three-ton elephant's basal energy consumption (20,268 kcal/day). The data shows that an average citizen in a developed nation consumes 8 or more equivalent tons of oil (ToE) a year, which equals 218,255 kcal/day[1], while an individual in a country with very low human development consumes 1 ToE, or less, equal to 27,282 kcal/day. Therefore, according to Kleiber's law, once the ancestors of *homo sapiens* incorporated other energy sources into their lives, such as wood fire[2], the species' energy consumption — which because of biological physiology only needs 7.3% of the energy that the elephant consumes, meaning 2,000 kcal/day — began to increase without growth of its body mass. Thus, our environmental footprint continues to grow in such a way that the equivalences for human lifestyles of 1 to 8 ToE represent the ecological footprint of animals weighing from 8.9 to 71.3 tons [3], while the heaviest African elephants only weigh up to 7.5 tons. In India and Africa, there is a discussion taking place regarding the sacrifice of thousands of elephants because some people believe their habitats' capability to sustain them is insufficient. Yet, any person from the 7.5 billion people that live in the world today leaves in his wake, no matter how humble his life may be, the equivalent ecological footprint that animals much larger than elephants would produce. And if they were to exist in nature, our planet could only sustain very small numbers of them.

According to the second law of thermodynamics, the order or value that the node generates is less than the disorder it produces. Therefore, the symbiotic or parasitic relationship that exists between the network's nodes and the substrate is immensely important. It determines if entropy is recirculated in the system or transferred to a sufficiently large sink such as space. The preceding statement forces every thermodynamic system to evolve toward more efficient configurations, whose search must be done with as few resources as possible within a reasonable time and within the trans-computational barrier — through a heuristic process that lets it evolve and capture larger possible futures (freedom). In the opinion of Wissner-Gross and Freer(124), this is the fundamental logic of intelligence as an evolutionary process.

This last factor is the one creating greater philosophical controversy regarding the strides that complexity science presents. For some people, optimization models like the constructal one or that of the causal entropic forces are evidence that the universe and the evolutionary processes follow an intelligence or underlying design. Undoubtedly, this idea clashes with the species' random mutation dogma — non-intelligent, trial and error. Nowadays, this discussion cannot be easily settled. No one knows why the universe is entropic, why it will probably destroy itself someday, and all the order it contains, nor do we know why there are processes such as life and culture that try to move in the opposite direction of entropy. What we do know with certainty is that persistent thermodynamic systems, such as life and culture, are as they are because they have embedded in them the logic of heuristic, entropic, or thermodynamic optimization. That does not limit the existence of systems with a different logic like the random or chaotic one. But given the physical laws of our universe, those operational logics do not manage to persist. It is very likely that the evolutionary or intelligent processes were created based on random processes and, once they appeared, despite mutation and changes, their descendants inherited the fundamental logic of optimization that makes them persist and characterizes the biological and cultural evolutionary process. Conversely, when these systems mutate and diverge from the logic enabling persistence, they simply disappear, which is consistent with the Darwinian postulate that only the better adapted agents (nodes, networks, and systems) survive.

Following this basic network model built by nodes, connections, and substrates that are founded on the laws of physics, the complexity in finite and persistent thermodynamic systems, emerges and evolves. So, any biological or cultural process may be analyzed according to the basic architecture of networks and thermodynamic systems. In a manner like that of the Russian dolls that are successively kept one inside the other (Matryoshkas), these processes are articulated in complex multilayer networks where the inputs and outputs of some nodes may come from nodes in a different network.

And now that the scheme's physical inviolability is clear to us, we understand the challenge of our time: integrating this natural logic into the operational logic of the networks built by human society. Although in the world economy global networks of information, goods, and services already exist — the catabolic part of the process — the intentional and deliberate construction of the recirculation flows is still pending — the anabolic part of the process. Thus, the main economic challenges of this era are

- Allocating prices to the externalities. Our ability to create a philosophy of the fantastic allowed us to move forward under the modern assumption that the sources of resources that we depend on and the sinks where we have accumulated our entropy until now were inexhaustible; and
- Finding a better network configuration. This will enable us to optimize the relationship between value generation and distribution (inequality and fairness), access to the network, and the substrate's resources.

Network properties

As previously said, the study of networks as a component of complexity science and complex adaptive systems is a work in process that has many outstanding issues. For the time being, we only have fragmented approaches. In mathematics, network theory has been developed as a branch of geometry and graph theory. In engineering and physics, there is a great deal of knowledge linked to the development of the electrical and telecommunications networks. In biology, the networks exist as the tools and methods to study ecological, neurological, and genetic relations. Nevertheless, reality provides us with examples that, added to the yet incomplete knowledge that we have, allow us to outline a few general concepts and properties:

1. **N**. Refers to the number of connections — edges, in the academic jargon — that a node can establish and manage. It costs to establish and manage each connection, so N will depend on the node's processing capability and efficiency level. Nodes with low connection efficiency, poor access to resources, or disabled by the surrounding entropy will have few connections (e.g., the survival strategy), whereas nodes with good access to resources, easy entropy transfer to a sink and efficient in establishing connections, will have a higher N (e.g., transformation strategy). In human societies, the maximum size of a person's social network, or N, which was observed empirically and is connected to the size of our brains' neocortex — the hardware's capability to process social computation tasks — is 150 individuals. That is known as the Dunbar number(174).

2. **Multiplexing**. Networks may have connections for a specific purpose, that is connections that only transmit one type of signal or material, or they can have general-purpose connections that allow different signals or materials to flow through the same connection. One example is the difference between a drinking water network and a river. The first is a specific-purpose network because it only transports drinking water. The second is general-purpose because it carries water, fish, sediments, ships, bacteria, algae, etc. A similar example is the traditional telephone network that is only used for voice conversations, and the TCP/IP or Internet networks that transport any type of digital information. In technical terms, a network that permits the simultaneous transport of various signals and materials has multiplexing functions.

3. **Network functions**. The network's functions are the properties, behaviors, protocols, platforms, and exchange mechanisms that nodes in a network share or accept. For example, in a multiplexing network, all the nodes must have the capability or the function to code, transmit, receive and decode the multiplexed signals. Although for the reasons previously explained, there is still no widely accepted classification of network functions. However, we will now present a list divided in two categories: the enabling functions and the control functions.

    i. **To enable, scale, and reduce costs.** The main benefit that the nodes or agents that participate in a network obtain are related to enabling, scale, and cost-reduction functions. Generically, these functions are called network economies:

a. **Enable, scale, cost reduction.** Cost reduction and the generation of economies of scale are some of the reasons networks exist. Nowadays, to participate in the English speakers' network using the English language function lets any agent reduce the interaction costs in the international business network. He who participates in a worldwide logistics network has access to countless locations with which it would be impossible to connect otherwise.

b. **Synchronize, socialize, update.** For a network to work, all the network's nodes must know the same protocol or algorithm to process the signals or act in a coordinated fashion against an environmental stimulus. The synchronization, socialization, and updating of functions are fundamental for network behaviors to exist. An example of a synchronization function in human society is mind theory, defined as the human beings' cognitive capability to recognize that other humans have mental states (viewpoints, opinions, ideas) that differ from their own(175). The mind theory is fundamental in construing an individual's identity because it turns him into an autonomous agent and lets him identify the others' autonomy. From this capability emerges the possibility and necessity to synchronize information periodically. The most common and universal manifestation of the use of synchronization functions in the human network is the gossip phenomenon(176), as well as those trends that become fashionable. When the networks' nodes have the capacity to synchronize with any other node, we say there is the capacity to interoperate or to have interoperability in the network. For example, fiduciary money is a platform that enables the exchange function in the network, and therefore, trade is interoperable.

c. **Validate, notarize, and trust transmission.** Given that the networks' nodes may be unknown or far from each other, there are functions of validation, notarization, or transmission of trust that save nodes from building trust on a case-by-case basis and incurring excessive costs of connection, transmission, and information management. In networks where the validation functions are cheap and efficient, the exchanges will be easy, and the networks will be able to grow, while networks where this function is highly centralized, expensive, or difficult to access, growth will be limited. In the analog world, the nodes that exerted this function had a limited size and reach. A part of the Internet's success is that trust sources, such as banks and social platforms, now have a global scale. The way in which these functions shift and are executed modifies the network's structure. Further on we will see in detail how the new blockchain-type technologies will introduce new validation functions to the network. In doing so, they will probably transform the structure or topology of the world's finance and trade network.

ii. **Control and intermediate.** Networks have complex control or intermediation functions that seek to fulfill various objectives:

a. **Managing risks.** Networks create advantages that also produce risks. The most contemporary example is that of the commercial aviation networks. While they enable business, tourism, political, and cultural networks, they, too, are susceptible of being used for criminal ends such as drug trafficking and terrorism. The intermediation nodes in a network, such as security systems at airports, seek to manage the risks inherent to the destructive use of network economies, but they also raise the costs.

b. **Noise filtering, signal amplification.** In telecommunications, and especially in networks with multiplexing, the signal to noise ratio is very important because, when transporting signals or materials, the networks are susceptible to being contaminated or transporting noise (parasite signals that reduce the main signal's quality). In today's world, filtering noise is one of the weakest functions of the Internet. As the information sources became decentralized, the noise increases, and then network users find it hard to discriminate between noise and signal. In the analog economy, book and magazine editors, museum curators, critics, opinion and fashion makers, and trendsetters oversaw filtering the noise and amplifying the signals. Nowadays, the noise and the signals are amplified or mitigated unexpectedly. This changes the risk conditions of the network in a way that is unforeseeable from one moment to another.

c. **To inhibit and restrict.** This function enables and disables connections, behaviors, and functions in the network's nodes and segments. At times, specific nodes exert these power and control functions deliberately and on occasions they depend on changes brought by environmental conditions. An example of a network with control nodes is the one we observe in the bee, ant, and wasp colonies, where the chemical signals that the queens emit affect the reproductive capabilities of other colony members(177). In the case of control functions exerted by changes in environmental conditions, we have the case of animals that hibernate in winter and respond to the signals of the environment.

When we place the enabling and control functions side by side (Table 23), we observe that there is symmetry between the different types of functions:

#	Enabling	Control
1	Reduce costs, scale	Manage risks
2	Synchronize, socialize	Filter
3	Validate, notarize	Inhibit

Table 23: Network functions.

The aforementioned tells us that to make balanced changes in a network's functions it is necessary to evaluate the effects of said changes together with the other functions. This topic is an extremely contemporary one: the introduction of version four of the TCP/IP protocol on which most of the Internet operates today radically changed the cost and synchronization costs, but it was left with no mechanisms for risk management, filtering, validation, and control. This imbalance in the Internet's functions produces most of the negative phenomena in the digital world.

4. **Topology**. A network's topology is the spatial and logical relation-
    ship that exists between its components. Normally, the topology
    is the shape that a network has in a diagram. It depends on the
    nodes' location in the substrate, the number of connections that
    each node can establish, and the way in which the network's func-
    tions are executed.

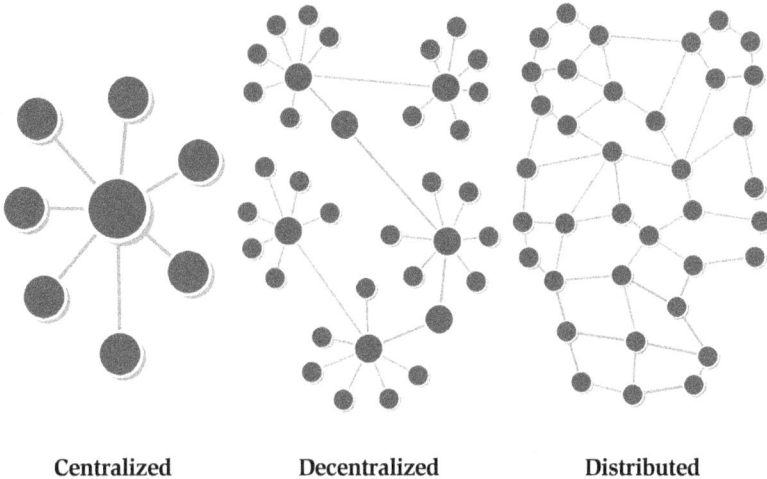

Centralized   **Decentralized**   **Distributed**

Figure 16: Network topologies.

There are many different network topologies (Figure 16). As it
can be observed in each type of network, the agents' possible
behaviors differ.

1. **Centralized networks.** The central node, concentrator or hub
    executes the synchronization, risk management, validation,
    filtering, and control functions. In this model, the central
    node is the intermediary in all the transactions, and for that
    reason it may obtain most of the benefits. The authoritarian
    networks and the free-riders of the status quo tend to create
    centralized networks with the master, the hero or the bandit
    at the center of the network, and the lackeys and serfs on the
    periphery. Metaphorically, the large size of the central node
    reflects the master's greater or superior dignity. The peripheral

nodes cannot communicate or transact among themselves without involving the central node.

ii. **Decentralized networks.** There are multiple control nodes that exert influence or control of a certain network function. The decentralized network shown in the diagram might well be a contemporary financial network with the banks at the center of the business ecosystem since they act as intermediaries in the credit and payment system. These types of networks are more productive, resistant, and resilient than centralized ones. While in a centralized network the loss or poor functioning of the central node signified the death of the network, in the decentralized networks the loss of one of the control nodes does not imply the entire network's collapse. In this model, most of the functions are intermediated by the control nodes, and for the very same reason, these are more important for the system's operation. The existence of several control centers stratifies and produces an evolutionary competence between the networks' different segments. The same happens in the competitive economy of conservatives, the control node with the higher number of connections will be the segment with greater influence in the network. The market economies of the second half of the 20th century are a good example of development and growth of decentralized networks at scale. In these networks, the nodes of a segment can communicate with distant nodes through intermediaries that must be paid for the interconnection service. An important aspect that made it possible to have decentralized networks in the modern era was function segregation, for example, the separation of power into the executive, legislative, and judicial branches. In economics, the decentralization problems of network functions have been addressed by research of principal-agent problems.

iii. **Distributed networks.** Here the nodes can connect with any other node. At first, they do so with those that are close by in the substrate and with which it is possible to establish physical connections. Furthermore, in this type of network there are agreements or protocols for the free flow of signals. The nodes let through without restrictions the signals going from one connection to another in the understanding that they all benefit from this type of arrangements. The iconic example is the Internet that was designed with distributed network logic so it could survive in a nuclear war. The idea is that without central connection points, the information flow can adapt to the loss of a significant number of nodes and surviving nodes that may reconfigure the routes and maintain communication. In hierarchical terms, network neutrality exists because communications are not discriminated. Hence, the operation is open and collaborative as is needed for a transformational economy to exist. We may also consider that public goods and open standards tend to establish distributed network arrangements.

The network's topology not only depends on the connections' physical dimension. Networks operate at different levels or layers, and although the network's physical or schematic structure influences its topology, it is possible that in logical terms these work differently at each layer.

5. **Network layers.** Diagrams oversimplify networks and they don't show that to establish, manage, and use network connections is costly and complex. The condition that justifies the cost of building a network is that the benefits — whether evolutionary or economic — are greater than the costs. This complexity is reflected in the different layers needed for some networks to work. In a neurological network, there is a physical layer that is formed by the link between axons and dendrites, a chemical layer formed by neurotransmitters, an electrical signal layer and a genetic layer that encodes and produces the proteins used by the network. In modern telecommunications networks, the best-known layered model is the Open Systems' Interconnection model (OSI)(178) that's divided in seven layers (Table 24).

OSI Model

	Layer	Protocol Unit	Function	Examples
Host layers	7. Application	Data	High-level APIs include shared resources and remote access to files.	HTTP, FTP, Telnet, SMTP, SSH
	6. Presentation		Translates data between application and network services, includes character coding, data compression and encryption.	S/MIME, TLS
	5. Session		Manages communications and sessions. For example, the continuous incoming and outgoing exchange in the form of transactions between two nodes.	RPC, SCP, PAP
	4. Transport	Segment (TCP) / Datagram (UDP)	Reliable transmission of data segments between points of the network, includes segmentation, recognition and multiplexing.	TCP, UDP, NBF
Medium layers	3. Network	Package	Structures and manages a multinode network, includes routing and traffic control.	IPv4, IPv6, ICMP, IPsec.
	2. Link	Frame	Reliable transmission of the data frame between two nodes connected by a physical network.	IEEE 802.11, Ethernet, PPP, ATM, MPLS
	1. Physical	Bit	Transmits and receives bitstreams in a physical environment.	IEEE 802, Ethernet, IEEE 802.11, ISDN, RS-232

Table 24: OSI Communication Model. Source: Wikipedia.

The OSI model clearly shows the implicit complexity at work within a multiplexed network. But what´s important is that, although any piece of information that the Internet transmits today passes through complex processing within the model's layers and protocols, these networks are malleable making it possible to configure different network topologies that coexist without trouble. For example, it is possible to develop a centralized network at the level of the seventh layer of the OSI model and for it to be transported via transport and network TCP/IP layers in the form of an executive information system, where executives from a company inform the CEO without having any communication among themselves. In the same fashion, with a distributed network topology at the seventh layer, financial institutions allow clients to carry out transactions among themselves by means of hubs to which clients have access via the Internet at the fourth and fifth layer. The above mentioned takes place even though the Internet is a distributed architecture protocol. In social terms, human beings have also shown throughout history enough cognitive flexibility to create networks with different cultural protocols and layers that are as different and diverse as monarchies and contemporary democracies. Therefore, to understand networks it is necessary to go beyond the apparent physical geometry and dive inside the networks inner workings — be they simple and passive like a river, or complex and dynamic as a neurological network — so one can understand a networks' true topology, the correlation of force between its functions, and the influence between the different nodes.

State of the Art

Before we go on discussing changes in human society's' topology, we need to recapitulate current scientific understanding about networks and its link to complexity science and the cultural evolution model. Network theory took off as a discipline in 1999 after the publication of Albert-László Barabási and Réka Albert work on scale-free networks(179), which made it possible to mathematically explain new phenomena such as the distributions of links and references in the *world wide web*. In that work, we first observed the phenomenon of the small world model or "the six degrees of separation" with which it was discovered that a person relates to any other person in the world through a chain of fewer than six people who know each other. Thus, despite our demographics and geographical dispersion, we could look at ourselves through the networks' metaphor as a single humanity that soon would be connected more closely due to the development of Information and Communications

Technology (ICT). On the other hand, the same results also showed that many network phenomena had scale-free behavior. In other words, some nodes named hubs had most of the connections and advantages whereas the rest of the nodes — indeed, most of them — had few connections and possibilities to benefit from the advantages of the network.

These first popular models and observations, though useful to describe the networks evolved or final structure, did not solve what we can describe as the network's "different problem" modules. They didn't explain the nodes' internal mechanisms, its functions and connections, the relationship with the substrate, and its evolution and persistence over time.

1. **Thermodynamic module**. Refers to the physical problems of the energy balance and entropy, the scarcity and abundance relationships with the substrate, the cost incurred and value produced by the nodes. The problems of environmental and social sustainability spin around this module, particularly in what refers to the anabolic flow or recirculation phase.

2. **Evolutionary module**. Relates to the node's problems of autonomy, adaptation, and evolutionary direction, such as collaborating or competing, and the development of the heuristic optimization solutions. For the most part, these are the problems that the cultural evolution model addresses: What degrees of freedom do we have? What strategies can we build and choose?

3. **Information module**. Refers to the node's capacity to process information, establish, and manage connections and exchanges with other nodes in the network. It relates to the functions of synchronization, acquisition, information processing, and value exchange at an operational level.

After the small world network models, other researchers like Lloyd Demetrius and Thomas Manke made use of ergodic theory, which studies the average long-term behavior of dynamic systems. This theory incorporated new elements into Network Theory when they analyzed networks' robustness and resilience, which is defined as the system's capability to maintain its performance despite the external perturbations. They discovered that network topology is the result of a Darwinian adaptation process that takes place due to evolutionary pressures in which the more robust configurations survive, and which are linked to the system's entropic information level(180). Hence, to become more robust and resilient, a network configuration depends on diverse factors such as the number of nodes, the cost of the connections, and the environmental restrictions like energy availability. In this model, the centralized or star-shaped networks are robust when N is low and fragile when N is high. In the latter case, the network's topology evolves toward more complex configurations because under certain conditions those are the ones that overall produce greater robustness and resilience for the system. However, this possibility does not prevent the opposite situation of networks evolving into less stable configurations.

This provides the guideline for us to plunge fully into the world that will cease to be. Clearly, the disintermediation processes driven by information and communication technologies dramatically changed the internal properties of economic, political, and social networks. The new technology modifies the number of nodes, the cost of connections and the filtering, synchronization, and validation mechanisms that in turn modify the topology of many networks that are vital for society. Therefore, the big question of our time is: "What do these changes mean?"

Network topology and history

For the time being, the state of the art in network theory and its connection with complexity science does not yet enable us to reach the point where we can build an empirical model in which to introduce real data, currently abundant in the big data environments, such as the number of nodes, the cost of connections, the processing speed of agents, and the hubs' influence level. Nonetheless, it is possible and probable that an amalgam of complexity theory and the holistic fusion of knowledge coming out of network theory — which begins in geometry, passes through engineering and reaches ecology — will soon bring new and powerful tools to help us better know and predict the evolutionary direction of many social processes that until now seemed, nomothetically speaking, unassailable.

Our knowledge about networks and our daily experience with them converts them into the mental model of our era, allowing us to build a discussion about human networks, changes in their topology and its probable implications. To start, we can examine two network diagrams that are relevant to the discussion (Figure 17):

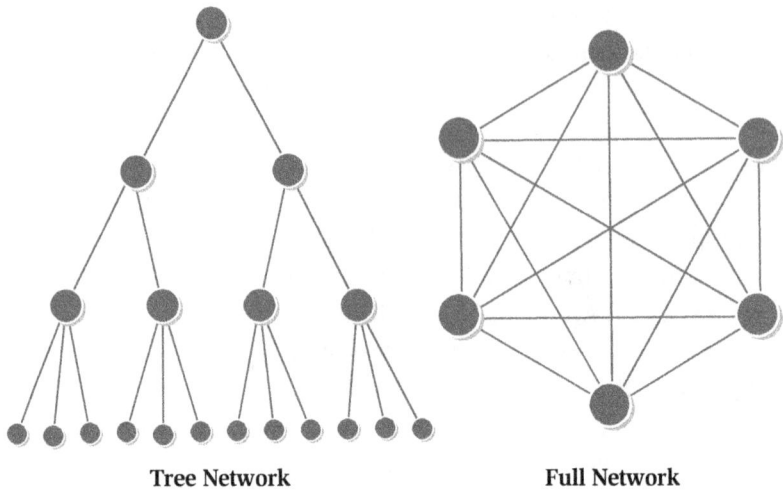

Tree Network   **Full Network**

Figure 17: Tree network and a complete network.

First, we present the tree network, the most common in society and in nature. Second is a complete network diagram that is currently being discussed as a paradigm of the new era.

Anyone who has explained an idea through a pyramid-shaped diagram or made an organizational chart intuitively understands tree topology. In nature, tree networks are part of the centralized and vascular networks family that are very common. They are observed in all types of phenomena such as in the tree's architecture that provides the name to this arrangement. They are found in hydrological basins, and in vascular systems of multicellular beings like the human circulatory system. In many cases, the tree-like patterns have a bilateral symmetry (Figure 18): on one side of the network, small flows are added to larger ones, so they can be moved from one part of the substrate to another, centrally processed and divided in smaller flows, and finally dispersed once again at the other end of the network. In closed systems, such as the mammal's circulatory system, the two extremes of a vascular network with a bilateral symmetry are joined, forming a loop where the network collects the oxygen-depleted blood at a capillary level, adds it to the venous flow, and transports it to the pulmonary circulation loop. Once there, the blood releases the carbon dioxide, is oxygenated, and then is transferred to the heart, the system's hub, which then pumps it to the arterial circulation that, in a descending scale, reaches the capillary circulation where it oxygenates the cells and collects the carbon dioxide.

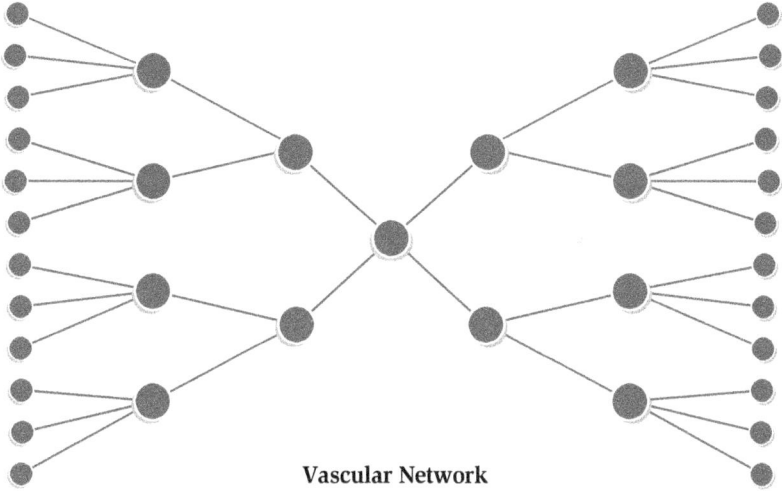

Vascular Network

Figure 18: Vascular network.

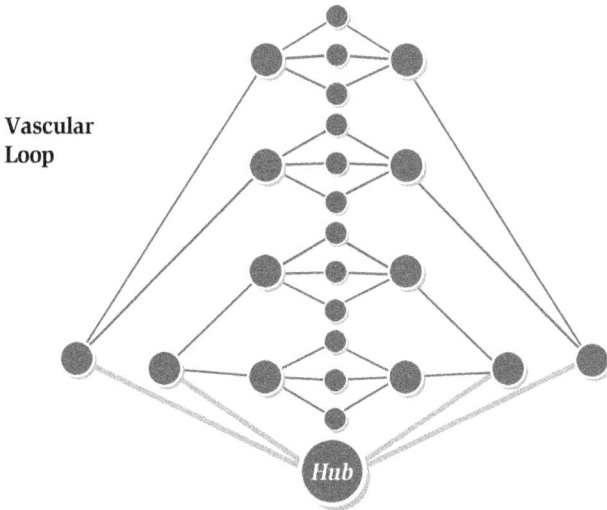

Figure 19: Vascular loop.

Vascular networks may be open or closed. The reason for their pervasiveness in nature, whether they are (open) vascular networks or (closed) vascular loops (Figure 19), is that this type of configurations is the most efficient, robust, and resilient arrangement for creating a large variety of scalable systems. Some of these systems reach the vascular configuration through passive mechanisms such as rivers and their basins, where the agents — the water molecules and the sediments — consistently follow the path of least resistance while others do so through active mechanisms, such as the genetic response to evolutionary pressures. In any of these cases, the ubiquity of vascular networks demonstrates that networks of this type organize themselves around the same mathematical functions of symmetry, flow and scale, given that at a microscopic level the agents are subject to the same physical optimization problems of the thermodynamic module.

In the case of human beings and their society, the novelty of this approach is to highlight that, through the cognitive flexibility that led us to curiosity, discovery, and the acquisition of a self-aware consciousness, the development of technology and an evolutionary culture, we managed to escape from the network's inertial and passive configuration model, like that of gorilla, chimpanzee, and wolf societies. This endowed us with the capability to create new and complex network arrangements, whose topological changes defined history's most important transformations:

1. **The tribal network.** Probably at the dawn of humanity our ancestors inherited and transmitted one of the two network arrangements that works well for social groups when N is low. They are the centralized patriarchal network, like the one that mountain gorillas have today, or a more equal one that leans toward the complete network such as the one that endures among the bonobos. Whatever the arrangement may have been, it became more dynamic as the volume of the cerebral neocortex increased, and the possible size of human groups was consolidated in the 150 members that the Dunbar number predicts(181) (Figure 20).

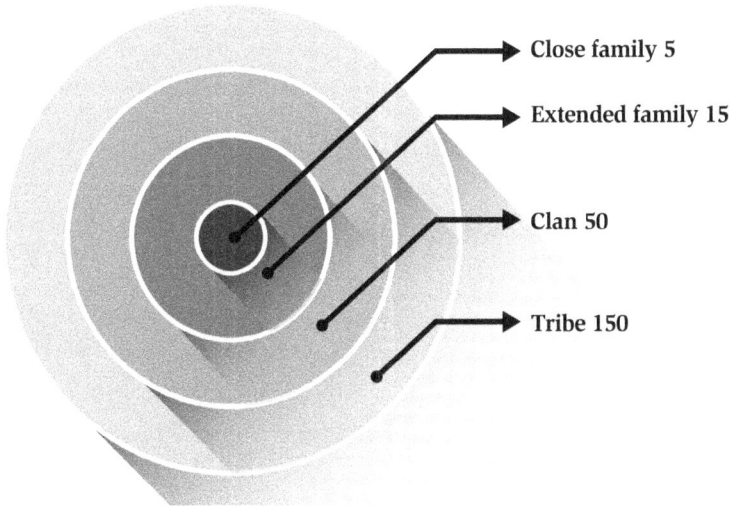

Close family 5

Extended family 15

Clan 50

Tribe 150

Figure 20: Layers and size of the human social group.

It is important to say that in the first phase of our history — the feral survival phase — the network began to change and become more flexible at the family and social layer levels. At first, human beings remained coupled at a niche level as an opportunistic omnivore for thousands of years and to the large ecological network with a tree-like topology called the trophic network. In the trophic network, the animals are stratified due to the role they play in the food chain (Figure 21). The nutrients and the energy flow from the pastures and plants found at the base of the pyramid; the next trophic level is that of herbivorous animals; and the carnivores and the omnivores are at the top of the pyramid. The genus homo change of position in the trophic network is still a topic of discussion among paleoanthropologists, who have different hypotheses on the moment when it happened and its triggering factors. Some hypotheses are related to the use of fire, solidarity, language, tools, mind theory, gender, etc. Although the causality is not yet well defined, in the end the new arrangements in the social and cultural network's layer of the species *homo sapiens* led to the emergence of hunter-gatherer tribes, who occupied a different or "artificial" position from the one they had a right to because of the biological evolution, but with which they managed to turn into the apex predators at the cusp of the trophic network.

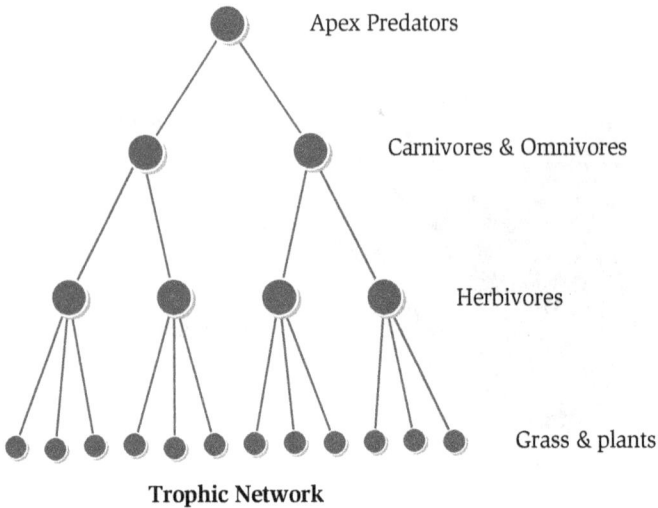

Trophic Network

Figura 21: Trophic network.

The impact of the tribe consisting of 150 homo sapiens on the ecological network was of such magnitude that it eventually provoked the fast depletion and extinction of mega fauna, like mammoths(182). Some researchers believe that agricultural development was an adaptation to the extinction of these prey animals since the comparison of hours worked to calories obtained between hunters-gatherers and early farmers, shows that most likely the former had an easier life than the latter(183). Over time, either the ecological change became a necessity, or it benefitted those who developed higher complexity levels through agriculture.

2. **The agricultural network.** Once the role of apex predator in the natural trophic network became unsustainable, agricultural development and animal domestication opened the door for human beings to begin a slow but inexorable hijacking process of the trophic network, which set the planets' resources at the service of our needs. By the year 2000, 38.1% of the planet's continental surface had an agricultural use(184), and according to Vaclav Smil(185), the ratio of mammalian zoomass was as follows:

#	Type of mammals	Millions of tons (live mass)	%
1	Human beings	305	30.5%
2	Domestic animals	667	66.7%
3	Wild animals	28	2.8%
	Total	1,000	100%

Table 25: Mammalian zoomass.

Thus, it became necessary to create a new trophic network — synthetic or artificial — based on the specialization, reorganization, and articulation of 150-member tribal modules. In other words, new forms of organizations were created that would control the substrate and expand the reach of the new human network that today we call "the economy." The problem was (and still is) that the new cognitive flexibility that enabled us to let go of our original position in the trophic network, scale it up to the apex and then take control of nature as our own network. That did not come coupled with the instinctive capability to identify the problems of the network module, the need for balance with the substrate and function configuration, turbulence, and stability. We were merely equipped with the autonomy to do all this and with the heuristic method of cultural evolution, which makes it easier for us try out different configurations (status quo, survival, transformation, and growth). Hence, this is how our long, colorful, tragic, and inspiring historical process began.

An interesting aspect in the way the human economic network was woven from the time when agricultural society was organized to just before the industrial revolution is the fact that, during such a long period, it was not possible to elude the main restriction that the thermodynamic module imposes on us. In nature, the trophic network, given the costs of thermodynamic transformation, productivity at each level can only be a tenth of the productivity at the inferior level. That is, if 100 units of plant biomass are produced at the base of the network, at the next level (the herbivores) only ten units of animal biomass can be generated, and at the last level, only one unit of predators' biomass can be sustained. This is a 100:10:1 ratio. Given that for millennia economic performance depended on the primary sector's productivity, society's stratification also became a trophic stratification. Most of the population worked in agriculture (>90%) at the base. At the next level, some merchants and artisans did more complex things, and at the third level, warriors and rulers became the apex predators, whose work was to defend, conquer, or repress.

Since productivity at the network's highest level depended on the size of the base, it is not difficult to understand that an apex predator (a master), the leader of a clan of 150 people (lackeys) who followed him aspiring to attain a higher social level, would seek to take over a network that two levels down had 15,000 farmers (150×10^2), as well as the necessary land for them to be productive. This without mentioning that the 100:10:1 ratio in nature is the optimum one, and that it is very likely many premodern agricultural societies had lower productivity levels. Based on this approach, it is easier to understand the pervasiveness of castes, war, and conquest in these societies. With a fixed productivity rate and the exponential costs of trophic transformation, there were only two ways to prosper: 1) to conquer the network's adjacent segments regardless of who occupied them (in other words, to make the base larger); and/or 2) to control the network's functions and stratify society in the most unequal way possible to benefit the upper strata. The extreme case of this stratification was slavery, in which human beings established authentic predator/prey dynamics. In most cases, both things happened, and the tree's centralized topology was consolidated as society's standard design, which in cultural terms was coded as a divine and immutable order one had to respect. Maybe this last idea that now seems so alien to us, at the time, probably intended to mitigate the number of "go-getters" within a trophic system in which it was impossible to fulfill said aspirations without incurring violence.

3. **The industrial network.** In the modern era, the introduction of new energy sources decoupled the economy from the ancestral trophic relationships of productivity. This enabled the human network's exponential growth in terms of the quantity, volume, and distance of the flows that the connections could manage. This new situation resulted in several changes such as the emergence of huge decentralized networks on which the economy works today:

i. **The vascular networks were built**. With the development of international trade and industrial specialization, driven at first by steam and coal, then by other fossil fuels and electricity, the vascular networks that created economies of scale came into being (Figure 18) such as the mining networks that extracted minerals, transported them via railways (connections) to the refining and production centers (hubs), distributed them as consumer products in wholesale shipments, and then sent them to distribution via retail chains so they could reach consumers. The market was the industrial network's great innovation. With this new arrangement, it made no sense to transfer the result of the economy's products, like the thousands of tons of steel and coal, to the pyramid's apex, where they were useless. It was necessary to seek the transfer and profitable use of the new productivity to the market network.

ii. **The network functions were segregated.** With democracy defined as a system in which State functions are separated into the executive, legislative, and judicial branches, control over the network functions was segregated, and the methods of checks and balances were introduced into the system. Thus, it became easier to find and take advantage of new growth and development opportunities because it gave the system greater flexibility and lowered the risk of making bad systemic decisions.

iii. **A human dignity was acknowledged.** When the fixed productivity rate was broken and new forms for value creation and distribution were opened, the divine order became anachronic — a barrier for expansion and change in the network's topology. Then the agents were freed to explore and experiment with the possibilities of a new economy produced by the vascular network.

iv. **The hub was invented.** An interesting aspect that the Dunbar number introduces is the network's maximum limit as a multiple of the tribe. In mathematical terms, the small world theory and the "six degrees of separation" reveal that the human network as a whole, despite being structured in fragments of up to 150 individuals, is able to manage a very large number of connections — 150^6 in the case of the "six degrees of separation." However, we must consider that a single individual finds it hard to manage more than 150 connections. In this case, the need to create and manage network nodes with thousands or millions of connections was added to the cognitive capability of the *mythos* (linked to the mind theory) to create and associate ourselves with abstract entities. That made possible the existence of useful metaphysical figures such as the juridical person, the institution, the political parties, and the commercial brands, which are the vehicles that allow for the existence of the hub. That is, the hub as an entity capable of simultaneously managing and intermediating millions of connections and the decentralized network's articulating component. Without this capacity to believe in and relate to the hubs, even though they are immaterial, it would not be possible for us to trust them and contribute our individual efforts so that banks, institutions, or corporations could work nor could or would we join a political party. To illustrate how fictitious but useful is the existence of the hub, one can only imagine how difficult it would be for a Neolithic or Dark Age farmer to understand the importance and inner workings of fiduciary money, life insurance, marketing, and political parties. For that individual, our contemporary metaphysics would not be accessible or comprehensible in the same way that for us it is no longer useful to believe in the ancient Paleolithic gods of nature, climate, and fertility.

v. **The vascular loops were kept open.** The shift from the tree's economic network, driven by agriculture, to the bilateral vascular network fed by hydrocarbons, led to economic productivity's biggest leap in history. The shift's impact was so profound that any action, idea, or concept that prevented maximizing productivity growth was cast aside (self-interest). This meant that the new vascular networks did not evolve toward the next level of complexity with anabolic recirculation phases (the common good). For two centuries, this omission made it easier for the network to grow and flow, but it degraded the substrate and diminished the system's robustness.

In a nutshell, network topology is an emergent result that provides clues about a system's interior regime. Today, the most visible change is the leap from a high intermediation model based on hubs to one with a lower degree of intermediation initiated by use of digital platforms, which is none other than a systemic change in the human network topology.

This is important because, according to what was laid out before in this chapter, topology changes reflect changes in the agents' behavior as well as their relationship with the environment and the utilization, renovation and destruction of the substrate. Those, at the end of the day, reveal a change so profound that we can say we're on the verge of one of the great shifts in history.

Random networks and dysfunctional networks

Before the 21st century network topology change is analyzed, we need to address two additional network cases: the random network and the dysfunctional network.

1. **Random networks.** In mathematical terms, these are networks in which a node has the same probability of linking with any other node, so that the interconnection between each other is statistically independent.

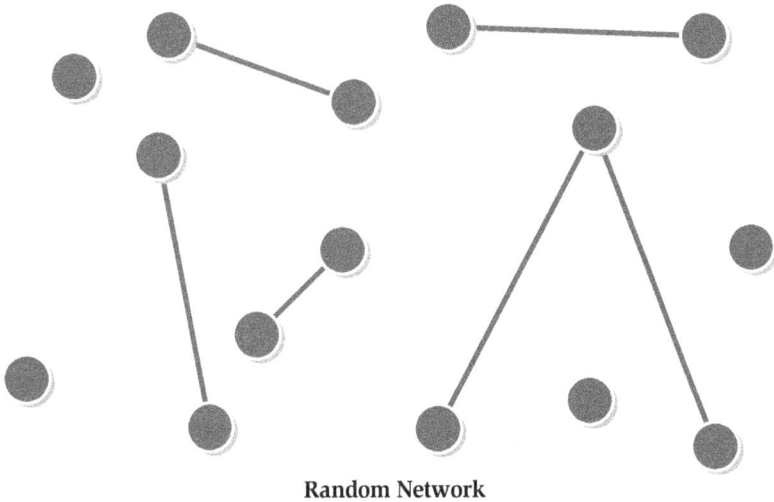

Random Network

Figure 22: Random network.

Examples of random network phenomena are the plants' pollination process that releases pollen into the air so that some grains manage to fertilize the flowers through the law of probabilities and large numbers; the reproduction of many fish species, where the female releases her eggs on the seabed (substrate) and the male fertilizes them by spraying sperm (agents) in the water; and the errant salespeople who — without any knowledge, help, financing, marketing, or market knowledge — go to busy places and try to sell their goods. In this type of network, the agents have a broad margin of autonomy (they are on their own), economies of scale work against them and, as a result, they are unproductive and not very efficient. In ideological terms, this would be the form of anarchic and libertarian networks if they existed, lacking any general network functions and platforms. The random networks would not be very important, but they are one of the key factors the modern era created and today affect us in a meaningful way.

During the premodern period, societies followed rules based on some type of natural order. In the medieval structure of masters, lackeys, and serfs, each character had a series of rights and obligations defined by the divine and natural order of things. Thus, even the serf had a place in the social order — a bad one according to our standards — but one he kept if he fulfilled his duties at the base of the agricultural network. This natural right to be part of society can be traced back to the Paleolithic societies of hunters-gatherers that probably engaged in initiation rituals to celebrate the integration of new members into the community. In fact, one of the worst punishments that an individual in one of the few remaining primitive societies can suffer today is to be disconnected from the trophic network and become part of the random network that equals exile and ostracism. In fact, in the biological networks that social animals form, the loss of one's place in the social group is very rare. In groups of large mammals, such as lions, only the adolescent males are expelled as a way of preventing inbreeding but, as time goes by, the young lions may re-enter the feline society and transmit their genes if they manage to defeat the alpha male in battle of any social group other than their own.

In the modern era, the definitive abandonment of the natural order and the serf's disengagement from the land through the urbanization process and the increase in land productivity that required less labor, enabled the existence of large random networks in the form of groups that no longer belonged to the agricultural tree network or to the industrial economy's vascular network. Just like in the agricultural era when more than 90% of the population worked in agriculture, the transition from the countryside to the city inverted the proportions 180 degrees. Currently, in a postindustrial economy like the United States, less than 5% of the population works in agriculture and, in developing nations like Mexico, this proportion is less than 10%.

Over time, groups of people who belong to society's random networks, who are in the subsistence, informal economy and underemployment sectors, have been given different names: proletarian, marginalized, indignant, and landless. More recently, they have been called "ninis" — they neither study nor work — and as mentioned before(186), one out of every four persons in the OECD member countries does not study, work, or receive any training. This is a serious situation because, even though human beings have a social, cultural, and cognitive flexibility to adapt to different network configurations, the only one that is alien and contrary to our nature is the random network.

Formally, the Universal Declaration of Human Rights that was ratified by the UN member countries protects the people's rights to be part of society. However, beyond the legal formalism, belonging to society and having the right to be someone relates to more tangible aspects such as access to education and health, work, and the banking system, certainty of ownership, security, and access to justice, among others. The reality is that by merely reviewing the inclusion level to the world economic network, we find that the random network today is gigantic. According to the World Bank, in 2014, 38% of the world's population older than 15 years of age had no access to any financial service other than the use of cash, and 73% had no formal access to a bank credit(187).

This shows the size of the risk and the instability in which humanity finds itself. Given that every human being tends to naturally coalesce toward the family, the clan or the tribe, belonging to a random network is unnatural. Nowadays, those who form part of the random network in terms of the economic layer but are connected with their mobile phone to the scarcely filtered global digital network, only need one point of convergence to act, rationally or irrationally, in favor of the solutions they believe will help them gain or maintain a place in the vascular network. As recently as 2016, the xenophobic phenomena such as Brexit in the United Kingdom and Donald Trump's campaign in the United States reveal problems resulting from the random network's growth and the weakening of the vascular network even in developed nations.

2. **Dysfunctional networks** may be defined as those systems that, although having a specific topology such as the nations *The Economist* classified as dysfunctional democracies, they work in conditions in which no homeostatic regime has been established. In this regard, the global economy is a dysfunctional network because, by not having a pricing system that internalizes the cost of externalities, it works at a very high systemic risk regime. Another simpler example is that of the differences observed between the open society economies and the closed systems economies. First, in the fully democratic societies, the random network is small relative to the size of the vascular network. Second, the scale and flow relationships are closer to a mathematical optimum, as in the case of South Korea where the GDP flow between large and small companies approaches a 50:50 ratio. On the other hand, in most economies that are part of the world's authoritarian spectrum, the size of the random network adjacent to the formal vascular network is enormous. The dysfunctional vascular networks do not grow, and that fosters the informal and subsistence sectors. In these systems, the hubs' control and the network functions have a centrist, free-riding, and predatory logic (the status quo strategy) that makes these systems, on balance and in the sum of random and vascular networks, famished and unstable. Thus, the presence and size of random networks in any type of society is a measure of the network's dysfunction. It can happen through the lack of resources in the substrate, as in the trophic networks when animals, berries, seeds and fruits are scarce, and/or due to a poor network configuration that produces high access and intermediation costs, as is the case in most of Latin America today.

To better explain the above, it is worth mentioning a high-level dialogue that various Mexican federal government officials had back in 2012. Their aim was to come up with a national digital agenda that would consider the challenges in shaping a public policy instrument requested by non-governmental organizations (NGO's) and that would be linked to the reform of the national telecommunications markets. In this setting, I developed and presented a methodology based on the idea that it was possible to make a diagnosis of the structural and operational conditions of network markets with a three variables approach: coverage, service quality, and market prices (Table 26).

Methodology for analyzing challenges in markets with network goods						
Case	Wide coverage / Access	High quality/ Technology	Buen precio	Diagnosis	Type of network	Random network
1	YES	YES	YES	Efficient market	Functional	Scarce or null
2	YES	YES	NO	Competitive market with heavy taxes and regulations	Functional in the vascular network	Due to market failure
3	YES	NO	YES	Poorly regulated and/or subsidized competitive market, price war	Functional but unstable	Due to poor service
4	YES	NO	NO	Nationalization	Dysfunctional	Large
5	NO	YES	YES	Competitive market with scaling problems: technological, physical or geographical barriers	Functional in the vascular network	Large
6	NO	YES	NO	Club goods	Dysfunctional	Large
7	NO	NO	YES	Competitive market with low investment level	Dysfunctional	Large
8	NO	NO	NO	Market with low competition and investment	Dysfunctional	Large

Table 26: Random and dysfunctional networks case analysis.

The analysis of Mexico's telecommunications sector in 2012 turned out to be a truism. For all participants the telecommunications markets' dysfunctionality was obvious: in fact, the specific case was a cartel, as described as Case 8 in Table 26. The interesting thing is that, even though these discussions were not made public, the coverage, quality, and price triad was disseminated in the hub of public policy makers and was adopted as the success measure for the telecom reform. In 2013, under a new administration, said success measures were top headline news(188). During this process, the cartel members entrenched themselves to prevent truly open and competitive markets, and consequently Congress only managed to pass some legislative bills. But the public perception of the reform was positive. If we assess the results with the same method used in 2012, we find that in the following years prices decreased, coverage increased moderately, and quality improvement stagnated. Moreover, the international indicators, such as the Networked Readiness Index(189) show that the progress made was insufficient to drive forward Mexico's digital transformation beyond the average pace in the rest of the world. Mexico's position in that index, from 2012 to 2016, was 76, 63, 79, 69, and 76, respectively. The reform did not change the dysfunctional character of the vascular network in the telecommunications sector, nor did it significantly reduce the size of the random network. Currently, only 45.1% of the population is an Internet user(190).

The conclusion is that as we revise the markets' operation based on the variables linked to the networks' structural properties like coverage, quality, and price, it is easier to see through the political, legislative, and media noise and diagnose a wide variety of issues. This approach also lets us establish reference lines to measure progress in different markets such as finance, health, and education. Besides having the capacity to understand the markets' structural operation through properties such as the network's topology, it also is possible to understand their operational and productivity conditions based on the relationship between the size of the random networks and the vascular networks. Finally, the discussion demonstrates once again that the impossibility for billions of people to have a place and be someone in society is one of today's most pressing problems, one that will either get worse or be resolved according to configuration changes made in this century to the economic, political, and social networks.

Change of Topology

To address the issue of change of topology in the 21st century, we must divide the system into rigid and flexible components. According to what we previously have discovered, in any system the components linked to the thermodynamic module form a network of rigid and inviolable restrictions. Therefore, in all cases in which it is necessary to take on economies of scale as in transport networks or transformations like raw material production or where we need to solve distribution problems, the networks will maintain the basic tree form. In other words, they will be pyramidal, vascular, and/ or vascular loops. In fact, the great revolution we need in our era because of the environmental sustainability problems (substrate conservation and degradation) is the change from open vascular networks (growth strategy) that has no anabolic recirculation flows to the construction of vascular loops (transformation strategy) that do have them since, in the universal order of things, that is defined by the laws of physics. This change is the only road we can take to increase the system's robustness, resilience, and persistence.

There is a "new age" idea today where the digital era will convert many physical flows of goods into immaterial flows of information that will generate a distributed economy independent of the thermodynamic module problems. Through the simple process of digitalization and thanks to more sophisticated technologies like stereoscopic or three-dimensional printing, anyone will be able to obtain and manufacture, on demand, the goods and services almost at the point at which they are consumed. Undoubtedly, said technologies have a great potential to build a more creative and decentralized economy. Although intuitively, the cost of moving bits through a fiber optical cable seems to be an option that is free of the restrictions of transformation and the movement of physical goods through the traditional information networks, the reality is that the information networks are also subject to thermodynamic limits.

Parts of these restrictions are quite visible: the manufacturers and consumers of portable electronics struggle every day with the trade-offs between the computing power, battery life, and the size and weight of their devices. While these lines are being written, Samsung — South Korea's most important information technology company — is suffering the worst scandal in its history: It had to withdraw 2.5 million Galaxy Note 7 devices from the world market because the greater energy and density required to deliver more robust features, under certain circumstances, caused some devices to overheat and spontaneously explode(191).

Another part of the thermodynamic module's effects on the digital world is not visible. In recent years, an important part of information processing began to move away from personal devices, such as mobile phones and personal computing equipment, to become concentrated on the infrastructure of large suppliers, such as Google, Microsoft, Apple and Amazon in their cloud-computing infrastructure. This means that energy consumption for information processing is being concentrated in remote data centers and remains hidden from the consumer view.

A recent estimate on indirect energy consumption in mobile devices says that watching one hour a week of high-definition video on an iPhone® or an iPad® demands the same energy use as that of two new refrigerators(192). Consequently, this reallocation in power consumption means that in physical terms the Internet hubs are getting increasingly closer to the power network hubs of the world because to subsist in the competitive world of utility computing it is essential to have access to cheap and plentiful electricity. Thus, in the first part of this century, the Internet that began as a distributed network of academic nodes is now more centralized at a physical level without having an alternative path for decentralization. And technologies such as three-dimensional printing are not exempt from the thermodynamic module's restrictions since the resins and materials they need to operate are subject to traditional production and distribution mechanisms.

What can happen and should happen with the economic network due to the influence of the thermodynamic module is the change of open vascular networks to closed vascular loops. In doing so, efficiency will improve, there will be new complexity levels, and the substrate's degradation will be reduced. Some functions will need to be centralized in hubs to take on the benefit of economies of scale, as is already taking place with cloud computing, and others will be decentralized because of scale, risk, security, resilience, and robustness issues.

For some futurologists, the thermodynamic restriction will be solved as new energy sources or technologies such as energy-efficient biological computers are developed. According to an estimate, the human average brain has a computing capacity of 38 petaflops (thousands of trillions of operations per second), a memory of 3,584 terabytes(193), and a consumption of 12.6 watts(194) that equals an efficiency of 3,015,873 gigaflops per watt, while the most efficient supercomputer in the world has an efficiency of 2.1 gigaflops per watt(195). Thereby, computation based on silicon and copper cables is 1,436,130 times less efficient than biological computing. With those rates, the operation of a silicon-based computer that had a capacity equivalent to the human brain would need 18 megawatts. Thus, this creates serious doubts over the feasibility to scale artificial intelligence (AI) systems, although the potential for improvement is clearly there. Meanwhile, if current silicon-based computation doesn't change or improve to become as efficient as biological computation, digital networks will continue to have the same scaling function within a vascular network topology at a physical level.

In the meantime, since the rigid elements determine a significant part of the system's configuration, the flexible elements (or degrees of freedom) allow the emergence of different configurations. These are the ones connected to the evolutionary model presented in the first part of the book under the cultural evolution model's strategies (status quo, survival, transformation, and growth). One way of bringing together the cultural evolution model with network theory is as follows:

Strategy

Description	Balance / Functional	Imbalance / Dysfunctional
Survival: Trophic Topology (tribe of 150 members, centralized or decentralized)		
Network functions are those prevailing in the trophic network. The ecosystem sustains apex predators in a 100:10:1 relationship.	If the natural law of the trophic network is respected, and the technologies applied to the substrate do not change, a network balance will exist.	When the load capacity is exceeded, the system self-regulates; either the number of hunters-gatherers goes down because of hunger or they migrate to new ecosystems.
Tree Topology Status Quo (centralized)		
The trophic network's homeostasis is broken. Society stratifies to take control of the natural network (agriculture, raw materials, captive markets).	When the tree functions well, members of society have a place and agree with inter-mediation rates, costs and advantages of stratification, for example, control of violence and defense of the substrate (land) against invasions.	With fixed productivity rates anchored to the substrate's productivity, the only network growth functions are the substrate's expansion by extension (invasion and con-quest) or the network's depredation (slavery, servitude, oppression).

Description	Balance / Functional	Imbalance / Dysfunctional
Growth: Vascular Topology (decentralized)		
The denser energy sources allowed the construction of bilateral vascular networks with new and varied enabling functions. On the one hand, the work is added to the primary production, transformation and manufacture networks. On the other, it is disseminated in trade and consumption networks. The energy and materials extracted from the substrate go in on one side; the entropy and the wastes that are deposited in the environment go out the other side.	Functional vascular networks are the ones that have cheap access to resources (energy and raw materials), low costs of access to the network, low intermediation rates that enable growth of the consumption network and the capacity to transfer the system's externalities and wastes to the substrate at a low cost.	The shortage and high costs of raw materials and the high cost of access to the network suffocate the vascular net-works, which generate growth of the random network, inefficiency in the hubs and high intermediation costs. That prevents the development of the consumption network and the inability or high cost to transfer externalities to the substrate.
Transform: Vascular Circuit Topology (decentralized)		
In this model, the open flow of bilateral symmetry vascular networks is discarded, and the closed flows model is adopted through the integration of externalities to the pricing system. The open flow model that starts in production and ends in consumption is called "cradle to grave." The second model that implies recirculation circuits, is called "cradle to cradle."	This model will achieve a balance if it triggers the reduction of random networks and the operation of "cradle to cradle" vascular circuits. To attain the inclusion of externalities into the pricing system, intermediation costs will have to go down with the introduction of new models, such as that of the platforms that will substitute the intermediation model based on institutions. Thus, the size, the profits rates and the hubs' cost will be different.	A poor design, too much rigidity or a slow or late implementation in the internalization of externalities to the pricing system may cause instability and an erratic behavior in the system that will increase the size of the random network. If the new intermediation model based on platforms becomes a network predator, the random network will increase, and the flows will be concentrated. Inequality and instability will then increase.

Table 27: Network strategies and topology.

It is interesting that when we talk about the coupling and the interaction of random networks and vascular networks as a complex system, there is a broad tradition of empirical measurements that point to the presence of these network topologies in human society. For example, in 1906, the Italian economist Vilfredo Pareto observed that 20% of the Italian population owned 80% of the property(196). Later, in 1941, Joseph Moses Juran(197), the father of the total quality culture popularized this relationship — the Pareto principle — to explain that 80% of quality failures stemmed from 20% of the causes and, ever since, the same distribution has been found in countless natural and social cases. Nonetheless, the ubiquity of this principle that has been accepted in social sciences as a curious phenomenon with no concrete explanation has not been a factor for us to think that the most important phenomena of social sciences, such as inequality and wealth distribution, are attached to a general network and systems theory.

While most social scientists did not delve further into the causality of the Pareto principle, during the 18th and 19th centuries physicists did use simple distributions and relationships to study diluted gases and, thereby, discovered the ideal or noble gas law that gave rise to the macroscopic thermodynamic laws by Kelvin, Joule, and Sadi-Carnot. In 1905, Albert Einstein was able to connect the microscopic calculations of statistical mechanics developed by Boltzmann and Maxwell with the macroscopic laws(198), thereby, discovering the so-called Gibbs distribution connected to random networks — also known as the Boltzmann distribution — that assumes all molecules have equal probability to access an energy level(199).

This distribution assumes that all molecules have the same probability of going from one initial energy level to a higher one and this, in turn, implies that each molecule moves independently of the others. For their part, Erdős and Rényi(200) demonstrated that for a network with a high number of nodes that are connected completely at random, the average chance of forming a connection follows a zero-order Poisson distribution that is similar to the Gibbs distribution. This result indicated that randomly connected complex networks follow mathematical inter-connection laws like the random collision of molecules in a gas. For example, when trade relations work randomly, the likelihood that a small retailer will attain a slightly higher sales level is the same, regardless of the initial level that is the equivalent of the Gibbs distribution, since in this case, all small retailers have the same opportunities to improve their sales, regardless of the market position they have.

In the 20th century, biologists and engineers found it convenient to model the complex relations of two variables through the allometric equation as applied to the study of adsorption or fixation of gas molecules or of a compound dissolved in liquid (a solute) to the surface of a solid support. The general form of the equation in the case of highly diluted solutions is called the Freundlich isotherm and is expressed as $f = Kc^m$(201). When m equals 1, we speak of the Langmuir isotherm that derives from a Gibbs distribution in which the adsorption takes place in a single layer of molecules (monolayer) and assumes that every adsorption layer is independent of the rest. But if the m exponent is greater than the unit, it is considered an indication of multilayer phenomena where there are so-called cooperative type interactions (network effects) that enable the subsequent adsorption of molecules once the sites have been occupied by the preceding ones. Then, in this case, they follow a Pareto distribution. All this reveals that when looking at a system in its entirety — owners and non-owners in the case of Italy at the beginning of the 20th century — many complex systems show two hierarchies, a diffusive one that follows a Gibbs distribution and a transport or convective hierarchy that follows a Pareto distribution. More recently, Albert-László Barabási and Réka Albert(179) indicated that the power function in networks like those we observe in phenomena that follow the Pareto principle, suggests how they grow since the new connections are linked, preferentially, with the nodes that are already well connected, or as Saint Matthew wrote(202): "For whoever has, to him more shall be given, and he will have in abundance (Pareto/vascular network); but whoever does not have, even what he has shall be taken away from him (Gibbs/random network)."

This way, when studying the distributions of many social attributes, we find analogy with the models emanating from physics and network phenomena. For example, the distribution of the number of citations of Mexican scientists — as in the rest of the world — follows the two patterns already mentioned (Graph 19):

1. When scientists have fewer than 1,600 citations of their work, these are distributed according to Gibbs' exponential model ($f \approx 95e^{-x/1000}$) and;
2. When they have more than 1,600 cites, they follow the Pareto model ($f \approx 99,500x^{-1.534}$).

The general explanation stems from the analysis of complex systems that are networks, in this case scientists connected among themselves. When a scientist has few contacts, the probability of establishing new connections — and having more quotes cited — is completely random and, therefore, follows an exponential function or Gibbs distribution. This explains why 90% of scientists are rarely cited. But if a scientist has many connections — he has been quoted more than 1,600 times — his chances of being cited increase more and more, something that is less and less frequent and explains why less than 1% of scientists have more than 10,000 citations. In other words, those who are ignored are more numerous and less known while those already famous are scarce and accumulate more references. This is a network phenomenon observed many times both in physical and social systems: few have a lot, and many have very little.

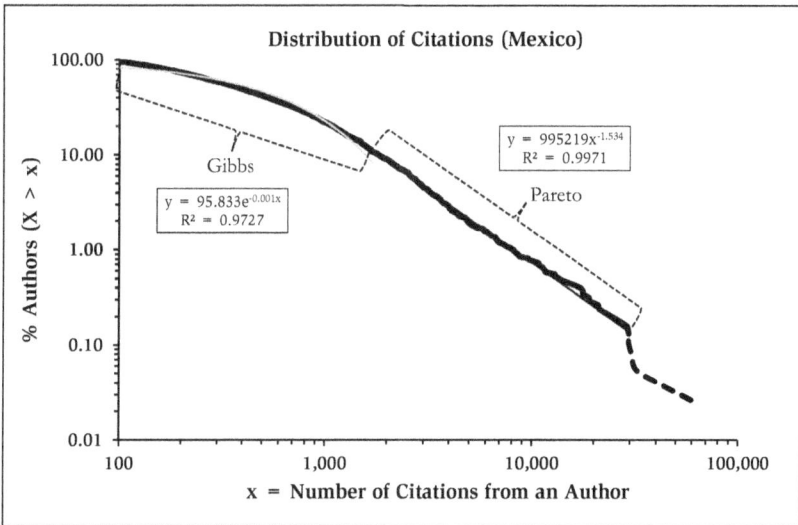

Distribution of Citations (Mexico)

$$y = 995219x^{-1.534}$$
$$R^2 = 0.9971$$

Gibbs

$$y = 95.833e^{-0.001x}$$
$$R^2 = 0.9727$$

Pareto

y-axis: % Authors (X > x)
x-axis: x = Number of Citations from an Author

Graph 19: Pareto-Gibbs distribution of academic citations in Mexico (log-log). Source: Graph is courtesy of Gustavo Viniegra G. and was made with Google Scholar™ data compiled by Webometrics (32).

In 2003, two Indian physicists interested in economics (econophysicists), Arnab Chatterjee and Bikas K. Chakrabarti, compared the predictions generated by the ideal gas equations with real data from social phenomena, such as money distributed in the economy(204). They discovered that in the same way that it happens in thermodynamic systems, many social phenomena follow the Gibbs-Pareto distribution pattern(205). When they focused on the inflection point where the distribution changes from Gibbs to Pareto, and they incorporated the propensity to save (λ) into the model, they found that the agents remained in the low distribution level segment or in the Gibbs partition when $\lambda=0$ (without savings) but entered the Pareto partition when $\lambda>0$ (with savings). This reveals several things:

1. Cultural networks (economic, political, and social) follow distribution and connection patterns that are knowable through network topology, so it's possible to mathematically model the state and size of the random network (Gibbs partition) or of the vascular network (Pareto partition).

2. The flow and scale functions, such as that of Gibbs-Pareto, are linked to the general laws of systems, such as the agents' diversity that produces modular network structures.

3. Other significant examples of unequal distribution are the 90:10:1 rule of unequal participation in social media and online communities that Jakob Nielsen observed. According to Nielsen, 1% of content generators contribute with 90% of publications, 9% contribute with 10% and 90% of users produce no content at all(206). And the relative distribution of family income available in all world economies can be seen here (Graph 20). In an average of 71 countries, 80% of households have access to 54.28% of the total income, while the superior 20% (deciles 9 and 10) has access to the remaining 45.72%, with very marked differences like the case of South Africa, where 80% of the population has access to only 33.83% of the income. In Norway, the same percentage of the population has access to 64.44% of available income(207).

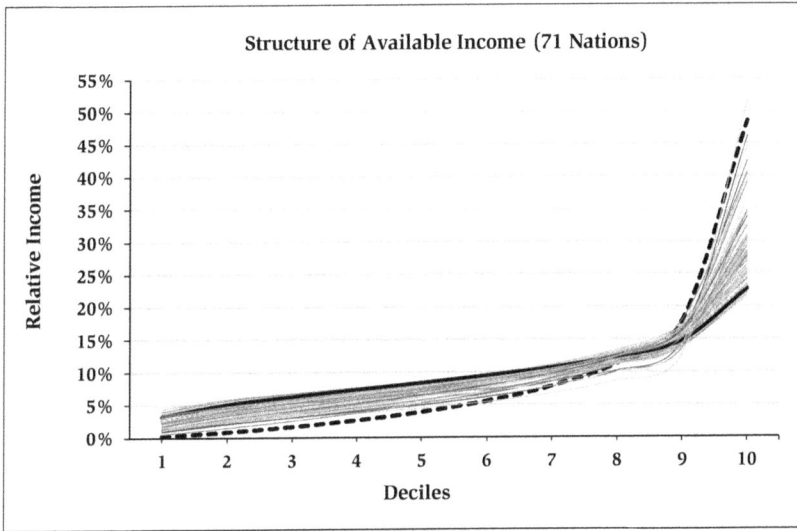

Graph 20: Relative structure of family income by deciles in 71 countries (2011). Source: World Consumer Income and Expenditure Patterns 2013, Euromonitor International.

4. The distribution of attributes, resources, and opportunities in human societies has a structure like that of the abundance of species in a habitat with segments that differ significantly among themselves:

   i. Approximately 90% of the population follows the exponential random distribution (Gibbs partition).

   ii. An intermediate segment, closer to 9% of the population, follows a power law with exponents lower than 4 (Pareto partition).

   iii. A superior segment, closer to or lower than 1%, follows a power law with an exponent larger than 4 (Super-pareto partition).

5. Although all societies are structurally or topologically similar — a few have a lot, and many have too little — small differences in the network's configuration, such as a greater savings capacity ($\lambda > 0$), transform the evolutionary configuration of systems and their conditions of stability and turbulence. Networks with very high inflection points and greater Pareto exponents are highly unequal and tend to be turbulent and unstable in the long term. In considering the relative distribution of available income in a group of selected countries (Graph 21), we observe that an apparently small difference, such as the first decile only having access to 1% of available

income in countries like Mexico or Egypt while the same decile gains 3% of income in Switzerland or South Korea, is linked with radically different conditions of development, stability, and growth.

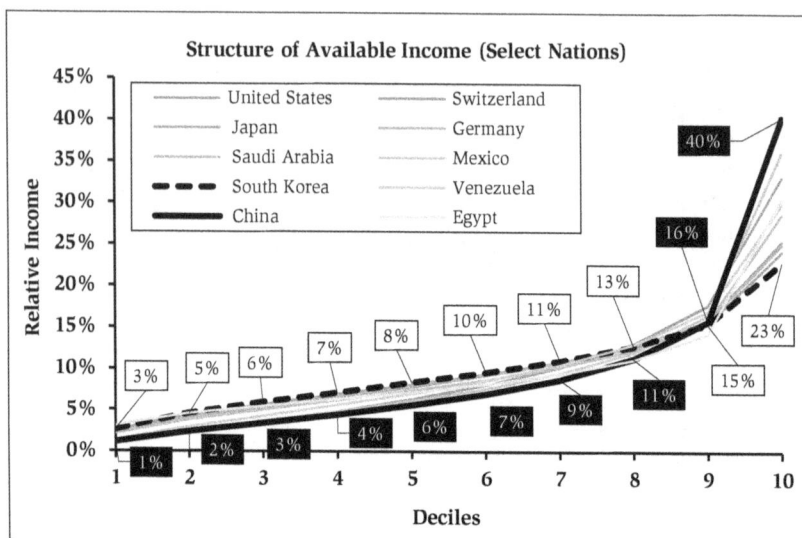

Graph 21: Relative distribution of family income by deciles in selected countries. (2011). Source: World Consumer Income and Expenditure Patterns 2013, Euromonitor International.

A practical proposal, coherent with the transition from Gibbs to Pareto, is that of Jeffrey Sachs(208), who estimated that extreme poverty can only be mitigated when people can pay for the minimum consumption needed for their survival and have the capacity to save ($\lambda > 0$). This is the idea behind the microcredit programs that the Grameen Bank in Bangladesh began in 1983 and that have now expanded all over the globe. Despite the generated benefits, aid programs have also been the objects of criticism because several financial institutions have been abusive by setting annual interest rates of more than 100%(209). It seems the problem lies in the simplistic approach that assumes credit will have a direct impact on poverty without realizing the high risk the new micro businessmen incur and who are devoid of technical and commercial capacities (access to the vascular network) to reduce the failure rate that, overall, raises the cost of money. In other words, the current approach does not consider the overarching relationship between masters, lackeys, and serfs prevailing in authoritarian societies nor their linkage with extra economic barriers that prevent the development and integration of micro companies to the vascular economic network. That integration would be the main factor for reconfiguring the network topology and transform it into a more democratic structure. This observation places at the heart of the discussion the importance of interactions and the micro-macro integration in the structure and the functioning of the social networks.

One example that illustrates the large systemic effect of the micro-macro relationship is Mexico. When transferring South Korea's income distribution to the income level in Mexico (Table 28), we observe a radically different situation. It suggests that although complex systems operate within immovable physical restrictions, such as the need to generate vascular networks, the degrees of freedom in social systems are sufficiently broad to reach completely dissimilar configurations.

Deciles	% México	% South Korea	Income in México (USD/year)	México as South Korea (USD/year)	Income in México (monthly pesos; USD 20x1)	México as South Korea (monthly pesos; USD 20x1)	% Change
1	1.19%	2.64%	$3,227	$7,158	$5,378	$11,929	122%
2	2.54%	4.57%	$6,902	$12,398	$11,503	$20,663	80%
3	3.68%	5.89%	$9,998	$16,000	$16,663	$26,667	60%
4	4.84%	7.09%	$13,129	$19,240	$21,881	$32,066	47%
5	6.10%	8.27%	$16,557	$22,452	$27,595	$37,419	36%
6	7.58%	9.53%	$20,567	$25,868	$34,279	$43,113	26%
7	9.44%	10.96%	$25,622	$29,767	$42,704	$49,612	16%
8	12.05%	12.76%	$32,710	$34,646	$54,517	$57,744	6%
9	16.51%	15.40%	$44,816	$41,822	$74,693	$69,704	-7%
10	36.09%	22.89%	$97,978	$62,156	$163,297	$103,593	-37%
	100%	100%	$271,506	$271,506	$452,510	$452,510	

Table 28: Income available in Mexico with income distribution of South Korea.

For example, if Mexico changed overnight and became a nation as economically democratic as South Korea in terms of education, health, credit, justice, and economic competition, but without a variation of its income level, 80% of families would have higher incomes (122% more in the case of the first decile), while the two highest deciles — currently overpopulated by masters, lackeys, heroes, and bandits — would have lower income (-7% y -37%, respectively). However, they would not lose their position of supremacy in the social hierarchy. In turn, that would probably reduce violence and social instability and demolish decades of economic stagnation.

Before reaching any hasty conclusions, it is worth saying that current available income measurements reflect the evolved structures. That is, the Korean and Norwegian people reached that distribution because the sum of their behaviors construed a different strategy from that of the South African, Mexican, and Egyptian people. Therefore, it is not possible to implement "Robin Hood" type solutions to change the network topology and the income distribution by decree. In fact, the discussion is broader and has to do with the way in which we build the dominant *quorum* in a society as well as the network structures that lubricate the operation of the cultural evolution strategy and that are preferred by each country's inhabitants. Without doubt, the numbers presented earlier demonstrate once again that given the networks' structure, universal equality is not possible. They also overwhelmingly show that unnecessary and scandalous levels of poverty do exist, as well as unsustainable and catastrophic levels of wealth inequality.

Once the analytical base of network theory has been described, we must delve into the analysis of the changes that are currently in process, the path that the new intermediation models can take, the reformulation of balance in network functions, and the limits the environment imposes on us.

11. The Two Challenges of the 21st Century

Sustainability

The sustainability issue, illustrated by the challenge of climate change — currently the most widely studied — is one among many global-scale environmental phenomena like drinking water scarcity and desertification for which overwhelming scientific evidence has been available for decades. The vascular economic networks that extract resources on one side and only produce externalities on another affect the substrate's renewal capacity, while every year we have fewer means of subsistence to accommodate a population that is rapidly approaching 10 billion people during this century(210). As always, we still have not reached a social consensus about the best way to address these situations. In my opinion, the process to do so has not even begun because we don't understand the source of the different attitudes fueling it, nor the ways to reconcile them. For the time being, we are looking for solutions in an improvised way, with no success, based on irreconcilable positions and without the *quorum* needed to move forward toward the deliberate construction of an economy built over the vascular loop topology. In facing this dilemma, currently there are four different social attitudes connected to the cultural evolution strategies:

1. **Preparationism (serfs/survival).** Preparationists or *preppers* are a subculture that devotes a significant part of its resources and energy gathering the necessary means, infrastructure, and training to survive a large environmental, biological, economic, political, and/or social disruption(211). The conviction of some *preppers* is based on a rational argument such as the possibility of a nuclear war or the collapse of the economy. But there are also those who base their preparations on a delusional idea, such as a zombie apocalypse or some sort of a supernatural event. Individuals with this perspective are not interested in belonging to society or making it lower its risks. For them, a future disaster is a certainty and the best path toward salvation is to remove themselves from society

and its course. That's why an important part of preparationists' efforts are focused on building bunkers and refuges where they can be self-sufficient for extended periods of time and isolated from world. This is not a feasible position for any significant portion of humanity, since redirecting our available resources to patiently wait for the catastrophe and, with any luck, survive the end of civilization, would halt the economy, create shortages and a chaos that would make a recovery impossible. However, despite seeming to be a fringe group, there are examples of preparationist nations. During the COP15 held in Copenhagen, a delegate from the Netherlands was saying to anyone who would listen, that the climate change disaster was unavoidable, at least for his country, because, along with Bangladesh, it's one of the lowest lying regions and, in turn, is greatly exposed to rising sea-levels. For that reason, said country already had a plan in place to invest $1.5 billion a year for the next 100 years, building new ocean barriers, that are expected to withstand rising water levels created by the melting of the polar ice caps. It turns out that what had seemed to be mere boasting really is part of the Netherlands climate change adaptation program, which was recommended by the expert group known as the Delta Commission (212). Toward the end of the Summit, when delegates from poor countries like Bangladesh, with no resources to build giant ocean barriers, faced him, saying that his was a selfish and cynical position, this representative simply said he was sorry for the situation in other countries, but that the impossibility of others to save themselves would not stop the program's development.

2. **Authoritarian denial (masters and lackeys/status quo).** These people, unlike preparationists, do not believe in the imminence of disaster. In the authoritarian world of the masters and lackeys, environmental problems are usually categorized in a state of denial. Several leaders have publicly taken this stance. The most prominent of our time is Donald Trump, who has stated that climate change is a hoax(213). As we saw earlier, authoritarian systems can't survive in highly restrictive environments, and it is unnatural for masters and lackeys to think that the environment is a resource one must take care of or that prosperity should be built by means of protecting common goods. For them, the evidence and explanations about environmental limits are a direct challenge to their worldview,

something that must simply be denied. An often-quoted anthropological example of a society that carried an unsustainable model to its final consequences is Easter Island. Its inhabitants went on logging palm trees, which sustained the ecosystem until the very last one was harvested. Consequently, their society collapsed into chaos to the extreme of even getting to a point where cannibalism was practiced(214). A similar case is that of farmers in Syria, who, during the first decade of this century, faced one of the worst droughts on record in the Middle East. In response, they extracted as much water as they could from the subsoil, at increasingly greater depths, and until the aquifers dried up(215). It's now believed this is a key factor that caused social unrest in the region, given that farmers, bereft of their livelihoods, migrated to the cities where they didn't find jobs either, and on the sum of all the conditions — economic, political and social — the outbreak of civil war became inevitable.

3. **Unfounded optimism (conservatives/growth).** Another attitude is that of genuine conservatives who trust that "science" and "technology" by themselves will be capable of solving the environmental restriction problems. As a matter of fact, the toughest part of the environmental problems we are facing, has to do with scientific and technical aspects, many of them thermodynamic and biological that have not been solved for decades. It's worth mentioning some of them. In 2008, CO_2 capture and sequestration (CCS) was a technological fad that attempted to reduce greenhouse gas emissions. The idea is relatively simple: emissions from large production facilities, such as the ones produced by a coal plant, are scrubbed from CO_2 that gets captured. Then CO_2 is compressed and pumped into deep wells inside porous rock formations where it will theoretically remain stored for millions of years. The problem is that any amount of work requires energy, and CO_2 capture, compression, and pumping involve the use of more energy to produce the same amount of electricity. This means that there's a thermodynamic penalty that, in the best-case scenario, raises the variable production cost by 40% and requires a tenfold increase in the capital costs for the construction of electric power plants.

A similar example is nuclear fusion reactors that, since the seventies, have been unsuccessful in their attempt to produce more energy than the reactor needs to sustain fusion. Another one is the use of algae to produce biodiesel that only works on a small scale, or the use of jatropha seeds as a source of biofuels that cannot be used at a large scale because the plant's life cycle is too long and the fruit's ripening is uneven, which then requires manual harvesting at a very high cost. Under any scenario, it's clear that today science and technology have no silver bullets that allow us to think that it's possible to remain under the open vascular network model. The consensus is that a diverse set of solutions is needed where vascular loop economic network topologies and a collaborative economic model are required. The challenge is that to achieve that, old conservative ideological models that are based on self-interest must be left behind, such as *homo economicus*, and that is very hard to accept. In fact, the current political situation in the United States demonstrates that many conservative billionaires found it easier to support and fund Donald Trump's authoritarian populism, clearly opposite to the open society's economic freedom, than to support a moderately liberal political agenda, which was not even attempting to change the rules that had benefited them for many years. *Fortune* magazine followed up on this issue and stated that investors like Peter Thiel of PayPal Holdings, Inc. and Woody Johnson of Johnson & Johnson Services, Inc. are some of a dozen of big business people who generously supported Trump's campaign(216). Robert Mercer, CEO of Renaissance Technologies, LLC, stands out among them. Apart from backing Trump, he was the key enabler of other initiatives like Cambridge Analytica, Citizens United, Breitbart and the Brexit movement. Thus, sustainability barriers lead conservatives to two different forms of optimism: one is the intuitive and unfounded belief in the supernatural powers of science and technology to sustain growth indefinitely, and the other is the untenable fantasy that allows them to believe authoritarianism has many hidden virtues that justify them to support it.

4. **Collaborative effort (liberals/transformation).** Any older adult who's gone through a long period of physical neglect and no medical attention will probably expect that on the day of a medical appointment, he or she will leave the doctor's office with a list of efforts to be made: eat better, exercise, sleep more, stop smoking, drink less. Nowadays, the construction of vascular loops represents a similar effort: sorting waste, carpooling, using the bicycle, turning

off lights that are not used, being interested in the downstream liabilities and effects of the products we consume, reducing our water consumption and, in a few words, assuming and paying the cost of the negative externalities we create. Like many patients, who as soon as they leave the doctor's office stop by the first convenience shop in their path to buy cigarettes, many other people feel that said list of efforts to address the environmental problems are a cost that detracts from their experience in the world. For the prepper serf, such efforts challenge them to abandon their paranoia and certainty that the apocalypse is near. To masters and lackeys, it confronts them with an unbearable world where — to become successful — involvement, care, and real work is required, instead of just taking away from others, mindlessly exploiting natural resources, and for the conservative, sustainability efforts, all of which would diminish their optimism about unbounded progress, accumulation, and domination.

In each case, the various characters experience a sense of fulfillment when they do things that agree with their world view, and a sense of resistance and frustration when they're immersed in a setting that challenges them. Preparationists must feel great pleasure every day they devote to build and stock their bunkers, as the same happens to liberals when they succeed in the construction of a new urban bicycle route, a reforestation campaign or a legal change that moves things forward toward the construction of the vascular loop economy. This is not a philosophical assertion. Those who leave the doctor's office and truly change their lives do so because they discover that the reward lies in the effort itself. Software developers who devote hundreds, sometimes thousands of unpaid hours to develop programs for open source communities; the countless groups that act guided by community service and solidarity, such as the Scouts and Rotarians; as well as all friendship and family relationships in which the aim is to create value, with no exchange of money and no attempt to control or dominate others, are all examples of the above-mentioned attitude. And naturally, it also is the case for all those economic transactions carried out in good faith, mutual benefit, and with low externality production. Hungarian psychologist Mihály Csíkszentmihályi described this sense of fulfillment, stemming out the accomplishment of difficult things, as a normal and desirable state of human beings. Described as the *"state of flow"*(217), it is an essential part of how innovative and collaborative people act in open systems, where the quorum is set toward the transformational strategy. President John F. Kennedy delivered the speech that best explains this attitude at Rice University in Texas on September 12, 1962(218):

> *We set sail on this new sea because there is new knowledge to be gained, and new rights to be won, and they must be won and used for the progress of all people. For space science, like nuclear science and all technology, has no conscience of its own. Whether it will become a force for good or ill depends on man, and only if the United States occupies a position of pre-eminence can we help decide whether this new ocean will be a sea of peace or a new terrifying theater of war. I do not say the we should or will go unprotected against the hostile misuse of space any more than we go unprotected against the hostile use of land or sea, but I do say that space can be explored and mastered without feeding the fires of war, without repeating the mistakes that man has made in extending his writ around this globe of ours. There is no strife, no prejudice, no national conflict in outer space as yet. Its hazards are hostile to us all. Its conquest deserves the best of all mankind, and its opportunity for peaceful cooperation many never come again. But why, some say, the moon? Why choose this as our goal? And they may well ask why climb the highest mountain? Why, 35 years ago*

> *fly the Atlantic? Why does Rice play Texas? We choose to go to the moon. We choose to go to the moon in this decade and do the other things, not because they are easy, but because they are hard, because that goal will serve to organize and measure the best of our energies and skills, because that challenge is one that we are willing to accept, one we are unwilling to postpone, and one which we intend to win, and the others, too.*

A defining moment like the one Kennedy's speech points to — and that we still don't know whether it will turn in the direction of the competitive or the collaborative model — is the long and devastating drought in the Middle East that, in 2008, even threatened to collapse Israel's economy. Given the urgency to face the challenge, researchers at the Zuckerberg Institute for Water Research achieved a substantial improvement in the efficiency of seawater desalination systems. This allowed Israel, in just a few years, to move away from danger and achieve a surplus in its fresh water supply(215). In this case, the question, yet unanswered, is whether Israel with this new technology and a water surplus will build better relationships with its neighbors and help relieve the regional devastation caused by the drought, or whether it shall exploit this advantage to exert greater regional control. The former will take place if all countries in the region manage to build a bond of trust and collaboration; the latter, if the *quorum* turns in the direction of arrogance in which the authoritarian Arab model butts heads against Israel's stubborn conservatism. Certainly, we don't imagine that in the long history of grievances and resentments that make the Middle East a difficult and volatile region, it is sensible to turn water into a weapon, but, as we've pointed out several times, we are not cast in stone. We have the liberty to choose our own destiny even if it's directed toward destruction.

Unfortunately, the Middle East drought and the different approaches taken both by Syria and Israel reveal the inevitability and unavoidability of the environmental dilemmas in this century. In Syria, backwardness and authoritarian denial made it impossible to follow a different route other than excavating of ultradeep wells. Apart from being sad, the case is paradoxical in addition to the death of thousands and the suffering of millions because of war. In 2015, an intentional attempt was made to destroy the millenary cultural treasures of the city of Palmira. In a region believed to be the cradle of civilization, authoritarians went out of their way to try to destroy the ancient history of humanity. Conversely, just around the corner from Syria, the same crisis met the legendary tenacity and innovation capacities of the Jewish people, who are empowered and enhanced by a *quorum* that tends to freedom and democracy. There, researchers dived into the unknown and solved the problem by means of creativity and reason. The environmental challenge is already here and it's *not* going away. At the end of the day, what we're still missing is a better understanding of our basic response models and the consequences they create in the environment so we can choose the most sensible one and, based on this decision, build with our peers what we need to survive.

The digital era

During most of the evolution of the human social network, information-based transactions were carried out exclusively between people. However, since 1960, with the introduction of the first transactional computing system for airline ticket management known as International Business Machines, Inc., IBM® SABRE®(219), we set out on a path that gave a new and strange shape to the industrial vascular network. Formerly, the airline *hubs* operation completely depended on human interactions; therefore, it had the advantages and disadvantages of tribal social codes. If we went to a customer service window at any analogue *hub* and made a transaction, said procedures were fully in the hands of the employee behind the counter and of the social relationships between the people handling them. Currently, this still is useful and that's why, despite the long faces, we try to treat well whomever is taking care of us at the Department of Motor Vehicles. But as time went by, the interconnection needs and the growth of the vascular network — coupled with the new concept that IBM and American Airlines, Inc. introduced with SABRE — shifted some network barriers like the maximum number of connections imposed by the Dunbar number, and a new structure emerged: the digital transactional *hub*. Thus, a break away from the canons of tribal transactions. With SABRE, the metaphysical idea of the *hub* or institution, powered by people, turned into a tangible and real agent different from humans. For the first time in history, humans made contact or transactions with a different type of information-based agent we now generically call *"the system."*

For the first time in history, we needed to interact, collaborate, and subordinate ourselves to an entity that was not a person. Once we established a relationship and interacted with SABRE and the many other systems that followed it, it became unavoidable to invent concepts and language that gave the system a tangible status such as: "Sir, the system says you don't have a ticket." "The system doesn't want to assign you a seat on the plane." "Without the system, I cannot help you." "I understand the situation, but the system won't do it." "It's because of the system." This means that through the electronic automation of processes, we invented a new type of intermediary that is not subject to the limitations and codes of traditional social relationships. Software is adaptable, flexible, and may be configured in countless different ways. However, it obeys Boolean mathematical logic, and consequently, is rigid, square, and without the ability to respond with flexibility to exceptions and uncertain situations.

Thus, a drastic and complex change began in the balance of network functions. In the first phase of digitization, the digital *hub* became a zealously guarded structure within private corporations and public institutions that helped establish rigid chains of command, standardized processes, reduced costs, and inefficiencies. This gave a great deal of control to those configuring the hub and took influence away from those operating the system. In fact, my professional experience has taught me that this change in influence is so important that in projects where a traditional transactional system, like SABRE, is implemented, the loss of autonomy and the requirement for the operator to become submissive to the system's rules creates immense resistance. Across hundreds of information technology implementation projects in which I've participated since the nineties, there was never any need to do much for users to adopt systems that provided them with autonomy, such as email, instant messaging, mobile telephones, and the web browser. But all over the world, the implementation of transactional systems that go against personal freedom always entail a slow, expensive, awful, and tough battle.

In the nineties, once the digital *hub* became the organization's transactional core and the dust from the person versus the system conflict settled down, the emergence and growth of the Internet and the commercial *world wide web* allowed the development of many more digital *hubs*. This finally shaped a new and versatile network topology called the bus network that, depending on the conditions of the configuration, may result in a centralized or decentralized network, a tree-like pattern, a vascular network or a vascular loop. It all depends on the way in which the network's functions are defined and controlled in the bus. Schematically, the bus network is represented as follows (Figure 23):

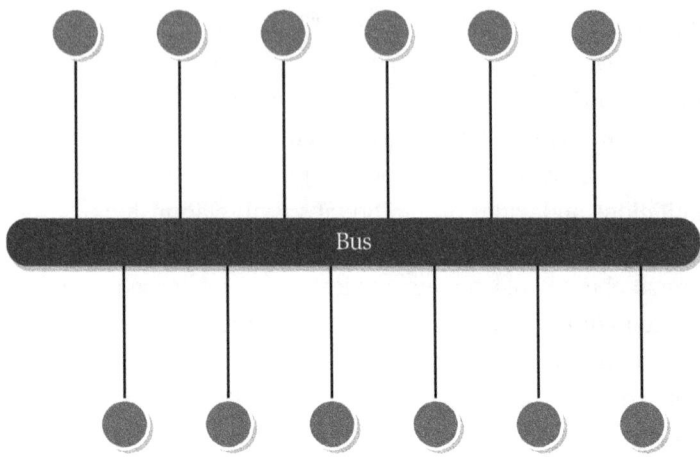

Bus Topology

Figure 23: Bus network.

At first glance, the bus network does not seem like previous topologies, but if we illustrate the case of American Airlines before and after SABRE's implementation, things become more clear (Figure 24).

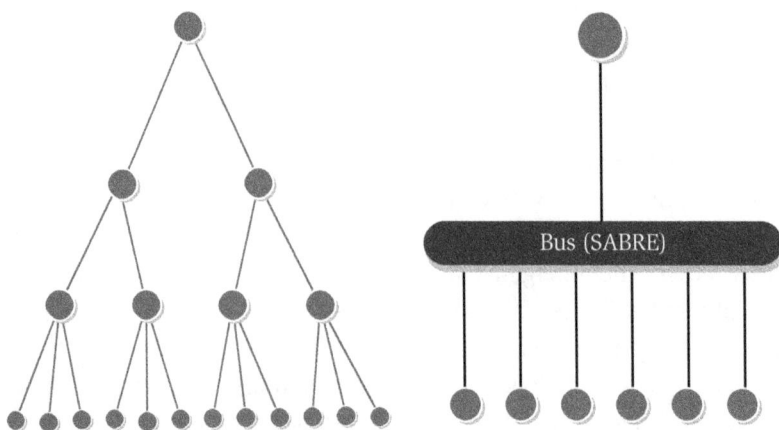

AA without SABRE

AA with SABRE

Figure 24: American Airlines before and after SABRE.

The traditional diagrams of a bus network do not illustrate the system's inner logical relationships, they only show a one-to-many network configuration — billions of nodes in the case of a bus like Facebook. But as said earlier, hidden from the apparent geometry of the network are logical relationships that govern the different operational modes and the topologies that emerge at every layer of a complex network with multiplexing functions. In the case of American Airlines, SABRE's introduction depersonalized the intermediation layer and established a different influence relationship between system designers, bus managers, and system operators. This in turn opened the door for the people-operated institution to become the bus network managed by the platform. In addition to producing efficiency and standardizing the processes, as was the case of airlines with SABRE, this introduced several important questions.

Table 29 contains a summary of properties for the four types of networks that emerge from the cultural evolution model. What's interesting in this exercise is that it's relatively simple to imagine all the properties of analogue networks. However, software's configuration flexibility has left many network properties, functions, and end results undefined such as the random network's size, risk management, filtration, node control (autonomy), robustness, resilience, and persistence.

The missing elements in the description of the new digital model provide clues concerning the current social levels of volatility and instability, which Moisés Naím correctly identified in *The End of Power*(220) and summarized in the phrase: *"In the 21ˢᵗ century, power is easier to get, harder to use and easier to lose."* The digital bus network is flexible enough to adapt to any of the cultural evolution strategies, but just as Kennedy said concerning space and nuclear technology, "It has no conscience of its own." Thus, it does not follow a pre-established path. The bus network is taking shape based on the intentions and ambitions of those who build, control, and use it. It's not something that is happening to us; rather, it's something we're doing to ourselves and that's why it's essential to solve the unknowns, examine the cases, and understand the consequences that the different network configurations and their use will produce in this the digital century.

	Survival	Status quo	Growth	Transformation
Network properties				
Topology	Trophic/ Tribal	Tree/ Agricultural	Industrial/ Vascular	Digital/ Vascular loop
Maximum N	Size of tribe (150)	Empire's surface	Consumer market	Value exchanges
Coordination	Centralized	Stratified	Decentralized	Distributed
Random network	Non-existent	Small	Large	?
Multiplexing	Yes	Yes	Yes	Yes
Layers	Spoken language Mythos Exchange	Spoken and written language Trade Mythos Art Logos	Spoken and written language Industry Telecommunications Marketing Trade Logos Technique Art Mythos	Spoken and written language Cyberspace Telecommunications Marketing Industry Trade Logos Technique Art Mythos
Network functions				
Network economies	Fixed	Fixed/ Growth by expansion	Exponential/ Growth by productivity	Dynamic/ Productivity and adjustments by sustainability
Synchronization	Symbolic/ Natural	Symbolic/ Institutional	Hubs/Rational	Diversified
Validation	Group	Hierarchy	Institution	Platform
Risk management	Group	Hierarchy	Institution	?
Filtered	Group	Hierarchy	Hubs	?
Node control	Group	Hierarchy	Institution	?
Network results				
Complexity	Low	Medium	High	Very high
Robustness	Very low	Low	High	?
Resilience	Very high	High	Low	?
Persistence (years)	90,000	10,000	200	?

Table 29: Summary of network properties for the cultural evolution model.

12. The economy in the 21st century

How can vascular loops be built?

To illustrate the paths that the post-modern society could take toward building an economy based on vascular loops, we will start with a simple example: the soft drink market that is connected to two important contemporary issues that embody the controversy between common good and self-interest. These issues are junk food's adverse effects on consumers' health and environmental pollution by disposable containers.

1. For preparationist serfs, the negative externalities the soft drink industry produce are but one more proof that humanity's end is near. For them, they examine sweetened beverages to determine which product has the longest shelf life and the best available price-amount ratio; or are there alternative methods to recycling liquids in the bunker that avoid the need for bottled drinks, including methods of storing the largest number of containers in the most compact way possible. Also, the more sophisticated preppers consider the nutritional aspects and the long-term effects on health. They may also care to take advantage of the high-energy density of said drinks to survive and the use of empty containers as fuel or as a means of storage. Other serfs, who do not follow this fanaticism about the end of the world, and who disproportionately suffer from malnutrition and undernourishment, will be open to any of two alternatives. First, should they join the authoritarian environmentalism movement and help restore the vertical order in the world, or second, should they abandon the existential prostration created by their external locus of control and join the construction of collaborative design solutions. An example of authoritarian environmentalism would be governmental prohibition, from one day to another, of industrialized beverages. Another example is the crisis that happened in Rwanda in 2008 when the government issued norms prohibiting the

sale of plastic bags. As a result, international environmental organizations celebrated Rwanda's decision, but this vertical and unilateral government choice did not consider the population's needs, particularly those of women who must carry the goods they buy and sell in markets across long distances. This change in regulations created a black market for plastic bags as well as a police system of harassment, extortion, and violence that has led to some housewives being accused and imprisoned for concealed carry of plastic bags(221).

2. For masters and lackeys, what's important is that the world's soft drink companies make investments in their countries, pay taxes that raise the public budget and help politicians on the side, to finance the electoral campaigns and the bureaucracy in exchange for letting them run their business without any government intervention. In this arrangement, the noise made by the media about the negative impact of soft drinks on health helps them gain leverage and negotiate higher tax rates with the industry. But it is also likely, for the same reason, that the regulations that control the direct targeting of children with ads and aggressive distribution and soft drink sales in schools hardly ever change enough to make a difference. In this model, negative costs overflow, provoking an increase of obesity's epidemiology, metabolic and cardiovascular disorders, and diabetes. In the case of the contamination of land, streets, highways, bodies of water, and coastlines due to the low recycling level of plastic containers, no systemic solutions will be found or proposed. Rather, only marginal but well-advertised efforts will be made that show some signs of progress. At the end of the day, the consumer will be held accountable for the problems. He will be the guilty party who requests and buys from industry that harms him and is irresponsible because he does not properly dispose of the containers he buys. Does this sound ridiculous? This is the situation in Mexico, the Number One country in the world in the children's obesity index(222). Moreover, not long ago, in one of those episodes that surpass reality — magic realism, as García Márquez would say — the president decided to capitalize on the Coca-Cola® prestige during an event in which he advocated, without anyone asking him to do so or it being necessary,

the virtues of the company's products besides avowing to be the brand's regular consumer(223). This took place when his popularity was at the lowest level, right after a disastrous and shameful meeting that helped boost Donald Trump's campaign, and at a time when social pressure was building up to change the country's dietary and health policy since seven of every ten adults is either overweight or obese(224), and per capita consumption of soft drinks is the fourth highest in the world with 137 liters a year(225).

3. For conservatives, every problem is an opportunity. Epidemiological data like that of Mexico indicates that sale of medicines and treatments related to the negative externalities created by junk foods can be good business. Unfortunately for the population, simple prevention measures and treatments have poor returns on capital, so investment in this type of solutions will be low. In addition to the medical industry, the problems related to the soft drink industry have a positive impact on beauty and personal care products, as well as in miracle products. In fact, malnutrition and undernourishment stimulate the growth of the vascular network. In the overall balance of corporate finances, the existence of chronic and complex public health issues that are difficult to resolve is a significant part of economic well-being. From this viewpoint, to make the externalities transparent and incorporate their cost into the transactions forestalls market growth and innovation, so the construction of vascular loops in the industry does not seem either viable or necessary. Environmental contamination is worse, but conservatives are optimistic. They believe a healthy economy and a degraded environment are better than a clean environment and a degraded economy. So, caring for the environment is opposed to a good working economy. And what they fail to see is that building vascular loops would translate into the explosive growth of a part of the economy that is underdeveloped. That is the most important growth opportunity we will have in this century; but to take advantage of this, it is indispensable to change the economy's topology.

4. It will take a while for liberals to review the different angles of problems like this one. They will seek solutions that close the vascular loop, so things change in favor of the largest number of

stakeholders with a lower level of negative externalities and a lower social cost. Thus, it would be necessary to use more effort and intelligence to explore and query the different and barely visible aspects of the problem, such as the following:

1) **Access to drinking water sources**. For many people — most unwilling members of the random network — packaged and industrialized products are the most accessible and safe options for hydration, but precisely because of the precarious situation these people live in, these products are expensive for them; resulting in this consumption impoverishing them even more. This means that part of the solution requires the reform of municipal water systems, the access to safe drinking water in schools and public places, and the reallocation of investment budgets in infrastructure, as well as making the public and private entities that manage these systems accountable for better results. It is evident that in many cases, government incompetence to build the public goods that guarantee access to drinking water is one of the growth pillars of the soft drink and junk food industries.

2) **Review of manufacturing practices for these products.** Sugary beverages, such as cola drinks, contain 34 milligrams of caffeine for each 354-milliliter can(226). This concentration can be enough to produce and promote a habit's progression, but not enough to compete with the stimulating effect of a cup of coffee that on average provides 150 to 200 milligrams of caffeine. This is important because for someone to become "hooked on caffeine," the abstinence syndrome can be severe with symptoms, such as intense headaches, if the daily consumption is less than 200 milligrams a day, equal to 5.8 cans of a caffeinated soft drink. The low caffeine concentration in soft drinks seems to be part of a hidden and unconscious stimulus for the consumer, who needs to attain a large enough dosage of 200 to 400 milligrams a day, equal to one cup of coffee in the morning and another in the afternoon. To meet that, such a person would need to drink more than 11 cans of cola a day, a common consumption pattern for some market segments. In the age of cognitive marketing and stimulus engineering, the technology behind product formulation must become transparent and monitored. In the

same way that we go to watch a magician's act, knowing we are going to be deceived through illusion, we now can consent to our senses being deceived in the market. But accepting deceit should be an informed, conscious, and personal decision. In the case of children, it is important to review the most reliable medical evidence on caffeine consumption, so parents can act accordingly. The same happens for refined sugars that, in certain concentrations and combined with caffeine, have metabolic and psychological effects that are not evident for the consumer.

3) **Health and environmental externalities cost assessment**. The difficult matter that needs careful reflection and probably a flexible trial and error process, are the many ways external costs can be internalized. If the costs are simply impossible to pay for one or all market participants, given the externality costs are greater than the sales volume, it will be necessary to completely rethink the market structure. For example, in the soft drink industry, there are three main packaging materials: aluminum for cans, polyethylene terephthalate (PET) for most products, and glass for some special containers. For each type of packaging, the recycling situation is different. Aluminum is easy to collect, recycle, and has a high recycle price. When it's not collected, it is chemically stable and not easily incorporated into the food chain. PET has a low price in the recycling market, is chemically unstable because it's light and fragile, easily scatters and fragments in water and soil, plus, has toxic effects on the terrestrial and marine food chain. Finally, glass is an inert material that is easy to recycle; it does not disperse nor is it easily dragged by water currents. Neither does it enter the food chain; but due to its weight and fragility, its handling is the most expensive. In addition, when used in returnable containers, environmental costs increase due to use of water used for washing the bottles and, in this system, there are higher capital and labor costs for the bottling plants, and an increased use of fuel to transport it. Probably, once all the direct and indirect environmental costs are considered as well as the resources needed to do the environmental remediation of accumulated damages, the costs saved by soft drink bottlers with the use of PET will be insignificant against the cost of the environmental damage.

So, in that scenario, using glass once again as the main container in the industry may become a more sustainable option, once all the costs have been tallied.

As it can be seen, it won't be easy to close the vascular networks in an economy in which natural resources enter on one side and trash comes out on the other with very little recycling. To begin, we will need to consider options that today aren't evident, can't be solved in a static way, and must change in an evolutionary fashion that adjusts to a shifting environment. For example, in the soft drink industry, we're still lacking the required data to reach a conclusion, but it's very likely that once similar cases have been analyzed, it will be more sensible to abandon some deeply rooted contemporary practices, such as the exaggerated usage of plastic. In some places, this has already begun. In September 2016, the French government issued legislation to eliminate the sale of disposable plastic utensils and urged the European Parliament to study the case and implement measures to reduce environmental pollution(227). It's essential that these types of decisions and changes be made in an informed fashion since the closing of vascular loops aims to make the network larger and more stable, not to break them apart.

Case 1: The digital tree or "Welcome to the UBER™ world"

In 2008, Travis Kalanick and Garrett Camp, technologists from Silicon Valley, were in Paris. They had problems finding a taxi during a snowfall, so they asked themselves: "Why can't we get a cab by just touching a key on the cell phone?" This is one of those cases where the right people posed the right question in the ideal conditions for it to be answered and further developed. At the time, three technologies had already matured enough to enable Uber Technologies, Inc. foundation and success. First, with the introduction of the Apple® iPhone® in 2007, a fast and explosive expansion of the mobile Internet took off via the *smartphones*. Second, these new devices had an "App Store", a virtual shopping mall or centralized *hub* for the retail sale of software created by manufacturers like Apple to increase the cell phones' functions in the post-sale stage. In the case of the iPhone, the App Store (called Apple Store) allowed hundreds of thousands of programmers, such as Kalanick and Camp, to gain easy and effective access to a huge consumer market estimated to have surpassed 2 billion iPhones in 2016. Third, technology transition of software services known as Application Programming Interfaces (APIs) became part of the smartphone functions enabling small software programs called *apps* to access and interconnect to a smartphone's sophisticated geo-location and navigation platforms such as Google Maps™ and Waze™ or to electronic payment systems like Visa® and Mastercard®. The APIs are interconnection interfaces with which a system can exchange messages safely and reliably with another system without any problems of compatibility or repudiation. That is, the APIs are a mechanism for creating interoperability capacities in an electronic network even when the systems' architectures and languages are different.

The above-mentioned means that Uber Technologies, rather than being a technology developer, is a technological orchestrator that builds the UBER™ service on a sophisticated multi-layered digital platform. At a physical level, the service runs on mobile telephone networks and users' smartphones. It is distributed and updated via the App Store and is made possible by API integration with Google LLC's navigation services (Waze™) and the international financial payment network. This form of innovation is called innovation through the disruption of the business model.

To understand how Uber Technologies works, we must first examine the workings of the traditional rental car market, universally known as taxis. The taxi precedes the automobile, and there are records of horse-drawn rental services of carriages and regulations in the United Kingdom as far back as the 17ᵗʰ century(228). The business model we know today as the traditional one took shape in the first half of the 20ᵗʰ century when, almost unanimously, city governments around the world decided to regulate such services at the dawn of the automobile era. The main aspects regulated by city officials were: 1) control and registration of drivers, 2) control of the number of vehicles in service to prevent an oversupply (color and labeling of units, ID plates), and 3)establishing a measurement mechanism based on time and distance that estimates the price of each trip (taximeter).

The interesting point about this traditional model is that despite government intervention to control the market in terms of network structure, taxi systems have remained working as a random network. Here, the role of government has focused on the access and control of suppliers into the substrate; in this case, substrate means the clients who needed the taxi services (Figure 25). Thus, within the substrate or market, supply and demand meet in a random fashion. Before Uber Technologies marketed it's UBER services, users had to go out to the street and randomly search for an available cab, like Kalanick and Camp did during that memorable snowfall in Paris. This way of doing things is changing, and it will definitely disappear in a few years with Uber Technologies and other similar companies.

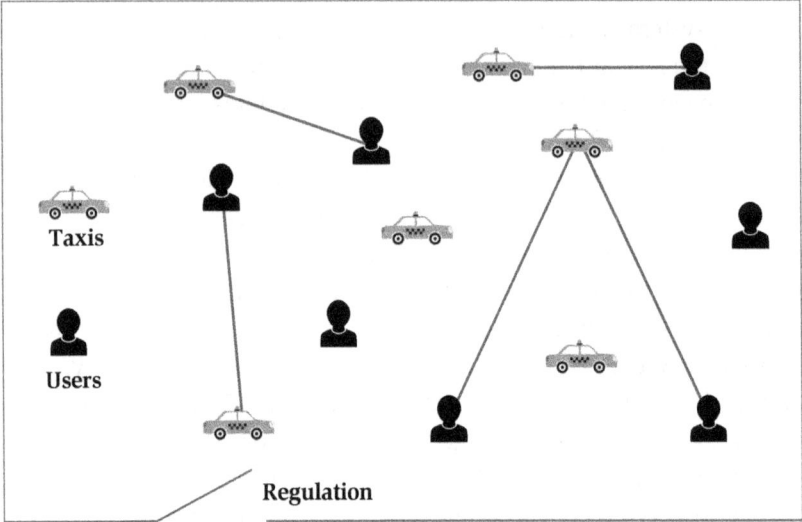

Figure 25: Topology of the traditional taxi market.

Besides the inefficiency of random operation, the traditional taxi model resembles an enclosure where the prey (consumers) are captive, while the government regulation only controls the number of predators (taxis) into the substrate, ensuring there are enough of the former, so the latter won't go hungry. In this system, the network functions are exclusively access and control, and they are fully in the hands of regulators and cab drivers. Given that there are no scale and synchronization functions, consumers are forced to use whatever service is provided. This means that in many cities across the world taxi services are insufficient, of poor quality, and maintain a high cost.

In the Uber model, the *app* and the new systems have given the market a new form (Figure 26). For starters, they bypassed government control of access to the substrate by using the telecommunications networks — literally through the air. That is, they managed to easily add new players to a market that once was very difficult to access. To further illustrate this, look at the prices taxi concessions reached in New York City between 2013 and 2014. A price of more than $1 million per unit was reached because only 13,605 taxi medallions (concessions) were available for the entire city(229).

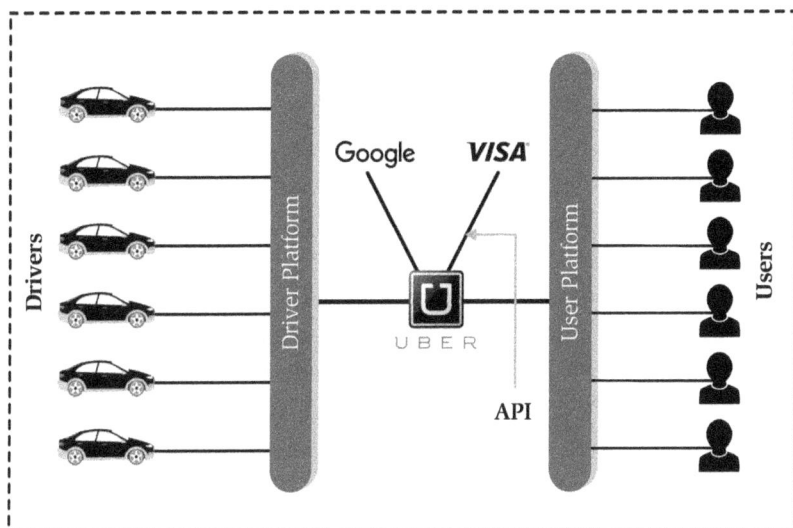

Figure 26: Market topology with UBER.

They created and centralized a network synchronization function that works by means of the Google Location Service™ and its geo-location platforms, the GPS (global positioning system) sensors incorporated in all smartphones and the optimization algorithms embedded in UBER software. In doing so, Uber Technologies was able to create an automatic dispatch system that efficiently linked supply and demand in real time. Moreover, it added new digital validation mechanisms, like the rating system that allows users and operators to evaluate each other recipro-cally; thereby, creating constant pressure to maintain service quality.

Although a change of a market's topology is a sufficiently disruptive in-novation, the new UBER model, based on digital efficiency, data gathering, and analysis, enabled new functions, previously unimagined, that really changed the 21ˢᵗ century economy. The capacity to know in real time the supply and demand conditions of the market allows for the establishment of dynamic rates that are adjusted by location and demand conditions. Combined, the elimination of market barriers and the dynamic rates allowed Uber Technologies to offer the consumer significantly lower prices with which the three variables of the network market improved: more coverage (by eliminating barriers and matching in real time the supply with the demand), better quality (with the evaluation system and driver navigation assisted by Waze), and a lower price (with dynamic rates and data analysis).

Besides the prior advantages, the company segmented the market with different types of vehicles: UberX™, UberBLACK™, and UberSUV™, and in some markets, even helicopters. It also introduced new products that stem from the shared economy concept to lower prices even further. With UberPOOL™, several passengers with a similar destination can share the same trip, and in some markets, UberCOMMUTE™ allows anyone on a daily trip, going from the suburbs to the city, to drive additional users and become compensated for the service with a fuel fee.

This way, in August 2016, Uber Technologies was the first global rental car company with more than eight million users and operations in 400 cities and 70 countries. Its market capitalization was estimated to be over $60 billion, more than 100-year old companies like The Ford Motor Company valued at a little over $50 billion at the end of the first half of 2016. It took six years for Uber Technologies to reach the first billion trips, but only six months to get a billion more(230). According to *Bloomberg News*, in that first half of 2016, the company lost a little over $1.2 billion investing in its growth(231). Nonetheless, it was able to achieve all that without owning either the vehicles or the telecommunications networks, without manufacture of any kind nor having drivers as formal employees or buying taxi concessions from the regulators.

So far, UBER seems to be an absolute, positive success of the digital economy that has benefited the consumer and won over the inefficient analog economy model. At a glance, the comparison between Figure 25 and Figure 26, seems to show that companies like Uber Technologies transform a costly random network into an effective digital vascular network. The problem is that the apparent topology of the network needs to be analyzed considering the network's internal or logical configuration.

To start with, we should point out that many of the new business models created and developed in the digital domain exist in an unregulated space since the discussion about the construction of governance in the digital era has not yet started. For now, some negotiations are just beginning to take place regarding the technical aspects (e.g., the Internet governance), but they are far from what's needed. In the case of Uber Technologies against the taxis, transport regulators don't fully understand the change, and therefore, they still don't know what their role is and what actions they should take.

Throughout history, the new areas of opportunity in misgoverned sectors, such as the conquest of the Western U.S., have followed three stages of development:

1. **The Gold Rush (short-term).** It is the time when players like Uber Technologies reach an exponential expansion that generates a gold rush, which, in turn, attracts countless players to the new market. This has been the situation during the first years of the new digital model, but it's already beginning to change.
2. **Law of the Gun (mid-term).** Uber Technologies impact on the market — the medallions' depreciation in New York and the lack of clients for the traditional taxi fleets — is going to produce despair, rivalry, and a free-for-all tension. Some participants will wage a price war, others will take aggressive measures (shutdowns, blockades, confrontations), and others who are unknown for now, will compete with Uber Technologies directly. This future competition will only exacerbate the confrontations which will go on until one of two things happens: 1) either Uber Technologies (or a similar company) monopolizes the market, or 2) the confrontation becomes unsustainable. In either of the two options, the space Uber Technologies services occupies, and where it expands will continue to be misgoverned. In fact, said confrontation already began in many cities. Some medallion owners in New York have filed legal actions against the regulatory authorities for their lack of action against Uber Technologies demanding payment for damages caused by a 50% reduction in the price of medallions. Other cities have imposed restrictive measures to the new system, and in others, groups of taxi drivers, desperate due to a drop in their earnings, have attacked drivers in the streets. Of course, none of the previous cases is viable in the long term nor is it the most positive one for the market.
3. **Institutionalization (long-term).** Because of the car rental service's importance in cities across the world, institutional mechanisms will be established to stabilize the market. For the time being, no

one knows what that form will be, and most likely, the issue will follow a trial and error process. This stage will arrive when the stakeholders get tired of living under the law of the gun and will depend on the maturity and common sense of those involved. In the Old West in the U.S., the law of the gun declined when the railroads arrived, the cities grew, and institutions such as courts, sheriffs, and the army were established. In the digital domain, this process will come with the construction of digital governance.

Another critical point the Uber Technologies case reveals is the company's dominance over the network functions, and consequently, over the real network topology. Given that Uber Technologies is not a public enterprise, there is no reliable data, only some leaked information and estimates made by different analysts; thus, it is difficult to obtain hard data. Nevertheless, it is possible to analyze the company's public behavior and compare Uber Technologies network configuration against the traditional taxi model (Table 30).

	Traditional taxi	Uber Technologies
Network properties		
Topology	Random	Digital tree
Maximum N	City	Global
Coordination	No coordination	Centralized, digital
Network functions		
Network economies	No	Yes, defined and intermediated by Uber
Synchronization	Poor or inexistent	Centralized in real time
Validation	Sporadic, centralized and partial (only taxi)	Permanent and centralized (taxi and user)
Risk management	Independent (for each node)	Centralized in real time
Filtered	Independent (for each node)	Centralized in real time
Node control	Centralized, reactive, based on policies	Centralized, based on data

Table 30: Network properties and functions of the traditional market against Uber Technologies.

What immediately stands out is the UBER identification as a tree-like network instead of a digital vascular network. This network occurs even though it has a vascular network's properties, when Uber Technologies matches supply and demand, then adds sharing network functions like UberPOOL, most of the important network functions are monopolized and centralized by the platform. The most relevant one, as well as the company's Achilles heel in the long term, is that the operators (drivers) and partners (vehicle owners) have no say in determining prices; they can only accept them or reject them.

Moreover, Uber Technologies has not modified another issue that is one of the weakest points of the traditional taxi model. Around the world, the traditional system usually lacks means to repay the capital that the partners contribute to the system. Uber Technologies' rates are structured in a way that allows for the payment of the variable operating expenses, a subsistence wage for the operator, and some income for the partner. And as the experiment with the marshmallow demonstrated, most partners are usually unable to save enough of their income to buy a new vehicle when their current one reaches the end of its life cycle. This partly explains the perpetual lack of investment and poor state of taxis practically everywhere. Conversely, in the secondary markets of medallions, license plates, permits, and taxi concessions, the partners' viewpoint before UBER was that most of the capital was in the concession's resale price. When UBER joined the market, prices dropped, and in the case of New York, it's said that the secondary market of concessions valued in more than $13 billion lost 50% of its value from 2014 to 2015. The unknown factor here is that we don't know what will happen when the markets become saturated. Will Uber shut down market access? Will there be a secondary market for places in the market? Will the partners be able to reinvest in the system?

Currently, various estimates say that Uber Technologies wealth of information and the analytic potential of its data enabled this company to find two numbers that allow it to grow explosively at the expense of the system's operators and partners. In Mexico City, a personal survey of operators and businessmen with units both in the traditional sector and inside Uber Technologies revealed that since the company's arrival, rates have been progressively and unilaterally declining, reaching a minimum subsistence wage of 6,000 pesos a month for an operator working 12 hours a day, and a return on investment that prevents even the most disciplined partners to recover their capital cost at the end of the vehicle's life cycle.

Through data analysis, Uber Technologies was able to find the minimum income level operators are willing to accept in Mexico City. Various organizations had estimated via different methods a wage level below which the worker begins to feel desperate for not being able to pay for his minimum needs, and this varies in every country. In other words, the data indicates there is a wage level at which people cease to be part of the vascular network and consequently fall into the harsh world of the random network. For example, many banks in Mexico don't think a consumer is profitable when his income is less than 6,000 pesos a month. Other studies reach a similar conclusion when reviewing the minimum income level that motivates the Mexican farmer to run the risk of migrating to the U.S. In 2010, it was estimated at 5,452.10 pesos a month ($3,271.26 a year), calculated by dividing the earnings from remittances(232) among rural households(233). In 2011, the Universidad Iberoamericana in Puebla estimated that according to price levels of that year, for the constitutional precepts of wellbeing to have been fulfilled, a minimum wage of 6,500 pesos a month was necessary(234). Currently domestic workers in Mexico City — one of the lowest levels of access to the labor market — earn around 6,000 pesos a month. On the other hand, the *Washington Post* published that the wage in dollars-per-hour for an UBER driver is $8.10 in Detroit, $9.93 in Houston, and $12.17 in Denver, which is very close to, or even below, minimum wage levels in those cities(235).

The conclusion is that the information asymmetry between Uber Technologies partners, drivers, and consumers lets the company know precisely all the market's elasticity functions and use them: 1) to bring down operators' earnings exactly within their tolerance limits of a minimum subsistence level and long workdays; 2) to squeeze the earnings of partners who already have an investment cost in the vehicle's value they extract a low income with no possibility of repaying the capital at the end of the car's life cycle; 3) to charge rates at a fixed intermediation rate of 25% over sales. That is, Uber Technologies earns the same if it sells one thousand $5-trips or five hundred $10 trips, although for partners and operators it's not the same to invoice the same amount with twice the effort; and 4) to subsidize low rates for clients, while the market's exponential growth is being fed at the expense of partners and operators. Thus, in the misgoverned digital world, companies like Uber

Technologies find new business formulas to restructure analogue markets and have enough leverage to configure the business models either
in a competitive or a collaborative direction. So far, Uber Technologies
has chosen a competitive design philosophy due to the absolute control
of network functions and information asymmetries that let it maximize
variables in its favor. But this makes the company repeat the economy's
classic agent and principal problems:

1. **Adverse selection**. The capacity to establish a fixed rate of 25%
    against the non-optional dynamic rates of partners and operators
    is a clear sign that what benefits Uber Technologies does not ben-
    efit the partners. If the sales volume grows with trips at a lower
    price, Uber earns the same, but the partners don't. This pushes
    partners and operators to work longer hours to earn more money.
    If, in the mid-term, Uber Technologies were to keep the hegemony
    in the market, the unilateral control of the rates could allow it to
    set prices at all sides of the market. Without long-term competi-
    tion, and because of the market barrier that represents matching
    the platform's size and functionality, there´s a real risk for Uber
    Technologies to consolidate as an international monopoly.
2. **Conflict of interest**. Uber Technologies could easily establish a fi-
    nancial mechanism so that each trip contributes a small percentage
    to a personalized fund, and after a certain period, the partner could
    withdraw his initial capital or reinvest it in the system. In the long
    run, this financial services part of the company could even become
    an important business line. But for the time being, Uber Technol-
    ogies is focused on expansion because the rate structure doesn't
    conceive the repayment of the partners' capital costs. This is clearly
    an example of a conflict of interest between the company and the
    partners. Uber Technologies, as a company, follows a plan that bet-
    ter serves the interests of risk investors who financed the platform
    development in Silicon Valley to the detriment of local partners who
    provided the capital goods that created the vehicle fleet.
3. **Moral risk**. The large information asymmetry lets Uber Technologies
    model and accurately forecast the operators' sensitivity and limits
    in terms of working more and earning less before they drop from
    the system. This new capacity to nudge the agents' behavior via the
    electronic platforms was recently called algorithmic management.

The observations that led to the adoption of this concept point out that platforms developed by Uber Technologies and Lyft, Inc. that provide their systems with autonomy to interact with humans, has made the machine the human's foreman(236). In Uber Technologies case, the digital system is programmed to assign work, give support (e.g., navigation), and assess the worker's performance, as well as send directive feedback to the operator — carrots or bread crumbs — that motivate him to remain connected and behave in a certain way on the platform. This problem is like that of caffeine in cola soft drinks. For a long time, business people have sought a way to manipulate employee and consumer decisions, but until recently there were no effective tools to do so. In this new era driven by massive data analysis in which the detailed and personal knowledge of our sensitivity is hidden, little by little we become more vulnerable to manipulation, and the evidence shows that said new capacity is being used without any restrictions.

For those who work in the field of contemporary management that fosters participative, creative, fair, and collaborative management for companies in the 21st century, the UBER model will appear to be a setback to the Taylorist era, which is hardly sustainable in the long term. In fact, because of the centralized and unilateral rates control, the asymmetry in the information, the agent-principal problems and the lack of control over exorbitantly long work hours, officials are starting to sympathize and work in favor of collective actions such as the creation of trade associations that are the forerunner of trade unions(237).

Currently, we are in the dark regarding the detailed discussions that made Uber Technologies's owners decide on the ongoing network configurations, but there are other stories we can use to make some comparisons. For example, in 2004, before Google's initial public offering, Sergey Brin and Larry Page adopted and propagated "Don't be evil" as their slogan, a phrase that guided their collaborators' ethical approach for years. For Jeff Bezos of Amazon, low profit margins of around 2% is a competitive advantage that pushes them to be efficient and protects them from the competition(238). In Uber Technologies, there is a global code of conduct that refers to the operators' behavior but says nothing about business ethics or the company's corporate behavior, which matches the evidence presented here.

The Uber Technologies model could have adopted elements from Google LLC's original slogan and "not be evil" in what refers to the use of information to determine wages, since the efficiencies it introduced into the market allow it to easily offer rates, so operators can earn above the subsistence level and work a reasonable number of hours. It, too, could have innovated with a financial mechanism for partners to gain back the capital invested in their vehicles. At the same time, it would have been terrific had it adopted a long-term business vision, like Jeff Bezos, and looked for a lower, dynamic intermediation rate with which the good and bad times would be shared with partners and operators. With the huge amount of data it processes, it would be easy to show all participants the real transport costs of passengers in urban areas and, thereby, put together a global innovation community and create collaborative value. But at the end of the day, despite the huge step implied in transforming an anachronistic random network into an efficient digital network that satisfies consumers due to the service's convenience and the low prices, everything indicates that Uber Technologies has decided to build an immense, authoritarian, and stratified digital tree network to effectively extract income from the base, add it through the bus and concentrate it in Silicon Valley.

Probably, Uber Technologies wager to consolidate itself in this way will be to build a strong alliance with consumers maintaining convenience, investing in advertising and low prices. However, the first adverse reactions to the model and the company have begun to emerge in different places, both from external stakeholders who have been alienated and affected by the change — the millions of taxi drivers at risk of losing their income and the wealth that the medallions' value represents — as well as the internal participants, the partners and operators, upset by the great effort they have invested in building the company that is not acknowledged in the rate structure. At the same time, government officials who are trying to understand the role they should play are starting to see that even in the digital world said changes come hand-in-hand with political pressure at a local level.

If in addition to all this, we consider the possible arrival to the market of the autonomous vehicle in the next few years, which will put at risk many millions of jobs in the world's transport industry when automation is already pressuring the labor market downward on different fronts, it's easy to see that a great storm is approaching linked to consolidation of digital networks configured like those of Uber Technologies. That is because currently many of the large participants in the technological industry (Google, Apple, Uber), as well as in the automobile industry (The Ford Motor Company, General Motors LLC, Tesla Motors, Inc.) are focusing their energy in transport automation, and they don't plan to stop. In fact, in August 2016 Uber Technologies ran the first commercial test with autonomous vehicles in Pittsburgh(239). In the long run, the whole idea is to eliminate operators since they are the biggest cost component in the equation.

With this configuration, the idea of a bilateral symmetry network topology collapses. The model transforms into a tree or a pyramid, without intermediation layers, a Parthenon (Figure 27). If we were to take this new configuration to the point of absurdity and present a world where only the digital platform and the users exist and there are very few jobs, income would rapidly concentrate like it did during the Victorian Era. The random network would explode, and social sustainability would be lost. So, despite the efficiency for the consumer and the technological innovation, the intended model moves us away from the construction of robust and persistent vascular loops.

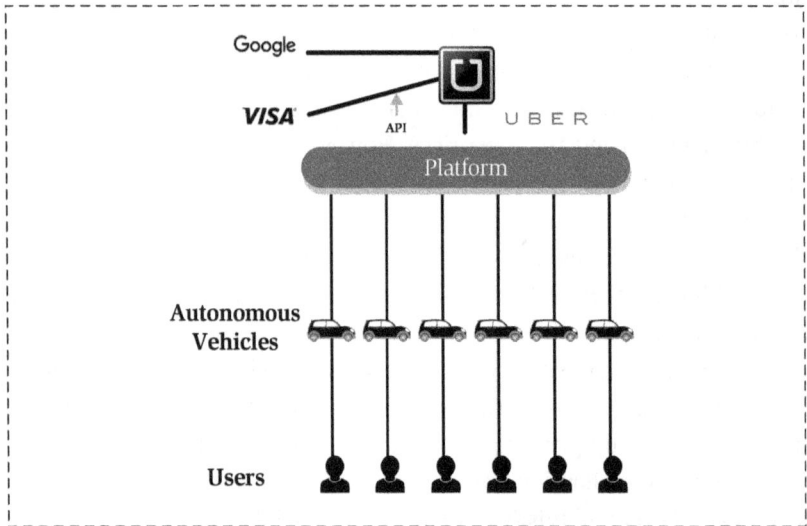

Figure 27: Automated passenger transport network or digital Parthenon.

In the past, the creative destruction of the old part of the economy to accommodate the productivity increase of the new economy resulted in employment and market growth. In 1914, Henry Ford made a highly questioned decision at the time: to reduce the working day from nine to eight hours and raise wages from $2.34 to $5.00 a day(240), which would equal $118.26 a day or $14.78 per hour in 2016(241). That is a substantially larger amount than what an UBER operator earns today in many U.S. cities. During Ford's time, the production line, introduced in 1913, created a massive automobile market with low prices. Ford's actions established a model that articulated and stimulated the industrial vascular network's development on both sides: they created millions of well-paid jobs and reduced the price of consumer goods.

Today, the companies developing autonomous transport systems that take examples from the past say that automation is a new, creative destruction phase that will produce jobs in the high technology industries. In Ford's era, blacksmiths, stablemen, and saddlers who made a living from the horse transport industry disappeared to give way to millions of more jobs in the existing rail, automotive and truck transport industry. It was a change from an agricultural tree network topology to a bilateral vascular network. But the evidence of the last decades points out that the destructive creation that produces automation is not being compensated by an equal or larger number of jobs in the advanced technology industries. According to *Businessweek*, in 2015 there were only 18 million people with software programming skills in the world, of which 11 million were professionals and 7 million, enthusiasts(242). And it's very likely that most of the systems we currently use, such as IBM® SABRE®, which is still in operation, were developed by a small fraction of the total number of those programmers. This shows there are cases in which the economy's automation and creative destruction can modify the network topology in a regressive way, such as going from a bilateral vascular network to a digital Parthenon. Hence, it is worthwhile to reflect on what Kennedy said: "Technology does not have its own conscience," which means that the path of technological development reflects our own aspirations of what we want to achieve and of our own conscience.

Case 2: The hacked economy or "Welcome to the Nespresso® world"

It is estimated that after 30 years in the market, Nespresso® — the affiliate company of Nestlé®, the Swiss conglomerate devoted to the production and sale of coffee systems in capsules or in single portions — sold $4.5

billion of product in 2015(243). Notwithstanding the current success of this segment of the world coffee market, the business model originated in a friendly marital battle. In 1975, Eric Favre, a Swiss aerospace engineer, joined Nestle's packaging department to learn how multinational enterprise works. At the time, his wife, originally from Italy, insisted that the Swiss "didn't know a thing about coffee," so Favre decided to show her he could produce the best espresso in the world. To do so, he explored Rome's coffee shops together with his wife until he focused his attention on the preparation technique of a coffee shop called Caffe Sant'Eustachio in Rome(244). Some months later in 1976, he built the first prototype of what would be the Nespresso system. For a decade, his invention suffered internal resistance inside Nestle, but due to his perseverance, it was finally launched in the market in 1986.

The rest is history. In 2015, after decades of double digit growth rates, Nespresso, the owner of several patents linked to Favre's invention, had sales of approximately 23% of Nestle's division of liquid and powdered drinks, which sold a total of $19.62 billion(245) of product. For us to have a reference of Nestle's magnitude and importance in the coffee world, the company's annual report for that year states that every second 6,000 cups of the NESCAFE® brand's soluble coffee are prepared around the world.

Conversely, in 1990, Peter Dragone and John Sylvan, two American entrepreneurs, founded the company named Keurig® (which means 'excellence' in Danish) based on the idea that they could solve a small, but persistent problem in offices throughout the country(246): the coffee prepared every morning under the standard modality of drip coffee makers kept its good taste only for a short time. Office workers were forced to drink bitter and burnt coffee the greater part of the day. Based on a similar logic as Favre's, Dragone, and Sylvan focused on the design and manufacture of a system of individual coffee portions. After many difficulties and failures, they finally released to the market in 1998 the capsules system called K-cup®. It's the single-serving coffee system with highest sales in the U.S., a market valued at $3.43 billion in 2015(247).

At first sight, Nespresso and Keurig seem to be classic examples of success in market economies. A pair of innovators identifies a problem or an economic inefficiency, develops a creative solution, finds the partners who provide the capital for implementing their idea, and their innovation becomes successful. Clients are satisfied with the efficiency, the investors and innovators assure a long-term success, their ideas are protected through patents, and the economy grows and becomes more efficient.

Coffee capsules are a good example that allows us to examine a situation that is part of the discussion of value, inequality, and the new models of the hacked economy. First, we must consider that the term *to hack* currently has two opposite meanings: one refers to the clever modification of a system or equipment to create something new and beneficial; the other is taking control of a system or equipment with insidious ends. That said, in our mental model of the market economy, a part of the social pact is implicit. People have the freedom to create and innovate because in doing so they introduce efficiencies that once they've expanded massively in the economy, produce a larger social benefit, greater even than the earnings the innovator captures, and which are also socially well-accepted like the equivalent of the respect and privilege awarded to the tribe's best hunter. Amazon Corporate LLC, Ford, and the PC industry illustrate this form of doing things. The companies innovate, transfer efficiencies to society, and most of their positive externalities are then transferred to the economy, which creates value while the company itself — its investors and innovators— capture part of the efficiency as earnings. This is a key part of the open society's operation. In the long run, innovations are disseminated, markets mature, products that were a novelty at first become generic, and sales growth rates and profit margins drop. However, the opposite model existed: that of opportunism and rentierism that makes the closed society turn around. In it, the intent is to maintain or generate a cost, an inefficiency in the economy that, when captured, becomes a profit for someone. This is when we can say that the economy, in the negative meaning of the word, has been hacked. In the first model, there is a positive-sum game (everyone wins) and in the second, we are dealing with a zero-sum game because one person's gain is the loss of another.

It was until the 20th century, with the dismantling of John D. Rockefeller's Standard Oil Company in 1911 following 30 years of legal battles, when in the Western world's democracies, the importance of fighting against the rentier and monopolistic business model was shown. After the Great Depression, President Franklin D. Roosevelt defined a new route for the government, strengthening the antitrust laws, and creating oversight agencies. Thus, in the second half of the 20th century, capitalism, innovation, and competition became the lynchpins of growth and development, with a tacit agreement that efficiencies had to be transferred to consumers. Little by little, different companies discovered that this unwritten market rule that fell outside the already established antitrust standards has a workaround: market rules can be followed on the innovation front while monopolistic prices can be charged in the market.

In the case of Favre, Dragone, and Sylvan, the coffee capsules eliminated the consumer, cited by some market experts as the biggest in the world: the kitchen sink where a substantial part of the coffee prepared with the traditional drip method is thrown away. With the new model, Nestle and Keurig discovered they could create great efficiency: while individual coffee consumption increased, the capsules reduced the amount of grains necessary for each cup. The problem is that the benefits were not transferred to the market, and we can easily prove this by comparing the cost per kilo of coffee. The Nespresso and Keurig capsules contain, on average, five or six coffee grams. In the retail world, that would be $133 per kilogram. The cost of a high-quality kilo of coffee beans varies from $30 to $65, that is, 2 to 4.5 times cheaper (3.25 times on average) than in the one-cup capsules. According to *Bloomberg News*(248), the effects of coffee capsule systems changed the market structure. Despite the capsules' sales increase, the new efficiencies pushed down the demand growth of raw materials and the reduction in coffee prices did not translate into a price drop for the consumer, which then guaranteed an additional benefit for Nespresso and Keurig.

That's why the results of this segment are so good. According to a *New York Times* report in 2012, a Nespresso spokesman explained that the coffee capsules market represented 8% of the volume but 25% of revenue(249). This is possible because of two things. First, Keurig and Nespresso have patents to protect both the machines and the consumables, so they could exclusively exploit the market. In the same way as many printer manufacturers, Keurig and Nespresso sold the only cartridges available on the market. Second, many consumers simply trusted them, asked no questions and became oblivious to the products they consume. Convenience was worth more than the family's economy as alienation and pleonexia took away the time and space for conscious reflection. In this case, the reflection is simple: to equal the water and coffee portions of a capsule, consumers only need to use six grams of coffee, preferably newly ground, for every 125-milliliter cup of water. In addition to the high cost per load, in the last few years, environmentalists have focused on the environmental cost of single portion coffee. The *New York Times* report cited earlier points out that from 1986 to 2012, Nespresso sold 27 billion cartridges that produce a particular type of trash — a mix of plastic and aluminum — that's neither easy to recycle nor does it break down in the environment.

And since no bonanza is ever lasting, as of 2008 and 2012 several Nespresso and Keurig patents began to expire. Finally, a new possibility emerged for new competitors to offer compatible cartridges and, in doing so, the consumables' price dropped. As was to be expected, Keurig and Nespresso took different actions to prevent more players entering the market. For example, in 2008, Jean-Paul Gaillard, a former Nestle employee, founded the Ethical Coffee Company, dedicated to the sale of biodegradable cartridges for the Nespresso machines but in 2010, he was charged in court for having breached the brand's intellectual property(250). Keurig, on the other hand, chose to design and sell a new machine at the end of 2014, the Keurig® 2.0 (K2.0) that validated the cartridges' authenticity and prevented others from being used. Naturally, consumers rejected, deciphered, and hacked this model, and went on to develop a simple method to use any type of cartridge, which consisted in attaching with adhesive tape a fragment of the original Keurig brand capsule to the machine's sensor. Thus, the unsophisticated coffee capsules market shows various conflicting elements: 1) the momentum of rentier innovation focused on hacking the economy; 2) the passivity of the alienated consumer who is willing to pay monopolistic prices despite availability of cheaper options; 3) the drive of proactive consumers who seeks to counter-hack the hack; 4) the lack of sustainability of a product based on convenience; 5) the inequality in value capture, risk exposure, and price divergence between coffee farmers and coffee industrialists; and 6) the large players capacity to use the legal system in their favor and forestall innovation and competition.

The case of coffee is only one among many. The *Washington Post* referred to a study published by Mark Perry of the American Enterprise Institute with data from the Labor Department. It shows that from 1996 to 2016 in the U.S., an interesting price evolution has taken place for various goods and services (251). On one hand, there are competitive products that previously were considered luxury items and now show a marked nominal price reduction, such as the mobile phone service (-46%), televisions (-96%), software and toys (-65%). In another segment are the goods that remain with the same price level, like automobiles, furniture, and clothing. Then there are staple goods and services whose price increase was higher than the cumulative 55% inflation. That is, they show a real increase, such as food, beverages — coffee included — and housing (over 60%). Finally, are the goods, also essential, with increments of over 100%, such as health (104%) and children's care (122%), and goods with increments of over 200%, like college tuition (196%) and textbooks (207%).

Moreover, there are two highly publicized cases of economic hacking that called the attention of the U.S. Congress: that of Martin Shkreli, the Wall Street investor, who purchased Turing Pharmaceuticals and raised the price of a medication called Daraprim® (which is used to treat illnesses produced by parasites and is indispensable for pregnant women or HIV positive patients) from $13.50 to $750 per pill. A second case is that of Heather Bresch, executive director of Mylan Pharmaceuticals, Inc., which sells a device called EpiPen® for the automatic administration of epinephrine, essential for saving the lives of patients susceptible to severe allergic reactions. In the last decade, she's raised its price by 500% (252). In this last case, public opinion flared when it was revealed that at the same time as the device's price increase (2007–2015), Bresch's annual salary rose 671%, from $2.4 million to $18.9 million(253). This disparity has become more and more newsworthy as cases of corporate abuse against consumers become public. What's more, despite the extremely severe financial crisis of 2008–2009, these markets continue to reward and encourage people with the temperament, skill, and lack of scruples to hack the economy. During the above-mentioned period, Mylan's shares rose from $13.29 to $47.59 per share.

At the same time, in 2015, the U.S. Department of Agriculture published the evolution of real prices in various food categories between 1985 and 2014(254). The study demonstrates that the prices of high quality food have risen substantially in the last few decades — red meat (18%), fresh fruits and vegetables (41%) — while the real prices of low quality food such as fats (-4%) and sugars (-10%) have dropped (Graph 22).

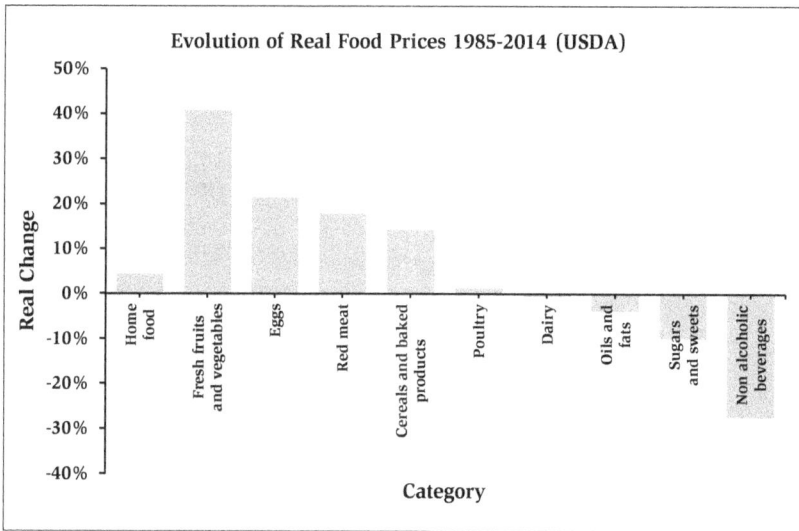

Graph 22: Real price evolution of different food categories in the United States, 1985-2015. Source: USDA.1985-2015.

This means that although we apparently live in a period of staggering innovation and efficiency, the reality is that a substantial part of the economy, the one of most concerns us, has been hacked. As sociologist Joseph Cohen from Queens University said: "The United States is the country in which luxuries are cheap and needs, expensive"(251). Although productivity has increased five-fold from 1965–2015(255), the average salary has remained stagnant at the same level of 1964: approximately $20 an hour at constant 2014 prices(256) as shown in (Graph 23).

The big mystery that has confounded and confronted economists is illustrated in the following question: Who has benefitted from the productivity increment? Piketty says it has to do with his model of $r > g$ inequality; Stiglitz and Vidal point to the inequality produced by collusion and mutual protection of corporate and political interests through *corporate welfare*. Hence, we say it's the control over network functions for the establishment of an authoritarian and conservative configuration by means of *hubs*, facilitated by a *quorum* that leans toward the way of being of masters, lackeys, superstars, and conservatives, that is neither sustainable nor robust or persistent in the long run, since 1) the size of the random network increases, and 2) it produces predatory dynamics that weaken the bilateral vascular network's behavior, and consequently, the open society. In the end, this style of contemporary technological change could well mean the involution of network topology toward undesirable authoritarian and vertical configurations such as the digital Parthenon.

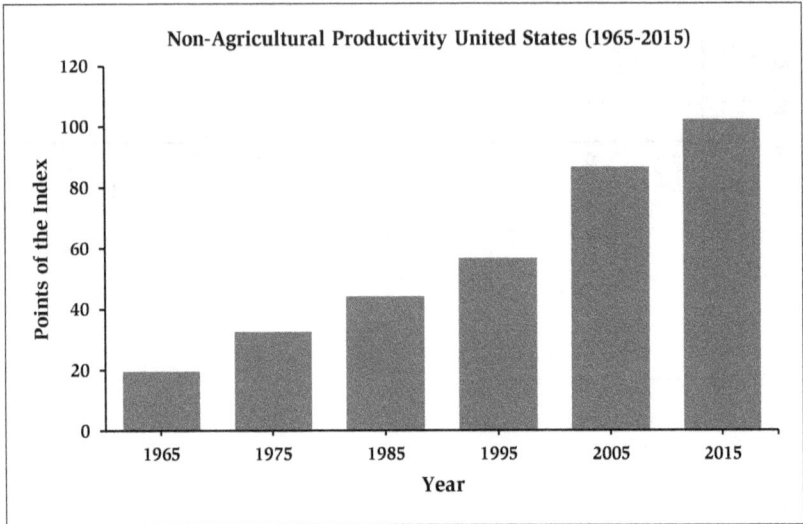

Graph 23: Evolution of non-agricultural productivity in the United States, 1965-2015. Source: BLS.

For decades, we have discussed ad nauseam how the effects of the hacked economy (the higher cost of education, food, and housing; the stagnation of real salaries for the middle class; the inordinate growth of executive compensations; the alienation, and subjugation of citizens (among others) increase the risk of eroding democratic systems. When social perception is that better times have been left behind and for the common man there is nothing better to pursue going forward, it can be said that we've arrived at the future. Although we'd have to say that the future has overtaken us, much like it happens to any head of a household who sees and experiences how hard it is to keep up with the price level of goods and services necessary for favorable progress and the development of opportunities for his/her children, even though now it's much cheaper to watch television and be connected to the mobile phone. For the same reason, it's not surprising that for lack of a logical and rational path, situations like that of the U.S. in 2016 take place in which large social groups, such as white males who have not attended college, voted determinedly for Donald Trump's fanatical and irrational political proposal, most likely because they saw that the 20ᵗʰ century road of democratic prosperity had come to an end. In other words, the closing of a vision of a future that will not be reached.

To conclude, it's urgent to review the areas and the specific points where the economy and democracy have been damaged so that we can understand from these weaknesses how some players have taken control over the network functions, and finally, of the topology itself. In the case of coffee capsules, the defect lies in the antitrust regulations as well as in those that protect obsolete intellectual property rights that treat the innovative product (the machine) and the consumable (the cartridge) in the same way. After several decades, captive consumers of consumables for all kinds of products find there's no indication of a rationale for maintaining indefinitely — and under obsolete laws — the consumables' prices at a monopolistic level. In fact, the historical evidence is overwhelmingly found on the side of standardization. From the industrial era through today, enterprises and consumers have benefited from the system's interoperability: standardized measures of bolts, the electrical system's unification at 12 volts in automobiles, the Internet's TCP/IP protocol, the HTML (HyperText Markup Language), a semantic markup language format that has enabled the *world wide web*, the Joint Photography Experts Group (JPEG) standard that universalized the exchange via compression technology of digital photographs, etc.

The case of Nespresso reveals the opposite side that has gained more momentum during this century: the fraudulent usage of legal protective measures for breaking the standardization process and creating inefficiencies and revenues that hurt the consumer. It suffices to look at what happened with the Nespresso and Keurig inventors. Favre was named director in 1986. Shortly afterward, he and some Nestle executives differed over the company's future: they forced him to resign in 1991. Since then, he has been developing his own business. Dragone and Sylvan lost control of the company in 1997 at the hands of the investors who financed it. And Sylvan merely got $50,000 for his stock liquidation. In a controversial interview published by *The Atlantic* in 2015, he confessed feeling regret for his invention of the K-cup and deplored the pollution caused by the billions of capsules used each year(257). He also said he doesn't own one of the machines because he believes the capsules are expensive, and for him, it's easy to measure the water and coffee he needs every time he wants to enjoy a cup of coffee.

Case 3: The shared economy or "Welcome to the AirBnB™ world"

In 2007, Brian Chesky and Joe Gebbia, who had been living together for a short time in a small apartment in San Francisco, were in dire straits to pay the rent. Since need is the mother of invention, their plight made them think of how to take advantage of the shortage of hotel rooms in town due to the celebration of the Industrial Designers Society of America's (IDSA) convention. They bought inflatable mattresses and advertised online that three airbeds with breakfast were available — Air Bed and Breakfast or AIRBNB™ — at $80 per night. Three potential guests responded quickly. After having tested their concept successfully (which allowed them to find a way out of their dilemma and pay the rent) Chesky, Gebbia, and shortly thereafter, Nathan Blecharczyk, began developing the project to seek funding for a web site through which the rental of any available space for short stays could be obtained easily(258). As part of the curious anecdotes of AirBnB, Inc.s first days, in the summer of 2008, the founders sought to benefit from the season of political parties' conventions to sell 500 boxes of a special edition cereal at $40 per box, the ObamaO's and the Cap'N McCain's with which they managed to collect $30,000 as seed capital(259). Shortly after, in the spring of 2009, Y Combinator LLC joined their effort and injected $20,000 to help the company take off. Afterwards, Sequoia Capital joined in with $600,000.

The idea underlying AirBnB, Inc. is that a large part of our own assets are underutilized. Our cars are parked most of the time without creating any value, and in the meantime, depreciating. At home, we have spaces nobody uses and yet they cost us due to maintenance and property taxes. Hence, in the digital era, the proposals of companies like AirBnB, Inc. — rooted in cooperatives and consumption clubs — have managed to create new markets via the new technology where a random network didn't even exist.

As those who live in cities like Paris, New York, San Francisco or London know well, those cities' big attractions and quality of living imply a high rental and lodging cost that makes every resident a highly appreciated and visited friend and family member. Before AIRBNB, outside family and friends, it was extremely rare, dangerous, and complicated to lodge unknown guests in the unused spaces of our homes. Trips, meeting strangers, and hosting guests have always been considered socially complicated and risky situations. That is why, over the course of history, lodging travelers has been a specialized and regulated business that evolved until it became today's hospitality industry, one shaped by different factors. First, a traveler care and service model was standardized. Thus, the complicated adaptation processes to the local culture ceased to be necessary, and an international travel culture was established, meaning an interoperability model. On the other hand, government officials were able to establish controls to monitor visitors. It's normal that in most cities, hotels register the travelers' passports and IDs. Value chains were created. All the consumption segments of travel — air, land, maritime transport, lodging, food, experiences, insurance, and financial services — were integrated into packages. The problem is that, despite the advantages of standardization and interoperability, the growing demand fed by the globalization of business and tourism as well as the increase in the scale of hospitality companies where large companies and the sector's excessive regulation, went on to create high-priced markets where local oligopolies were created. In addition, they have lessened the travel experience's authenticity.

The AIRBNB model is simple. One side of the market has people who rent their properties and the other market side is the consumers. By means of a platform, supply and demand meet in a reliable and safe manner through validation, rating, insurance protection, and payment retention mechanism known as *escrow*. In the current model, AIRBNB guarantees the parties the rendering of the service and payment. On one side, it retains the payment for the lessor until the service has been delivered, but it guarantees it through the *escrow* mechanism. The tenant is not anonymous, and through a mutual rating system between the lessor and the guests, it creates a prestige and honor system that informs the network about the quality of the property and the reliability of the guests. In terms of the network structure, the AIRBNB market is a digital bilateral vascular network (Figure 26). The difference between the UBER and the AIRBNB model is in the configuration of the network functions (Table 31).

	Uber Technologies	AirBnB, Inc.
Network properties		
Topology	Digital tree	Digital, bilateral, vascular
Maximum N	Global	Global
Coordination	Digital centralized	Decentralized
Network functions		
Network economies	Yes, defined and intermediated by Uber	No, each property has its own conditions
Synchronization	Centralized in real time	One to one (peer to peer)
Validation	Permanent and centralized (taxi and user)	Permanent, centralized and decentralized in the community
Risk management	Centralized in real time	Collaborative
Filtered	Centralized in real time	Collaborative
Node control	Centralized, data based	Communal, based on prestige

Table 31: Properties of Uber Technologies network against that of AirBnB, Inc.

The key to this difference is that AirBnB, Inc. cannot standardize the product because each property is different, and for that reason, each owner controls the price. In technological terms, the transactions in this platform are easier than those of Uber Technologies. It uses the same APIs to interconnect to the financial services and to the maps for potential renters to easily locate properties, but it doesn't have to solve the navigation problems nor the rate estimate in real time. Neither is it involved in the labor complexity that UBER has because the object of the transaction is mainly the lease of an asset, and secondarily, complimentary services like cleaning. Since this market was practically nonexistent before AirBnB, Inc. — except for properties being offered in classified ad pages — there are also no entry standards and barriers as in the taxi market. However, the platform's scale has already elicited reactions from the hospitality industry in different cities. In 2016, the estimate was that AirBnB, Inc. had a market capitalization of $30 billion(260), 2.3 million rooms and 100 million guests, after surpassing the mark of a million rooms rented per night in the summer of 2015(261). This figure would place it over the nearly centennial Hilton Hotels &

Resorts® chain, established in 1919 and considered the most valuable lodging group with a market capitalization of $22 billion. Furthermore, a recent forecast stated the platform could reach 500 million rooms rented per night in 2021 and, by 2025, reach one billion(262).

The platform's rapid growth has been clearly felt in many tourist destinations around the world. Hoteliers claim that the AIRBNB model prevents them from benefitting during the high seasons since the competition's prices do not increase nor vary much even when the demand peaks. This is problematic for those assets specialized in tourism that compensates for poor sales during the low seasons with extraordinary revenues during the high seasons. AIRBNB hosts don't have the cost structure that hoteliers have during the low seasons, that is why they're able to offer better rates year-round.

Another component of the AIRBNB experience is authenticity. As hotel chains standardized their processes, became automated and reduced their costs, the client's experience worsened. Little by little, from the moment they left home to when they returned, travelers were trapped inside every link of the industrial travel and hospitality chain. Thus, it was possible to roam around the world without really learning anything about it. With AIRBNB, hospitality has once again been put in the hands of local hosts and the travel experience has recovered human contact and authenticity. That's why one of the model's strengths is the users' loyalty, the majority of whom say in surveys that AIRBNB is more fulfilling, both for business and pleasure than the traditional hotels(262).

However, not everything has been rosy for this company. In the summer of 2011, a hostess' home was the first of many properties that was sacked and trashed by guests, and in 2014 and 2015, Harvard University studies showed issues with service denial in some properties for racial motives. In cities with a strong tourism industry, like Barcelona, New York, and San Francisco, legal actions seeking to limit space rental for short stays and the company's expansion, have been undertaken(263).

In 2016, AIRBNB's room inventory was higher than the sum of the three largest hotel chains in the world (Hilton, Marriott® International, and InterContinental Hotels Group) and eight times larger than its closest competitor, HomeAway, Inc.(260). On top of that, while its organic growth continues, the company is also pursuing a significant acquisition program(264) (Table 32).

#	Date	Company
1	June 1, 2011	Accoleo
2	March 20, 2012	Crashpadder
3	July 2012	NabeWise
4	July 24, 2012	DailyBooth
5	October 3, 2012	Fondu
6	December 1, 2012	Localmind
7	December 2, 2014	Pencil Labs
8	September 11, 2015	Vamo
9	September 29, 2015	Lapka
10	April 13, 2016	ChangeCoin
11	September 19, 2016	Trip4Real

Table 32: AirBnB, Inc. acquisitions.

The above complies with Silicon Valley's pervasive logic. Companies like AirBnB, Inc. that emerge literally from nowhere and grow meteorically in a few years rely on the digital era's public and common goods, such as the telecommunications protocols, the APIs, and the standardized data formats. This means that the market is open, and others have the same chance to compete. But as markets grow and mature — assuming that a similar technological capacity exists between competitors — the access to capital determines the growth limit. In AirBnB, Inc.'s case, 2012 was the critical year of expansion because the company had the financial capacity to acquire five competitors (Table 32). Unfortunately, the digital platform environment is one in which the winner takes all and though AirBnB, Inc. cannot configure itself as a digital Parthenon since it cannot take control over the basic network functions like price, it has a mixed growth strategy, both organic, and acquisitions, which seeks to establish a world supremacy in the shared hospitality economy. This did not happen by chance. When reviewing the lists of Uber Technologies investors(265) and those of AirBnB, Inc.(266), the two have eleven shareholders in common (Table 33), something quite frequent in Silicon Valley where there's a high degree of endogamy among investors, executives, and companies' board members who control the largest platforms in the world.

#	Investor	Investors in Uber Technologies (Total 76) Round	Investors in AirBnB, Inc.(Total 39) Round
1	Citigroup	Debt	Debt
2	CrunchFund	B series	B series
3	Fidelity Investments	D series (Principal)	E series
4	General Atlantic	D series	E series (Principal)
5	Jeff Bezos	B series	B series
6	Jeremy Stoppelman	Angel	A series
7	Kleiner Perkins Caufield & Byers	D series	A series
8	Morgan Stanley	Debt	Debt
9	Sherpa Capital	D series	D series
10	TPG Growth	C series	D series
11	Wellington Management	D series	E series

Table 33: Common investors in Uber Technologies and AirBnB, Inc.

The complicated issue in this discussion is that while these platform companies innovate, expand, and add efficiencies to the economy, the development of new business models may be very positive, as it has been for home owners and travelers around the world. But the problem arises when supremacy is created for the control of network functions, like Uber Technologies, or for market expansion via acquisitions, like AirBnB, Inc.; then, the transmission of efficiencies stops. In the long run, income concentrates, as it occurred with Nespresso. In the case of AirBnB, Inc., there are already some signs of alarm. The company's platform generates income by charging two fees: the host pays 3% per night booked for the processing, which probably originated in the initial cost that credit card operators charged for each transaction, while guests pay anywhere from 6% to 12% for the service. Although both don't add up to the 25% that Uber Technologies charges, the expectation has been that the 3% fee per night booked would drop as the transactions' volume expanded, especially since credit card operators typically charge big users less than 1%. All the same, that efficiency has not been transferred to the market. In the meantime, the client's service fee that could remain stagnant or increase if only AirBnB, Inc. remains in the market is part of a more in-depth discussion.

Moore´s Law drove the digital era. But instead of a law, this insight from Intel Corporation's co-founder Gordon E. Moore is an observation of the speed at which economies of scale are created in the production of micro-processors. Basically, this theory says that the number of transistors in a processor doubles every 18 months, and since 1965, one can buy twice the computing power for the same amount of money every two years. After 51 years, an Intel® Core i7® processor with 1.75 billion transistors contains 760,000 times more transistors than the Intel® 4004 of 1971 with 2,300 transistors. This means that the efficiencies created by the semiconductor industry, and that are diligently transferred to the market by companies like Intel, have allowed hardware and software manufacturers and entre-preneurs to develop increasingly powerful solutions, but at lower prices. However, in certain key parts of the economy, a part of these efficiencies has not been transmitted. For example, although the cost of transmission, validation, and exchange of electronic messages has dropped by a factor of hundreds of thousands in the last 50 years, down to a level that allows transactions as sophisticated as Uber Technologies that contain satellite navigation and dynamic rates estimation in real time, in the financial sector of credit cards, intermediation rates have not dropped as much as is technically possible. This leads us to identify some in-depth questions regarding the digital economy of the 21st century: How much does digital intermediation cost, and how much is it worth? What are the limits and the risks of digital supremacy? Can it be avoided? And what's the balance between the big and the small parts of the economy?

Public goods in the digital era

The questions regarding the new economy, though part of a new and different context, are not separated from the main questions of the old economy: What is public? What is private? and What is scarce? What is abundant? A model to address these questions and answer them that adheres closely to the complex systems' analytical approach, gives rise to the definition of public goods in the economy(267). For economists, goods may be classified in terms of two categories or principles:

1. **The rivalry principle.** It occurs when an agent consumes a good, and thereby reduces the available amount of that good for the other agents. All the consumer goods we buy in the grocery store, like oranges and tomatoes, are goods subject to this principle because a pound of oranges that someone buys and takes home lessens the

number of oranges available in the store for others. Conversely, the air we breathe is a low-rivalry good, since the air one person breathes does not diminish the amount of air available for others.

2. **The exclusion principle.** An agent's capacity to limit other consumers from having access to a good through physical or legal means. The laws that define private property let the consumer buy oranges and tomatoes and prevents others from accessing them, so they become high-exclusion goods.

In a schematic way, these principles help classify the goods into: (Figure 28)

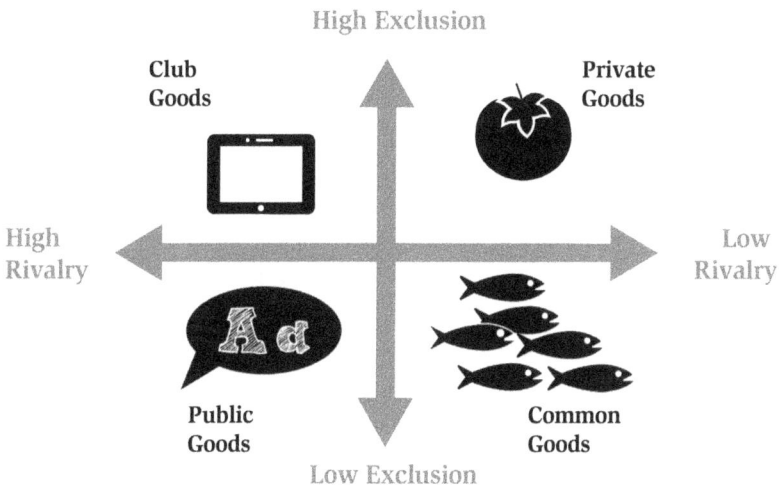

Figure 28: Types of goods.

1. **Public goods.** They are low-exclusion goods; one cannot forestall consumer's access to them, and low rivalry, since the good's consumption is not reduced to the amount available for other people (e.g., the air and national security). In the network model, public goods equal network functions because, as previously stated, they are the properties, behaviors, protocols, platforms, and exchange mechanisms that all the nodes of a network share. The best examples are a country's language and its overall literacy level.

2. **Private goods.** They're high exclusion and high rivalry, like oranges and tomatoes, and correspond with each node's scope for action.

3. **Common goods.** They're low exclusion and high rivalry; one cannot limit the agent's consumption, though this diminishes the amount available for others. Some examples are wood in public forests and the exploitation of fish stocks in the open ocean. Common goods represent a part of the environmental problem still without solution. The impossibility of generating effective exclusion for acceding to many environmental assets, such as fish stocks in international waters and high rivalry in the market — greater demand, greater earnings — create a problem called the Tragedy of the Commons. It's defined as the negative effects that imply the destruction of a shared resource through individual actions based on self-interest. The network model links common goods with problems of usage and access to the substrate.

4. **Club goods.** They're high exclusion and low rivalry. For example, a subscription to a digital magazine where consumption is limited by the payment, but the consumer reading it doesn't reduce the available amount of the electronic goods for others.

During the analogue era, the goods' classification was fundamental for the design of nations, public policies, and governance. For example, the 20th century communist regimes denied and repealed without success and at a huge social cost, the economy's private goods, and tried to solve the Tragedy of the Commons based on State control. In open societies, the defense of freedom and private property enabled the market economy's development, but to date, we have not found a satisfactory solution to solve the Tragedy of the Commons. Currently, in the digital era, the goods' classification became technically more complicated, but there are two attitudes concerning the digital goods' classification. On one side, most agents ignore the need to construct digital governance, and on the other, those who benefit from this situation do what they can, so the new digital environment remains misgoverned.

Even so, it's already evident that for some time now we are in the law of the gun phase where digital space has increasing risks and dwindling earnings for its inhabitants. As these lines are being written, a confrontation between the U.S. and Russian governments is at its peak, in which the first accuses the second of trying to sabotage its last election via the publications in Wikileaks of thousands of emails from Democratic National Party (DNC) members. There have also been reports of attempts to intrude the electronic voting systems, so that the Central Intelligence Agency (CIA) announced electronic and symmetrical retaliations against Russia(268)The latter is compounded by Russia's accusations months earlier that the U.S. government was behind the publication of the Panama papers that incriminated and shamed distinguished members of the Russian oligarchy for acts of corruption(269). This means that 2016 was the year in which a new Cold War was inaugurated, the digital one that has placed us on the verge of the first cybernetic war. Many of these issues have their roots in the design deficits of the Internet TCP/IP protocols because they lack functions that we have gradually discovered are indispensable for the public goods' development in the digital era.

Since the invention of the telegraph and, of the telephone in the 19th century, the history of telecommunications has been the history of private invention and patents. A history filled with chapters on plagiarism, disloyal competition, monopolies, expropriations, and the provision and exploitation of common and private goods concessions to individuals. It wasn't until the end of the 20th century, with the privatization of state telecommunications in Europe and Latin America, that the exploitation of telecommunications stabilized under the definition of private goods, which until then had been regulated because they were considered strategic and of public interest. The same also happened with The Bell Telephone Company in the U.S., which was divided in 1982 because of its large monopolistic market. In the case of digital networks, in the 1970s and 1980s, everything indicated the industry would follow a similar road. Therefore, the network topologies and network protocols such as X.25 and Frame Relay proposed by telecommunications equipment manufacturers had a greater number of users than the Internet, and industry competition ensued. The most important difference between these protocols and the TCP/IP is that they were centralized and oriented toward connection, which means that all connections and network routes had to be explicitly defined, configured, and charged by the operator, based on each segment of the network, and which emulates the same logic used in the traditional telephone system's measured service. Thus, this required the design of protocols with a high level of control and functions' centralization in the telecommunications companies, which meant these networks were expensive and difficult to build and manage. Moreover, they could only be used within a narrow range of large-scale corporate and institutional applications, not at a domestic level or in small companies.

In the 60's, the U.S. military research complex was focused on solving a single question: How to win and survive a nuclear war against the Soviet Union? Answering this question allowed for the creation of a project within the Defense Advanced Research Projects Agency (DARPA) that broke with the traditional telecommunications model with which the Internet's open architecture was built. To guarantee the operations' continuity, only the minimum exchange functions of information packages were defined, and as a result, the Internet nodes are like cockroaches: simple, resistant, and able to survive and adapt to a nuclear war, but unable to determine the evolution of the network's complex behaviors.

The concern is that since the first public presentation of this type of network in 1972(270), and with the release and transfer to society of the IPv4 protocol in the form of the digital era's first public good, the Internet's ease of use and the open architecture enabled the fast digitalization of innumerable interactions. It was easy to create and integrate functions, patches, and new protocols, like HTML, over the TCP/IP (the Internet's protocol stack) without needing to update the base network's protocol. Therefore, today there is no governance that defines borders between public and private, large and small. Namely, each time we enter the network, we go into a self-help world where we don't even know how to classify, utilize, and manage the goods we create and migrate to the digital environment. A case in point is when we see that network nodes are identified merely by the IP address from which any node may execute, without restrictions, all the functions defined in the protocol and direct them toward all other network nodes. That's a positive when it's a matter of protecting freedom of expression, but it's a negative when it breaches the right to privacy and enables crime through anonymity.

Since 1994, the Internet Engineering Task Force (IETF) had set out to create a new version of the protocol named IPv6. The group started publishing its results beginning in 1998 and ending in 2006. However, this new protocol's adoption and implementation is still in process and it's estimated it will still take many more years. The new specification was created primarily to broaden the space for the IPv4 addresses that ran out between 2011 and 2014 and to facilitate management of the increasing number of devices connected to what is known as the Internet of Things (IoT). Apart from some technical changes, IPv6 didn´t include new functions for the advanced and distributed management of the network. For the time being, the development or update of a further version is not being considered nor is it in process.

This deficit of explicit network functions at the protocol's highest level has allowed the Internet to turn into a version of the Old West. In other words, an immense space, open to conquest by anyone who is willing to draw on the model's open architecture to build and exploit the use of functions by means of centralized platforms. That's why it was easy for the banks to make a facsimile of themselves on the Internet that let them maintain their role and grow as money intermediaries in the digital realm. No one thought (and it wasn't possible at the time) that it was essential to create a general and distributed network function for value exchange. In fact, from the strictly technical point of view, the way in which world financial institutions exchange money through electronic means is primitive, even comical, because it's like what would happen if sending money via fax were legal and viable. Contrary to the paper currency system, in which an authority issues every bill with a unique serial number and certain properties that prevent its duplication or forgery, in the current model there is no data structure for electronic currency that defines it as such. There is only one piece of data correlated with some metadata, like the account number and the beneficiary's name. Thus, when a bank complies with a customer's order to transfer a certain amount to an account located in another bank, the two institutions need to have a previously established trust relationship, usually through the central bank, and execute a complicated series of processes to avoid what is known as the *double-spend* issue. Both institutions must reach an agreement that the data in the source and target accounts will be updated to reflect the transaction's amount, which is the same as two people who agree to transmit via fax a bearer value certificate in the understanding that the original will be destroyed once the operation is confirmed to avoid the *double-spend* of the same certificate. Technically, electronic money doesn't exist — unlike digital photos defined in JPEG files — just like other general network functions such as identity and trade don't exist either.

Consequently, even though the 21ˢᵗ century is well underway, we don't have all the public goods we require like, as an example, the cash of the analogue world where the State subsidizes its cost in the form of distributed network functions. That's why, in the digital world, the lack of public goods has been remedied with private goods that force us inevitably to use and pay costly intermediaries such as Uber Technologies, Visa, Paypal® and AirBnB, Inc. In fact, until very recently, it was thought that it was not technically possible to create diffuse functions or distributed platforms in the digital space. Now we are seeing the contrary.

Case 4: The distributed economy or "Welcome to the Blockchain world"

In October 2008, Satoshi Nakamoto, a libertarian digital activist, published in the Cryptography Mailing List an article titled "Bitcoin: A Peer-to-Peer Electronic Cash System"(271), in which he describes the development of an electronic version of cash that can be exchanged from point to point without the intermediaries' intervention. To solve the *double-spend* question, the author proposed a distributed database to store the records of all the exchanges.

To explain this system's operation in parts, the following scenarios explain: User A, Juan, who lives in one country and needs a document translated, and user B, Maria, a translator who lives in another country, agree on the service price in a Bitcoin. Once Maria delivers the translated document, Juan opens the mobile phone's electronic wallet, inputs Maria's chain or electronic address that she previously shared and identifies the wallet in which she requested the payment transfer, and he executes the transfer instruction. Up to this point, the way users perceive the transaction is practically identical to the electronic transactions to which we are used to with traditional banks. The difference lies in the hidden part of the transaction. Behind the Bitcoins' wallets lays a distributed system called Blockchain.

Blockchain is a database that contains the record of all transactions carried out with Bitcoins. To simplify the process, we shall say that the Bitcoin Juan takes from his wallet to pay Maria has number 001, so that once the transaction is executed and validated, it's registered in Blockchain's database as a transfer to Maria through a cryptographic key in Juan's possession. A new key is generated for Bitcoin 001 that Maria now has, and she keeps the keys linked to her Bitcoins in her personal electronic wallet. If Juan would try to reuse the Bitcoin 001 key, this immediately alerts all network members that Juan no longer owns it, and his attempt to use the same Bitcoin twice is rejected by everyone.

What's interesting about the Nakamoto model is that through cryptographic techniques and a distributed consensus-based system that is not centrally intermediated, it changed the balance between the public, the private, and a transaction's unequivocal validation, the same as a bank does, although in a centralized fashion. Albeit Blockchain's registries are public and all participants know who owns Bitcoins, no one knows the real identity of the wallet owners, since they're protected by sophisticated cryptographic techniques that, besides guaranteeing at all times every Bitcoin's uniqueness and ownership, allow for the voluntary and collaborative participation of thousands of computer nodes. The so-called miners, at the same time they are producing bitcoins, maintain Blockchain's operation, integrity, and security as a system. Considering that the idea behind Bitcoin is that there is no authority with the capacity to arbitrarily determine the monetary offering, Blockchain's software is programmed to produce new bitcoins, up to a pre-established limit of 21 million, every time that the miners solve increasingly complex cryptographic problems that are an intrinsic part of the network's operation.

Bitcoin's core software, that in the old model is the equivalent of the banks' core banking software, can be downloaded, installed and modified by anyone in the world. Once installed, the computer(s) that have the software may be registered as a Bitcoin mining node. To enter, a new node must accept as valid the last copy of the Blockchain and start working. Transactions, such as the example of Juan and Maria, are added, transformed, and distributed to the network nodes in the form of mathematical problems of hash cryptography whose solution can only be solved by tedious methods of trial and error. This means that the node providing the greater computing capacity has a bigger chance of solving the problem. Once solved, the node adds a new block of records to the *Blockchain* — thereby its name — that contains the results of the mined group of transactions. The reward for the effort to solve the problems or "mine the block" is the production of new bitcoins that are assigned to the winning node. The new block spreads in the network and is validated against the cryptographic keys of the previous blocks to guarantee that there are identical Blockchain copies and a distributed consensus about the registrations' historical integrity. This means that Blockchain's integrity is harder to breach than a bank's, and once the transaction becomes part of a block and is added to the chain, it's practically impossible to break the distributed consensus regarding the chain's properties because each block is converted into a result concatenated to previous blocks.

The technological solution that gave life to the Bitcoin is, without doubt, brilliant and innovative, but there are aspects of this currency that still raise doubts. One of the most germane is that the model for determining the monetary supply, with a limit of 21 million Bitcoins, is arbitrary, probably linked to Nakamoto's libertarian ideas regarding the use of precious metals as a means of exchange disconnected from an estimate of the real monetary demand.

The result is that because of Blockchain, it was possible to create the first electronic currency in history. Under this model, the chain of blocks becomes a public good capable of supporting a similar function to that of paper money in the analogue economy, but without the support and intervention of an authority or a financial institution. The oddest thing is that eight years after the publication of Nakamoto's article, no one knows the origin, location or identity of the person who led the system's development until 2010 when he left the scene. But the concepts he contributed to the world of technology led to the takeoff of a new technological race to build decentralized platforms that can dramatically change worldwide dominion of financial institutions on money intermediation. Currently, more than 75% of the total number of bitcoins to be produced with a market value close to $10 billion, is already in circulation. The efficiencies Blockchain generates are so large that, paradoxically, some of the most important financial institutions, like Goldman Sachs, have not been able to ignore them. On November 15, 2015, that institution requested a patent registration titled "Cryptographic Currency for Securities Settlement," based on the same Blockchain model(272). In addition, there are already thousands of start-up companies based on Bitcoin and Blockchain that develop open-source distributed technologies like Ethereum (developed by Ethereum Foundation as a decentralized platform that runs smart contracts) with which it is possible to develop new functions such as self-executing contracts and property registries that are bullet-proof from dictators, civil wars, and coups d'etat.

For those who believe it's unnecessary to solve the problem of goods' classification and governance on the Internet, here are some of Blockchain's consequences and potentials that make this task even more urgent. The first that should attract attention is that technologies like Bitcoin substitute functions the State has traditionally monopolized and monitored. That's why Bitcoin has turned into the electronic means of preferred payment by criminals and a large part of the shadow economy. Moreover, even though Blockchain lets us trace always the Bitcoins' routes, the complete concealment of the owners' identity is an extraordinary facilitator of tax evasion and illegal exchanges. For example, Bitcoin's original price in 2010 was $0.06, and although the price fluctuates considerably from one day to the next, in 2016, it varied in a range close to $500, but at times it has been more than $1,000 (in December 2017 price spiked above $19,000). Whoever invested $100 from the start, then sold it at $500, obtained $833,233 in earnings that have not been traced or accounted for.

Those properties foster the dismissal or demonization of innovation, as in Uber Technologies case: In some places, the new models will be prohibited, and, in others, the authorities will let them pass without any analysis, restriction, or intervention as if change were a natural and irremediable consequence of technological development. Neither of the two positions is desirable. And it's quite likely that at some point the Bitcoin will stagnate since the lack of a mechanism to adapt to the needs of monetary demand and connection with the fiscal and judicial systems forestalls it from converting into the great currency of the digital era.

Twenty years ago, a conference speaker, expert in technological development, insisted that the impact of disruptive technologies is usually produced in two phases. First, they're used to improve on what we already know how to do — like PCs that were used to replace the typewriter in writing documents and the calculator by facilitating accounting tasks via spreadsheets. Afterwards, when we discovered the real potential of this technology, we found the way to stop doing things as we had done before and paved a way to new forms of work and interaction. With PCs connected to the Internet, activities that we could not have imagined with the typewriter and the calculator became possible. In the case of the Internet, platforms like AirBnB, Inc., Uber Technologies, and Google, for lack of native and distributed functions in the TCP/IP protocol, turned into the facsimile representation of the analogue network hubs. With them, we now have improved the quality and quantity of the things we already did. But with the Blockchain model, despite its current deficiencies, a new door opens for doing things in a radically different manner like creating a currency without the State's backup. This can create results as different as a chaotic anonymous network of tax evaders and criminals — consistent with the law of the gun — or an efficient, secure, and robust value exchange network with insignificant intermediation costs. It all depends on the way we build and classify goods, especially public and private ones, and whether we decide to subject ourselves to the rule of law and define a digital governance model based on the identification and analysis of the following issues:

1. **Public goods.** The fact is that the Internet was built upon the public goods that DARPA released. The main one is IPv4, and to it others like Java® (owned by Oracle Corporation), HTML, and KML were added together with all other standards, protocols, languages, and

services that followed soon after. These included aspects such as military declassification and the free use of the global positioning system network (GPS). Despite the wealth of goods that thousands of people and civil, military, or government organizations have contributed, we still need to define and build many more, particularly those that facilitate the identity, trade, property, cash or currency, search, and information use functions. Some already exist in a centralized and private fashion, but as the new independent and anarchist developments show, like Bitcoin, we're still far from solving the challenges of public goods in the 21st century. These begin with the property and control of the Internet's technical standards and protocols, give rise to network functions, and come to and in the end allow for the existence of international peace, national security, and public security in the digital environment.

2. **Private goods.** One of the most surprising changes that took place during the last 20 years was the weakening of the protective regime to the individual's property and privacy rights. There is a phrase that says: "If you don't pay for the digital service you use, you are the product." This exemplifies cases such as Facebook® and Google that, by offering free-of-charge services, have taken for themselves, to the detriment of the person, the users' time, information, habits, and knowledge. In part, this is caused by the public goods' deficit in the digital setting. Every time we use a device connected to the Internet, our identity — for the other nodes — is merely the IP address of the device we use, and that forces us to pay third parties, like Facebook, Google Gmail® and LinkedIn® for the identity credentials we need to interact with different services at the expense of our time and privacy.

3. **Common goods.** In the digital economy, these relate to the issues of network access. For example, in the case of mobile communications, access depends on the assignment and use of the radio frequencies (RF) as well as the telecommunication companies' permits and concessions. In some countries, there is an effort to classify Internet access as a right that will convert it into a public good, but at the same time no viable or compatible business model is being proposed. In other countries, there are problems regarding a monopolistic and oligopolistic exploitation of telecommunications. Probably, the effective solution to these problems will follow the

parameters given in other network markets (like utilities), like that of electricity, which work well when there are private, competitive, and open markets above the market's failure, and subsidy mechanisms for the strata beneath it.

4. **Club goods.** Not much attention is usually paid to this type of goods in the traditional economy, but, in the digital space, a worrisome trend exists. The goods that existed 10 or 15 years ago had the option to be transformed into public goods, like knowledge, today are club goods. In the last five years, the editorial industries that control culture's dissemination through academic journals and textbooks have consolidated into large entrepreneurial groups. Since then, access to knowledge has been closed via the use of *paywalls*. This explains in good measure, as we mentioned earlier, that the price of textbooks in the U.S. has increased by 200%.

13. Government in the 21st century

The knowledge society, electronic government, and digital governance

The relationship between governments and information and communication technologies (ICTs) can be conceptualized through two different and separate frameworks. The first seeks to make progress toward a Knowledge and Information Society (KIS), and the second is known as E-Government (E-Gov). In spite of the widespread use of both frameworks, none of them has succeeded in integrating a coherent public policy with regards to the digitalization of society. While the labels of KIS and E-Gov frequently overlap or are (wrongly) used interchangeably, the problems of definition run more deeply than the terminology. Conceptual frameworks are still forming, and policies are at a crossroads.

This chapter posits that, rather than being on top of the challenges of the digital era, governments have *muddled through* the requisites and complications of the new technologies. Since the start of this century, new government organizations of higher and higher rank — including national ministries — deal with day-to-day projects with E-Gov and KIS. These organizations may perform at satisfactory levels or not. However, it is difficult to assert that a strategy is in place when every new project reconfigures the mandate and the overarching goals of the organizations are ever changing.

In sum, when it comes to the role of government in the development, adoption, and diffusion of ICTs, we can only say that attention to short-term decision-making has crowded out long-term strategy and planning. It is incumbent upon us to revise and discuss the current conceptualizations on these two subjects and to establish a new starting point to build public policy for the digital age:

1. **The Knowledge and Information Society**. Economist Fritz Machlup used this term before the beginning of the digital era. He observed that societies that managed to convert scientific knowledge into new technology and economic value in the market also attained higher

levels of social welfare, in addition to higher levels of employment and income(273). Over time, various authors borrowed the term to frame their observations about change in post-industrial societies: that is, in developed nations where the work force started to move away from manufacturing and toward services. The KIS conceptual framework successfully explained the link between economic growth, welfare, and the start of the digital era in post-industrial societies. Today, the most widely accepted definition is the one established in the Declaration of Bávaro, Punta Cana, during a preparatory meeting in advance of the World Summit on the Information Society, which took place in Geneva (1st part) and Tunisia (2nd part). The Declaration reads: "Education, knowledge, information, and communication are at the core of human progress, endeavour, and well-being."(274)

That said, it is noteworthy that the contemporary academic literature explains the economic transition from manufacturing to services as a process that involves multiple factors. High levels of development in post-industrial economies cannot be attributed exclusively to the digitalization of society(275).

2. **Electronic government**. Although the concept is still in want of a more robust definition, the OECD has proposed one that is widely accepted: "The term *E-Government* focuses on the use of new information and communication technologies (ICTs) by governments as applied to the full range of government functions. In particular, the networking potential offered by the Internet and related technologies has the potential to transform the structures and operation of government."(276)

    Understanding that E-Gov is that which governments do with ICTs can be taken as a definition, but it begs the question because it does not lay out what the public policy goals for this field should be. The frequent misunderstanding that planning and budgeting can make for a strategy reveals a confusion of means and meaning.

As we pointed out above, there are two separate — and unmet — overarching imperatives in the process of digitalization of societies. These imperatives have a common root but belong in two different branches. One refers to the diffusion of ICTs in society, and the other refers to the diffusion of ICTs in government. The former addresses the need to bridge the digital gap and to create governance instruments for the digital technologies. The latter refers to the goals and management processes of ICTs for governments.

Thus, we can say that the digital age results both from the digitalization of society and government. Both trends converge and produce social benefits — although not for everyone. In the interest of clarity, it is essential to separate and organize the characteristics and needs that digital public policy must advance. What follows is a conceptual organization that goes from the global idea of digitalization to the management of technology:

1. **Digitalization.** Beyond government actions, it results from a society that develops, adopts, and diffusses ICTs. The factors that enable and foster digitalization are:

    i. **Education.** The primary global measurements (indexes) on digitization, such as the E-Government Survey of United Nations, use general literacy and schooling as factors that enable (or constrain) digitalization. Digital interaction requires skills to read, write, express, and interpret abstraction and complexity.

    ii. **Coverage.** The availability of ICTs in all jurisdictions brings about issues of economies of scale and monopoly that resemble those of telecommunications, electricity, and transportation. A tension of goals is inherent to these issues. On the one side, there are attractive possibilities to make efficiency gains that translate into lower prices. On the other side, there are public service obligations: firms must deliver service to areas of less dense economic activity where the costs of serving each additional user are higher, but prices must not rise proportionally.

    iii. **Quality.** Speed is the current parameter of quality in ICTs. It is technically determined by the general process of innovation in ICTs and Moore's Law. But access to it depends on specific local market conditions. To illustrate this point, consider how the parameters of broadband have changed throughout the years. It went from 512kb/s (kilobytes per second) some years ago and increased consistently, in competitive markets, to the point that some countries now enjoy domestic speeds of 100mb/s and beyond.

    Other quality parameters are gaining ground in addition to speed. For instance, data compression rates — on digital TV — and access to diverse content have become more relevant. The rule of thumb is to assess the quality of ICT services by comparison to the satisfaction of consumers in nations of reference.

iv. Price. The digital basket of an individual or a family refers to that set of services and goods that users prioritize according to their preferences and budget. It includes mobile telephones, portable personal computers, Internet access, software, and content. Families use between 3% and 5% of their income to integrate their basket, and do without it — partially or completely — when the price of the basket goes above that level. In affluent societies, demand expands as prices drop as a consequence of Moore's Law and of highly efficient and adaptive markets. Hence, digitalization gains ground constantly. However, it is noteworthy that efficiency of ICTs markets is not a sufficient condition to guarantee accessibility or affordability to digital services and goods. In most jurisdictions, governments need to deploy subsidization and other mechanisms to expand access to ICTs for people in poverty that use most or all of their income for basic needs.

2. **Digital Governance**. The interconnected society has been learning to carry out all kinds of digital activities. Thriving networks attest to the progress of digitalization in all areas of human interest: science, entertainment, philanthropy, and unfortunately, the digital equivalents of all imaginable anti-social and self-destructive behaviors. Of course, the emergent landscape of a digitally interconnected society has brought a new relevance for the role of government and governance. Governance instruments enable the construction, protection, and access to public and common goods. They also protect and regulate markets. The social need for digital government and governance instruments is no different from the general social need for government and governance instruments. A digital society needs digital government and governance to build, protect, and guarantee access to digital public and common goods. Finally, and just as it occurs in the non-digital, or *analog* world, digital governance is expected to lay the foundations for markets in the digital economy.

Approximately two decades ago, governments started to create new organizations with authority to implement overarching policies for the digital society and government. Today the agenda of issues and problems of digital governance has spread throughout the spectrum of social and governmental activities. The relevant question is no longer who is in charge, but who can coordinate all the different actors in charge of all the parcels that form this diverse and often contradictory landscape. What mechanisms of governance should governments put in place?

The answer is that there is no answer. Yet. As shockingly as it might sound, there is no established response to this question because even the most advanced governments are continuingly pioneering efforts. We can take for granted, however, that approaching the problems of digital governance requires a mixture of adaptation and ingenuity. Public and national cybersecurity, for instance, echo pre-established notions and areas of policy. However, a fresh and inventive approach is indispensable for other fields and problems, like the deadly accidents caused by the use of mobile telephones or addiction to the Internet and video games.

That said, perhaps the most disruptive phenomenon we all are witnessing in these years refers to the massive and profound disintermediation enabled by digitalization. This process comprises the disappearance or the transformation of all kinds of economic, political, and social roles. Uber, AirBnB, Blockchain, and even the traditional media are cases in point. The electronic media and the newspapers, in particular, have been losing audience and readers to the digital media at a massive rate. Another example of this is how the idea of the brick and mortar — public or private — service offices have become obsolete now that we have access to transactional digital services.

The advantages of disintermediation, however, also bring along new complications and challenges. They make imperative the recognition and definition of new rights, obligations, and responsibilities for citizens and governments alike. Furthermore, these new definitions will loop-back to force some adjustments in the traditional mechanisms of governance beyond the digital world. Some of these challenges already show as looming or visible tensions and contradictions. For instance, several nations are making headway to fight cybercrime and to put up cyberwar programs at the same time they expand policies of citizen participation and open government with features of co-government and open data.

In 2011, the federal government of Mexico issued one of the antecedents in the construction of digital citizen rights. The Federal Government Open Data and Interoperability Schema postulates the following tenets(277):

(ARTICLE XI.)- As regards the provision of digital services, all government organizations will oversee and implement their activities in a way that facilitates citizens to:

I. *Freely choose the channel and type of technology that enables digital communication with government organizations;*
II. *Interact through applications or systems based on open standards;*
III. *Receive simplified attention through exclusive, and preferably digital channels;*
IV. *Know, digitally and remotely, the state of their administrative processes;*
V. *Obtain electronic copies of documents related to digital services;*
VI. *Participate in digital mechanisms of public participation;*
VII. *Be identified only once through digital media;*
VIII. *Enjoy access to open data.*

As digitalization moves forward, governments will have to revise the ensemble of functions they carry out. Some of these functions will have to disappear. But the critical task will be laying out the foundations of digital governance, which will involve government and society, together with new government functions for the transformed environment. (Table 34).

Intermediation functions that may disappear	Digital functions to develop and nourish
• Closed data • Opacity • Regulatory complexity • Bureaucracy • Dissociation (citizen/government)	• Cybersecurity • Trust sources • Legal certainty • Interoperability • Protection of rights • Digital common goods • Integration and cogovernment citizen-government)

Table 34: Extinction and development of functions of government in the digital age.

3. **Digital government.** According to the Inter-secretarial Commission for the Development of Electronic Government (CIDGE, after its Spanish acronym), the overarching goal of digital government is: "To give direction and meaning to how governments use ICTs to improve social welfare." This goal encompasses the following tenets of action:

    i. **Improving the operational efficiency of public institutions.** Most internal government activities produce, transform, and/or use information. From this perspective, institutional problems actually reveal operational inefficiencies in the exchange or transmission of information that, in turn, affect the decision-making process. Thus, the use of ICTs in government aims to make public institutions more efficient.

    ii. **Reduce transaction costs in the interactions between citizens and government.** High transaction costs in government processes — such as paperwork, red tape, and services — are often tantamount to a barrier in the relationship between citizens and government. These problems constitute an efficiency loss that translates into economic losses for everyone. Moreover, they take a dramatic toll on society in jurisdictions, like Mexico, where government programs often have millions of users, and institutional structures are insufficient to address the demands and needs of society with an adequate quality standard.

    In representative democracies, governments have the prerogative of creating the organizations that constitute bureaucracy. However, as embodiments of a public mandate, bureaucracies cover a political function of accountability that frequently eclipses or overwhelms their service to society. Enacting laws and procedures and appropriating funds is one thing; creating value for society is quite another.

    The good news is that ICTs are abating transaction costs in the access to services and public goods. ICTs have a high potential for the generation of social value, not the least because they are enabling the disintermediation (that is, the de-bureaucratization) of government institutions. This transformation can also affect, positively, the relationship between citizens and their elected representatives. Bureaucracy is not a synonym for government. But ICTs may transform both. Block-chain has shown that it is possible to disintermediate the State and banks. In like manner, digital governance seeks to disintermediate bureaucracy and to build a different relationship between citizens and government. This new type of relation is called *Open Government.*

iii. **Building interoperable information public goods "info-structure."** Information public goods exist and are necessary for the adequate functioning of the analog world. In fact, they are the enablers of citizen rights. For instance, public registries are information public goods par excellence. Thus, if moved into the digital domain and made interoperable in an API environment, civil, public property, mercantile, and criminal registries can also become the foundation of the trust sources needed for the expansion of the digital economy. Other digital public goods include information structures whose construction and management must be exclusively for governments — like the digital monetary system. Therefore, in the wide array of ICT investments, *Infostructure* should be atop the priorities.

4. **ICT governance.** Governing ICTs encompasses the processes, rules, systems, and controls to manage and utilize ICTs. Some models have emerged to harness and give coherence to all these tools:

   i. **Project Management Body of Knowledge (PMBOK).** A methodology for project management proposed by the Project Management Institute.

   ii. **Information Technology Infrastructure Library (ITIL).** A methodology of practices to manage ICT services, developed by the Trade Office of the United Kingdom.

   iii. **Control Objectives for Information and related Technology (COBIT).** Seeks to bridge the gap between goals of government, on the one hand, and goals of control of ICTs, on the other side. This methodology was developed by the Information Systems Audit and Control Association.

   iv. **ISO-27000.** This is the standard for the administration of security and information technology risks, published by the International Organization for Standardization (ISO).

v. ISO-38500. This is the standard for the administration and government of ICTs, published by the ISO.

Methodologies and systematizations of good practices have flourished because they address the growing and complex array of problems in the adoption of ICTs. Two paramount problems are the very high rate of failure in automation projects (>50%) and also the grave problems of information security and privacy protection. This last problem, and the difficulties it entails, are indicative of the need to create digital public goods, such as public cyber-security. Security is perhaps the dullest, most technical and specialized aspect of the use of ICT. But the list of problems related to it is painfully long, and its importance cannot be exaggerated. Some high-level scandals that illustrate this are the Snowden case, the theft and publication by Wikileaks of the emails of the Democratic Party during the U.S. presidential campaign of 2016, the theft of 500 million passwords from Yahoo!, and the failure of the first version of the U.S. government site, healthcare.gov.

Based on these concepts, the following table illustrates the size of the gaps and the action government must take as a response (Table 35):

Concept	Definition	Current state
Digitalization	The adoption and use of ICTs by society at large.	Until June 2016, only 50.1% of world population used the Internet(278). Dispite technological advances, the analog society still comprises 3.8 billion people who inherited the digital divide as part of poverty and marginalization. For them, the digital divide grows more significant by the day, and with it, their inability to understand what the new digital society is.
Digital Governance	What government does in and with respect to the digital world.	The discussion of the issues of digital governance needs an international lever. Unfortunately, international organizations have not identified with enough clarity the scale and importance of the challenge ahead. Instead, the thin and poor space of international negotiations on digital governance has only served to protect the interests of corporations. A case in point is the negotiations of the failed TPP (Trans-Pacific Partnership) that addressed the issues of digital governance behind closed doors and without including the international society.
Digital Government (E-Gov)	Government`s use of ICTs	Between 2000 and 2010, several nations took serious steps to promote cooperation and development of solutions to the challenges of E-Gov. The OECD and United Nations established departments for that purpose. However, interest has subsided in recent years. Some nations, like South Korea, have stabilized at high levels of development, while analogical processes, inefficiency, and corruption persist in closed societies. Paradoxically, technology has become a resource for authoritarian models in nations with a strategy to preserve the status quo. In those nations, ICTs have become vehicles for massive surveillance and espionage. In those societies, masters and lackeys have taken control of technology to serve what they define as a superior rationality that is not subject to accountability mechanisms and that does not create value, i.e. digital colonialism.

Concept	Definition	Current state
Governance of ICTs	Management of ICTs within organizations	The absence of public goods allows anonymity, the systematic loss of privacy, and precludes interoperability. Disarray can occur as a result. The adequate management of technology becomes increasingly complex and costly at all levels, from the domestic and individual sphere to the corporate and international. This situation suggests that we are sliding back into a new Law of the Gun period.

Table 35: The roles of government in the digital era.

As we prepare to enter the third decade of the 21ˢᵗ century, it becomes increasingly evident that ICTs will not necessarily drive democratization. The enthusiasm of the early 2000s on that count has dwindled. In authoritarian societies, like China and Mexico, technology has become an integral part of the mechanisms of social control in the hands of the state. Correspondingly, higher economic concentration and a growing alienation process — along with the diffusion of digital technologies — has been undermining democracy and fueling instability in open economies geared toward the conservative quorum. All of this means that little by little, analogical governance is weakening while the creation of adequate replacements at the digital level does not seem to be within reach. A new governance model must foster and strengthen collaboration and openness in society. As we have explained in previous chapters, that model must be founded on a sustainable economy where agents link to one another in vascular loops. In sum, a new digital governance model must rise to the challenge of the digital age.

Three models of digital governance

When we use complexity and network theories to analyze the problems of economy and government in the 21ˢᵗ century, we find there is a *quorum* that tries to keep the authoritarian aspects of the *status quo* and the inequality of digital conservatism. This occurs even when the status quo and the conservative models are, under current conditions, inherently unstable in the long term. As explained in previous chapters, authoritarian systems are not efficient in the long run because they require too many resources, and they become unstable with innovation and the free flow of ideas.

On their part, conservatives also need a lot of resources to expand, and they produce inequality, stratify society, and have no collaborative capabilities to build anabolic recirculation circuits that are indispensable to solve the sustainability problems. This is so because conservatives try to transfer negative externalities to the substrate without a cost, and that goes against the system's persistence rules dictated by the thermodynamic module. Therefore, an open society with collaborative design offers the best probabilities to find durable solutions, and that — in the cultural evolution model — points to the liberal society quorum.

A question we can formulate at this moment says: How can we think of different paths for policy and social activity when most of what we know has followed the paths of authoritarianism and conservativism? The best answer that we had in the 20th century were the vascular networks, regulated by *hubs*, because large institutions and corporations were indispensable to make things work. However, we are now in a different era. Today, the *hubs* of the 20th century have been hacked by special interests and are only delivering diminishing returns while accumulating imbalances that imperil the whole system — as we have learned with the cases of Uber, Nespresso, AirBnB and the H1N1 postcard. The technology to bypass these *hubs* and reconfigure society's networks already exists, but the public decision to put that technology to use has not taken place. Disintermediation has not occurred and will not happen spontaneously.

It is very likely that bureaucracies today will not understand the disruptive impact of Blockchain and other distributed network technologies. But that would not be different from what occurred decades ago, before the disruption caused by microchips, the Internet, and social networks. Changing the role of government and its relation with the digital society has become one of the most urgent challenges of our time. It is an indispensable condition to address the long list of unsolved issues and turbulence of the new century (e.g., digital governance). The differences between models of governance and network configurations can be laid out in the following taxonomy (Table 36):

	Conservative Analog	Authoritarian Digital	Conservative Digital	Liberal Digital
Network characteristics				
Topology	Bilateral vascular	Digital tree	Digital bilateral vascular	Digital vascular loop
Maximum N	National	National	Global	Specific scale for each problem
Coordination	Decentralized with specialized hubs	Centralized: analogical and digital	Centralized in private platforms	Distributed on digital public goods
Network functions				
Network economies	Specialized by type of network: manufacturing, services, etc.	Depredation of common goods and markets	Maximization of rent-seeking through centralized data analysis	Optimization of social value through distributed analysis
Synchronization	Corporate and governmental hubs	Governmental hubs	No synchronization (Law of the Gun)	Distributed platforms
Validation	Governmental	Governmental	Weak as a result of centralized platforms and correspnding loss of privacy	Strong, thanks to digitally distributed public goods
Risk management	Centralized on specialized hubs	Centralized through State hubs special-izing on security	Weak; everyone manages own risk on their own	Strong; digital governance proscribes anonymacy and guarantees privacy
Filtering	Centralized on specialized hubs	Centralized through State hubs specialized on security	Without filters but with massive surveillance (public and private)	Individual freedoms and guarantees to exercise rights; there are limits and legal consequences to enforce compliance
Node control	Through specialized hubs	Governmental	Centralized in private platforms	Through specialized hubs

Table 36: Governance and network functions for the three models of digital governance.

There is no way to overstate the urgency of change. We are witnessing turmoil, lack of effectiveness, and erosion in the influence of political systems. How to defend the current state of things? Two examples can illustrate the perils and consequences of the absence of filters in a network and the incapacity of the political system to hedge risks.

The first is Brexit. In January 2013, David Cameron, then Prime Minister of the United Kingdom and campaigning for re-election, committed to carrying out a referendum on staying or leaving the European Union. This proposal sought to create a sense of familiarity and connection with that share of the British electorate that distrusted the membership of the UK in the European common market and even thought of it as a toxic, pervasive relationship. For Cameron, the political calculus might have implied the assumption that the UK citizens would be rational enough to vote for continuing in the European Market. On the 23rd of June 2016, 51.8% of the UK electorate voted to leave the European Union, and 48.11% wanting to remain. The consequences did not wait. The British pound lost 20% of its value against the American dollar. Public polls show that there is a substantial number of people who regret having voted to leave the European Union(279). Several analysts illustrated their feeling of frustration by reproducing the tweet of *@LauraTopham*, a leaver: *"I am shocked and worried. I voted leave but didn't think my vote would count- I never thought it would actually happen."*

The second case occurred in Colombia. After five decades of guerrilla warfare, the national government and the FARC (Fuerzas Armadas Revolucionarias de Colombia) attained a complicated but workable peace agreement. In the purpose of cementing the agreement, Juan Manuel Santos, president of Colombia, proposed to carry out a plebiscite with the question: Do you support the final agreement to terminate the conflict and build a lasting and stable peace? Just as it occurred in the UK, the calculus of Santos might have been that, after all those years of violence, the Colombian people would vote in favor of the peace agreement. The referendum took place on October 2, 2016. The no votes carried the day with 50.22% of the ballots versus the 37.44% of registered citizens voting yes(280). Similar to the events in the UK, the political movement that favored no thrived with all sorts of theories that created apathy and disinformation without any checks or control. Interestingly, the yes option won in the regions that had suffered the most from the guerrilla(281). This clearly shows that the people who had been directly affected by the conflict did not see the attractiveness of seeking a more perfect but uncertain future agreement. They were more ready to accept peace under the circumstances, whatever its imperfections.

Other common denominators are noteworthy. The first is that Cameron and Santos did not think they had sufficient political support to make the decisions themselves. Also, the leaders of both nations resorted to referendums in spite of the quality of their legal institutions and to the electoral procedures that gave place to their mandates. As sensitive (but not sensible) political leaders, Cameron paid attention to skeptics of the UK membership in the European Union. Sadly, he validated the conspiracy theories about that membership and gave those theories a chance to become the center of public deliberation. On his part, Santos imperiled a fragile but valid agreement by resorting to the electorate, when voter turnout in Colombia hovers around 55 % (282). The paradox is that these leaders perceived the seeds of the current turmoil and intended to appease it. Unfortunately, their actions only made the problem worse.

The second common denominator in these two cases points to a new phenomenon. Twenty years ago, widespread credit was given to the opinion that a higher flux of information through open networks would produce better-informed citizens. That happened, indeed. But mostly for citizens who were already informed and who would have been informed regardless of the new technologies. These citizens have utilized the networks to strengthen their critical judgment, productivity, and purposefulness in society. However, the most significant share of uninformed citizens in the old model have also stayed uninformed in the current model. Inadvertently, most of these citizens have fallen prey to platforms — like Google and Facebook — that validate and confirm the pre-existing views of users. These platforms seek to keep the interest of users by adapting the content that these users can see more easily, including news and opinions, that other users share, and take as real or valuable. That is how *echo-chambers* appear and grow strong.

Of course, shortly after Brexit and the triumph of "nay sayers" in Colombia, the xenophobia and blatant racism that festered throughout the presidential campaign of Donald Trump created the paradigmatic case of *information bubbles* and *echo-chambers*. These cases show us that, sadly and in spite of and because of the circumstances, a significant share of citizens do not grow up to a level of rational and emotional maturity. Instead, the political attitude of millions degrades to immaturity. Adults of all ages can end up behaving by impulse, just as some adolescents get emboldened by the validation of their peers — gang effect — enthroning emotions above responsibility and foresight. Cameron and Santos behaved as the insecure parents who reward their violent adolescent children by appeasing them with more power in the form of a car or a credit card. Tweets such as that of *@LauraTopham* transpire the usual claim of repented adolescents who do not take responsibility for their actions: *"Why did not you stop me?"*

It is fair to generalize that, in the past, *hubs* put some boundaries to irresponsibility and disinformation. Newspapers presented a repertoire of authors, a variety of views, even selecting the opinions of readers' letters to the editors. Importantly, professional media paid and notarized their pieces of information, taking responsibility for them. By contrast, today we have the technological capability to express ourselves without filters and as we please. The current digital environment is an enormous sphere of online noise — a Babel-sphere. Luckily, there are alternatives to exit this inertial path. And they are not necessarily regressive. Put differently: We need mechanisms of citizen-participation and citizen-government interaction that reward good behavior on both ends of the system and that filter the noise and prejudices that incite bad behavior.

Open government

Open government is an ideal of liberal democracy, and open government can (and must) be reformulated to rebuild the ideals of citizenship and democracy. Inherent to the history of liberal democracies is a tension between the ideals of the State as an instrument of society, on the one hand, and the ideals or imperatives of the State as a reality with ends of its own, on the other. Throughout the recent centuries, as economies grew and transformed into bilateral vascular networks, the institutions of governments also transformed and grew into enormous and complex *hubs*, operated by specialized bureaucracies, rife in opacity and difficult to understand. However, the principle that the State is an instrument of society has served as a counterweight to foster transparency, participation, and accountability. Hence, the principle that the institutions of government should be open is one with the checks and balances that characterize modern constitutions. Open government has become a postulate in the improvement of governance through the adoption and diffusion of best practices — the *raison-d'être* of organizations like the OECD (Organisation for Economic Co-operation and Development).

In the old model, good governance was also complicated, specialized, and distant from the interphase between citizens and governments. But success ultimately depended on the robustness of constitutional fundamentals. In open societies, bureaucratic professionalization and intermediation succeeded. Governmental *hubs* facilitated the construction of public goods, which in turn enabled solutions to problems of allocation and protection of common goods. Private markets developed in these favorable conditions and functional vascualar networks emerged while the random networks subsided. The story was different for closed societies. There, incompetent bureaucracies did not develop public goods. Instead, they allowed predatory behavior to rule private markets. Inadvertently — although not without liability for the consequences — bureaucracies fostered or tolerated dysfunction in vascular networks and random networks expanded. That is one of the reasons that academic institutions and think tanks in closed societies so energetically promoted the transference of good practices from open societies.

Not all went nicely for open societies. Special interests captured *hubs*, the vulnerability of which grew in tandem with their complexity, opacity, and their embedded tendency to concentrate power and responsibility. The hacked economy and corporate welfare stand as cases in point. The debasement of politics as a result of *information bubbles* and irresponsible citizens came in recently as a corollary to the gradual but consistent erosion of (analog) governance.

The silver lining of these unintended and undesirable consequences is that they have reinvigorated the projects to reform and improve governance based on the old, but sound, principles of open government, but now using the new possibilities of digital technologies.

Since the start of his administration, President Barack Obama embraced and championed the ideals of liberal thinkers worried about the promises and perils of digital technology. In his campaign for the presidency, Obama surrounded himself with people like Todd Park, who had a trajectory of promoting new interaction models based on digital technologies such as open data and collaborative, self-regulated, and free-of-charge platforms such as Wikipedia.

The most important contemporary antecedents of open government are the Memorandum on Transparency(283) and the Open Government Directive(284), issued by the administration of President Barack Obama in 2009. In the Memorandum, Obama wrote:

> *"My Administration is committed to creating an unprecedented level of openness in Government. We will work together to ensure the public trust and establish a system of transparency, public participation, and collaboration. Openness will strengthen our democracy and promote efficiency and effectiveness in Government."*

Obama's embrace of open government legitimized and resurrected the concept and led to the Open Government Declaration, proclaimed by Brazil, Indonesia, Mexico, Norway, Philippines, South Africa, and the United Kingdom(285):

> *As members of the Open Government Partnership, committed to the principles enshrined in the Universal Declaration of Human Rights, the UN Convention against Corruption, and other applicable international instruments related to human rights and good governance:*
>
> *We acknowledge that people all around the world are demanding more openness in government. They are calling for greater civic participation in public affairs, and seeking ways to make their governments more transparent, responsive, accountable, and effective.*
>
> *We recognize that countries are at different stages in their efforts to promote openness in government, and that each of us pursues an approach consistent with our national priorities and circumstances and the aspirations of our citizens.*
>
> *We accept responsibility for seizing this moment to strengthen our commitments to promote transparency, fight corruption, empower citizens, and harness the power of new technologies to make government more effective and accountable.*
>
> *We uphold the value of openness in our engagement with citizens to improve services, manage public resources, promote innovation, and create safer communities. We embrace principles*

of transparency and open government with a view toward
achieving greater prosperity, well-being, and human dignity in
our own countries and in an increasingly interconnected world.

Fifty-four nations form the Open Government Partnership (OGP) today. The Partnership works online to foster the principles of transparency, participation, and collaboration with a special emphasis on open data initiatives. The Partnership relies on active participation of civil society and the private sector, and it has become one of the few international institutions with capabilities to counterbalance the degradation of analogical governance. This instrument only needs the challenge and mission of creating instruments to improve digital governance. It is easy to establish intentions and goals, but the devil is in the definitions, the instruments, and the community rules and values to put them to use. No doubt, there is competition between the three models of digital governance (authoritarian, conservative, and liberal). In the case of Obama's U.S., the original intention to create a new alliance with society failed to contain the noise, the rage, and the disorder we all witnessed in 2016. Two years later, it is remarkably apparent that the failures of governance of the digital world contributed to cultivating a new breed of authoritarianism.

Problems of the social contract

The essential purpose of governance is to address and serve the main issues and deficits of the social contract. What are these problems and how are they affecting society?

1. **Value-creation versus rent-seeking.** Inequality stands as a paramount, overarching — and yet not sufficiently addressed — problem of society in our time. To illustrate the importance of inequality today, let us consider the over-developed and bloated state of the financial sector that is not a sign of health. The value of financial assets has grown far above the value of the world's GDP, while 89% of the world's population has no access to financial credit. In 1990, Deutsche Bank estimated the total value of the world's financial assets at around $51 trillion(286). That year, the world's gross product stood at $23 trillion(287). Now, looking at the same proportions in 2013, we can observe that financial assets represented $242 trillion and the world's

gross product stood at $76 trillion (Graph 24). However, if we consider the nominal value of all securities — derivatives and others — their value hovers around $500 trillion. Along with the value of tradition-al financial assets, we get to a (hard-to-believe) estimation: The total value of the financial market is more than to $750 trillion or 10 times the value of the world's gross product. What this data says is that, at least in the most recent two decades, the growth of the financial sec-tor has accrued more benefits for itself than for the rest of the world.

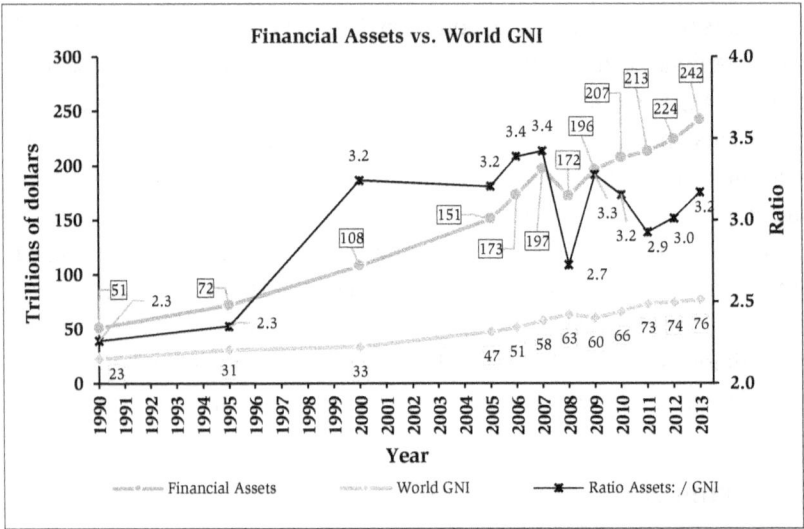

Graph 24: Financial sector against World's gross product. Data from World Bank and Deutsche Bank.

The above-mentioned figures can only underscore the extent of rent-seeking in our time. The irony is that, in spite of the magnitude of this problem, societies have not adequately come to realize and acknowledge how inequality affects us all. Recent research carried out in the U.S.(288) illustrates the gaps between how we think about economic fairness and the economy. This study had its respondents (n=5,322) select one among three charts that represented the distri-bution of wealth in the U.S. One showed an equitable distribution in which each quintile had 20% of national wealth; a second chart dis-played the actual distribution of wealth in the U.S. (without mention of the fact), and the third chart showed the actual distribution of wealth in Sweden (also without mention). Asked which of the three options participants preferred, 92% chose the Swedish chart (Graph 25).

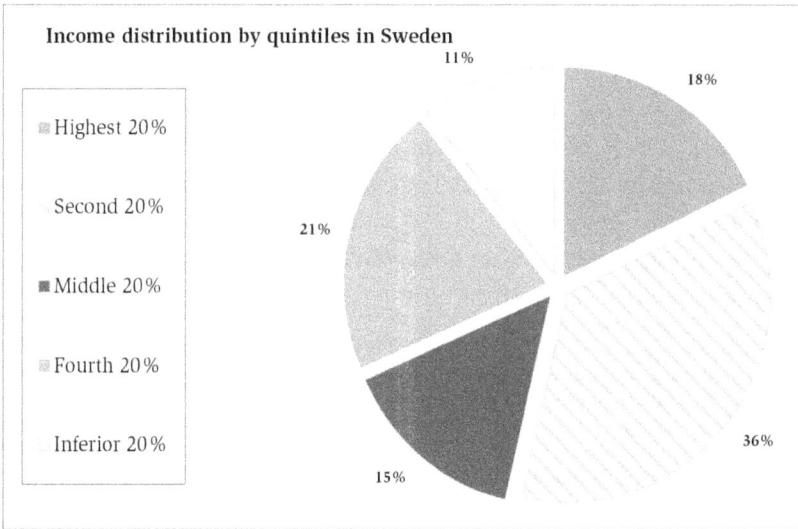

Graph 25: Wealth distribution in Sweden. Own elaboration with data from Dan Ariely and Norton (2011).

In a second part of the study, respondents were asked to guess the distribution of income for the U.S., and they also were asked to define what an ideal distribution of income would look like.

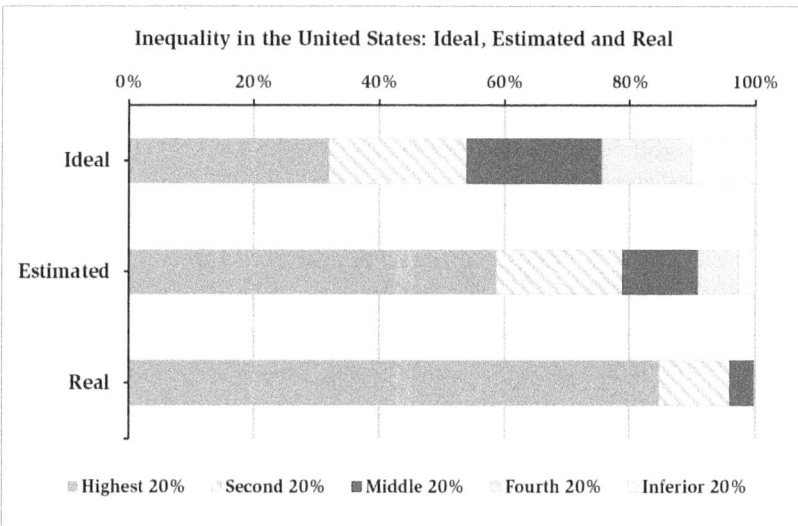

Graph 26: Perception of inequality (ideal, estimated and actual). Own elaboration with data from Dan Ariely and Norton (2011).

The results show that people tended to underestimate the levels of inequality (Graph 26). The difference between the income perceived as ideal for the top quintile and the real income for that same quintile was more than 50 points — and twice that of the real distribution in Sweden. In other words, Americans validate inequality, but never to the extent that they suffer from it. How to explain these gaps in what people know about the social reality? These disparate results could be a consequence of widespread lack of information, of disinformation, or even of denial. Further research can clarify that. However, what we can assert without ambiguity is that the long-run stability and health of the social contract require that society engages in informed conversations and deliberations about the real situation of income, and the causes of inequality — such as economic rent-seeking and the reforms that could mitigate inequality — like changes to taxation.

2. **Short-term vs. long-term.** Currently, short-term decisions tyrannize political and entrepreneurial systems. Executives of publicly owned enterprises listed on the various stock exchanges have to respond to their shareholders with quarterly results and profits. The public quarterly reporting requirements of stock companies in the U.S. constrain work and thinking, precluding the development of long-term vision and implementation. On their part, politicians are also too busy surviving: scoring on every news cycle, raising funds for their campaigns, and fighting in competitive elections. Even if they are well intentioned, politicians and entrepreneurs struggle to find a little time to analyze problems and think of reforms and changes that could improve things. Sadly, the opposite rule prevails: long-term considerations become the enemy of short-term, critical goals and gains. When maximization becomes the organizing principle, the environment favors the automatic selection of a particular type of individual: self-centered, transactional, and exclusively respondent to their own interests. These are the profiles we described in previous chapters: masters, lackeys, serfs, heroes, bandits, conservatives, and superstars. The financial crises, the depletion of the environment, and the destruction of public goods are the collective equivalent of short-term self-indulgence that kills honest efforts and precludes valuable achievements in the future: taking that marshmallow now and foregoing a greater reward later on.

3. **Scale and government levels**. In 2006, the Minister of Agriculture in Mexico asked me to design and execute a plan to create a new national digital services and telecommunications network. The request meant to improve the government for millions of agriculture workers already on the list of beneficiaries of the most important social programs in Mexico. At that time, the ministry had a network of 1,000 service offices spread across the nation, but a telecommunications network that only reached a quarter of those locations. Mexico was 80% an urban society and 20% rural. Demographic density and geography are the usual crux for service providers in rural areas. This case was not the exception. For 76% of the population in rural areas, most was scattered in 182,675 population centers with fewer than 1,000 inhabitants that spread across a territory of more than 1.8 million square kilometers. Importantly, this request coincided with a streak of natural disasters and high prices for energy, grains, and cereals as a result of the booming demand from the BRIC nations (Brazil, Russia, India, and China). The public finances were suffering the pressure and that reduced the budget for our project. Scarcity forced us to do more with less, trying to reach as many beneficiaries as possible through a consolidated set of local offices.

    After pondering an array of solutions, we discovered a study on the distribution of beneficiaries. This study, authored by the Colegio de Postgraduados, had found that Mexico had a network of 450 nodes —which they called micro-regional centers — where 80% of beneficiaries were up to 1 hour away from the nearest node, regardless of the means of transportation — boat, horse, truck, or other. Fifteen percent were between one and two hours away from the closest node, and the remaining 5% were dispersed at longer distances. The economy of this reasoning was striking. We had been used to seeing the nation as a territory — and that is why we had been seeking to solve coverage for more than 190,000 population centers (Table 37)(233). After reading this study, we understood that the nation — and therefore the State — was only relevant and capable of holding a permanent presence in the very last node of the network: exactly where the economic density allowed the existence of Sunday markets. When we estimate the average number of networks of 150 inhabitants (or Dunbar networks) in each level of the network, we can observe that at level VI, which corresponds to places with fewer than 1,000 inhabitants (83% of the total number), the density was inferior to a Dunbar network, and that convinced us not to dilute resources by trying to reach population beyond in the interphase between levels IV and V.

Scale Level	Dunbar Networks (average)	Population	Range	Accumulated population	N	% N	N (cumulative)
I & II	8,987	14,829,346	1,000,000 +	13.20%	11	0.01%	0.006%
III	2,158	16,363,103	500,000-999,999	27.77%	25	0.01%	0.019%
		13,873,211	250,000-499,999	40.12%	39	0.02%	0.039%
		8,599,450	100,000-249,999	47.77%	56	0.03%	0.068%
IV	168	5,946,088	50,000-99,999	53.06%	86	0.04%	0.113%
		4,150,450	30,000-49,999	56.76%	109	0.06%	0.170%
		3,664,946	10,000-14,999	60.02%	300	0.16%	0.326%
		6,417,488	15,000-29,999	65.73%	304	0.16%	0.484%
V	46	6,081,738	5,000-9,999	71.15%	882	0.46%	0.943%
		6,360,949	2,500-4,999	76.81%	1,839	0.96%	1.899%
		8,976,755	1,000-2,499	84.80%	5,921	3.08%	4.979%
VI	0.62	6,507,030	500-999	90.59%	9,264	4.82%	9.798%
		4,822,134	250-499	94.89%	13,590	7.07%	16.867%
		5,743,850	1-249	100%	159,821	83.13%	100%
		112,336,538			192,247		

Table 37: Populational structure of Mexico. Source: Population and Dwellings Census 2010 (INEGI).

At the end of the day, the strategy that we decided on centered in the consolidation of personnel and resources. It consisted in the construction of a high-speed voice and data network, covering 450 micro-regional centers that could be reached by 95% of the users.

The strategy also proposed mobile centers to reach the remaining 5% marginalized users in the rest of the territory.

This case illustrates how the new and growing knowledge and information about the interplay of demographic dynamics and economic structures reveal the inconsistency of some current institutions. This incongruence refers to the scale of some political divisions, levels of government, and public policy.

Water represents another case in point. Depletion of water resources underlies innumerable economic and social problems all over the world. In numerous occasions, divisions of jurisdiction constrain or preclude the adequate scale for the instruments to manage water resources. Syria represents an extreme and grave case, where failure to manage water resources contributed to political instability and war. Harmonizing scale with jurisdiction and ownership (public or private) is a prerequisite to protect common goods such as water basins.

Cities also offer another example of the importance of scale for government. According to the *World Urbanization Prospects*, published by the United Nations(289), 6,388 million people will live in cities by 2050. This figure represents an increase of 2,458 million people from that of 2014. Therefore, most of the opportunities and problems of society will concentrate in cities, since 66% of the world population will be urban and up to 85% in the case of the most developed regions (Table 38). Although cities represent only a small portion of the land, they are the locus of the most consumption of resources and energy. Therefore, they have a considerable role in the solution of problems such as curtailing greenhouse gas emissions.

Most large cities, however, still consist of a multiplicity of smaller jurisdictions that struggle to coordinate their separate administrations and give unified responses to their inhabitants. The scale of the urban networks, therefore, requires an adequate scale of government organization. Some degree of administrative consolidation can improve the functions that municipalities are managing separately, such as water, transportation, urbanization, public safety, and air pollution. But that does not necessarily mean *going big* again. Moreover, attention to network dynamics and scale should prescribe, in several cases, the empowerment of mayors and communities. With adequate governance tools, local actors can be more effective than prime ministers or presidents.

Region	Population (%)			Population (millions)		
Year	1990	2014	2050	1990	2014	2050
Most developed regions	72	78	85	830	980	1,113
Less developed regions	35	48	63	1,454	2,899	5,225
Regions of less development	21	31	49	107	283	895
World	43	54	66	2,285	3,880	6,338

Table 38: Evolution of Urban Population, 1990-2050. Source: United Nations, World Urbanization Prospects

4.   **Management issues**. The first business school in the world — L'École Supérieure de Commerce de Paris (ESCP) — will turn 200 years old in 2019. Its anniversary will honor a discipline that has used two centuries to try to discover the best ways of creating value through leadership, human capital, management, and the development of strategy. Schools and doctrines, like Taylorism — authoritarian and vertical — and holocracy — horizontal, post-modern, and based on self-management — have emerged and decayed. The vagaries of management reveal the competitive or collaborative air of each time and place. But the legitimate concerns for management and leadership traverse all times. Leaders, managers, and workers at all levels suffer every day from problems they cannot even identify or name. Like sub-clinical cases, they stay as non-recognized, non-diagnosed syndromes that only get worse in a vicious circle that has pleonexia and alienation at the center.

Until the 1980s, the image and the capacity of leaders depended on their qualifications and competencies to make decisions, not on the number of tasks that they could manage. Leaders were not expected to *grind stone* in the trenches, to work more hours than line operators, or to be as hectic as a nurse in an emergency room. Starting in the 1980s, and perhaps as a way to prove themselves to the boomer generation, the *Yuppies* generation (young urban professionals) focused their energies on doing the best, having the best, and living the best — an approach of maximization. This generational shift interwove the notions of professionalism with those of leadership. The expectations about leadership transformed. Professionalism acquired new, multiple meanings: shielding work from all emotional or domestic perturbations, making work a priority above everything else (including health), demonstrating vibrant energy and readiness to work under all circumstances, getting straight to work without previously learning or asking the basics of the job, giving self-appearance an overriding place, and in sum, becoming the best product and brand of one's self — not the least, by promoting, consuming, or thinking about what one considered to be the best products, the best brands, or the best ideas. The disastrous consequence of this social trend was nothing less than the repression and concealment of human needs, desires, and limitations. The social contract — its definition and functionality — have been consequently affected.

Today, the *Millennials* are building their values by opposing the obsolete ideals of professionalism of the *Yuppies*. It is worth taking a look at some diagnostics and prescriptions about professionalism that we received at the end of the 20th century (Table 39).

Directives of professionalism	
1. Family matters must not interfere with work.	
Problem	*Millenial* **solution**
Many women of the Yuppies and GenX generations could not have the time or support to take care of their children. Unwilling to interrupt or put their careers off, a lot of these women did not breastfeed their newborns and fed them with synthetic formula. Lack of adequate care produced problems of socialization and public health for that new generation. The supremacy of work above family ended up as a woeful work-life imbalance, for mothers and fathers alike, because it overlooked the importance of non-renounceable aspects, such as child rearing.	Some parents in the new era have fostered a legal and media campaign to promote the normalization, the recognition, and the respect of fundamental rights of mothers, fathers, and children. Breastfeeding in public and in work places is one aspect of these campaigns. Part of the new activism seeks to make enterprises facilitate work-life balance through benefits and time flexibility. Part of the new generation is pressing for firms to adapt to the needs of a family, while the old generation adapted their family values to work.
2. A professional person must work as much as it is necessary and keep high levels of productivity over long working hours. Professionals can work adequately without adequate sleep, and manage as many tasks as required (multitasking).	
Problem	*Millenial* **solution**
Scientific evidence is conclusive about multitasking: • The human mind can only be attentive and concentrated for a limited time. People that work for long hours in multitasking mode are less productive(290). • Lack of sleep is one of the main aging factors. An adult needs between 7 to 8 sleep hours every day to stay healthy(291). • Constant low-key stress impairs judgment and is a risk factor for mental illnesses(292). • Chronic fatigue produces lapses of judgment and bad decisions by executives(293). • Multitasking does not exist. Trying to solve two tasks at a time is a sure method to solve none(294). • Saturation forces the delegation of functions to people that do not have the capabilities to deal with them.	Work for life (instead of living to work).

Directives of professionalism	
3. A professional knows what she is expected to do. No need to ask questions.	
Problem	*Millenial* solution
The risk of incurring bad decisions grows in proportion to the complexity of problems, personal interactions, and unintended consequences(295).	Organizations are encouraging horizontal, collaborative relations characterized by diversity and multi-disciplinary teamwork. Even the highly vertical and compartmentalized services of intelligence in the U.S. have adopted these practices to improve their decision-making processes and to reduce risks(296).
4. Professionals are mistake-proof experts.	
Problem	*Millenial* solution
• Information and knowledge grow at exponential rates. Infallibility is a delusion, even for highly specialized professionals. • The social expectation of infallibility creates unsustainable and unnecessary pressure over individuals. It incentivizes deception, rewards refractory stubbornness, and favors isolation in the process of making decisions. • It encourages the reinforcement of established knowledge and practices and discourages innovation of ideas and experimentation.	There are two ways to counter the delusion of professional infallibility: • Demystify mistakes. Making mistakes is part of life. The Obama administration adopted the motto: fail, but fail fast. • Evolve through collaboration. Science, for instance, seeks specialization along with multi-disciplinary, inter-disciplinary and trans-disciplinary values and practices. Trans-disciplinarity occurs when specialists get involved in a discipline other than that in which they have specialized.

Table 39: Management and ledership directives, problems and solutions. Yuppies vs. *Millennials.*

Some people seem to think that public policy and even international negotiations and decisions reflect meticulous planning and even surgery-like deliberation or premeditation that only involves professionals and experts. Maybe that is the view of a significant, if not a majority, share of the people who have not had first-hand experience in government, diplomacy, or politics. But the people that have had experience in these spheres — I count myself among them — hold a very different, and not as optimistic, view of things. Someone who manages a large and complex hub, like a ministry that serves tens of millions of citizens. On average, belongs to more than 20 boards of directors, leads hundreds or thousands of collaborators, oversees the design and compliance of tens of normative instruments, and is responsible for the results of tens of strategic indicators. That person must also comply with hundreds of administrative procedures, present information to the media for every news cycle, and travel to attend conferences and work meetings. Add emergencies to this picture and the outcome, reasonably, shows over-worked and stressed out leaders who have no time to learn or think or to develop a strategy and oversee its implementation. Managers of today have little if no management capability at all.

In sum, it is time to replace the management system that centered on closed, individualistic, and antagonistic leadership. Unfortunately, the institutionalized consequences of that model — in government and private sector alike — persist today, affecting all levels of organizational and personal life from the opportunities and restrictions of breastfeeding or personal health to the quality of high-level decisions. Today, *Millennials* lead their attention to the recovery of moral values that uphold humanity: community, fallibility, openness, and appraisal of leadership and success through parameters of added benefit, and not of simulated value.

Releveling Asia

The universal history we learned at school was incomplete because it ignores or underestimates the importance of the history of Asia as parallel to that of the West. Of course, there are specialized courses in many universities, but they were not popular, at least until recently. Therefore, our general perception of the historical evolution of the world is limited. Graph 27 illustrates the growth of the GDP of modern Western powers and ancient nations in close relationship to Europe: U.S., France, the UK, Spain, Italy, Germany, Russia, Greece, Egypt, Turkey, and Iran(297).

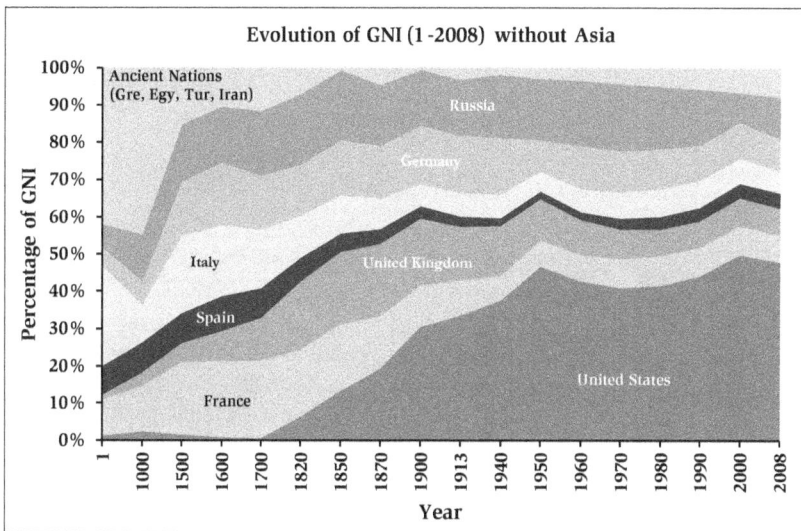

Graph 27: Evolution of GNI without Asia (A.D. 0 - 2008). Source: The Maddison Project, http://www.ggdc.net/maddison/maddison-project/home.htm, 2013.

This is universal history from the viewpoint of the Western Civilization. It essentially states that during the first millennium of our age, there was high tension between the old civilizations of the Middle East and the Medieval Europeans. At the start of the second millennium, the former began to decline in favor of the hegemony of the latter. Modern states emerged from Medieval Europe and turned into great nations that competed and made war upon one another to control the world during the 19th century. Two world wars gave way to the dominance and supremacy of the U.S. during the 20ᵗʰ century. Since then, and until recently, the world economy divided into two blocks of economic power: the European and the American. Today we have a more complete and balanced view of the economic history of the world, thanks to the academic work of Angus Maddison (1926-2010), a renowned economist at the University of Groningen in the Netherlands.

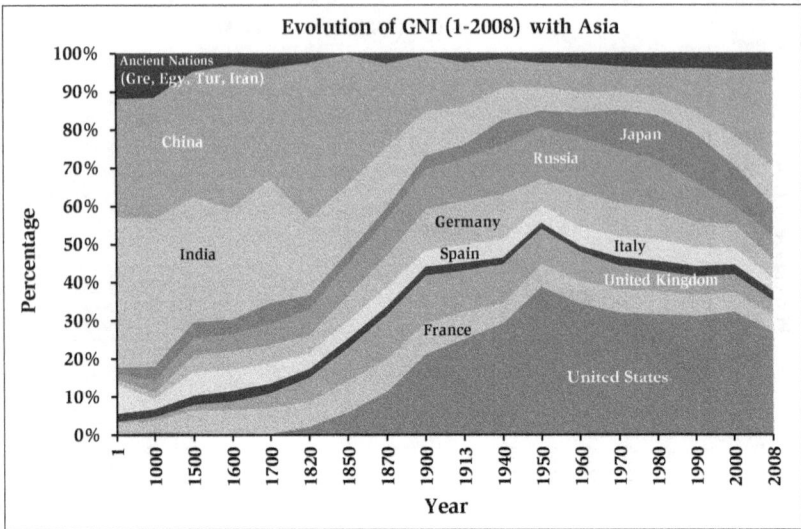

Graph 28: Evolution of GNI with Asia (A.D. 0 - 2008). Source: The Maddison Project, http://www.ggdc.net/maddison/maddison-project/home.htm, 2013.

His research shows that the civilizations of the Middle East were not the only powers in the first millennium of our era: that was, instead, the position of China and India (Graph 28). While these two nations stayed anchored in the agrarian economy and lost their economic preponderance in the industrial era, they are bound to recover a central place in the world economy. The reassertion of the economic power of the Asian economies is not a surprise today. China started an ambitious process of economic reform and industrialization in 1980, and India followed suit in 1990. Together they represent 36.5% of the world's population: the central drive that explains their economic transformation into the industrial era and away from the agrarian and feudal era.

The problem is that, after World War II and especially after the end of the Cold War, the U.S., the European powers, and Japan, occupied a disproportionately large space in the world economy. Just as with China and India at the start of the first millennium, the preponderance of the Western powers and Japan was uncontested. But today the emergence of China and India is reshuffling the pieces in the board and is pressing for accommodation by all players.

There is no question that these shifts in the international system are also affecting government and governance in the 21st century. But the effects and consequences are so vast and complex to understand that we can only lay out the key concerns that guide the analysis of students and specialists:

1. **International Public Goods.** International peace is more difficult to manage today than it was in the near past. After the use of atomic weapons and the destruction of Hiroshima and Nagasaki at the end of World War II, non-proliferation of nuclear weapons became a central international public good. Other international public goods are the fight against terrorism and piracy in the oceans. By definition, the international community should cooperate to build and protect international public goods. However, neither China nor India have shown eagerness to do that. Some economists would say that they are "free riding." These nations get the benefits of the public goods that facilitate international trade, but they are not cooperating to maintain them. For instance, China has a strong influence over North Korea, but has not pressed enough to stop its nuclear weapons program. Instead of centering its enormous resources on international collaboration to stop proliferation of nuclear weapons, China has been playing the complicated and perilous games of the Cold War.

2. **Environmental common goods**. The economic growth of Asia has taken a high toll over the environment, just as it occurred in the U.S. and Europe in the 19th and 20th centuries. Environmental restrictions are very high for China and, in particular, for India. These two economies do not have enough natural resources to fuel their economic growth, and for that same reason, have been searching for alternatives everywhere in the planet. China and India are planning to expand their power generation capacity with coal. These additions will weigh heavily in the CO_2 inventories of emissions for China and India, in spite of the also significant additions of clean fuels, like solar. The dilemma, however, is that while the new powers must have all the right and opportunities to pursue their development, there is not more environmental space to support that economic growth. All nations must act responsibly to find solutions. China and India must protect the few common goods that are still left, and the Western nations cannot deny the reallocation of environmental rights.

3. **Open society**. In the view of many people, the economic success of Asia puts in question the viability and the need for open societies. The appearance of order supports these views: economic reforms in China don't get hobbled by democratic competition (because there is no such democratic competition), public and national

security in the digital space are guaranteed by State surveillance over communications, and drug trafficking is a minor problem because traffickers are summarily executed.

When defending the efficacy of State capitalism, Chinese leaders get to the point of publicly stating that Western notions of individual freedom and dignity are inefficient, alien to Chinese culture, and not a necessity for Chinese citizens. However, the reality is that China is playing an opportunistic and pragmatic role at this moment. China uses technology, knowledge, and the markets of the open society at the same time that it controls and represses its population. Deng Xiaoping laid out the ideology behind this strategy. One of his sayings captures its pragmatism: "No matter whether the cat is black or white, as long as it can hunt mice, it is a good cat." Mao Zedong had also contributed to this philosophy with the doctrine of "one country, two systems," when referring to the place of Hong Kong in the Chinese system. On the other hand, China's millenary history indicates that every time it opens to the world, the coastal cities prosper while the inland population lags in poverty and marginalization. In time, the differences and tensions between both sides become unsustainable bringing about a national collapse. Currently, the problems of inequality in China and India are too big. Inequality, coupled with the inflexibility of their political and social structures, put both nations at high risk of systemic failure.

In the second half of the 20th century, the Cold War forced nations to define and align with one of two blocks (although there was resistance of the so-called *non-aligned nations*, among which China and India were members). There is not a comparable bipolar rivalry in this century — and probably there will not be something as such. However, the relation of the Western nations with the new Asian powers, and especially China, is already one of the most important themes to consider when we think of government in the 21st century, and one with too many sensitive aspects: Tibet, Taiwan, human rights, intellectual property, dumping, and fair access to their markets.

There are not lost causes, there are causes waiting to be won.
Katrina vanden Heuvel

14. The Society of the 21ˢᵗ century

Zombieland

The new technologies and their effects over society have opened a discussion about the transformation of human nature. Some authors, like Giovanni Sartori(298), propose that alienation through TV and the media has brought about a new type of human being, the *homo videns*. Others, like Ray Kurzweil(299), herald the era of transhumanism — identified as H + . For Kurzweil, the exponential advance of technology will enable a singularity in the history of human progress by the year 2045, when some humans will have conditions to live comfortably for more than a hundred years, and when the human-machine fusion will even allow loading consciousness to computational networks. Unbound by natural restrictions of the brain, the evolution of the intelligence would be exponential.

There is little doubt that the current technological processes are alienating people and are as dangerous and comparable to the religious and political fanaticism that brought about social destruction in other eras of human history. However, scientific evidence says that the current technology and media cannot transform and dominate human nature in the ways that Sartori worried about. Nor is it true that information technology can develop exponentially and indefinitely. In 2012, for the first time in 50 years, the reduction in the cost of production of transistors stagnated, and as of 2014, the cost of electronic miniaturization began to increase(300). This indicates that we are in the final phase of Moore's Law, which has been driven by silicon circuits. This limit signals that the exponential economies of scale of the digital age will stop. Besides, the before-mentioned difference between the 12.8 watts of energy required by a human brain and the 18 million watts (megawatts) required by an equivalent computer, represents a barrier against exponential and unrestricted development of artificial intelligence.

Taking these considerations into account, we may agree that the analysis of society in the 21ˢᵗ century is still, essentially, the analysis of the formation and transformation of the *quorum* related to the four strategies of cultural evolution (survival, status quo, growth, and transformation). If we consider the network topologies they produce, we see that positive feedback is critical for their functionality. Tribal networks work well in small modules of low complexity, low productivity, and high equity with centralized-patriarchal or decentralized-communitarian network topologies. Authoritarian networks are functional when they contain violence and poverty, structuring order in the form of tree networks. On their part, conservative networks are functional when there are possibilities for expansion and growth in the substrate, linked to competition, effort, and personal achievement within bilateral vascular networks. Finally, although they have not been brought to existence, liberal networks and their characteristic vascular loop topology support the development of the open society, successfully rising to meet the challenges of sustainability and the digital era. Additionally, our analysis of the economy and government leads us to conclude that two of these four scenarios of cultural evolution are against the wall. On the one hand, the *quorum* is not going to move toward the preparationism or the existentialism of the serfs. On the other side, the tools and the solutions of the conservative strategy have become obsolete, nevertheless there´s value in some of the alternatives trying to overcome the current restrictions. The commercial production of electric power by nuclear fusion is a case in point.

Therefore, authoritarianism and liberalism are mostly the only alternatives left on the table, in addition to chaos. But these paths are absolutely antagonistic to one another. The 2016 campaign in the U.S. is an example of the magnitude of this clash. For the first time in modern American history, and after decades of alienation and desperation for failing to get the rewards that millions felt entitled to get, the Republican electorate, historically aligned with the optimism of conservative expansion, abandoned all reasonability along with the desire to pursue the open society. Instead, millions of political conservatives turned with enthusiasm toward the demagoguery of Donald Trump, the consummate authoritarian master.

The terrible examples of the Brexit decision in the UK, and the failure to support the peace agreements in the plebiscite Colombia did not suffice to stir cautiousness in American voters. In a scenario impossible to imagine just a few months before, Donald Trump triumphed, leading a base of what once was the Republican Party. Just 46.1% of the popular votes was sufficient to give him 306 electoral votes against the 232 of the Democrats, who led a heterogeneous mixture that included old conservatives, minorities, and members of the ruling elite. The popular vote of 48.2% representing a 3-million vote lead over Donald Trump did not suffice to give victory to Hillary Clinton. Before the horrified eyes of millions of Americans, and the rest of the world, the U.S. became the first banana republic with a nuclear arsenal.

Lackeys and serfs relished in optimism the arrival to power of a master who promised to restore them with what they thought they deserve and others — especially immigrants and competitors in the globalized economy — have taken away. Trump scandals and misogyny should have contributed to coalesce the unanimous opposition of women and minorities, but, incredibly, even 29% of Latinos and 42% of women voted in favor of the Republican candidate.

For those who remained on the liberal side, what happened resembled the end of an apocalyptic movie where survivors contemplate from a precarious shelter that everything falls under the control of the zombies. This has happened many times before when democracy has perished in the hands of demagogy. Or as it is said in the Star Wars film series the *Revenge of the Sith* by a tearing Senator Padme Amidala when the creation of the galactic empire is approved: *"So this is how liberty dies, with thunderous applause."*

In this last respect, it is worth reviewing the evolution of the problem of alienation as a degradation factor of the democratic society. After World War II, consumerism in open societies nourished the concept of convenience as an engine of consumer satisfaction. On the institutional side, the message was the same. Institutions are there to give total satisfaction to individuals without requiring any effort from them. Passive consumer-citizens reflect the exaggerated external locus of control society has. Too many people are expecting that corporations or established institutions give — external — satisfaction and solution to their problems and desires, as illustrated by documentary maker Davis Guggenheim in *Waiting for "Superman"*(301). While the U.S. trails all other developed countries on educational indicators, young Americans report to have more self-confidence than young people in other nations. It does not take much to identify a disconnect between personal ambitions and the effort that is necessary to achieve them. That disconnection pervades the mood of the voters who supported Trump.

The exploitation of the gap between desires and needs is fundamental in the relationship between the consumer and the market, be it a market of goods or a market of political options. Today, the best publicity on Earth is that which identifies a feeling, need, or a sense of lack in the consumer's mind and uses it to build a brand around it, seeking to capture the emotions of the consumer by offering a relief or satisfying experience. Coca-Cola is an iconic example of the evolution of marketing throughout the decades: gradually moving from concrete value propositions to attitudes toward life. In the course of a century, Coca-Cola transitioned from a brand that invited many to enjoy a beverage to portraying the product as a sign of good taste, and then to a reason to smile, and finally, a feeling that can be tasted(302) (Table 40).

Year	Slogan
1886	Drink Coca-Cola and enjoy it
1908	Good 'til the last drop
1937	America's favorite moment
1957	The sign of good taste
1979	Have a Coke and smile
2009	Open Happiness
2016	Taste the feeling

Table 40: Coca-Cola Slogans.

As some psychologists say, the problem is that self-esteem, self-determination, independence, motivation, and will to achieve can only come from within the person. If we think of this from the opposite perspective, a way of undermining, submitting and destroying someone or of leading someone to self-destruction would be to convince that person that the solution for his or her problems could only come from external sources, immediately and without need of effort. People who live with an external locus nurture an enormous internal vacuum that makes them excellent and credulous consumers like — zombies — because external solutions only appease their emptiness for a moment, then it constantly reappears, stirring a recurrent need to consume, sometimes compulsively. The marketing that has brought us up in the most recent half century resembles an anxious and overprotective mother that charms, spoils, and flatters consumers, to the extent of draining out their personality. Sadly, many people do not relate to others through authentic feelings, but through a repertoire of brands and the attitudes attached to them. From that perspective, Donald Trump is more a brand than a person. His brand attracted voters with inclinations toward authoritarianism and emboldened them to act accordingly. Just as it occurs with soda drinks, what matters are the feelings that the drink provokes, and not their ingredients nor their negative health effects. What matters the most is the validation that people get to express and act in ways that would have been otherwise inadmissible, in the old *quorum*.

Add to this that we have a hacked economy. It is easier to collect rent when consumers are convinced that value equates convenience. The case of Nespresso is one among many where convenience gets more social appreciation than adverse effects over the environment or the family budget. In our time, convenience is so overrated that it makes it look reasonable to pay three times the cost of coffee than adding a couple of spoonfuls of coffee to the coffee machine. Despite their seemingly greater concern for society and the environment, the millennial generation often limits its efforts to attaining convenience and fun, thereby creating a vicious circle in the search of solutions that balance the greatest convenience with the least effort. At the end of the day, these attitudes lead nowhere (e.g., the storms of protests in social networks, which make a lot of noise, but cannot provoke change). This is what we call couch activism or *slacktivism*, the main benefits of which are simply to produce a positive psychological sensation of release.

The degradation of analogical public goods and the absence of digital public goods aggravate the situation. Good education, health, and nutrition are even more costly and difficult to access, factors that militate heavily against maintaining the liberal quorum. That is disastrous but gets even worse with the possibility of higher income concentration propitiated by the emergence of automated networks of the digital Parthenon type. Two Oxford scholars published in 2013 a piece of research on the future of employment and vulnerability toward automation(303). Among their conclusions, they state that 47% of employment in the U.S. is at risk of disappearing to automation within the next two decades (e.g., works in the transportation sector). Notwithstanding the bottlenecks that are hobbling automation in many jobs, the reality is that several of those barriers are in the process of being defeated. On October 19, 2016, Tesla, Inc. announced that all its vehicles would be fully geared for total automated driving(304). Two days afterwards, the firm Emolument published a study where most respondents said that they did not feel that technology threatened their jobs. Of the study's respondents, 82% were workers with no college education or diploma (305). In sum, we cannot but conclude that a meaningful part of the system — that goes from the interaction rules followed by the agents, to the hubs' control of the networks functions and topology — has accommodated to make the random networks grow while generating more rent-seeking and predatory behavior in vascular networks. It is this configuration that opened the door, with acclaim, to the renaissance of demagoguery through digital authoritarianism; for contemporary democrats, this is just the equivalent of a zombie apocalypse.

Tomorrowland

Another paradox of our time is that, while some factors facilitate the movement of open societies toward the authoritarian *quorum*, liberal tendencies persist even in closed societies. On the night of March 14, 2012, while representatives from Iran and Israel used the mass media to trade accusations and invoke war, two Israeli graphic designers, Ronny Edry and his wife, Michal Tamir, decided to take advantage of technology to bypass the hubs of government and international diplomacy. That night, in their Facebook account they posted an image of Ronny and their daughter that said: "Iranians, we will never bomb your country. We love you"(306) (Figure 29).

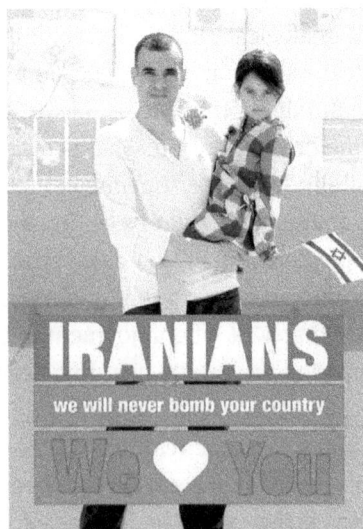

Figure 29: Israel loves Iran Campaign.

In the same post, Edry published the following message:

> "To all the Iranian People: to your fathers, mothers, sons, brothers and sisters. For us to get into war, it takes that we fear one another and hate one another first. But I do not fear you. And I do not hate you. I do not even know you. I have never been hurt by an Iranian. I have not even known Iranians. I met only one Iranian, in a museum, in Paris, a good type. Recently, on TV I have been seeing an Iranian. He talks about war. I am sure that he does not represent the entire people of Iran. If you see someone in your TV talking about bombing your people, rest reassured that that person does not represent the whole People of Israel. I am not an official representative of my country. But I know the streets of my city. I talk to my neighbors, my friends, my relatives, and in the name of all of them, we love you. We do not want to hurt you in any form. On the contrary, we want to meet you. To take coffee and have a chat about sports. For all of you that feel the same, share this message and spread it among the People of Iran".

A few hours after this message was sent, the poster and the message became viral. And other Israelis soon replicated different versions of a poster with the same message. Forty-eight hours after that, the message had crossed national boundaries and the responses on the side of Iranians began to appear (Figure 30). "Israelis, we do not want to have a nuclear bomb. We want peace and democracy. We are your friends."

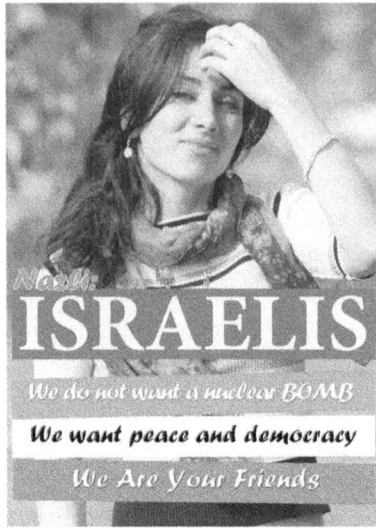

Figure 30: Answer to the Israel loves Iran Campaign.

Within a few days, the idea of Edry and Tamir became an international trending topic and it probably raised the eyebrows of many diplomats and bureaucrats. For centuries, diplomacy was a highly specialized, regulated, and centralized activity. People knew about the opinions and feelings of other people through the statements of ambassadors, chancellors, and prime ministers. In the places where international trade is absent, and where there is no artistic or intellectual exchange, people from one place are an enigma for people abroad, even if these people are geographically close to one another. They do not drink coffee and they do not *talk about sports,* to echo Ronny's words. It is hard to believe that a modest graphic designer could have bypassed such a millenary international diplomatic tradition with only a Facebook post. The new technologies are capable of empowering citizens who are determined to disintermediate diplomacy, block warmongers, and help to keep peace in a novel and distributed fashion.

The emergence of activist consumers represents another form of positive change. As a trend, activist consumers antagonize basic aspects of the markets, which are not built to allow the participation of consumers in the processes that satisfy their needs. It is noteworthy that the participative consumer has an internal locus — liberal or conservative —and vies to go beyond the passive satisfaction of needs, endeavoring in the recovery of autonomy and control over processes and thereby cultivating values of intimacy, community, belonging, accomplishment, and authenticity. Those consumers want to know options, select possibilities and personalize the experience linked to the value of a transaction. Examples of these new consumers and their patterns of consumption are micro-brewers, hobbyists, sports people, adventure tourists, foodies, hackers, makers, and activists.

Thinking about these new patterns of consumption, we can say that a brand is the tangible representation of the feelings consumers experience when they relate or use a certain product. Since those feelings belong to the consumers, in a strict interpretation of things, brands are the property of those who live a psychological experience when they buy or use the branded goods and services. Thus, we can also say that those in charge of managing a well-established trademark are only the stewards or Sherpas that strive to keep alive and well the feelings and connections between the consumer, the product, and the community linked through a brand. A counterintuitive implication of this is that consumers can take away the brand — meaning their feelings — when they want. This in turn makes brands — as we conceive them today — susceptible to hacking or hijack when there's a divide between what they represent to the consumers and the satisfiers provided by its managers.

A first example of *brand hacking* or *brandjacking* in the hands of a participative consumer is that of the Ferrari P4/5, financed by James Gilckenhaus and developed by Pininfarina(307). Glickenhaus, a wealthy consumer of the Ferrari S.p.A. brand, felt nostalgic about the Ferrari cars of the 1960s, and especially for the P2/3 model. In Glickenhaus' view, Ferrari had distanced itself from what he saw as the essence of the brand. Hence, he decided to finance the designers of Pininfarina to create a new series P model over the last Ferrari Enzo ever sold. Marking a contrast against the traditional closed design process of Ferrari, Glickenhaus opened and shared the project on Facebook. He quickly captured the attention of hundreds of thousands of fanatics who had similar feelings about the Ferrari brand. As the project became notorious, the CEO of Ferrari S.p.A., in an unprecedented decision for a company centered on the strength of its brand, felt compelled to officially certify Glickenhaus' new car with an official "Ferrari P4/5 by Pininfarina" denomination.

Afterward, Glickenhaus commissioned a second unit of the P4/5 to compete in races. Once the new car was delivered, Ferrari learned about the situation and threatened legal action in case the second car raced as a Ferrari. Glickenhaus who wasn´t disposed to abandon his feelings or objectives because of a potential legal matter, decided to rename the car "P4/5 Competizione." That is how he ceased to be an aficionado and became a new competitor in the racing car market as the owner of the Scuderia Cameron-Glickenhaus, which has thousands of followers that want to recover the lost essence of automobilism.

The P4/5 example shows that communications in their present state can massively diffuse a project and ignite the direct participation of consumers — owners of the brand or owners of the feeling that constitute the brand — and have relatively easy access to industrial design and manufacturing capabilities, thereby diminishing the control brand representatives have on their assets. Either because of the proliferation of piracy or because of the new tools of digitalization and 3D printing, new competitors are now able to bypass traditional entry barriers — like upfront investments of hundreds of millions of dollars — and cater to the imagination and feelings of dissatisfied consumers. We can paraphrase the slogan of Patek Phillipe & Co.: "A firm never owns its brand; it merely looks after it for the next generation of consumers."

In sum, the digital citizen and the digital consumer, like Ronny Edry and James Glickenhaus, are examples of a new and powerful collaborative disintermediation force of change that can be the center of a new quorum that allows us to escape from the social apocalypse and enables the construction of the land of tomorrow.

Community, participation, and co-creation

Institutional relationships have changed throughout time. In the 1960s, their structure was vertical and departmentalized, known as the silo model. The following era was more open because it sought to identify and integrate all the steps of the value chain within organizations. Nevertheless, the new complex interactions escape the control of organizations, giving rise to the campaigns of "Israel loves Iran" and the "Ferrari P4/5 by Pininfarina." Together the porosity of the digital networks and the fracture in the corporate and institutional intermediation model show us that the development of new models, such as those based on communities, is indispensable as a safeguard against more confrontation and fracture.

One option to make things better is open government and the other one is co-creation. Co-creation is a model in which a firm or institution enables the involvement and participation of clients and other stakeholders in the development of products and solutions. For instance, by the end of the 20th century, The Lego Group, the LEGO® toy maker from Denmark, was facing great pressure on their production costs and losing market share to the competition (308). In 2003, The Lego Group hit bottom when it reported losses of $240 million. Partners broke with family tradition, injected capital, and hired a professional CEO. In the process of rebuilding its brand, the company discovered that some of its products had attracted participative consumers with specific interests such as electronics and robotics enthusiasts who hacked — in the sense of making something new or better — the electronic LEGO Technic products. Those enthusiasts created robots and software that The Lego Group had not brought to the market.

What matters in this story is that Lego company executives, while worried about managing the crisis, kept their minds open to new possibilities and had the sensitivity to understand that the communities of enthusiasts and their goals and interests were, in fact, the strength and the future of the brand. Against what other firms with a different culture could have done, like Ferrari, Nespresso, and Keurig, The Lego Group made the decision to follow a business philosophy of co-creation based on open technology and a supportive relationship with the communities of creative and enthusiastic consumers. In a few years sales recovered, and new markets were discovered thanks to the active participation of its clients. Examples are the production of films, video games, and educational shows. In 2015, The Lego Group had sales of $5.4 billion, with profits of $1.4 billion.

Co-creation depends on active citizens or consumers. These agents meet in communities that further their interest, create scale, reduce costs, and keep their motivation and interest alive. In sum, communities require a variety of support components, just as any other network. The components that help to build communities, networks, or active markets include:

1. **Community.** The quintessential characteristic of these markets is the existence of groups of active consumers that give life and meaning to a goal. The key is to understand that communities get their thrust from the interest and motives of people, and not the reverse.

In some places it is believed that communities create the interest and motivation of people because external influence is what makes people move. However, extrinsically motivated people — a group of lackeys and serfs that follow a master — are not a community.

2. **Platforms.** All industries have a scaffold and an infrastructure that enables processes and actions. For instance, ports form the backbone of that infrastructure in the maritime industry. In the sports industry, that infrastructure can be equated to runners and the public and private spaces where they train and compete. The platforms enable the work of a community. Each industry has different platforms, real or virtual. For instance, electronic auctions depend on software platforms; LEGO consumers depend on the thousands of exchangeable pieces made of plastic.

3. **Activity.** To keep their vitality, communities depend on concrete and permanent activities that allow members to attain their goals: for instance, baking bread that tastes better and looks better, building a new airplane, getting the best from practicing with a musical instrument. Without activity, communities perish.

4. **Rewards and positive feedback.** Members of communities reward themselves with participation in competitions, projects, prizes, and recognitions. At the center of this is the intimacy members attain through a shared feeling of belonging and achievement.

5. **Knowledge and good practices.** Communities evolve by creating knowledge, establishing good practices, traditions, and rules. When they don't translate experiences in knowledge that allow to preserve their vitality and creativity, they stagnate and fall into vicious traps that, in time, reduce the benefits of participating in that community.

6. **Supplies, tools, ingredients and inputs.** Just as it happens with an organism or the node of a network, communities use resources from the environment and need tools, raw materials, and ingredients to work. It is a fallacy that communities in the digital world can be created and developed at no cost. For instance, while a meaningful part of the interaction of The Lego Group with its consumers is virtual, the firm nonetheless invests seriously and steadily in the communities. In turn, communities stay with the brand because the brand is sensible to their needs and feeds them with prototypes, software, platforms, manuals, blocks, and ideas.

In conclusion, although there are important factors that continue to strengthen the model of passive and alienated agents, the transformation of society is viable and possible with active, participative, and creative agents. Change, innovation, and the development of solutions toward a liberal and open society centered on the creation of value depends on these agents and not on those that are submissive to technological change and can pave the way to digital authoritarianism.

All this said, the path toward the open society needs the deliberate and determined construction of new spaces, components, and relationship models that can facilitate its functioning and allow it to prosper.

Leadership, value and innovation

In addition to the leadership of masters, paladins, and superstars, we mentioned and borrowed from popular culture three styles of leadership: *baby boomers* who base their lives on social position, economic status, and educational or professional credentials; the yuppies, driven toward the maximization of results and professionalism; and the innovators of the new millennium, or millennials, who are centered in attaining development through shared value. These three types work as generalizations, and are not intended to pass judgment over individuals. Instead, the types make clear that only two generations past, the leadership style that tended to prevail in organizations was distinctively conservative. The pioneers of the digital era — who were scorned as *nerds* in the early days of their success — introduced new models of leadership. Some of the new technological firms that vanquished the established corporations were created by non-conformist rebels that thrived on the rich mosaic of counter-culture of the West Coast of the U.S.. Poised toward technological innovation, these leaders succeeded against large corporations, and in so doing, they shattered the confidence of the status-centered culture of the baby boomer generation and the professionalism-centered culture of the yuppies. These new leaders also showed that leadership could have different foundations. In time, even the term *nerd* acquired new and positive connotations, linked to capacity and creativity. In fact, it is worth noting that within *nerd* counter-culture, the virtue that matters is technical capacity. All the rest is superfluous, including the façade of professionalism cultivated by yuppies. The transformation of cultures of leadership in organizations is, therefore, a profound change.

373

As corporations and institutional bureaucracies grew and became more complex, they also became more opaque. Knowing and understanding the value created or contributed by each participant became more and more difficult. An irony can be observed at this point. In recent decades, as international manufacturing processes or business units turned obsessively toward abating costs and increasing their productivity and efficiency, they mainly sought results through enhanced controls over raw materials, labor, waste management, times, and processes. On their part, the management, decision-making, and marketing business units lost sight of what productivity and added value meant and started to allow and develop new master and lackey dynamics. Moreover, the introduction of digital technology brought about a wide array of non-productive activities, embedded within productive activities. For instance, email connected all the members of the organization and reduced communication costs in a dramatic way. However, electronic communication also led to endless and pointless threads of conversation, *spam*, and security risks, like *phishing*, that cannot be filtered out efficiently because of their entanglement with relevant and valuable messages. In my professional experience, I could corroborate that when organizations inventory and rationalize their reporting and messaging, they believe that more than 70% of that effort, which makes up a significant part of the payroll, was useless and unnecessary. Today, the crafting and use of Microsoft® PowerPoint® presentations and the growth of work hours through telecommunication systems and smartphones have become important causes of low productivity and time loss in contemporary organizations.

This context of bureaucratic lack of productivity, work overload, and forced use of innovation to survive in the market has helped to demystify old leadership styles while encouraging the flourishing of new styles of leadership centered on value and not on image. Some of the studies inspired by the Great Recession of 2008 throw light on these developments. For instance, the research firm MSCI(309) points out that the size of the remuneration CEOs receives have no correlation with better market performance. Seen in more depth, this incongruity underscores the link between extrinsic motivation and bad results, as we have pointed out before. According to the study, firms that have the highest executive pay and practice cult to the CEO, in the long term, deliver the worst results to shareholders.

Despite the evidence about the problems in the formation of leadership and in the process of value creation, archetypes have strong roots, wired in our biological structure. Different ethological studies(310) indicate that humans have a natural proclivity to identify leaders according to their image and behavior. Lacking the concrete references to measure the capacity to create and contribute value, we primitively make our choices by considerations of physical height, vocal tone, and the symmetry of face. In other times, those stereotypes were useful to identify the attributes of the best warrior or hunter, but they are no longer useful in today's information-based society. Hence, the construction of a different *quorum* requires a new method that fosters transformational leaders and solutions. Thus, we propose to organize an approach to generate value and innovative leadership by centering attention on three aspects or levels: the style of leadership, the process of innovation, and the spaces of innovation.

1. **Components of transformational leadership:**

i. **Focus on value (identify and measure the contributed value).**
The transactional and management systems developed from the old IBM® SABRE model is now useless to foster and measure productivity in institutional and bureaucratic environments. These systems are more anachronistic when we consider that digital technology is powerful enough to support the existence of commercial autonomous cars and the automation of office tasks by means of artificial intelligence. In fact, a meaningful part of the problems of opacity and productivity in organizations have to do with learning difficulties, interoperability, filtering, translation, and interpretation of information. That is what occurs when, for instance, information, residing in a multimillion dollar transactional system, is extracted, transformed, and interpreted in Microsoft® Excel®, to be rendered again in a Microsoft® PowerPoint® presentation for a meeting. Even though these activities are often made by highly skilled workers — information workers — most of these tasks require little creativity and constitute a waste of talent and imagination. At the same time, this dynamic reinforces the authoritarian operation model. In this process, lower rank workers mine data from data mines like SABRE; they extract information gems and deliver them to manager-level crafters who cut them, polish, and complete the PowerPoint final incrustation. The result is bestowed like a tribute of new knowledge to the masters of bureaucracy, who assimilate them into their trove of managerial wisdom.

This process only replicates, in a very inefficient and costly way, the filtering and synchronization of information inside a network. It could be different, but changing these dynamics implies breaking away with the culture of bureaucratic submission and embracing open and collaborative models of organization with distributed networks.

Jeff Bezos embraced the transformation and shattered the old model by resorting to a frugal innovation. In 2004, he defined an important aspect of the work culture of Amazon® by means of the narrative(311). Amazon workers do not use PowerPoint; it is not well appreciated. Instead, for their meetings — especially if attended by J. Bezos — collaborators must craft a text called narrative, which contains the context and data, identifies the problem, proposes a solution, and requests a decision. Narratives are not sent in advance through email. To the contrary, every participant in the meeting gets the text at the start of the meeting because that ensures that everyone can have time during their work hours to read it carefully. Once everyone has synchronized with the same high-quality information and there is a clear goal to attain, they discuss the subject and arrive at a decision. In an email sent in 2004, Bezos explained why abrogating PowerPoint and using other more complex mechanisms is in fact a more efficient method to promote value creation at Amazon:

> *Well structured, narrative text is what we're after rather than just text. If someone builds a list of bullet points in Word, that would be just as bad as PowerPoint.*
>
> *The reason writing a 4-page memo is harder than "writing" a 20-page PowerPoint is because the narrative structure of a good memo forces better thought and better understanding of what's more important than what, and how things are related. PowerPoint-style presentations somehow give permission to gloss over ideas, flatten out any sense of relative importance, and ignore the inner connectedness of ideas.*

Some modest measures have enormous potential to transform bureaucracies and all types of organizations. Actions like requiring workers to express through narratives can be crucial to the objective of discovering, measuring, stimulating, and creating value. A narrative, for instance, can immediately help to reduce opacity and favor innovation by identifying those workers that can create and articulate complete ideas while siding out the — less capable — PowerPoint *free riders*.

ii. **Evidence-based decision making.** By method, Jeff Bezos continually asks of his collaborators at Amazon: "What is the best counterargument to your text?" This question forces whoever is presenting an argument to find flaws in it — like prejudices, or substitution of anecdotes for hard data. Self-criticism is always a challenge. We struggle to see things beyond our experiences and pre-established ideas. In this respect, the DIKW pyramid describes the hierarchy and level of complexity that information can have. The first level is that of data; the next corresponds to information, then knowledge, and finally, wisdom, at the highest layer of the pyramid (therefore the acronym DIKW). The quality of evidence-based decisions improves when: 1) data noise (e.g., prejudice) is identified and eliminated; 2) experiences and personal anecdotes are assimilated and balanced through contrast with contextual data turned into information; 3) rigorous analysis of evidence prevents rushing to conclusions; 4) processes arrive to a decision, and results are evaluated and shared as new knowledge that adds to a wealth of collective wisdom in an organization.

iii. **Balance between focus and curiosity.** Balance between present needs and future opportunities is a recurrent issue for leaders. For some corporate leaders, the discussion has to do with the difference between effectively running day-to-day operations, on the one hand — like promoting and selling products and services, making production lines work, fulfilling orders — and innovating and creating new opportunities on the other side. From a strictly managerial point of view, the discussion is between keeping in place the things that work well and that it is not convenient to stop — processes — and developing initiatives to change things — projects. However, from a sociological perspective, the balance must be struck at some point between traditions — things that should not change, like child-rearing — and innovation — discovering new opportunities beyond the limits of the community.

All these discussions aside, transformational leaders are those who can keep things from getting stuck while at the same time promoting new ideas without getting distracted. These are the people who find the balance between focus on the present and curiosity to seize the future.

iv. **Learning by doing.** People and organizations learn in two ways: using things (*learning by using*) and doing things (*learning by doing*). The first method relates to technological assimilation and the second to technological development. Each model is valid in a specific context and it is important to take the differences of each approach into account, even if users may take themselves as innovators regardless of which scheme they apply.

The model of passive technological assimilation can be useful when there is no previous knowledge about something that is already established or when learning something new is not indispensable. However, learning by doing is the sensible alternative when the situation requires developing a competitive advantage and producing an authentic innovation. Assimilation requires low effort and yields little learning. Doing requires considerable effort, but much can be learned on the way, and that is the key characteristic of open societies and self-determined people. In authoritarian bureaucracies, where work has been organized to digest information and reproduce it in reports, meetings, and PowerPoint presentations, directors seek to subsidize their process of learning through the — old and inefficient — learning-by-using model. Meanwhile, each member of a creative team is responsible for his or her own learning, including leaders. Learning involves a personal and individual effort that becomes an asset for collaboration and active participation in authentic innovation processes.

It might be worth recalling how things were during the government of Mexican President Felipe Calderón (2006-2012). In those years, PowerPoint became the main tool for the directive team in the office of the president. Teams of advisors were under constant — and even anguishing — pressure to create and edit the PowerPoint presentations that the President revised in cabinet meetings, even amidst crises and emergencies, such as that of the H1N1 influenza outbreak. Hundreds of people in the bureaucracy dedicated thousands of hours to prepare slides for the president. Through this practice, the president implicitly signaled to the bureaucracy that political status depended on intervening at key moments of decision and not on investing time for analysis and reflection. Naturally, ministers and deputy-ministers mimicked the presidential habit and relayed the work of analysis downstream until it reached the lowest levels of the hierarchy. The end consequence was that the quality of documents was low — as the rank of the people who prepared them. Moreover, decision makers did not have an informed opinion about the issues because they had not participated and reflected upon them.

Paradoxically, aides conveyed obsessive and minute attention to parameters of form. These existed, and the president took them seriously. Even if the cabinet often did not address the issues of fundamental importance, nothing could make the president more frantic than a PowerPoint slide with an acronym: they were banned. In 2012, the final year of the presidential term, the director of the National Archives (AGN after its name in Spanish) asked for the help of our office to consolidate the historical archives of the administration of President Calderón. She commented that a substantial share of the decisions and executive discussions of the presidency did not have adequate documental support because they had been based on PowerPoint presentations. Logically, that represented a challenge for the National Archives, an office with the mandate to compile and conserve documents. Through *detectivesque* travails, her collaborators had managed to secure some files from the computers and emails of a handful of aides. But the team of archivists could not assert the origins and authorship of the documents, and they even doubted that those documents were the final versions used by the president. In sum, archivists considered that a substantial part of the documents used to make decisions had been lost forever.

Former British Prime Minister Sir Winston Churchill and his working habits offer an example in the opposite direction of the Mexican presidential story. According to his memories and to biographers like William Manchester, Churchill had the habit of dedicating hours — usually at night — to write long articles and cabinet papers (proposals of policy) that forced him to formalize and bring his thinking down to earth. By conveying the reflections of the prime minister, these documents also clarified and gave input to the cabinet, war cabinet, and even the leaders of other nations (e.g., U.S. President Roosevelt in the most critical moments of war). The contrast is clear. Churchill did not expect bureaucracy to give him an interpretation of facts. A known megalomaniac, Churchill looked down on documents produced by the bureaucracy and considered that infusing his knowledge into the public service was part of his duties as a statesman.

v. **Management of unexpected consequences.** There are no perfect solutions in economic, social, and cultural systems. Complex systems are subject to emergent phenomena and perturbation. However, the knowledge of network functions and the restrictions over a system increase the possibilities of better understanding the probable consequences of decisions: What are the filters? How does the network synchronize? What contention mechanisms exist? The answers to questions like these improve the risk management and diminish the possibility of catastrophic failure. By contrast to conservative or authoritarian systems, that center narrowly in the maximization of results, the liberal systems are forced to be holistic in their decision-making processes and flexible to modify the course of action as response to unexpected consequences.

2. **Components of the innovation process.** According to Fred Dust, from IDEO, the process to make innovation can be broken down as follows:

i. **Make the right question.** There is a widespread — although wrongly attributed to Albert Einstein — phrase that says: "If I had one hour to save the world, I would use 55 minutes to define the problem and five to find the solutions." It is true. Defining the question is the critical point in an innovation process: its implicit and explicit assumptions can either frame success or replicate mis-judgments and prejudices. As way of illustration, let us think of someone premeditating innovations to transportation at the start of the 20ᵗʰ century, when automobiles existed already but horses still dominated. A bad question would have been: How to improve horse transportation? The right question would simply be: How to improve transportation? That question is more open and lends opportunity and space to consider the automobile as part of the solution. The key to innovation, therefore, resides on the definition of the problem and in presenting premises and assumptions with transparency that allow the collaborative scrutiny of peers, as occurs with the narrative-based method of Amazon.

ii. **Ideas can come from anywhere.** In large and stratified organizations, many innovation initiatives fail when participants weight ideas according to the rank of the people that generate them. Although the engineers and designers of The Lego Group can boast about being the only world authority on the subject, the open process of co-creation in which they participate does not make a differentiation between the ideas of a kid and those of an aerospace engineer.

iii. **Many ideas, and the freedom to dissent.** A good process of innovation produces a lot of ideas and gives the opportunity to freely reject bad ones, even if they come from the directive levels. In the innovation processes operated by IDEO, ideas do not get tagged to names to limit personal affinities or rivalries.

iv. **Ideas have no owner.** If there is not an owner for each idea, then it is easier and simpler to accept failure and to search for new solutions.

v. **Short development cycle.** Innovation has a high rate of failure. To test as many different solutions as possible, it is better to develop proof-of-concept examples with short development and development cycles, while understanding that prototypes must be cheap.

vi. **Focus on value, fostered by results.** If the definition of the problem — question and premises — is adequate, then the definition and measurement of value and of the results of the solution must be simple too. All solutions should be formulated by responding the question: What is the measure of success?

vii. **Fail, but fail fast.** Before their implementation, all solutions must have clear metrics of success and failure under the motto "Fail, but fail fast." Processes of innovation are built to accept trial and error and failure. However, to resist several testing cycles, it is indispensable to have the capability to overcome the phases of error. This can only be achieved through the rapid identification and acceptance of failure.

viii. **Permanent process.** Innovation is a difficult discipline, and first-time success is extremely uncommon. Once an organization establishes a practice of innovation, it is better to transform it into a permanent and iterative process and not to reinvent the practice every time it is necessary.

ix. **Adapt the recipe.** There are several methods and recipes to innovate, but there are none that helps all organizations in the same way. Recipes must be customized through flexible methodologies.

3. **Components of a space or an innovation lab.** According to Edgar Barroso, a consultant from Cutter Consortium, the organizations and offices specialized on innovation:

i. Promote collaboration between, within, and across-disciplines (multi-, inter-, and trans-disciplinarity).

ii. Dedicate flexible working spaces that adapt rapidly to the changing conditions of work for individuals and teams.

iii. Create solidarity within communities by seeking solutions together.

iv. Engage in strategic partnerships continuously with business sector key organizations at the local, national, and international level.

v. Create a permanent program of activities that keeps the community and the space of innovation alive: innovation challenges, competitions, conference, workshops, and consultancy.

vi. Maintain a permanent staff with high levels of adaptability and resilience.

vii. Work to attain specific goals.

viii. Recruit the most creative people and create an ecosystem that makes specific projects flourish.

If it exists, it is possible
Anonymous

Conclusion

To summarize, the future offers three possibilities: 1) chaos, if the world cannot get rid of the inertial conservative model — the sustainability of which is not granted by planetary conditions; 2) the involution to the authoritarian apocalypse; 3) the deliberate construction of the transformational world of tomorrow. Nothing is written in stone, and the results will depend on the sum of our decisions and actions. The victory of Donald Trump in the U.S. presidential election of 2016, the choice of the UK electorate for leaving the European Union (Brexit), and the defeat of the peace agreements by Colombian voters have turned on the alarm: authoritarianism is gaining momentum. Authoritarians have the advantage that low complexity social organization — their recipe — can be attained rapidly, instinctively, and without reflection and careful proposals. Albeit with the disadvantages of inefficiency, violence, inequality, and long-run instability. Meanwhile, the path to open society is difficult, but not impossible in the long run. We are amidst a chaotic transition because the configuration of social, economic, and political networks gained flexibility to the extent that the existing system became unstable. We are witnessing and experiencing a total reconfiguration of human society. We are living a *tabula rasa* moment in history, where everyone — liberals, conservatives or authoritarians alike — lives in uncertainty and ignorance about the future. That is the reason why we have the opportunity to capture it.

The present is a unique opportunity for all of us interested in maintaining the open society and making it grow. Complexity science, the cultural evolution model, and network theory allow us to better understand the configurations of different systems while we can develop tools to propel change, from an abstract and general level that speaks to social science, all the way to the specific aspects of transformational leadership, the innovation processes, communities, and collaboration spaces. Regardless of the very challenging circumstances, there are ways to maintain the open society and to make it grow. We only need to imagine it and work toward its creation.

III

The world
as it can be

We tend to overestimate the effect of a technology
in the short run and underestimate the effect in the long run
Roy Charles Amara

15. Internet II

Anachronisms of the Internet

On March 19, 2016, at 4:34:30 a.m., John Podesta — campaign manager of the Democratic candidate Hillary Clinton — received an email, apparently from Google, informing him that someone had unauthorized access to his email account and prompting him to follow a link and change his password. Urgently.

Podesta — a *Baby Boomer* born in 1949 — requested the technical team of the campaign to review the email. At 9:54:05 a.m. on the same day he received a response from Charles Delavan — from the DNC help desk — which contained the following statement: "This is a legitimate email, John needs to change his password immediately."(312) Confident in the response of the technical team, Podesta clicked on the link that took him to a page where, inadvertently, he gave his password to a group of Russian *hackers* called *Fancy Bear*(313). Months later, thousands of messages downloaded from the Podesta account were gradually published by WikiLeaks during the final phase of the campaign. The scandal contributed importantly to the loss of confidence in Hillary Clinton's candidacy. Delavan's blunder will probably transcend the annals of U.S. electoral politics as one of the costliest mistakes in history.

This case highlights that the technical complexity, anonymity, lack of privacy, and in general terms, the insecurity experienced by many within the network, is a consequence of the high degree of obsolescence in many of the components that make the Internet work. In all this shame and pain, Clinton and her colleagues discovered that the advantages of the Internet to handle an election campaign might not be worth the associated risks for public and national security. Although the Internet we know, use, and love is incredibly useful in comparison to the analog technologies it replaced, the reality is that several of its components, including email, are as obsolete as fax machines (Table 41).

Component	Function	Flaw	Year
DNS (Domain Name System)	Translates the numeric addresses of internet in names of domain (e.g. 148.206.32.5 in www.google.com).	The hierarchical and centralized structure of the network of DNS servers increases vulnerability to attacks. The most common of these attacks deny service by saturating the server's capacity of response and preclude users from finding and solving the addresses of the services that they are looking for. It only has support for American alphabet in ASCII code.	1984
SMTP (Simple Message Transfer Protocol)	The base protocol to exchange email messages between servers.	Originally designed without security functions. Lacks verification of senders, encryption, and authentication of users.	1981
POP3 (Post Office Protocol)	The protocol for downloading email messages from a server.	Carries out all transactions without encryption. Obsolete functions to authenticate users.	1988
IMAP (Internet Message Access Protocol)	The protocol to download and manage email messages.	Complex to implement operators and use for users. Generates downloads and unrequested message copies. Lacks robust security functions.	1986

Table 41: Obsolete components of Internet.

The state of the Internet today can be compared to the state of the Ford Model T automobile against the horse more than a century ago. The Internet is already a massive, useful, and integral part of a new economic paradigm. However, it is far from being a mature, reliable, safe, and comfortable technology. Extending the illustration, we can say that today's Internet resembles the first cars that did not have all the sophisticated gear with which we have become familiar: air conditioning, anti-lock brakes, seat belts, independent suspension, heating, airbags, satellite navigation, impact absorption zones, electronic injection, and systems to control emission of polluting gases. Clinton, Podesta, and Delavan became yet three more victims in the growing statistics that remind us of all that is still left to improve with the Internet.

Identity, anonymity, privacy, and freedom of speech

Complex problems, such as the disasters that surpass the available capabilities in the system that must solve them, can be managed in two forms: one is declaring them unsolvable and finding consequential ways of adaptation; alternatively, complex problems can be dismantled. The Ancient Greeks used to call for "cutting the Gordian knot" when a problem got out of hand and needed to be solved without more complications. We need to confront the problems of our obsolete Internet. Where to start? Should we live completely without it and start over? Or, can it be reformed gradually, one step at a time?

To continue with the analogy of disasters, we might imitate an established principle of first response: triage, the process of prioritizing patient care based on need and available resources. This principle gives way to tenets that must be championed above everything else. For example, in the case of disasters and emergencies, the highest principle is the preservation of human life. Triage also recognizes that, by definition, in a disaster the necessities exceed the capabilities of response in a system. Triage adheres to the premise of using available resources to save as many lives as possible, regardless of the economic, political, or social background of the people affected. During triage, the first respondents catalog the patients into five categories (Table 42):

Color	Description	Action
Black	Dead people or patients that will die within minutes.	No need to give care, but they are identified in order not to waste time and resources.
Blue	Catastrophic patients with little chances of surviving and that need massive use of resources.	No effort or resources are given to their attention. These patients are third priority.
Red	Critical patients that can survive if they receive simple but immediate measures.	Most resources go to these patients. They are the priority.
Yellow	Patients that will probably survive if they receive attention within hours.	Second priority. If they get worse, they can be re categorized as red color and receive attention.
Green	Patients with minor injuries that can wait for treatment.	Third or fourth level of attention.

Table 42: Triage. Classification of patients.

Many might consider the classification as bad, unfair, or inconsiderate because it is expressly designed to not examine aspects such as the family or political background of the affected. However, these rules of decision-making constitute the most-used technique in the world to face problems that have no apparent solution with a limited amount of resources. In disasters, triage officers are the highest authority, and their decisions about life and death cannot be contested or appealed.

The Internet is a complex system that has evolved without an established direction. Today, several factors continue to impact its evolution: the obsolescence of protocols, imbalances in the network's functions, the prevalence of private platforms over individual rights, and the absence of digital public goods constitute a new, complex Gordian knot. Many people — and the experts above everyone else — see these intricacies as impossible to unravel. The discussion is not new, and it is likely that similar conjunctures have existed before. For example, at the beginning of the industrial era, the abandonment of the economic, political, and social institutions of the agricultural era led the promoters of industry and urbanization to think that the new model of social organization had strong and reliable mechanisms of self-regulation — a principle that was regarded as logically superior. A corollary of this view held that the society that was emerging had to be free of parochial rules. Unfortunately, not all things could be left to manage themselves. As discussed in other chapters, lack of attention to the foundational rules of the industrial economy paved the way to the era of dysfunctional vascular networks, robber barons, and to the imbalances and instability that eventually culminated in two world wars.

To some extent, the current problems of the Internet resemble the imbalances of the industrial age and the collapse of institutions in the first half of the 20th century. One of the most important responses to that collapse was the Universal Declaration of Human Rights and the Western constitutions that put individuals, their dignity and rights in the center. Today, we must follow principles like those of triage to select the first rules of action as we rise to the challenges in Internet governance.

The analogy between triage as a response to disasters and the governance of the Internet allows seeing more clearly the obsolescence or absurdity of present practices. Today, the protection of data flows, online traffic, and Internet Protocol (IP) addresses seem to have become more important than protecting individual rights such as privacy. In the analogy that we have chosen, this would be tantamount to putting the protection of goods above the protection of human life. It seems that, little by little and without fully realizing the consequences, the digital era refurbished the answer to the foundational question: Is the human person the center of society?

Of course, put in that way, the right answer can only be clear-cut: The person is the center of society. Therefore, the basic principles to config-ure any network should be the preservation of dignity, freedom, and all other human rights. Unfortunately, some recent events have revealed that the information networks displaced the citizen from their center and gave in to the faulty digital governance that is fueling the resurgence of authoritarianism. This point can be illustrated — not without a flavor of tragicomedy — by the wave of "fake news" that circulated on Facebook during the U.S. presidential campaign in 2016. Titles like "WikiLeaks killed Hillary," "Imminent criminal accusation against Hillary," "Hillary in 2013: I would like Trump to run," and others, reinforced the views and the disinformation of Donald Trump's followers. The astounding fact is that many of these inaccurate news stories were produced by groups of teenagers located in places as far away as Macedonia. These improvised hustlers of political misunderstanding took advantage of credulous citi-zens and made handsome economic profits through the advertisement(s) linked to the booming traffic of their messages(314). This scheme of de-ception is not new. It reinforces tactics of manipulation of public opin-ion that also took place in the analogical era, but that were solved then through a balance and compromise between anonymity and privacy.

One social reality that newer generations do not seem to entirely rec-ognize is that anonymity in advanced democracies is legally prohibited. The legal identity of individuals is, at the same time, a fundamental right and the source of all obligations of the person (i.e., children have the legal right to be recognized by their parents, and parents are obliged to register their children). This identity is one pillar in the construction of citizenship. In the analogical institutions, all members of society have the right to know with whom they are dealing and cannot conceal their identity to their peers. Identity can be conceived of as a public good. It exists without economic costs, and the authorities can require citizens to identify themselves at all times without a court order and risking a penalty — like arrest — should they refuse to identify themselves. The sole principle of banning anonymity enables other virtuous consequences.

For instance, it enables and gives robustness to network validation and filtering functions that allow journalists and media owners to be identified by everyone else. These conditions reduce the dissemination of false or dubious information. Conversely, the right to privacy and freedom of speech balance the proscription of anonymity.

These fundamental freedoms imposed limits on the State and defined spaces of self-determination for the person. A paradox of the contemporary world can be illustrated by the following example: if a citizen in an advanced democracy, such as Denmark, takes to the streets, he will be protected by analogical governance. He might not be able to hide in anonymity, but his rights to privacy and freedom of speech will be granted. However, if he uses his smartphone and browses the Internet, he immediately earns the right to be anonymous and carry out all kinds of illegal activities — especially if he hides in the *dark web*. On the other hand, if he utilizes his real identity, that person will lose his right to privacy and will weaken his freedom of speech to programs of massive vigilance, ransomware, and groups of anonymous harassers — trolls. He also risks that his personal information will be sold because of *big data* tracking of online purchases, and that obsolete or shameful information about him stays in the network and can be mishandled. In the Internet, there is no right to be forgotten.

The solution to the problems of anonymity, privacy, and freedom of speech on the Internet is binary and does not admit middle-of-the-road options. At the time of laying out the Constitution of the United States of America, the Founding Fathers tried to compromise with the practice of slavery in some states of the new federation. They discussed arguments of all types, from economics and technology to religion and culture. At the end of the day, there was no way around the dilemma: Slavery cannot coexist with democracy. A compromise was not a solution. But that is what the Founding Fathers settled on. The fault line in American politics stayed until the Civil War. Could this war have been prevented? In fact, it is also a paradox that the legal prohibition of slavery restricted individual liberty on both ends to prevent people from voluntarily surrendering into servitude. Similarly, in the case of the Internet, the person must be front and center or individual rights will succumb.

The preservation of human life is the foundation of triage. In like manner, a solution for the problems of the Internet requires establishing first principles of action. Since the Internet is not an end in itself,

and the person — his dignity, freedom, and rights — is the center of
the open society, it is necessary to ban anonymity, defend privacy and
freedom of speech by:

- Transferring public goods of identity to the digital domain so that
  they become legally valid and interoperable.
- Technically delimiting a new public sphere where anonymity is
  prohibited, and the actors are legally responsible for all their activity in commercial, educative, academic, cultural, political, and
  media spaces.
- Legally defining property rights of personal data, privacy, and freedom of speech in the digital domain, along with the definition of
  legal boundaries for private and institutional actors (e.g., the prohibition of massive surveillance programs and big data projects
  involving involuntary, uninformed, or harmful participation).

There are no technical barriers to fulfill these principles of action.
Nothing stands in the way of new platforms and components in the
open architecture of the Internet. Moreover, there are no arguments to
defend the actual course of things. To the contrary, the present course
is only growing more and more uncertain and risky. The problems of
the Internet hurt everyone, including those who have profited with
the digital gold rush and now must confront the new law of the gun.
Facebook, for instance, was suddenly caught up in very difficult spots
when it censored the publication of a historical picture taken during
the Vietnam War(315) and, later on, for allowing the spread of "fake
news" that facilitated the campaign of Donald Trump(314). It also committed other blunders by declaring several million of its users were
dead(316) and mismanaging the metrics that serve to charge advertis-
ers. It was found that these metrics did not reflect the actual traffic of
the platform(317). Facebook failed, on its own platform, as a measurer
of the media and as a normalizer of rules. In this vacuum of digital
governance, *hubs* like Facebook must get out of their way constantly,
step into emergencies, and often, extend their functions toward those
previously held by institutional regulators.

Things are not getting any better in the public sector. Negligent responses to the above-mentioned contingencies are the visible consequences
of technological illiteracy of institutional actors and of the absence of a

deep reflection about the implications of the digital world in the transformation of society. Thanks to generalized ignorance, and counting blindly on the experts of the industry, public authorities have taken for granted that the new digital spaces can function in a legal void. Sluggishness to translate analogic governance into digital governance has brought about an ungoverned digital world. With the intention of lessening these problems, the experts of several governments — engineers, not constitutional lawyers — are devising unsophisticated responses with the purpose of fighting fire with fire. A deep-seated problem with apparent solutions such as massive surveillance programs is that they do not introduce elements to reconfigure the system in a coherent form. Instead, these counterattacks have an inbred authoritarian strain that exacerbates mistrust in government agencies and creates more instability. Another lamentable result is that these false solutions undermine public confidence of the institutions in an open society because they contribute to the perception that governments use technology in oppressive ways and without caring to improve people's lives.

To make things worse, it is very unlikely that these types of actions will render any desirable results for public safety or national security. Despite the USA Patriot Act of cyber spying programs and the cyber war underway since 2001, the largest democracy on Earth has been left in shambles thanks to a handful of ambitious adolescents in Macedonia, the email gaffes of Clinton, Podesta, and Delavan, plus Wikileaks, a team of Russian *hackers*, and a narcissistic sociopath armed with a Twitter account.

How will the new Internet be? (a tale)

In a not very distant future...
One Saturday morning, overwhelmed by the unceasing questions of his two children, Mateo tried to understand what was going wrong with his motorcycle. The children kept on asking questions: "Is it true that grandfather was afraid that you used the Internet when you were a kid? Is it true that years ago you had to get to a page called Google if you wanted to find something on the Internet? Is it true that kids could be attacked online? Did you ever suffer anything like that? What was the worst thing that happened to you? Is it true that you could have lost all your money without even noticing? What was a troll? How did they troll?"

Suddenly, Mateo stopped and smiled. The flow of questions from his children made him recall earlier times. More than 30 years ago, he bombarded his father with similar questions: "What is a fax? How could you do your homework without Wikipedia? Is it true that there existed black and white televisions?" Mateo set his tools aside, cleaned his hands, and sat on the floor with his kids.

Mateo was born in the first decade of the century. He is part of the first generation that lived all his life surrounded by the digital world. And, even when he did not live in the time of faxes and black and white TVs, he witnessed the decadence of the old and savage network, now known to be as friendly as the Model T. Mateo also witnessed the transition to the new Internet II, a more hospitable and much less colorful than the former version, but much more useful for everyone. The questions his kids asked made Mateo think about a time when he spent hours on Google and YouTube searching for information and trying to find useful results, then copying and pasting information from one place to another to keep what he wanted. He took a while to realize that his two kids were still there, all ears to listen to more answers from their father.

"It is true," Mateo said. "When I was your age, the Internet was very different in comparison to the Internet today. When I was growing up, the network was a wild place. First, every time that you used it, you could be a different person. Nobody knew who was who! And, naturally, you could not trust anyone there. Some messages looked as if your parents had sent them, but they were hoaxes to rob all your money. That made your grandparents very nervous, of course. And they were locking everything with passwords. Accessing the network as a kid was like going out to the garden and see that all the toys were locked with a chain. Another problem was that information on the network was in different places, and you needed to memorize a different identification for each system. It was difficult to keep track of all that. If you wanted to search for something, you had to use search engines such as Google. Sending messages was even more complicated because there were several types of messages. Long messages required that we use special applications, and we had to manage our contact list for each of them. If you had a picture in the system, sharing it could become troublesome. Some systems stole your information without informing you, and they sold it to other companies that contacted you to bother you with advertising that you did not want to see. With all those problems and mistrust, you had to pay a lot of money to intermediaries that facilitated secure ways of advertising, selling, or buying online."

Mateo added, "People worked for the Internet, instead of having the Internet working for the people. We had thousands of 'spam' messages that we did not want. Every time that you used a new service you had to spend hours writing back the information that was already stored in other places. I think that I wrote my name and address thousands of times in many different websites. But one day all of that changed, thanks to a wise public decision. Now, when we use the Internet, we all say who we are, and it is simply not allowed to say that you are Iron Man or The Hulk. And what matters the most is that our ID says who we are and how we want to be treated by everyone in all the systems online. For instance, your IDs tell everyone that you are kids and that nobody can offer or give you things that are not good for you or that your mother and I have not previously authorized. I do not like to participate in marketing studies, and my ID tells all the companies on the Internet that nothing about what I do can be used to bother or distract me. Nobody can utilize or keep my information without my authorization. In the past, the companies that provided the services controlled my security and my privacy. In the new network, only we determine what we want. In the beginning, a lot of people did not understand the new model, until they saw that they could not use most services without an ID. Then they thought that they could do the same things that they did before, and some of them received penalties or were jailed." "Like Juan's dad!" the kids said. Mateo continued, "In government, some people did not understand that it was no longer valid to spy on others, and they also received punishment. You will be able to do more and more things with your same IDs as you grow. And just as it happens in life, if you do something that is not right, you will get in trouble."

As always happens when adults answer kids' questions, Mateo realized that he was divagating on themes that he worried too much about, but that kids simply did not care. Suddenly, he changed the conversation — "Why don't you help me fix the motorcycle?" He stood up and reached for his toolbox.

After that talk, and with the help of the kids and of Jarvis — his intelligent digital assistant that resembled the gadgets of Tony Stark in The Iron Man franchise — Mateo rapidly found and dismantled the malfunctioning part of his motorcycle. He took a snapshot with his smartphone camera, and asked Jarvis to locate the replacement. Within seconds, the assistant answered that the replacement part was available at a nearby repair shop. Although the repair shop was small and closed for business on Sunday, immediate delivery was available at a reasonable price. Only half an hour later, a delivery boy was at the door of Mateo's house with the replacement part. This boy did not work for the store. He took the job as a *gig*, only for that specific delivery. *Gigs* like these had turned common thanks to the new possibilities of transferring trust easily. The transformation in the way people trusted each other also helped to increase the efficient utilization of all goods: movables, estates, and vehicles. Most people now rented goods to or from their neighbors, and it was common now to have multiple *gigs* in the district. Moreover, *gigs* impelled everyone to develop skills, and not having gigs was a negative sign with which nobody wanted to be associated.

It was incredible! The solution to the problem, the localization of the replacement, the logistics of delivery, and the payment all pieced together in a secure and trustable manner, not least because all the communication and the protocols were encrypted. No information was typed into the system, and all intermediaries and platforms ran smoothly and efficiently. The new interoperable public goods in the network, and the electronic assistants with artificial intelligence had changed the Internet to serve the people. The new configuration was centered in the agency, and focused on the needs of the person, just like Mateo and the owner of the small repair shop.

Years ago, it would have been impossible to use a simple snapshot to locate a replacement part only a few blocks away from home. The high costs of intermediation, publicity, transaction, and logistics made it very difficult for a small business to offer competitive processes. The search model of Google would have made finding and purchase of that replacement part more difficult. That inefficient and old model was based on probabilistic estimations and influenced by advertising. Luckily, the builder of the motorcycle had an open data and co-creation business model that allowed the intelligent assistants of clients like Mateo to access the location of replacement parts services. In the past, the *hubs* had been designed to capture the user, take away its agency, and deliver a little portion of value at the very end of a transaction that also included layers of processes for the exclusive benefit of the platform.

In those times, the platforms were not capable of creating a different business model, one that put the delivery of value to their clients above all other priorities. Advertising was beyond the reach of small businesses. But now, with the new scheme, publicity became a public and self-regulated good without anyone having to manage it. The inventories of small businesses competed automatically for clients and purchases. Additionally, owners could opt to have their products participate in biddings and make direct offers to clients.

The Act for the Governance of the Internet (AGI) prodded this technological revolution. The key to overcome the technological sluggishness and the abuse of users at the hands of *hubs* was the enactment of public goods on the Internet and the deployment of financial mechanisms to create a payment system for their activities. Interestingly, the financing of the new network used a similar taxation instrument as that which the U.S. implemented in the mid 20th century to finance the expansion of its network of highways. This time, governments taxed telecommunications, not gasoline, so that everyone contributed to the financing of the new platforms.

At the moment of this revolution, many people expected — and feared — that the public institutions would take over the control and develop another poor and incompetent technology, aside from mismanaging the budget. But, that did not happen. The success of the new network was based on a model of open government. The government laid out general parameters of design (e.g., the defense of privacy and the interdiction of anonymity) with the guidance of constitutional lawyers and experts in public policy. Each of the following played a part: academic institutions, businesses, and citizens developed the technical specifications and the systems. Several of these new platforms followed the *blockchain* distributed design. The responsibility for the operation and maintenance in the new platforms had a distributed configuration that worked through paid contracts with the private sector and non-governmental organizations.

Other services, like email, messaging, social interaction, and cloud data storing were categorized as basic services. Internet service providers (ISPs) had to offer these services to their clients under the conditions of the new regulation. In some cases, an ISP created its own interoperable services. But in many other cases, an ISP outsourced the service to other providers like Gmail, Outlook, and Facebook. However, this time they also had to comply with the applicable regulation.

Of course, this great transformation had a major economic impact. To maintain the vitality of markets and to rebalance the economic weight of the different actors of the technological sector, the institutions of economic competition restructured the relevant markets. They utilized the *rule of three* to analyze the maturity and the concentration of the markets: In the long run, the mature competitive markets need at least three large — also called generalists — competitors, and none of them must have more than 40% of the market. Regulators also determined the unbundling of conglomerates of media and telecommunications. The separation of these conglomerates gave way to four new sectors: telecommunications, content, hardware and software, and platforms and services. This was the way to break up the vertical and horizontal concentration that the largest corporations had utilized to capture markets, slow down innovation, and preclude the development of more efficient markets.

In the new arrangement, telecommunication firms had to center their focus on transporting bytes and in providing basic services. Also, the content sector thrived and became much more creative, in part because the new regulation had strong protections of the principle of net neutrality. Producers of content, from educational applications to soap operas, did not have to find a way around the telecommunication enterprises to get to consumers. And users gained the right to access all services and content from any device or telecommunications network.

As part of all these changes, the platform and services enterprises had to abandon their old model, where they took advantage and plundered the consumer. This time they really were forced to innovate. They created services like Jarvis, which builds on each user's activities and expands capabilities of the person. This was a radical departure from the old model, which sought to manipulate, supervise, and even take over the user. Other firms specialized in network infrastructure to focus on creating and providing support to digital public goods, such as the new legal electronic currency. The transference of value thrived with the reduction of intermediation costs and the scaling down of artificial, rent-seeking processes that acted like customs agents.

It is worthy noting that a meaningful part of institutional bureaucracies dissolved as an effect of the new digital public goods and their platforms. Many institutions and functions that had been ubiquitous in life disappeared, like cab licenses. The new times were labeled "the post institutional age." Public organizations kept their role as guardians of the rule of law, but they also transformed into stewards in the implementation of laws and public policy. What matters the most: The new platforms were run by society and the markets.

The new collaborative dynamics of co-creation, open access, distributed platforms, and digital governance finally paved the way to build economic vascular loops with anabolic recirculation flows. Perhaps the most fruitful consequence of the digital governance revolution was that it enabled the economics of sustainability to crystallize. The digital revolution facilitated the adequate and efficient estimation and recovery of costs of negative externalities. These transformations were, in turn, the result of the proscription of anonymity, the drastic reduction of transaction costs, the build-up of digital public goods, and the transition toward electronic currency. Thanks to the reduction and by-passing of bureaucracy, the revenues from charges to negative externalities flowed back through the digital platforms — and not through bureaucracy — to a new and dynamic economic sector for environmental services and recovery.

Exceptional projects, such as the self-financed recovery of the Amazonian rain forest led by the prominent photographer Sebastião Salgado, became normal and widespread, and allowed the economy to compensate for the loss of employment that resulted from automation, aside from giving a sense of purpose to the new generations beyond the Millennials — the generation of Mateo.

It is also important to point out that the great imbalances and risks that had imperiled the world economy became evident when the new networked economic paradigms diffused, and people finally understood the effects that each topology had over society and the environment. The great transformation — formed by shifts in currency, property rights, and trade in *blockchain-like* platforms — revealed how the largest part of wealth had been stagnated in humongous and dangerous economic aneurisms. It also became evident that in the highest strata of the economy there was far less entrepreneurship than was formerly assumed, and this discovery eased the reform of fiscal systems. Progressive taxation recovered momentum and with it came other sensible policies, like penalties for fixed, immobile, assets, and the diffusion of credits for people entering the workforce in the social security network. The new network paradigm made clear that the health of the economy depended on keeping it in flow without stagnant wealth, and at the same time, avoiding the growth of the random network because of extremely low wages.

Finally, the new scheme of participative government and co-creation of public goods became the best educational space for democratic behavior and helped to create a virtuous circle of participation, change, and improvement that strengthened the liberal *quorum*.

The best free education is given at home.
Claudio Lerma

16. New generation analog solutions

Frugal innovation, habits, and neurosciences

Apart from the high-impact projects and innovations — *moon shots* — that change the network's structure, such as the Internet's modernization and the incorporation of the negative externalities' price into the economy, there *are* some interesting solutions for changing things by means of a bottom-up approach. That is, solutions made by the individual that if widely disseminated, can become part of the social behaviors that change the *quorum* of the evolutionary strategy, which in turn changes the network configuration. Don't eat the marshmallow, the KonMari method to treat pleonexia, Amazon's narrative, *Israel loves Iran*, the LEGO® co-creation communities, and Common Sense Media's recommendations to leave the mobile phone aside when with others in the car, at the table, and in the bedroom(318) are simple low-technology innovations that — by being personal decisions that relate to the close surroundings — do not depend on big systemic changes, government initiatives, or a social revolution. Furthermore, whoever assimilates and executes them, quickly obtains specific personal benefits. And yet, every day we witness, even among people who want to change, that although simple and requiring little effort, these recommendations are difficult to carry out. As we already know, for those persons who relate to the world through an external locus of control, the change is practically impossible because, above all, it requires a deep internal change. For those people, the external stimulus is the one that prevails; the marshmallow and the mobile phone are the ones that rule over their free will. On the other hand, there are those who, although they are in the internal locus gradient, also have a hard time changing. The answer probably lies in the neuroscience of habits.

According to Charles Duhigg(319), the best-known communicator on the neuroscience of habits, studies point out that more than 40% of a person's decisions are the result of automated behaviors that are indelibly coded in the brain's basal ganglia; what we call habits. Apparently, habits are optimization strategies that, by automating routines, let us reduce the use of brain capacity and exert less mental effort when doing repetitive things. This can be useful when we want to use that capacity to do other activities or reduce the brain's energy consumption. According to neuroscientists, habits have three main components: 1) a signal or a trigger, 2) a routine, and 3) a reward. The main problem with habits is that, since they are automatic routines, we carry them out unconsciously, so a bad habit like drinking a half bottle of wine every night may soon produce significant damage.

Once coded in the brain, habits are difficult-to-impossible to eliminate, so looking out for those moments when they form is crucial (e.g., learning as a child that you have to wait before you get an additional marshmallow). Although once created habits can't be destroyed, they can be transformed. The mechanism for habit formation is sufficiently flexible to allow the transformation of a harmful habit into a beneficial one. In *The Power of Habit*, Duhigg provides us with a recipe based on current neuroscience for habit re-engineering:

1. **Identify the routine.** Many negative and repetitive behaviors are driven by habits. Since these are executed unconsciously, we need to examine what is not working well in our lives through a state of full attention or *mindfulness* that can allow us to identify the routines associated to a habit.

2. **Experiment with the rewards.** Habits take place because we yearn to obtain a reward at the end of the routine. In the habit of drinking half a bottle of wine every day, it's possible the reward is not the wine itself, but the company of friends at the bar. Once the routine has been identified, we can experiment with different rewards — maybe going back to the bar but drinking a non-alcoholic beverage instead and discovering the reward we truly crave. Although in a state of full attention it is easy to identify routines, uncovering the signal and the reward may require more work; thus, experimentation is needed.

3. **Isolate the trigger.** Habit triggers may be any kind of signal: a time of day, an emotional state, a location, the presence of other persons or an action preceding the habit. To isolate the trigger, the author proposes writing down five things once we identify that we are craving the reward. Where are we? What time is it? What is the emotional state? Who is nearby? What happened right before the

craving started? As the days go by, probably the answers to some questions may change, but those answers that are consistent every day point to the habit's likely trigger, for example, something that it occurs the same time every day.

4. **Have a plan.** To overwrite a bad habit with a better one, it's important to have a plan. In the case of the half bottle of wine, if we discover that the trigger is when we leave work and the reward is the company of friends, the plan could be: go to the bar at 7 p.m. and drink some mineral water with your friends.

The conclusion is that a substantial part of the positive changes relate to frugal aspects of personal behavior, which, rationally, should be easy to modify. However, they are not because many behaviors that are harmful are linked to bad habits that neurologically are very hard to change. Looking out for routine behaviors, especially in children, is fundamental. With children, it's necessary to pay attention during the formative years, particularly in light of the new technology that is intended to create dependence since, overall, it seeks to attract the user's attention through signals, the establishment of routines, and the provision of rewards to consolidate repetition. This means that part of our constant state of distraction and alienation is the result of the habits subconsciously induced by behavior reengineering. Notwithstanding, we should be aware that it's relatively easy to hack them. We simply must develop and practice a state of complete attention or *mindfulness* about our everyday routines.

Cure violence

On December 11, 2006, President Felipe Calderón announced a joint operation named "Michoacán" as the start of what he himself called "the war against drugs." At the same time, he defended before the Chamber of Deputies (Mexico's lower house of Congress) the need to raise the security forces' budget by 60%(320). One month later, on January 4, 2007, the front page of newspapers showed him dressed in military garb (Figure 31). From the start, the security cabinet, driven decisively by him, determined that the only way to confront the problem of organized crime, violence, and the weakness of the State was to follow the orthodox method — dating back to the era of Salazar Viniegra —

of maintaining the prohibition of drug use and sale, as well as the use of the military to carry out police duties against drug trafficking to restore the State's role in society.

Figure 31: Front page of the Reforma newspaper, January 4, 2007.

The rest is history: The official strategy was to decapitate Mexico's organized crime groups. Shortly thereafter, those groups fragmented into smaller and more violent ones, and an escalation of violence and homicides began. Ten years later, even after Calderón's administration has passed, violence continues.

Behind this "war" is the debate that Paul H. Thibodeau and Lera Boroditsky(321), researchers of the psychology department at Stanford, define as the dilemma of combatting crime as a beast or a disease. When decision-makers characterize crime as a beast, they adopt the hunter's tactics as the solution to confront it — retributive justice. A beast is on the loose and the hunter's responsibility — in this case, the armed forces — is to kill it. Therefore, society is excluded from the solution and is forced to take refuge and wait until the hunters catch and kill the prey. The other model — rarely used — sees crime as a disease. Thus, solutions are implemented in which both government and society address the malady as if it were an epidemic.

Modern precedents to the latter approach are mainly related to the mechanisms of transitional and restorative justice, such as the commissions of truth and reconciliation in Chile in 1991 and in South Africa in 1993. The latter is especially important since the main obstacle for achieving the transition from apartheid toward democracy was the fear of South Africa's white population that the black population would take revenge after the abuse and mistreatment it had suffered for decades. The transitional and restorative justice processes focus on discovering the truth — to the greatest possible extent — paying special attention to the needs of the victims who actively participate in the process. To the offenders who provide the opportunity to repair the damage, ask for clemency, and seek mechanisms that help prevent a repetition of the behavior and/or the conditions that provoked the damage — such as preventing the army from taking on police duties — all are within the framework of society's participation and involvement. The archive of the public hearings that the Commission of Truth and Reconciliation of South Africa held is online. More than two decades later, it is a powerful testimony that ratifies the breakdown of the violence cycle through a humanitarian and participative de-escalation. The result is that Chile and South Africa managed to achieve their transition to democracy without violence, with justice and with no State repression and crimes.

In the same vein as the reconciliation processes that beholds violence as a problem requiring a social solution — but with a focus on urban violence — is the Cease Fire Model from the Cure Violence Organization created by Gary Slutkin, a physician graduated from the University of Chicago. In the first part of his professional career, he headed the tuberculosis treatment program in San Francisco (1981-1986). During that period, he discovered that most of the new infections took place among immigrants newly arrived in the U.S. who had no easy access to the institutional care and prevention programs. In time, he concluded that it was possible to reach them with the help of well-established members in their communities whom he hired as first contact workers. Consequently, he raised the treatment rate from 50% to 95% (322). After that experience, he moved to Africa to participate in different public health programs in complicated areas like Somalia. During conflict and chaos, he learned and helped improve the techniques for control of epidemics, especially of cholera and AIDS, through the training and engagement of community participants. He was an instrumental agent in reverting the HIV epidemic in Uganda — a unique and exemplary case in Africa — and after 10 years of living in the midst of the worst human tragedies, he left Africa and returned to Chicago. There he became interested in the violence that was taking place in the city's marginalized areas where weapons were common. After studying the data, he concluded that this presented the same contagion pattern of the transmissible diseases, and he proceeded to adapt the techniques he learned in Africa to the issue of violence in Chicago.

For Slutkin, the main predictor of an act of violence is a past act of violence, just like the main risk factor to get a contagious disease is to meet someone who previously had it. According to the public health techniques Slutkin used(323), the epidemics are averted with three measures:

1. **Interrupt the contagion.** To this effect, one must locate the first patients (*patient zero*), those spreading the contagion. In the case of violence, Slutkin trained community workers — many of them former gangsters with a criminal past — so that empowered with their knowledge of the community and mediation techniques, they would locate and calm down the victims along with violence prone and angry people who were involved in recent violent cases.

2. **Prevent the future contagion.** Around the first patients, there are others who get infected as carriers, that is, people close to them who, although they do not display violent behaviors, are filled with resentment and grievances that easily can turn into violent behaviors. The community workers also intervene in those cases by using mediation techniques; they seek to dispel and transform the anger into other emotions.

3. **Change the standards.** In the last phase of the process, the Cease Fire cells develop community programs on violence, conflict management, and change of social standards. Just like the use of the condom in the HIV case in Uganda or the basic hygiene measures in countries with gastrointestinal epidemics, the change of social standards concerning violence is fundamental.

According to the studies published by Cure Violence and audited by independent sources, the method of community intervention and conflict mediation reduces the shootings and the homicides between 41% and 73%. On the other hand, the organization's figures(324) show that when there are insufficient funds to maintain the program due to budgetary cuts, the violence returns and gets out of control, as it happened in 2016 (Graph 29). This agrees with the conclusion that society requires permanent and stable mechanisms to contain violence (Chapter 4).

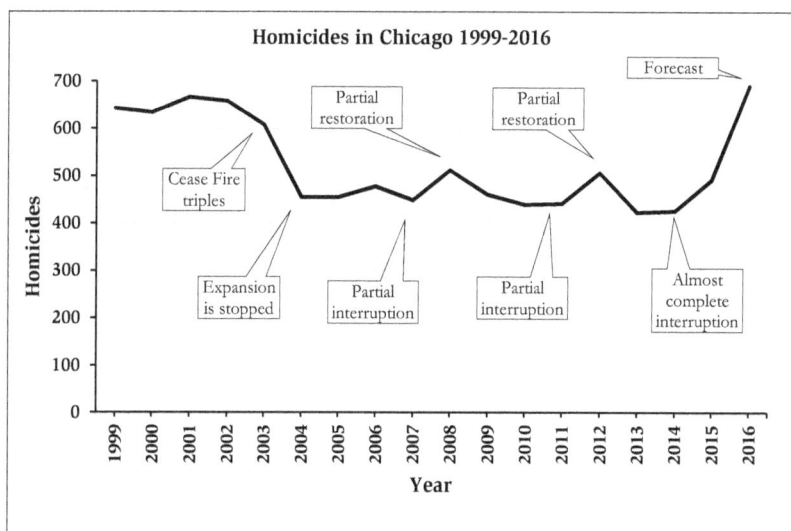

Graph 29: Relation between financing of Cease Fire and homicides in Chicago. Source: Chicago Police Department and cureviolence.org.

In cases like the "war against drugs" in Mexico and the urban violence that exists in some big cities of the U.S., the peaceful transitions of South Africa and Chile clearly show that the habit of addressing violence as a beast is obsolete, the same as its institutional counterpart, the hunter strategies. In fact, it's cheaper and the results are better when we treat violence as a disease. Curing violence means that the communities, the victims, the justice system, and the reconciliation mechanisms need to evolve and have a place as a comprehensive part of the solution.

The citizens' revolution in Colombia

During the 1980s and 1990s, Colombia was the emblematic case of failure in Latin America. Besieged by the drug cartels, the guerilla, and the economic crisis — and on the verge of becoming a failed State — this country tried with little success and at huge costs all the measures that the police, military, and political orthodoxy had prescribed. The trauma and despair of society and the country's leaders was of such magnitude that they ventured to try out inclusive and heterodox solutions, which would have seemed unimaginable in Latin America's authoritarian culture a few years before. Colombia's efforts and results have a common denominator: They are based on the idea that the construction of citizenship at the base of society is essential for the good progress of democracy, and it shows that — even in the highly difficult conditions they suffered — the implementation of analogue tools for strengthening the open society in the postmodern era is still possible.

1. **The police agent as builder of citizenship.** After Felipe Calderón declared the war against drugs in Mexico, it was not long before a part of the national security cabinet acknowledged a rapid increase in violence and began thinking that the strategy was mistaken. Silently, a group of public officials interested in the rational and professional development of public policies — with whom I stayed in touch to discuss the country's challenges — began to examine other international experiences in the fight against organized crime and the containment of violence. They soon discovered that in Colombia, particularly in Bogota and following years of failures, new philosophies linking the police and the community had been adopted. In the planning documents that the Colombians shared, their aim was to make the police agents into honorable officials, akin to the community and able to build citizenship in their social environment. That attitude was totally the opposite of the Mexican strategy encouraged by the warmongers.

    At the outset, the latter entailed the militarization of the federal police's equipment and image. Within a few months of the Calderón Administration, the image of the police was transformed. With Calderón in command, the solid colors of the uniforms were changed to a tactical camouflage, the caps were replaced with combat helmets, and bulletproof vests replaced the ties. The agents' faces were covered with balaclavas and paratrooper goggles, and the policemen became popularly known as *robocops*. Years later, in a meeting with an important and award-winning advertising agency, its main partner proudly told me the story of how his agency had overseen designing the *robocops'* image. Officials who had studied the problem in depth and tried to convince the president to change the strategy were cast aside, while the publicists — experts in the sale of cosmetics, but ignorant in public security issues — obtained *carte blanche* to define the hunter-beast strategy of Calderon's administration. The results are there for everyone to see: As time passed, Mexico's armed forces, and the federal and local police, have been tarnished due to serious cases of human rights abuse. This also happened in the U.S. when the local police departments followed the "new" orthodoxy of purchasing military equipment and promoting a hunter's mentality among police agents(325). In the meantime, Colombia, after having traveled and abandoned that road, has become pacified.

2. **You have a place.** In 2006, after 42 years of conflict with the guerrillas of the Revolutionary Armed Forces of Colombia (FARC), which led to more than 200,000 deaths and 5,000,000 people displaced, the government of Colombia decided to try a different approach. It requested the creative board of MullenLowe, an international advertising company, to develop a communication strategy to promote the guerillas peaceful demobilization. From the start, the creative team headed by José Miguel Sokoloff, a Colombian, was unassuming, and acknowledged that they did not fully understand the conflict: "We immediately decided to be part of this because it's an opportunity to impact the result of the conflict with the things that we do, with the tools that we have. But we didn't know much about it. We didn't understand it."(326) Therefore, they requested access to those who were living first-hand the consequences of violence, and they paid more attention to the stories of the soldiers, the former guerillas, and their relatives than to the rhetoric and opinions of Colombian politicians and journalists. Thanks to their openness to learn about the problem's human dimension, they were able to develop campaigns that left people with a profound impression:

> And we talked to about 60 of them before we felt we fully understood the problem. We talked about why they had joined the guerrillas, why they left the guerrillas, what their dreams were, what their frustrations were, and from those conversations came the underlying insight that has guided this whole campaign, which is that guerrillas are as much prisoners of their organizations as the people they hold hostage.

In the first phase of the strategy, the publicists found that after many years in the guerrilla forces, the best possible spoke persons were precisely the former guerillas:

And at the beginning, we were so touched by these stories, we were so amazed by these stories, that we thought that maybe the best way to talk to the guerrillas was to have them talk to themselves. So we recorded about a hundred different stories during the first year, and we put them on the radio and television so that the guerrillas in the jungle could hear stories, their stories, or stories similar to theirs, and when they heard them, they decided to go out.(327).

In time, this campaign lost its effectiveness, but the effort they made to understand the problem allowed them to comprehend that nostalgia played a big role during the Christmas season, and was the time of the year when most desertions occurred from the FARC. Then, in 2010, they developed the "Christmas Trees" campaign. At night, nine huge trees that had been placed in strategic points of the jungle lit up with a message that said: "If Christmas can come to the jungle, you can come home. Demobilize! At Christmas, everything is possible"(327). Although few guerillas saw the trees, many of them learned about them and that Christmas they demobilized. In total, 331 guerrillas — the equivalent of 5% of the total guerilla force at the time — returned home. Shortly thereafter, a former guerilla remarked that although the idea of the Christmas trees was fine, the guerillas moved through the rivers and not so much through the jungle paths. Immediately, the campaign was changed to "Rivers of Light." Former guerrillas, their relatives and the general public sent thousands of reconciliation messages with the slogan "Come home for Christmas." The messages and some small gifts were put inside floating airtight capsules that lit up at night and were released in the rivers in the conflict areas. As a result, the desertion rate increased to the point where there was one case of demobilization every six hours.

In 2011, when the peace process began, Sokoloff and his team realized that the guerrillas' concerns had changed. They had stopped worrying that the army would kill them and had begun thinking about the rejection they would be forced to endure back home. Thus, Sokoloff decided to seek out the mothers of the guerrillas who were still active and ask them for photos of their sons/

daughters when they were young, so they could publish them with the most loving message the mothers could write, and that, broadly speaking, said: "Before you were a guerrilla you were my son. Come home, I am waiting for you." Years later, during the World Cup in Brazil in 2014, the Colombian team went through a good phase that energized and unified the country — and in the same sense as the previous campaign — they launched a massive campaign in which all kinds of Colombians participated: "Come out, leave the jungle. We're keeping a place for you," referring to keeping a place for them at home so they could watch the matches.

At the time when those campaigns were developed, from 2006 to 2014, at least 17,000 guerrillas demobilized, and though not all of the credit can be given to the advertising campaigns, it's believed that the use of the advertising tools was an important and significant component of the peace process because it changed the terms of the conversation and reintroduced the guerrillas' personal and human dimension into the national discourse. It's inevitable to contrast this case with the Mexican *robocops*. In Mexico, the agency did what the president requested; in Colombia, it did what the country needed. In Mexico, the publicists only saw the transaction's economic dimension and gave themselves over to the banality of evil to "give the client what he asked for." They did not understand the problem or even thought of the consequences. In Colombia, they were more unassuming, collaborative, creative, and sought to fulfill the wishes of the Colombian nation — its client — and, consequently, create a true social value.

3. **Mobility and democracy.** Bogota experienced a process that's not very common in Latin American politics. After a phase of great decline and violence, it became an international example of renewal thanks to a succession of mayors who transformed it. From 1992 to 1994, Jaime Castro tried to clean up and organize the public finances, saving the city from bankruptcy and creating a budget for new programs(328). His successor, Antanas Mockus, from 1995 to 1997, set up the basis of a new civic culture of respect for the law (e.g., the police agent as builder of citizenship)(329). From 1998 to 2000, Enrique Peñalosa leveraged both the financial order that Castro established as well as the citizen building foundation that Mockus implemented and launched an aggressive modernization program

based on the democratization of the public space(330). To date, Peñalosa's program is a worldwide example of urban transformation. It is based on the idea that the citizen is the city's protagonist — the owner and shareholder — and that justice and the levels of democracy become tangible in the way in which public space is shared and used for the first time in Latin America, Peñalosa reverted the privatization of public spaces in favor of the citizen. As an example, he implemented measures to prevent automobiles from parking on the sidewalks. (In Bogota — as in many other cities — the shops used the sidewalks as a private parking space for their customers; thus, pedestrians were forced to walk in the middle of traffic). From the city of Curitiba in Brazil, he imported the integrated transport network model — currently known as the rapid transit bus systems — with which he reassigned the streets' public space in favor of mass transport and in detriment of the automobile's private use. He created good quality public spaces in the most marginalized areas of the city and reconnected these areas to the city center with bus routes, green corridors, and bicycle routes. He reordered informal trade and recovered historical spaces that are part of the people of Bogota identity.

It's not clear how or when the citizens' revolution in Colombia began. For now, we can only see how it's developing and the effects it produces. Probably, its main cause was that, after decades of failure and violence, a significant part of Colombian society simply reached the conclusion that it was necessary to leave the confrontation behind and change the old way of thinking and acting, as well as enable new leaderships and such radical ideas as those of the Ministry of National Defense and its messages of reconciliation and inclusion for the guerrilla. Nevertheless, the history of transformation in Colombia is not over. The plebiscite's failure to ratify the peace agreements in 2016 indicates that the new citizen's *quorum* is not yet fully consolidated, and a broad and influential segment of society has no desire to leave the old forms behind. Fortunately, the main actors already have a vision of things with better results than any other country in Latin America; thus, it's likely — and desirable — that the citizens' revolution of Colombia reaches its objectives.

The cities' social capital and the right to a good administration

In 2015, the Mexican Congress passed a bill for constitutional change to modify the legal status of the Federal District, the Mexican capital and one of the largest and most populated cities in the planet. The capital was then renamed Mexico City with the idea that it would gain the legal organization of a state. As part of the reform, Congress called for the creation of a constituent legislative body in charge of drafting the first constitution in the city's history. Foreseeing that the National Action Party (PAN) would naturally participate in the process and that, given its current state of prostration, the party and its representatives would not be able to articulate and present a sound and interesting constitutional draft, I wrote a proposal on the right to a good administration and the preservation of the city's social capital, which I delivered and discussed with the party's top officials and members of the constituent congress. Months later, the head of the Mexico City government, in accordance with what is stipulated in the reform, sent Congress a draft that, apart from presenting serious technical deficiencies, did not consider things as fundamental as the protection of private property or the citizens' individual rights. On the contrary, it sought to define an authoritarian system based on collectivist rights that the State would administer, much like the old Soviet systems of the Cold War. Although no one expressed their satisfaction over the draft, and some experts denounced it as abhorrent, the twisted and lazy logic of the Mexican politicians prevailed. The members of the legislative body, despite having all the legal powers to do so, did not create their own project, and for months tried to straighten out a controversial monstrosity that was incompatible with the federal constitution.

The contrast is interesting. On one side, the politicians are in despair due to the postmodern instability, but on the other they continue to hold on to the burning pillar of the status quo and authoritarianism. When drafting the proposal to strengthen the social capital of the city (meaning the sum of private and public capital)(331), I did not think it would be opposed to the official proposal, though maybe it was not such a big surprise that it was. Mexicos City's populist and collectivist constitution is one more indication that, increasingly, there are fewer people who understand and advocate for the implementation of an open society. Thus, we must keep building and putting forward collaborative design laws and policies aimed at improving city governance in the 21st century.

In a medical analogy, many of the negative aspects and the problems in authoritarian countries like Mexico are symptoms of a complex condition with a common origin: the syndrome of economic and political rentierism. Roughly, the low quality of public services, the weakness of the State, the endemic corruption, and the poor economic performance, among many other problems, are related to an authoritarian model of economic and political development based on obtaining personal unlawful gains and not on the construction of public and private value. The examples are many in all spheres of public and private life:

1. In terms of the formal economy — the vascular network — many of the big corporations prosper based on negotiations and public concessions that enable the extraction of income in the market, not through innovation and international competitiveness as it occurs in the telecommunications, construction, and transport industries. Said situation is favored by the political and economic support that the rentier businessmen contribute to politicians during the electoral processes. The public administration then pays them back through diverse mechanisms of corruption that guarantee the protection of large-scale economic rents.

2. In terms of government — the network configuration — access to public power is marked by private favors and the use of public budgets with electoral purposes. Public office is defined as the opportunity to extract revenues of all types through acts of corruption that range from making it difficult for citizens to have access to public goods and services, to charging fees and commissions for the use of the budget in public works, the non-transparent provision of concessions, and a long etcetera that is only limited by the corrupt officials' endless creativity.

3. In terms of the informal economy — the random network — the high access barriers to the formal economy for the lower income sectors feed a complex cycle of codependence with the government. Thus, a significant part of the informal economy can only function with mechanisms for the extraction of income, such as the use of public spaces for the illegal sale of products, the use of social programs in favor of groups with specific electoral interests, and the illegal and destructive use of public wealth, like the illegal exploitation of public land and natural resources.

At the end of the day, the formal and informal sectors of the economy, as well as politicians, are brought together as a network thanks to the electoral processes, the government's corrupt acts, and the economy's rentier and dysfunctional operation mode. The syndrome has as a common denominator the existence of sufficient, coordinated and like-minded actors with the power to control the *hubs*. Together, they work relentlessly to identify, seize, and extract income with no concern for the preservation, construction, and enjoyment of public and private value. Therefore, it is no surprise — given international benchmarks of value and innovation, rule of law, formation of human capital, economic growth, and inequality — that the dysfunctional democracies are stuck in a situation that for decades has been below their true potential.

Furthermore, there are many examples of how well-established mechanisms facilitate the rentier model, like the complex network of fiscal provisions that produces null or very low effective tax rates for the low-income population (50%), high effective tax rates for the middle-income population (49%), and low effective tax rates for the high-income population (1%). Therefore, this guarantees the flow of low average public resources — approximately less than 20% of the GDP — for the clienteles and the political class without imposing any excessive burdens for the sector with the greatest political and economic influence, and without the possibility of effectively building public goods. This is the circular operation of the rentier authoritarian economic model.

In contrast, during this century, the cities' development will be crucial because an increasingly large number of the population will reside in them. Therefore, most of the problems will concentrate there. Thus, it is essential to create ideas and solutions that help to govern them more effectively. In an abstract way, cities are the dense and compact aggregate of public capital, specifically public and common goods as well as private capital, which is the individual and collective property of those who live in and use the urban spaces. This sum of capital can be called the cities' social capital, whose combined benefit translates into tangible well-being.

Generally speaking, the aim of those of us who live in a city is to preserve, increment, and enjoy the social capital of our cities by developing a large and diverse array of public and private activities. Based on the democratic process, we citizens elect and appoint the authorities whose central mandate should be to create and promote conditions that foster the conservation, expansion, and enjoyment of the social capital.

Apart from the division of social capital into public and private, there are other tangible and intangible subcategories (Table 43):

	Tangible	Intangible
Public capital	Urban infrastructure: sidewalks, streets, sewage systems, drinking water systems, public transport systems	Mobility, public safety, beauty, ease to undertake and do business, rule of law, sustainability
Private capital	Homes, land, office buildings, automobiles	Business culture, civility, citizens' participation, respect for the law, social activities

Table 43: Division of cities social capital.

In the legal traditions of Latin America and many European nations, the constitutional frameworks are based both on abstract legal principles and on the definition of obligations and rights, particularly human rights, over which the action space of authorities and citizens is defined. Thereby, constitutional objectives are coded in terms of general principles (e.g., article 3 of the Political Constitution of the United Mexican States: "Every individual has the right to receive an education. The State — Federation, states, Federal District, and municipalities — will provide preschool, primary, and high school education."

The shortcoming of this kind of wording ("to receive education") is that the attainment of the objectives is interpreted in terms of the "best effort," rather than of specific goals, which ends up being the main pretext of incompetent authorities when they're asked to be accountable. They can always argue: "Yes, there are poor results," but they made their "best effort." That is why it is interesting to think that this legal approach could be complemented or rectified through a new generation of proposals that clarify the legal mandate with more precise performance-oriented responsibilities that impose restrictions on the rentier public administration. An example is to incorporate the right to a good administration. A new generation right — from which would stem the constitutional responsibility to preserve *ex ante* the cities' social capital and not only *ex post*, as it currently occurs with traditional accountability and anti-corruption mechanisms.

In terms of comparative law, the right to a good administration has for years had support and formal justification. It is not a new idea. It is part of the new generation of rights that were incorporated into different constitutions in the last few decades as a mechanism that strengthens and makes more viable the construction of the rule of law. The most important example of the use of this right in a constitution is in article 41 of the Charter of Fundamental Rights of the European Union(332). For authors like Jaime Rodríguez Arana(333), the good public administration is:

> ...a right of citizens, none less than a fundamental right, and, also, a principle of administrative action. The citizens have a right to demand certain patterns or standards in the functioning of the Administration. And the Administration is obliged, in every democracy, to distinguish itself in its daily actions by its objective service to the general interest.

In the same manner, Pablo Dermizaky Peredo(334) remarks on good government:

> Once the premise is set that the rule of law and democracy are inseparable, it is without doubt, nonetheless, that not every democracy is a "good government." What should we understand by "good government"? One that executes the State's aims through a democracy as it is defined in Article 3 of Mexico's Constitution. And just like not every democracy is a "good government," not every rule of law is one either. Herein appears the need to introduce a concept of good administration, of the efficiency of the rule of law that Ulrich Karpen speaks of.

The social capital and good administration proposals are focused on the idea of breaking the rentier mental model of government that sees public power as the appropriation of the space being governed for personal purposes and where the citizens are mere inhabitants, beneficiaries, and tenants of the governing administration. The mental model of the good administration and the social capital is opposite to the rentier model. It stems from the principle that citizens, through the electoral process, put each new administration in charge of the social capital of our cities — capital that we own, has a specific value, and productivity — and that elected authority, coupled with its corresponding bureaucracy, must act in a way that, during its administration, the social capital is preserved, increased, and its benefits are effectively enjoyed by all of us who *are* and *make* the cities. To that effect, we must redefine the legal framework that gives life to the cities' government based on the following:

- **Constitutional law.** In presenting the reasons for constitutions, we must have a long-term view on the right to a good administration, the cities' social capital, and the rights and responsibilities that both citizens and authorities have to create it, preserve it, and increase it. At the same time, in the constitutional legal corpus, we must incorporate the right to a good administration at the level of a fundamental right.
- **Definition.** When there is a right that establishes the legal foundation for developing the concept of the cities' social capital, we will have to define this concept and outline its components at the level of laws and regulations. In a conceptual sphere, the definition of social capital can be as basic as "the accounting value of all of the cities' infrastructure added to the accounting value of private property," or as complex as a formulation that incorporates intangible aspects like those that Bogota has (e.g., mobility, sustainability, and urban beauty). In fact, international standards already exist that are aligned with this idea like the ISO 18091, promoted by the TrustedGov.com organization. The point is that a definition of social capital implies reaching a measurable, concrete amount whose evolution can be measured throughout time and in response to the government's actions.
- **Mandate.** The reform must incorporate the constitutional mandate, so the authorities work to preserve, increment, and facilitate the enjoyment of the cities' social capital and its productivity. Regardless of the political actors' ideological idiosyncrasies, a consensus concerning this point would mark a principle of concrete action for the creation of a long-term development agenda.
- **Measurement.** The measurement of social capital is crucial if we are to learn about the authorities' performance, and thereby, reduce those practices that enable public rentierism. For example, a city's infrastructure has an accounting value that is maintained or reduced in terms of the assets' depreciation and the reinvestment made in said assets (maintenance). In the current model, the infrastructure

is built at high costs that, at the end of the construction period, are not assessed in real terms. Moreover, said values are not updated based on the technical debt that the poor execution of the work and the lack of reinvestment produce. An example of technical debt that reduces the social capital is the case of Line 12 in the Mexico City subway system. The technical deficiencies in its construction produced greater maintenance costs, hidden costs, and service failures that negatively affect the city's social capital. Conversely, the mandate's component of "preservation," in addition to the measurement system, would force reinvestment of a significant part of the public budget in the cities' social capital so as to compensate the annual depreciation of the assets that wear down, and pay the technical debt that negatively impacts any city's infrastructure. This would mean a lower possibility of waste in expenditure programs that are geared to the electoral political process. Therefore, we could obtain legal directives so that priorities, budgets, and government programs can justify their existence in terms of demonstrating positive effects in the preservation, increment, and enjoyment of the cities' social capital.

- **Standards.** The best cities in the world, like Paris, were built and rebuilt based on organized design processes that have at their roots standards that guide their development. The preservation, incrementation, and enjoyment of a city's social capital are intimately related to the standards that define it. Without standards that mark the purpose of the cities' different areas, there is no framework that enables us to call on the authorities to render accounts or to focus the private actors' economic efforts for fully developing the social capital.
- **Automatic feedback mechanisms (citizens centric approach).** The cornerstones of the rentier model are the control of a valuable resource and the coercive capacity to extract an income from that resource without reinvesting or rendering accounts until its depletion. An example of this is found in the rules for estimating the property tax in Mexico City, which classify property in terms of its value according to the finishes and furnishings. That is, the value of the property tax has more to do with how a citizen chooses to live, than with the public services he has. Thus, in the same city block two taxpayers who enjoy the same public services and own a property of the same size pay different amounts according to their

lifestyle, without taking into consideration the public services they effectively have and enjoy. Likewise, a house with good finishes (what real estate agents call "curb appeal") and in an area arbitrarily classified by the authorities as medium level, can pay a higher tax despite lacking daily drinking water, potholes in the street, and street vendors at the corner. The aforementioned occurs because the legal framework includes no consideration to index either the government's performance or the services' cost to the estimation of taxes. Thus, there is no sanction for the elected authorities or the bureaucracy due to their incompetence or inaction. To this effect, we would have to establish measures that, linked to the measurement of the cities' social capital, allow the citizen to automatically sanction the authority. For example, the citizen should be able to pay a significantly lower tax or not pay the taxes for services in the event that these do not comply with the standards for guaranteeing a quality service or a clean, well-regulated environment like in those streets and neighborhoods where trade on the streets is forbidden, and yet it takes place anyway.

Currently, the citizens are captive, and despite the provision of poor services, the authorities and the bureaucracy live in an ideal situation: They have the double benefit of charging and utilizing the tax income, and at the same time they benefit from the votes that corruption and clienteles give them linked to the depletion of the social capital of the city. A change must take place, a watershed moment, which, in legal terms, imposes a cost *ex ante* to the inaction and the execution of the rentier model.

The best TedTalks in history

In 1984, Richard Saul Wurman, architect, author, and book designer, realized that technology, entertainment, and design were on a path of convergence. This encouraged him to organize a conference that he named TED (Technology, Entertainment, Design)(335). The first TED Talk had little success and six years went by before the second was held. Since 1990, public interest in this type of conferences grew and they became an annual event held in a single place that preserved the original topics the founder defined. In 2000, Wurman, then 65, decided to leave

TED in the hands of a successor, and in 2001, he sold the organization to Chris Anderson, who incorporated the organization into the Sapling Foundation. Then, in 2002, Anderson laid out his vision to the members of the TED community and the role from that moment on and to date he would play as the conferences' "curator." That same year Wurman disengaged from the organization. In 2005, the organization tried to create a TV program, but it met with rejection by several TV stations, so Anderson and his team decided to put online, and with no charge, a selection of conferences under the open copyright license known as Creative Commons. Months later, the collection of online conferences increased to 44 and had been watched more than 3 million times. This initial success produced a radical change in the conference's strategy, which turned its online platform into the core of its business model. In 2006, the cost of attending the conference was $4,400 and one could only attend by invitation. By 2007, TED.com was launched, and in 2015, the site had more than 2,000 conferences that had been watched altogether more than one billion times. Under the slogan "Ideas worth spreading," TED is maybe the most important publication platform of new social, political, and academic ideas in the world. Its scope is even greater through programs such as TEDx™, where any person, following the platform's *ethos* and with a free license, can use TED's format and push even further the growth of the audience in the platform. In 2017, the cost of attending the main conference, TEDGlobal™, was $10,000.

TED's presence is of such importance that it has become difficult to avoid its influence. In the same way as we hear "There is an *app* for that," it is likely that any topic of interest that an academician, activist, or politician follows in specialized journals and books has a TEDTalk™ associated with it: for example, the genetic edition with CRISPR, the multiverse theory, Twitter's introduction to the world or a young man's innovation in Africa to produce electricity with scrap. Are you interested in a particular topic? Most certainly there is a TEDTalk about it.

In 2008, iTunes® recommended me to subscribe to the then new TED *video podcast*. That week, Hans Rosling, professor of public health in Sweden, gave his now renowned and acclaimed TEDTalk. Thanks to the impact of that presentation, Rosling became a global academic star and, probably, his was the best presentation of demographic and public health statistics in history. Since we generalists are omnivores, and we like to be on a diet of varied information and abhor information bubbles

— academic or digital — the TED podcast soon became a daily treat like the ones children enjoy during recess. As time went by, the list of TEDTalks™ grew and soon exceeded 100, then 1,000, and nearly reaching 2,000 talks. From the start, I acquired the habit of sliding the cursor over the stars indicator and rated every conference: I used the five-star rating only for those of great value. In 2016, only 100 conferences on my list had five stars. Every two years I update the list of the best TEDTalks in history published at (http://wp.me/p36ut2-4K). Within that list there is an even smaller subset of conferences that present, advocate, and propose what I call "new generation analog solutions," and which, of course, are aligned with the collaborative design philosophy of the liberal *quorum*.

1. *A lukewarm hug that saves lives*, Jane Chen, November 2009, TEDIndia, 650,000 visits(336). A graduate with a Master of Public Administration degree from Harvard's John F. Kennedy School of Government, Chen discovered that thousands of premature babies around the world died in their first days of life for lack of access to incubators. In the developed world, incubators have an initial cost of $20,000, require stable and continuous sources of electricity, and the service of specialized technicians. Under this paradigm, it was impossible to save the babies because the problems related to the lack of incubators — capital, electricity and qualified technicians — had to be solved first. Chen decided to focus on keeping stable the newly born babies' temperature. Thus, she invented a type of blanket in which one could put hot, encapsulated paraffin blocks in plastic packages. Paraffin is a cheap and safe material that absorbs and retains the heat obtained from accessible energy sources. Moreover, when it cools, it releases the heat slowly and constantly enabling the stabilization of the newly born babies' temperature and a quick replacement of a depleted heat source — a cold paraffin block with a new, warm one. The paraffin blocks can be heated with anything that is used to heat a pot of water, such as wood, and do not need electricity or the service of specialized technicians. The price of those heaters called EMBRACE is $200 per unit. They show that many problems of life or death have no solution under the costly and highly "technified" Western paradigm but can be solved with good enough and frugal means that provide a life opportunity for thousands of babies.

2. *How to fight desertification and reverse climate change,* Allan
    Savory, February 2013, TED 2013, 3.7 million visits(337) and *For
    more wonder, rewild the world*, George Monbiot, July 2013, TED
    2013, 835,000 visits(338). Savory and Monbiot, who had different
    and independent viewpoints, discovered the complex network of
    emergent behaviors in ecosystems. In his talk, Monbiot explains
    that at the beginning of the 20th century, the wolves were extermi-
    nated in the Yellowstone National Park in the U.S., and since then,
    the landscape began to change. First, the young willow trees dis-
    appeared, the pasturelands expanded, and the small water creeks
    eroded. In 1995, the wolves were reintroduced to the park, and in
    a few years' time, new willow trees sprouted and grew, and the
    small water streams had well-defined banks once again. The park
    recovered its vitality. Biologists discovered that changing one sin-
    gle variable, like the reintroduction of apex predators, allowed the
    resurgence of many species affected by the lack of control of the
    herbivores, like the willows and the grasses that keep the river-
    banks defined. When the wolves came back, the behavior of most
    of the animals changed: The moose and the deer ceased grazing in
    the open valleys and the riverbanks. This emergent phenomenon
    was called a trophic cascade. On his part, Savory — a member of
    the first generation of professionals dedicated to the conservation
    of parks in Africa — studied the problems of sustainability and
    erosion of grasslands as well as the number of animals that an eco-
    system can sustain. At first, he followed the agronomic orthodoxy
    and reached the conclusion, along with other colleagues, that thou-
    sands of elephants had to be sacrificed to preserve the health of the
    national parks. As time went by, even with the lack of elephants,
    the grasslands degraded, and the desertification continued, so Sa-
    vory decided to look for other alternatives to manage the flora and
    wildlife. Years later, he discovered that the relationship between
    herbivores, the soil, and the health of the ecosystems had not been
    understood. He created a new management system called planned
    holistic grazing that consists of reintroducing livestock to the grass-
    lands and letting them graze briefly, but intensively, in different
    parts of the land. The concept is to replicate the conditions gener-
    ated by the large herds of wild herbivores that consume, trample,
    and fertilize the land with their feces until they move on to the next

area. The results and testimonies of Savory and his followers are encouraging, although there is a fierce debate against them from the traditional specialists in agronomy and soil management. Now that the traditional methods have failed, Savory's and Monbiot's experiences show that the emergent phenomena that take place when we change one of the system's interaction rules — such as the existence of apex predators in Yellowstone or the herds of herbivores grazing in the African grasslands — can open a new and exciting door to address the problems of sustainability.

3. *Everything you think you know about addiction is wrong,* Johann Hari, June 2015, TEDGlobal London, 5.9 million visits(339). Hari, a journalist with a family past affected by addictions, decided to travel around the world to research the current situation concerning scientific knowledge on drug addiction. Soon, he learned about Portugal's experience and results. (It was the first country in the world to create a review panel of the scientific evidence on this topic.) Under the leadership of Dr. João Goulão, the panel's conclusion was to break away from the international consensus on prohibition and completely decriminalize drug consumption. Moreover, Hari analyzed the studies of the Canadian scientist Bruce Alexander, who reviewed the original experiments carried out on rats and discovered that the high addiction rates that decades earlier had served to harden the war against drugs, were correlated to the situation of isolation, confinement, and alienation of the rodents during the experiments — "controlled conditions," the scientists would say. Alexander carried out new versions of those experiments, but he decided to put the rats in an enriched environment, that he dubbed *rat park,* with games, labyrinths, and dens where the animals could socialize in a "normal" way for the species. The results showed that when the animals are in an enhanced context, the tendency to engage in an addiction is dramatically lower. It was this new knowledge that partly drove the Portuguese to change the strategy. Instead of pursuing and ostracizing addicts, Portuguese society — working jointly with the government — sought to redirect the use of resources to recognize the addicts, take them in, and keep them connected to society. According to Hari, the statistics of European institutions that monitor the addiction rates show that 15 years after the new policy was implemented, "The overdoses

and HIV [...] went down massively," general drug use went down by 50%, and overall, a significant reduction took place regarding addictions. Portugal's social consensus changed and "practically no one wants to return to the old system."

4.   *What makes a good life? Lessons from the longest study on happiness,* Robert Waldinger, November 2015, TEDx Beacon Street, 11.5 million visits(340). In his talk, Waldinger explains that 80% of millennials in the U.S. said in a recent survey, "A main goal in their life is to be rich," and "...another 50% said another important goal is to be famous." He then adds that in 1938, Harvard began a project titled "Study of Adult Development," which has been the longest of its type in history. Since then and to date, the academicians have followed two groups of men: one made up of sophomore students at Harvard — most of whom finished their studies and served in World War II. The other was a group of kids from the poorest neighborhoods in Chicago. After 75 years, the big conclusion was: "Good personal relations keep us feeling happier and healthier. That's it." The three lessons they learned about relationships were: "Social connections are really good for us and loneliness kills;" "It's not only the amount of friends you have or whether you're in a stable relationship, what matters is the quality of close relationships;" and "Good relationships protect the brain." Unfortunately, this contrasts a great deal with the answers of the American kids: "One of every five American kids reported they are isolated."

5.   *Why ordinary people need to understand power,* Eric Liu, November 2005, TEDCity 2.0, 1.7 million visits(341). Author, lecturer, political science professor, and director of the non-government organization Citizen University. Liu makes a passionate defense of ordinary people's involvement in politics. He explains the double process of the professionalization of politics and the simultaneous disconnection and estrangement of the citizen, or what he calls the "civics of power." He proposes the construction of a new power, that of the ordinary man, which must take place from the local to the national level, by making the citizens power-literate. As a first step, he shares the development of a study program for the ordinary citizen. With it, he purports to establish a path that allows the voter to reintroduce himself in political engagement and build a local-influence network that will later produce changes at a national level.

6.   *Social services are broken. How we can fix them?* Hilary Cottam,
     September 2015, TEDGlobal London, 649,000 visits(342). Cottam
     narrates the story of Ella, a woman who lives in a rundown area
     of a British city. Although she's not starving, she is trapped in the
     middle of social and capacities poverty, like millions of people
     in the most developed countries. She says that, even though she
     had no intentions of doing so, she repeated the same cycle of bad
     decisions and dead-end streets as her mother. Thus, she depends
     for her sustenance on the social services programs of the welfare
     state. When Hillary meets Ella, her city has 73 social services
     available to which she can have access to via 24 different institu-
     tions. Most of the agencies are well aware of Ella's family and her
     issues, but Hilary realizes that, after 30 years of interventions and
     despite the diverse programs, there is no plan, no final objective
     on how to help this family. The speaker explains that, according
     to the British government, a family like Ella's has an annual cost
     of £250,000 sterling, and the problem is that most of that cost is
     consumed by the social services system itself. That is, one of the
     workers who looks after Ella "...must use 86% of her time in pro-
     viding service to the system: meetings with colleagues, filling out
     forms, more meetings to discuss the forms, and maybe 14% of the
     time is actually with the beneficiary." This takes place in a large
     number of government programs around the world. Despite the
     enormous operating expenditures, little or none of the resources
     actually reach the beneficiaries.

     In what may be called a post-institutional intervention, the city
     where Ella lived decided to find the way to change the proportion
     between the system's cost and the user's benefit. After making
     the rules more flexible and finding out what Ella's family truly
     needed, it created an aid group and rediscovered the very ancient
     wisdom that human contact and the deinstitutionalization of re-
     lationships were important to understand and find solutions to
     the complicated problems of people like Ella. Cottam also under-
     scores loneliness as a public health problem that "damages and
     kills more people than smoking." She reports a terrifying piece
     of data from the United Kingdom: "One person out of 10, among
     those over 60, that is, 850,000, does not talk with anyone in the
     course of a month." The report extrapolates the data to the rest of

the developed world and the big urbanization processes that are taking place, as in China. For the speaker, the elements that allow us to turn the equation of the ineffective institutionalism on its head and toward a community based on relationships of mutual support are easier than to think of making the institutional processes even more formal, structured, and efficient. To this effect, she proposes less structured processes, such as Circle, a free-of-charge service hotline, founded by Cottam and managed by a small and autonomous team that provides all kinds of support to the elderly, from assistance setting up a DVD player to helping them care for their sick pets. Apart from the calls — and thanks to the users' meetings that Circle organizes — they were able to create new groups of friends between people who were disconnected and had no possibility or the tools to be part of a community. These new friendships enhanced the users' overall situation and lowered their dependence on the costly governmental welfare programs. For this social entrepreneur — as she likes to call herself — the three factors that forced the change of the institutional model to one based on relationships were: "First, the nature of the problems that have changed and require different solutions; second, the human and financial cost of doing things the same way as always; and third, the technology. [Since] the technology we use is very simple, it consists of things that are already available such as databases and mobile telephones."

In 1992, James Carville, the strategist of Bill Clinton's successful presidential campaign, hung a sign on his office wall that read: "The economy, stupid."(343) The phrase, directed to the team he was heading to focus on the economic message they wanted to transmit, was disseminated and became popular through *The War Room*, a documentary that was an Oscar nominee (1993). Over time, the phrase changed to *It's the economy, stupid!* Since then, it has been used in the most diverse variations to underscore unassailable truths, the main cause of an issue or the crux of a solution. Altogether, the Internet II, the best TedTalks in history, and the new generation analogue solutions appear to paraphrase Carville and scream out at us that the heart of the solution: *"It's the person, stupid!"*

17. The Democracy Innovation Network

The middle-scale

Attention to the middle-scale is often left to the side in the analysis of complex systems. Thus far, we have defined the agent's behavioral system through its essential aspects — interaction rules, cultural evolution strategies, and design philosophies — as well as through structural aspects, the network functions, topology, and hub characteristics.

The sum of all these factors is sufficient to explain the different evolutive paths a social system may take. Other mid-level parameters, however, can accelerate or slow change. For chemists, an agent that accelerates a reaction is referred to as a catalyst and an agent that slows down a reaction is called an inhibitor. The intermediate-level agents in a network stimulate or slow down changes in its configuration. We can draw examples of social catalyzers from our every-day experience. Some examples are the academics who often don´t do research, but act as connectors or hubs for other colleagues promoting collaborative relationships. These professionals frequently make a significant difference in innovation and scientific discovery. Other types of social intermediate-level agents are collectors, curators, and organizers — like TED's Chris Anderson, the think tanks, lobbying firms, and impertinent relatives and friends with matchmaking inclinations.

The influence of intermediate agents must not be underestimated. For instance, the prohibition of consumption and commercialization of drugs and the militarization of the police forces are two notoriously defunct public safety paradigms. Specialists continuously advocate for the demilitarization of the police forces and the decriminalization of a meaningful part of drug consumption and commercialization. Why have new public paradigms not emerged? Why has not a new quorum consolidated on these issues? Part of the reason resides with intermediate level agents — warmongers and bureaucrats — who make a living from the war on drugs and actively work to inhibit change.

Even if it does not seem to be true, over the last century the world has become more peaceful: there are fewer international wars and internal armed conflicts. The market economy has developed at an exponential rate, and military might has waned, although it is still huge. And, as is widely known, the militarization of police forces and the war on drugs made the arms industry thrive. At the same time, these policies distract attention and resources from institutions and programs that could yield more promising results, such as the reform of the criminal justice systems, the prevention and treatment of addicts, and the education and training of the young in vulnerable circumstances.

To be sure, once the quorum changes, the emergent configuration of a complex systems does not stop. However — borrowing again from the chemical reactions metaphor — it is not the same to wait for days until a reaction is complete instead of using a catalyzer to speed it up to finish in minutes or hours.

The role and influence of inhibitors and catalyzers in society can be so meaningful that their stories very often transcend to popular culture in the form of books and films. For instance, the satirical movie *Thank You for Smoking*(344), portrays the activities of Nick Naylor, the vice president of the Academy of Tobacco Studies. Staged in the 1980s, Nick Naylor puts all the resources of his organization to the service of denial, manipulation, and distortion of the science that linked the consumption of tobacco to health risks. Ironically, at that same time, Mr. Naylor tried to excel as the parent of a teenager, developing the ethical dilemma of the plot. On the other hand, the movie *Erin Brockovich*(345) illustrates the role of a social catalyzer. This real-life story features a bold and audacious woman who defies all the unwritten laws of legal practice and makes a big corporation pay fairly for the damage inflicted on the health of an entire community. More than an irony, the fact that Mrs. Brockovich did not have education as a lawyer underscores the importance of ingenuity in the acceleration of change.

If we see the U.S. as a networked system, we would have to agree that nowadays the middle-level is infested with inhibitors and wanting for catalyzers. On the side of inhibitors, the operational premise is simple: investments in the mid-level of the network protects sales and generates income. For instance, the financing of distorted science to reinforce the seek-and-hunt paradigm of policing does not solve the problems of public safety and worsens the issue of the militarization of the police forces. But that is not a problem that affects the intermediaries that profit from procurement contracts with governments.

On the side of the catalysts, things are more difficult. Given that value and cost have a complicated relationship because everyone wants to access and enjoy value, but few want to pay the price of creating it. For example, Nick Naylor wishes to be an example for his son and build a good relationship with him if that doesn't compromise his job as a lobbyist for the tobacco industry.

This takes us back to our discussion on responsibility, guilt, and the banality of evil. As discussed in other chapters, the leader of the teachers' union in Mexico, the Germanwings co-pilot, Adolf Eichmann, and the businessmen that finance harmful special interests are completely guilty for their actions. However, the irreparable consequences of their actions are of such enormous magnitude that they alone cannot be considered responsible for them, given that they lack the capacity to face and solve the consequences. Thus, our tolerance to leave in the hands of sociopaths or incompetents matters that entail catastrophic risks should be zero. Sadly, American voters will learn this with President Donald Trump, who has high probabilities of committing acts that will find no repair, even if all his fortune was confiscated to redress damages. Instead, American voters as the ultimate bearers of the country's sovereignty will have to accept the consequences of his actions. As it always happens in societies that make the mistake of confusing demagogy with democracy.

The point could seem unnecessarily polemical. But it is not. Someone who causes damage and lacks the financial, mental, or physical capabilities to repair and redress the affected can be considered guilty, but not responsible. On the other hand, a responsible person is someone who can face and search for solutions to a problem, regardless of who caused it. The sphere of social responsibility for each of us depends on the reach of our influence and capacity to act. For those reasons, the best argument for us to get involved in the development of network catalyzers isn´t economic. On the contrary, it resembles the answer U.S. President John F. Kennedy left us more than 50 years ago to justify the trip to the moon: We must do this effort, not because it is easy or convenient, but because we are those who have the capability to do it.

Do Tank

In the same way technology and the problems of post-modernity have changed the markets, politics, government, and society, it is necessary to change the mission, tasks, and methods of intermediate actors. For a long time, the activity of these actors was constrained to intellectual specialization and emerged in the form of think tanks. They are formed by specialists dedicated to research and divulgation on specific areas of public policy, such as civil rights and economic freedom. Think tanks can receive funding from the government, but they also raise revenue from people, foundations and corporations with specific interests in public policy. Two prominent examples are, on the conservative end of the political spectrum, the Heritage Foundation, established in 1972 with a yearly income of $112.7 million. On the liberal end is the Brookings Institution, established in 1916, with an annual budget of $107.5 million(346).

Another type of actor are advocacy groups dedicated to promoting policy and legal changes as a direct means of furthering specific social causes like the working conditions of mothers. On the same level, we have lobbying firms that are more interested in seeking legal protection for commercial or industrial interests such as the militarization of the police forces. Finally come the organizations that carry out specific and localized projects, such as the promotion of voting or community action (e.g., Cure Violence). In this three-layered system, think tanks lay out strategic guidelines, the tactics of which are spearheaded by lobbying firms and advocacy groups with social activists carrying out experiments and specific projects at the operational front.

In the analog world, this arrangement was functional because there was a consensus about the validity of the analysis based on facts, and that the discussion and decision-making would be rational and based on evidence. In this slow, institutionalized system, think tanks reviewed and developed new ideas; lawmakers, advocacy groups, and lobbyists discussed and crafted policy, and activists experimented or carried out projects at the specific, community level. For all its sluggishness, that process had the virtue of adhering to evidence and facts. But it could not adapt to the digital era and collapsed. A prominent example that shows how the system became fractured is known as the myth, the lie, the humbug of vaccines and autism(347).

In 1998, "The Lancet," a renowned medical journal founded in 1823, published an article signed by Andrew J. Wakerfield et al. that correlated some cases of autism with a substance called thimerosal, which is used as a conservative in the MMR vaccine — measles, mumps, and rubella. The date of publication is crucial because it coincides with two factors: first, the consolidation of infotainment as a new style of report-ing, stimulated in part by former Preseident Ronald Reagan's suspension of the Fariness Doctrine (1949) more than a decade before. The Fairness Doctrine was a public policy that had required the media to "present opposite views on controversial public issues in a balanced, honest, and equitable form." Second, 1998 was one of the critical years when the use of the Internet exploded. Thanks to these factors, the article co-authored by Wakefield found an unprecedented divulgation and resonance. A mix of sensationalism and information put that scientific publication at the center of alarm in vast sectors of society.

During the following three years, medical doctors, public health experts, and authorities revised the results of the article and proved it false. But the damage was done. The alarm that the media propagated, and that the Internet replicated, took an uncontrollable life of its own, separate from the views and opinions of academics and professionals. In 2004, 10 of the 13 authors of the article issued a partial retraction and explained that their report had been misunderstood because their research did not causally link vaccines and autism. In 2010, after a careful 12-year investigation, "The Lancet" published a formal and complete retraction. Too late. The false information had continued to multiply unchecked, and parents of the digital age, empowered by the Internet, felt better informed than the analog specialists and decided to reject vaccination for their children. In 2014, San Francisco — ironically, the cradle of the digital era — registered an epidemic outbreak of measles (132 cases) that might have originated from an international visitor to Disneyland. The experts conjecture that the low rate of immunization among local kids contributed to the propa-gation of the virus(348). Comparisons with other outbreaks — 1982 with 14 cases and another in 2001 with 5 — indicate an apparent regression in the conditions of public health in the State of California.

Another outstanding crack in the system of intermediate influence oc-curred with the legal victory of the conservative group Citizens United in 2010. That year, the U.S. Supreme Court determined that the group had the right to publicize a film against Hillary Clinton during the 2008 cam-paign. The judgment established that Citizens United, as a legal person, could enjoy the same right to free speech as that of individuals. The le-gal consequence is that, nowadays, that group or any other similar one, cannot be the subject to spending controls in political campaigns. This unfortunate decision paved the way for corporations to spend as much as they wished in electoral campaigns(349) and reinforced the capture of politicians and politics — the government hubs — in the predatory model of economic and political rent-seeking.

These examples abound in ironies, just as does our current situation. For instance, in 2011, the Fairness Doctrine, suspended by President Ronald Reagan in 1987, was finally abrogated by President Barack Obama. These decisions facilitated the conversion of informative spaces into info-entertainment shows, and Donald Trump and his spokespersons enjoyed thousands of hours of unlimited broadcasting during the campaign and used those spaces to deny reality and make unfounded allegations to whomever they pleased. The leaders of Citizens United — David N. Bossie and Stephen K. Bannon — were key players in the Trump campaign. Bannon was a campaign manager and chief strategist for the Trump administration for the first eight months of the President's first term. It is noteworthy that, for years, Bannon had run Breibart.com, an ultra-conservative news platform rife with xenophobia and racism. Many consider that Breibart.com is the news outlet and main communication channel of the Alt-Right movement. Of course, this website was one of the principal echo-chambers that spawned the popularity of Donald Trump in the dawn of his bid for the presidency.

In sum, 2016 was a hallmark year in the collapse of the analog, stratified, and specialized world of intermediate organizations. In that year, the thorough and well-balanced reflection cultivated by think tanks had much less influence on the public debate than the fake news invented by teenager charlatans in Macedonia. And, crucially, professional analysts did not foresee the outcome of the election and the factors that produced it. The technical and operational capacity of traditional intermediate groups failed to promote voter turnout: only 55% of citizens cast a vote — the lowest level in 20 years(350). At the end of the day, the context, the dynamics, the tools, and the speed of influence in the intermediate levels of the network changed, and the precepts that used to work became obsolete. This is not an aberration. A business-as-usual return to the old state of affairs does not seem feasible for the immediate or long-term future.

What to do, hence? Start over. It is time to redesign and revitalize the intermediate associations that can hold and support the open society. To continue with paradoxes, it is intriguing that part of the solution can actually come from the adoption of the operative model financed by

Robert Mercer and utilized by Trump, Bannon, and their accomplices in Citizens United and Breitbart. Some observations are in order. In the first place, barriers of specialization did not stop these actors. Citizens United used to produce films, but it went out of its established business to imagine, build, and execute a legal strategy that changed the history of the U.S. Another irony is that Breitbart, an instrument of authoritarianism, copied the news aggregation model of the "liberal" *Huffington Post* and adapted it with discipline, hence building communities of opinion with people who felt marginalized by the messages of the traditional media.

In general, Trump's team of media manipulators were agile and disciplined. They thought of what they wanted and acted consequently. One of the things we can learn is that the progress of the open society can be defended through a new, intermediate model of intervention — a model that can bridge the space between experimentation and takeoff of social projects with agility; a model that is more centered in obtaining concrete results and less centered on rewarding best efforts, capable of experimenting, innovating, making mistakes and acknowledging them rapidly.

A new model for intervention at the intermediate level must establish meaningful relationships in society and with society and make them grow. This implies a departure from the rather ethereal, aseptic, and (until recently) safe model of the think tanks and pioneering into that of the more grounded "do tank," one geared for dealing with all the complications of innovation in democracy. It is the necessity of democracy, and inspiration can draw examples from the MIT Media Lab and the diversity-welcoming ecosystem that pushed forward the digital age from Silicon Valley.

Components of the project

In recent years, as the political and social situation in Mexico and other places worsened, I started to discuss with people of all walks of life about the ideas in this book. The question was always: What is the solution? As if there was a silver bullet that could bring about a rapid and systemic solution to authoritarianism. This seems to be the common denominator of "slacktivists": the expectation to find silver bullets or hacks and don't play unless you have one. There is no hack for this situation. And, as a matter of fact, while I was writing this book, the historical events were taking a more accelerated pace, and we moved from witnessing possibilities and dangers of regression in the open society to the certainty of a new authoritarian tide. We also transitioned from thinking in paths to expand democracy to the need to imagine new tools to bring it back. The U.S. is the eye of the storm today, but the situation is not reassuring in the rest of the world. In Mexico, the possibility of a comeback of populist authoritarianism is just before our eyes. A dictatorship has strengthened its grip over Venezuela. The nationalist and extreme right tide is also rising in France. In the midst of these changes, "the solution" I propose has three main components: 1) A change of the quorum — the cultural evolution strategy; 2) Digital governance — the network functions configuration; 3) Vascular loops — the network topology. Each of these components has sub-components of different size and complexity. Let them be moon shots or frugal changes. Outlined below are the components for the Democracy Innovation Network project. It is more of a roadmap that helps us think about new, intermediate level organizations, as well as refurbishing the ones that already exist in a way where they can explore and build the solutions that will shape the future.

1. **Changing the quorum.** No doubt, the central piece and drive of this method is the development of projects that reinforce and amplify the interaction rules that favor the liberal quorum. The most important contribution of complexity science to the social sciences is the knowledge that emergent phenomena, like power and violence, depend on the behavior and attitudes of the agents that aggregate in a quorum. If the quorum consolidates in the authoritarian strategy, there is nothing left to do. Conversely, if the quorum changes toward a collaborative design, maybe the development of other components won't be necessary, given that people will discover and build them on their own.

    i. **Find the liberals.** All through the years that I participated in political campaigns, I heard over and over, in the voices of international political consultants hired to advise Mexican political campaigns, that the segmentation of the electoral market in advanced countries like the U.S. had attained such a degree of perfection that it had become almost an exact science. However, according to what we discussed in Chapter 2 about perceptual science, the initial segmentation of moral, social, commercial, and political identities used in academia, government, and commerce is arbitrary. Markets are segmented when someone — often a guru using some intuitive or invented criteria — has an "eureka" moment with which he or she defines the characteristics of the segments. With these characteristics or taxonomies, people create messages, proposals, and campaigns. They are also used to make forecasts and gauge preferences. In 2016, electoral experts in the U.S. failed when they became locked inside the traditional segmentation of red Republican states and blue Democratic states. They were incapable of seeing that in the old industrial regions different unidentified segments existed. Those segments did not fit with either of the pre-established party categorizations.

In Mexico, millions of voters continue to back political parties that have lost most if not all their prestige (approximately 9 million in the case of the PAN). However, I know from first-hand experience that many members of the leadership in those parties don´t know who those voters are and why they vote for their party. Their opinions, moral identity, and even specific location stay ignored.

The interaction rules, the cultural evolution strategies, the design philosophies, and the concepts of locus of control, optimization, and maximization add up to a new way of doing segmentation. This new, first-principles approach seeks to isolate, at the highest possible level, the cognitive biases from the social taxonomy construction process. The proposal is in line with recent developments on the side of neurosciences, cognitive marketing, and behavioral economics. There is also internationally valid research on human behavior — like that of the marshmallow experiment cited above — telling us that as much as a third of humanity has the capability to delay rewards. This is, however, only a first step. What befits us is to use the categories of the new taxonomy — masters, lackeys, serfs, heroes, bandits, liberals, conservatives, superstars, and paladins — and put them to the test in experimental research. A string of derivative questions have to be addressed. For instance, Is this a valid segmentation? How do we identify them? Who are they? How many there are? What do they think? How do they relate to one another? and What do they want?

ii. **Create a new pedagogy of freedom.** In the same fashion, many people are unhappy and want "someone to do something," but remain stationary even to solve their own problems. They are dispersed, and many times hidden in the mass of pleonexia, alienation, and acedia. There are true liberals out there. They are the people that wait to eat the marshmallow. They change the broken lightbulb, pick up the garbage in their doorstep, and act in a responsible way, no matter that in their environment it is easier and more profitable to behave to the contrary. These people really seek to own their problems and make an effort to solve them. They want to do something, but very frequently don't even know how or where to begin. This is totally understandable because most of them are overwhelmed by the pedagogy of authoritarianism and acedia. If they Google™ "how to be part of change?" it is unlikely they will find the adequate outlet and response to validate the deepest feelings of their moral identity. They won't find accessible explanations on the value of freedom or collaboration or content that can help them verbalize, articulate, define, and defend their identity in their social environment. We need to create and propagate a pedagogy of freedom that is accessible and useful for all citizens, just as Donald Trump normalized and encouraged radicals to express themselves, and Breitbart News created and diffused a pedagogy of authoritarianism. Liberals must act fast to keep their message alive.

iii. **Create methods and tools (moon shot).** As people get more and more isolated, developing more intimacy with their mobile phones than with their neighbors, it is also more and more difficult to create mutual help and social participation networks. These losses of human and social wealth imply that knowledge and techniques of how to relate with one another disappear. However, it is highly probable that there are many people out there — a quantification is in order, and urgent — with the capacity and willingness to escape slacktivism. However, they simply lack the method to overcome their situation. In these post-modern times, liberals must avail themselves of methods — let them be modest and analogical (e.g., organization of neighborhood gatherings, inviting people door-by-door at the right time of the day) — or sophisticated and digital. Liberals also require tools and platforms to create distributed collaboration networks, to manage projects and achievements. Put simply: It is necessary and urgent to create organizational methods and systems that allow the development of platform-based, distributed political parties — emergent, self-managed, self-regulated, and transparent. These new political parties must break away from the old analog intermediation model of the political parties of last century.

2. **Digital governance.** Digital governance as a subject must be at the center of the discussion table. Recent events — like the effect of fake news on Facebook®, or the hacking of email accounts and the ensuing WikiLeaks' scandals in Hillary Clinton's campaign — catalyzed interest to start a conversation about digital governance. However, because of its novelty, the subject needs to be approached at different levels:

    i. **Awareness.** The conversation must start at some moment, and the first step is to raise awareness about the problem and the need to discuss the challenges of digital governance. This conversation must rely on a divulgation stream — studies, books, reports — plus a discussion and divulgation stream — conferences, forums, and public meetings of stakeholders.
    ii. **Development of new knowledge.** The two above mentioned streams must rely on research and network collaboration for the development of knowledge on digital governance.
    iii. **Development and promotion of innovative solutions.** A philosophical premise in the world of innovation says: "If it exists, it is possible." Therefore, even at a small scale — but scalable— it is important to develop innovations that will give viability to improvements in digital governance. Today it seems feasible to create blacklists of fake news outlets, just as IP addresses of pernicious websites have been blacklisted for many years. These lists can feed apps connected to our social networks so that when the users opt-in, the app could analyze the records to locate and purge — disconnect — the outlets that promote fake news dissemination. These new systems could create a rating system showing the amount of fake news that has been shared. It is interesting to think about all the changes that would be

set in motion if we realized our degree of naive credulousness and that of our friends. The open and collaborative nature of the global projects also lead to find and promote solutions from other independent innovators like the platform Ushahidi, Inc, created by volunteers to collect information during disasters. What matters the most is that programmers and systems designers join the ambition to improve digital governance.

iv. **International collaboration.** Once an international problem is recognized and defined with a set of clear and distinct principles, the next step is to catalyze collaboration. Normally, this stage takes the form of government directives or joint development of declarations or agreements. An Internet Governance Act could be a sound foundational document for that purpose. While phrasing a guiding document can be easy, mustering social and political consensus around it involves a great effort of persuasion that takes time and determination to foster international collaboration.

v. **Development of digital public policies and social activism.** The law of the gun will continue to create problems in the digital world as long as the responses of governments continue to replicate the expensive and ineffective logic of retribution and control that mirror the failed paradigm of the war on drugs. This scheme can be counterweighted with a mixed entailment program. It needs on one side decision-makers to craft public policy and on the other social activists to catalyze change. Every day there are more victims of robbery, abuse, and digital blackmail, but for them there are no viable solutions in sight. We should bear in mind that victimized citizens without a voice to harness their cause constitutes a latent risk for democracy. Their frustration and desperation can embolden authoritarian policies to limit freedom of speech and eradication of privacy in the digital domain.

vi. **Digital public goods (Moon Shot).** Although the task of building digital public goods looks appalling, there are several ways to make it happen. If the other components of the digital governance come to existence, then three scenarios are possible. In the first possibility, a local or national government spearheads the effort to develop specific digital public goods at a small scale, but with the possibility to upscale them. Besides being successful, these projects must also be open, easy to expand, and have the proclivity to become de facto standards (e.g., a civil registry based on blockchain). Another viable path can consist in the independent development of platforms that secure the principles of digital governance. In other words, while they add users, platforms stay on a route propitious to attain legal recognition, for example, by adhering to the tenets of a hypothetical Internet Governance Act. The ultimate goal for platforms in this path would be to grow and develop to a level that enables their recognition as digital public goods (e.g., the Ethereum platforms). The third option, less probable at this moment, would be to launch an ambitious program, with all the political and financial support from a national government in an endeavor that mirrors a U.S. NASA Apollo-type space project: an almost literal shot to the moon, with ambitious and clear goals, deadlines, and adequate political and financial backing.

3. **Vascular loops.** What the discussion of complex systems, network theory, and new generation solutions (e.g., the trophic cascades) suggest is that we still don´t understand enough about the relationships between the economy and the environment. Contemporary examples are the negligible progress with the international agreements on the environment and the likely withdrawal of the U.S. from the international consensus on climate change. The network-theory based proposal of creating vascular loops is promising (Chapter 10), but it still needs further development to formalize, consolidate, and integrate network theory into economics. It is worth saying that there aren´t many alternatives. The internalization of negative externalities has been discussed for decades, and there are only two ways out: give a price to said externalities or do nothing and leave externalities as they are. But that is clearly an inadmissible and self-destructive course of action. Fortunately, the option of internalizing externalities through the price system can trigger positive and significant changes — even considering the state of institutional underdevelopment that is hobbling more ambitious innovation.

i. **Knowledge.** Recent knowledge about complex systems and network theory can be used to develop new models in different branches of economics (Chapter 10). Academic institutions can contribute by collaborating to study — formally and experimentally — aspects such as the behavior of nodes, the network functions, and the relationship of use and destruction of the substrate.

ii. **Innovation.** Payment of environmental services is not a new thing, but it is not scaling as required. Some international programs, like the REDD+ (Reduction of Emissions from Deforestation and Degradation) have achieved good results, but their management systems are still limited by the intermediation of governmental bureaucracies. In the private sector, fair-trade and organic certification programs have also contributed to create a more environmentally sustainable and human economy. Innovation for the disintermediation of these programs through distributed platforms stands as an ideal field to build and scale-up vascular loops.

iii. **Development of public policy proposals.** Historically, environmental issues have been of exclusive concern for governments and multilateral international organizations. The entanglement of environmental problems with government management is a reason why the solutions for these issues do not scale-up in size. Too many initiatives exist that depend on the intermediation and control of the government, but there are not enough initiatives that rely on the evolutionary dynamics of markets (Chapter 11).

iv. **International collaboration.** Despite the Paris agreements on climate, we need to recognize that the contemporary architecture of international cooperation has achieved too little, too late. The international conversation needs more ideas and solutions to give effectiveness to international collaboration on environmental and economic issues (e.g., the use of network theory and distributed management models).

v. **Experimental public policy.** One of the contributions of China to public policy is the so-called experimental public policy. In the traditional model, public policies are developed based on technocratic and bureaucratic principles. The ensuing implementation relies on complicated changes in normative frameworks, and their results undergo evaluation after a full government

cycle. One of the deficits of these models is that they only identify problems of design and unintended effects after a first cycle
of implementation, when legal changes, are already in place,
impeding corrections and even the possibility of backtracking
and starting over. In the Chinese model of experimentation, the
institutional actors have latitude to implement trials at a small
scale before proposing legal modifications. They also have instruments to abrogate and easily eliminate public policy that
gives bad results. These features should inspire a corresponding imitation in open societies. The construction of an economy based on vascular loops needs a much more flexible policy
environment, where experimentation and co-creation allow the
discovery and development of new economic models.

The way solutions get built matters. The three components and their
corresponding sub-components are part of a coherent ensemble with
mechanisms of mutual reinforcement. These operate as follows: if there
is an open and collaborative quorum, then it is easier to approach and
solve the problems of digital governance. In turn, a new digital environment with an architecture based on principles of distributed architecture and disintermediation can bring about an environmentally
sustainable and socially responsible economy. In a vascular loop model,
recirculation currents can pay with efficiency and without intermediation to new economic actors for the environmental services they provide.
Seen from the perspective of network theory, the great breakthroughs
of history tell us that changes in the three components — the quorum,
network configuration, and topology — are the key factors that under-
pin those changes. Human societies are complex systems with interrelated components. That means we can´t afford to address change in
a fragmented fashion.

18. Zeitgeist

The rebellion against freedom

Today's Zeitgeist escapes definition. My generation (X) has seen too many changes. In 1982, as kids, we lived in fear because of the escalation of the Cold War as a consequence of former U.S. President Ronald Reagan's Star Wars defense program. Only a few years after that in 1989, the very concrete Berlin Wall and the abstract Iron Curtain fell after some years of economic and political opening (Perestroika and Glasnost) in the former USSR led by Mikhail Gorbachev. For months, we followed with enthusiasm the downfall of tyrants like Nicolae Ceausescu, the rise of Lech Walesa in Poland, and the reunification of Germany led by Helmut Kohl. The worst environmental problem for humankind was the depletion of the ozone layer, but international cooperation crystallized in the Montreal protocol, which sufficed to address the issue and provided a a solution to implement. At the end of the 1980s, ideologies and utopias expired. Francis Fukuyama dared to coin the term "The End of History." All that was left to do was continue the democratization process, making globalization deeper, and taking advantage of the new technologies like the Internet, the portable personal computer, and the mobile telephone. By the start of the 1990s, the U.S. had become the undisputed hegemonic world power. In 1991, observant of the forms of international law, it organized a multinational coalition to liberate Kuwait from Iraq's invasion. Saddam Hussein, then Iraq's leader, was forced to retreat without the region falling into chaos. For their part, financial institutions were confident they had found a failproof method to stimulate growth and to solve economic crises through programs of adjustment that nations could administer with rigor and discipline. In Mexico, financial crises broke out in 1988 and 1994, although a dirty electoral process in 1988 made the country miss the wave of democratization — and yet the nation caught up, with enthusiasm, in 2000.

While all of this occurred, some pessimists refused to join the enthusiasm for the end of the Cold War and insisted on building a view of their own, examining and measuring reality with skepticism toward institutional propaganda. They fueled their criticism by pointing at the obvious problems in globalization, inequality, automation, unemployment, economic growth, and environmental degradation. These pessimists frequently crowned their argumentation with sentences that began "If this goes on like this, in the future we will…," and then added a complement of the sort: "destroy the climate patterns," "…weaken democracy," "…have social problems," "…create enemies," "…worsen public health," "…reduce the opportunities of future generations," or "…alienate the youth." Some even dared to specify the date of their prognosis. Although the date of the prophecies did not come true, the cumulative effects of these concerns transformed the collective imagination about the future into a distant dystopia, one that nobody thought to witness. WELCOME TO THE FUTURE!

It is sad to get here as if we had concluded our mission for this life. And as if there was nothing left to do now. A future is one of the most valuable and essential ideas because it motivates us to pursue and capture it. We are terrified to be caught and immobilized by the future. However, we can recognize that the future is now. And some of us may be scratching our heads with some questions: Why did we accept this slow but decided path to disaster? Why did we stop dreaming of a brighter future? Why are we working so hard to make a living and so little to live? Did our imagination fail? Are we suffering the self-fulfillment of our prophecies? What defines victory or success in new endeavors of culture, politics, economics, and society? From the most widespread and cynical perspective, the answer is simple: None of these questions really matter. That is today's Zeitgeist: rebellion against freedom. For masters, lackeys, and serfs, the open society is evil because it forces them to be responsible for their actions, to collaborate with others, and to accept diversity. Just like teenagers asserting themselves; these masters, lackeys, and serfs burst bullishly to get what they feel entitled to, and they enthrone the authoritarian master who will promise exactly that.

The generational shift as an opportunity

When we look at world leaders' ages, 90% of them are above 50 years old(351). The most numerous group was born between 1942 and 1967, and only 9.74% were born between 1967 and 1982 (Table 44). This means that, by the start of the next decade, those born in the 1970s will take command. If nothing else changes, the worldview of those leaders will stay in the center of decisions in the decades to come.

448

Generation	Age range	Total	%
1967-1982	< 50	19	9.74%
1957-1967	50 to 59	70	35.90%
1942-1957	60 to 74	89	45.64%
1924-1942	75 or more	17	8.72%
		195	100%

Table 44: Age ranges of world leaders in 2016.

If we observe the U.S. 2016 presidential election through the prism of generations, we can appreciate that the baby boomers and their interests prevailed. The members of Generation X lost, and millennials didn't show up in sufficient number to make a difference. All this said, for natural reasons, the influence of baby boomers will start to wane in the next few years. Generation X will take over part of the control, and in time, the relay will be complete and will start giving way to the millennials' takeover. Thus, the intergenerational relationship between Generation X and millennials is critical to shape a shared idea about the future.

The calling of history for the generation born in the late 1960s and 1970s is still a mystery. We have a historical experience and social programming that the millennials lack. Historically, we lived the apogee of the space era and the withering of the sexual revolution — halted by HIV at the start of the adolescences of members of Generation X. We can recall the last episode of the Cold War, and we built, explored, and pioneered the Internet. We lived the world tragedy of 9/11 of 2001 as adults, and we can vividly recall its consequences. Socially, we are optimistic about technological progress because when we were children we were told that cars would someday fly, that people would inhabit in other planets, or live below the oceans, and that all of us will live to be or past a hundred years because medicine would vanquish diseases. For our generation, divorce, rock, sex, rebellion, and pop culture have been a part of life, not a novelty. Our parents were more conservative than us. They did not understand our music, our video games, and our habits. Ironically, from our perspective children today, actually look more conservative than ourselves.

With baby boomers who rode the wave of the hippie movement, Woodstock, and the sexual revolution, the ancestral stable dynamics of generational change became fragmented. From then on, people aged (and were classified as "squares") the moment they did not understand new changes in technology, music, and fashion. You were not young if you did not infringe on the habits and values of the old generation. But those born after 1970 are part of a new generational re-encounter. Our historical circumstance made us holistic: we like and understand the classic rock of the baby boomers and the disco music of the 1970s. We are loyal without remedy to the rock bands of the 1980s, and we are also content to see that millennials develop a love for the music that we considered ours. We can talk about the music of the band Queen with our nephews. To be sure, our omnivorous affinities make the new generations uncomfortable: we happily go to concerts by Taylor Swift and Muse as if they were Guns N' Roses. We consider ourselves the silver backs of video games. We know them all, starting with Pong in the 1970s. We have used all the platforms and we play with our kids online, although we always take precautions to prevent a millennial eliminating us within minutes. By contrast to the generation of our parents, we understand that the world is a changing and even convulsive place. We do not want or demand the new generation to imitate us: we are truly interested in their independence and future.

Symbolic center

Processes of historical change have symbolic centers that — like beacons — help to channel the social energy: "Land and Freedom," "No taxation without representation," "One man, one vote," "Effective suffrage, no re-election." Sadly, the symbolic centers of the open society have lost their power to fuel the people's imagination. When my generation was born, humankind had just landed on the moon, smallpox had been eradicated, and we were told that the world of the future — our world — would be one of optimism in which success could be reached with effort. As always happens, things occurred differently. Utopias faded; thus, we also ran out of catalysts to build the future. If we tried to locate an idea to synthesize the symbolic center of our era, we would discover that a myriad of exciting mottos had already been used by other generations. When we carefully observed the catalysts of other times, it is striking to realize that most of them upheld a programmatic or instrumental theme that includes a solution, such as "One man, one vote," while the classic and powerful "Equality, liberty, and fraternity" have not been practical and solid enough to satisfy the need for concrete results in our times. In other words, some are too operational, and others are too ethereal.

According to our analytical proposal, everything ultimately gravitates around human dignity and human nature. That is the ardent issue of all times, that the contemporary breakthroughs on artificial intelligence and biotechnology have rekindled in our time. Hence, and given that in other times, symbols have facilitated change in social organization, the way to explore ahead in the construction of a symbolic center relates to the person and the place of the person in society. A symbolic center must be convincing as a sign and practical as a catalyzer of change.

It could take hundreds of years to solve this issue from a philosophical approach, and there are no guarantees of success. Also, the odds are against popularizing a plan that draws on the theory of complexity, including thermodynamics, biology, and information theory in the way that we have defined and described intelligence as "a physical process of optimization that vies to capture the largest number of possible futures through entropic and heuristic optimization." This challenge must therefore be approached through the eyes of a marketing specialist.

In just the same manner that Sokoloff approached the problem of the FARC in Colombia, inquiring what were the goals of the guerrilla fighters. In essence, we may as well ask: "What is a person?" "What are the ends that a person pursues?" If we may respond heuristically, we can aim only to get a "good enough" response. According to philosophers Ken Taylor and John Perry(352)

> *"for Aristotle, the understanding of something requires knowing its final cause, or its purpose, and the final cause of a living being is the function that it normally performs when arriving to maturity. Therefore, to understand what a person is, it is necessary to know what is expected from mature adults."*

These thoughts are tremendously useful because they connect to what we have stated about the dignity of the human being: that a person only has possibilities for self-fulfillment through the right to be someone and to have a place in society.

- Being someone encompasses the notions of opportunity, freedom, and dignity, expressed through rights such as education, health, justice, and everything related to the person and the protection of his dignity.
- Having a place relates the right to enjoy the benefits and fruits (value) that people create with their effort. It is linked to the real and tangible mechanisms of the social contract (taxation, property rights, access to the economic network) and with the interaction of the person with other people — that is, with society.

This is the central discussion for open societies. It is the point where traditional conservatives and liberals have fallen short because they solved the problem of freedom from the perspective of the individual, overlooking the collaborative interaction with others (i.e., the protection of common goods). Both parts — being someone and having a place in society — are essential to approaching the problems of the future. For instance, in our century billions of people live on the margins as part of the random network — without identity, education, credit, work and security — and are not considered to be someone in society. Their right to vote — or be voted for — cannot and has not made a difference in that respect. They do not have a place in society. And the situation can only get worse because of the processes and problems of automation, alienation, hacking of the economic network, and the resurgence of authoritarianism. To be someone and to have a place in society is nothing more and nothing less than reasserting — as it has been said many times before — that the only thing that supports humanity as a concept is the belief that human dignity exists and must be preserved.

Annexes

Trademarks

AIRBNB is a trademark of AirBnB, Inc.

Amazon is a registered trademark of Amazon Group Companies.

American Airlines is a registered trademark of American Airlines Group Inc.

Coca-Cola is a registered trademark of Coca Cola Company.

DARAPRIM is a registered trademark of GLAXOSMITHKLINE, LLC.

EpiPen is a registered trademark of Mylan Pharmaceuticals, Inc.

Facebook is a registered trademark of Facebook, Inc.

Google, Gmail are registered trademarks of Google, LLC.

Google Maps, Waze, Google Location Service are trademarks of Google, LLC

IBM is a registered trademark of International Business Machines Corporation.

Intel Core i7 is a registered trademark of Intel Corporation.

iPhone, iPad are registered trademarks of Apple Company.

Java is a registered trademark of Oracle Corporation.

Keurig, K-cup are registered trademarks of Keurig Corporation.

LEGO is a registered trademark of The Lego Group.

MasterCard is a registered trademark of MasterCard, Inc.

Microsoft, Excel, PowerPoint, LinkedIn are registered trademarks of Microsoft Corporation.

Nestle, Nescafe, Nespresso are registered trademarks of Nestle, S.A.

PayPal is a registered trademark of PayPal, Inc.

SABRE is a registered trademark of Sabre Corporation.

UBER, UberBLACK, UberX, UberSUV, UberPOOL, UberCOMMUTE are trademarks of Uber Technologies.

Visa is a registered trademark of Visa, Inc.

Glossary

A

Acedia. Apathy or mental sloth to do good or what is right.

Anocracy. An unstable and incoherent government system that mixes democratic and authoritarian practices.

API. Application Programming Interface, a set of software functions that allow the exchange of messages between different software systems.

Autotroph. Capacity of some living beings to produce organic nutrients from inorganic substances. For example: Using light or chemical energy. Green plants, algae, and certain bacteria are autotrophs.

B

Baby Boomer. Demographic group, especially in the U.S. and Europe, born between 1943 and 1961.

Big Data. Practice that includes the collection and analysis of large and dispersed digital data sets within which patterns and tendencies are discovered, and that could not be found with traditional data analysis techniques.

Biofilms. Mass or film made of bacteria that aggregates in response to environmental factors, e.g., biofilms increase the resistance of a bacterial disease to treatment with antibiotics.

Biomimetics. Imitation and use of designs and patterns that exist in nature to solve human problems.

Blog. Contraction of the word "weblog;" a text and/or audio/visual log published on the world wide web. Collection of periodical publications that people, and businesses, create on their web sites.

Boolean logic. Logical analytic system grounded in algebra. It has one or two variables based on operators: NO, YES, AND, OR.

Bottom-up. Dynamic systems change from the bottom to the top. Processes and phenomena that are built from the base to the apex.

Brandhacking or brandjacking. Identification and use of the gaps that exist between the expectations a group of consumers has for a brand and the value they receive from the enterprise that holds it.

Brexit. The result of a British referendum on June 23, 2016. The process followed by the United Kingdom to leave the European Union.

BRIC. Informal acronym for a group of economically emergent countries — Brazil, Russia, India, and China. In 2011, South Africa was included, thus it is also known as BRICS.

C

Chaebol. A large conglomerate of businesses in South Korea, typically family-owned.

Co-creation. It's the economic process in which different actors come together to create new products, e.g., consumers and professional designers.

Convective network. Network configured to maximize the efficiency in the transportation of a flow.

Cradle-to-cradle. Process that seeks the recirculation and use of materials through recycling circuits or cycles.

Cradle-to-grave. Process that follows a product from its creation until final disposition in a responsible manner.

CRISPR. Genetic engineering techniques that allows gene editing in an organism.

Crony-capitalism. Economic system in which business people and government officials collude to obtain personal advantages to the detriment of the rest of the citizens.

Cryptography. Set of techniques that try to hide the meaning of messages in a way that only intended users can understand them.

Curators. People that care for, organize, and keep a collection of valuable objects.

D

De-anonymization. It is the use of data analysis techniques, generally Big Data, to identify by indirect means individuals linked to a data set. E.g., it is possible to identify users of a drug from a pharmacy when comparing a drug sales data base with another one that contains credit card transactions by means of the time and date identifiers.

Decarbonize. Actions that tend toward less use of economic processes that create emission of greenhouse gases.

Decile. Division of a population in 10 equal parts referenced to a variable such as income or age. Usually the first decile is identified with the group with the lowest value in the variable and the tenth decile with the highest value of the variable. In the case of age in a population, the first decile will contain the younger population and the tenth the oldest.

Diachronic. Relative to time. Dynamic data analysis to which the time variable is added to observe behavior of a system in a defined period.

Diffusive network. Network configured to maximize the diffusion of flows over the substrate.

DIKW. Acronym of "Data, Information, Knowledge, Wisdom." It relates to the levels of complexity in information and knowledge.

Divest. Action of selling or parting from the property of a business or financial asset.

Double-spend. Possibility of using a valuable certificate in the market once it has been used because of the lack invalidation mechanisms.

Dumping. Trade practices in which a product is offered at a price below its production cost as a means of displacing competition and eventually obtaining higher profits once the competition has left the market.

Dystopia. Imaginary state where nothing works or does so in a dysfunctional manner.

E

Endogamy. Reproduction among relatives or things that are closely related.

Entrepreneurship. Dynamic capacity of a person to develop or establish a business.

ENVIPE. National Public Safety and Victimization Perception Survey (Encuesta Nacional de Victimización y Percepción sobre Seguridad Pública), produced by the Mexican National Statistics and Geography Institute (INEGI).

Ergodic. Related to a process or system in which a sample or part is representative of the whole, thus, it can be studied by statistical means.

Escrow. Contractual arrangement in which two or more parties agree that a third party keeps the money until the conditions of the agreement are met.

Ethology. Scientific study of animal behavior

Ethos. Set of values, principles, and ideals that give direction to a society.

Evolved. In thermodynamics and systems theory, it refers to the configuration or form a system acquires after operating for a long period of time. E.g., a tree is evolved from the seed.

F

Feral. Savage, rustic.

Foodies. Fan or enthusiast of good food and drinks.

G

Genomics. Science that studies genomes.

Gigaflops. Unit that measures the speed of a microprocessor or a computer expressed in billions (Giga) of floating point operations (FLOPS).

Glasnost. Transparency or frankness in Russian. It was the process of opening the Soviet system, started in 1985 by Mikhail Gorbachev.

Governance. What government does. It relates to the quality and functioning of public matters.

Granularity. Size of the particles that form a whole. In data analysis and statistics, it refers to the level of detail in data. e.g., in sales data, low granularity would be monthly sales figures and high granularity would be sales made by the hour.

H

Hardware. Physical components of a system.

Hash cryptography. Irreversible cryptographic technique. To solve the decryption requires computationally intensive techniques that search all possible solutions (brute force).

Heuristics. Art and technique to discover or gain insight in a quick and practical way.

Hoarding. Compulsive and self-destructive accumulation behavior.

Holocracy. Self-managed management system that has no hierarchy.

Homeostatic. Capacity of a system to maintain a regime or balance by means of constant configuration changes.

Hub. Concentrator or meeting point; central or neuralgic point in a network where a great number of exchanges are made.

I

Ideographic. The study of specific and delimitated cases.

Infostructure. The contraction of informatics and infrastructure. It refers to the large-scale information structures a contemporary economy needs to operate.

Infotainment. Mix of information and entertainment. Strategy used by information and news broadcasts that fuses entertainment techniques with serious news to keep high ratings.

IoT. Internet of Things. Interconnection and management of devices through the Internet.

Isotherm. Graphic representation of the curve that joins the same temperatures in a plane.

K

Knowable. That which can be known.

L

Libertarian. Individual who follows the libertarian ideology based on personal freedom, self-interest, no intervention by the State in personal affairs, and even the disappearance of the State.

Lobbying. Action by a specific interest group to create pressure to influence government institutions and decision-making individuals and bodies.

Logos. In philosophy, the understanding of reality through reason. In theology, it is the search for truth.

M

Millennials. Generation born between 1980 until 2000 that started reaching adulthood with the new millennium.

Mindfulness. State of complete attention in which an individual is aware of his actions and the motives behind them.

Moonshot. A project of great ambition that seems impossible to realize.

Multidisciplinary. Research techniques that gather specialists from different disciplines to work on the same problem.

Mythos. Development of histories and explanations based on intuition and beliefs that don't require support by evidence or rational thinking.

N

Neocortex. The recently evolved layers in the brain of primates and human beings.

Nerd. Originally a derogatory term given to people with few social and athletic abilities, but with above average intellect.

Neuroplasticity. Capacity of neuronal systems to adapt to stimuli and experiences.

Newtonian. In systems theory, it refers to systems that behave in a predictable and linear way and that can be explained by means of Newton's mechanics.

Nomothetic. Effort to study reality through a general and systemic approach that tries to discover and define general laws.

Notarize. Action of certification or validation of a piece of information or event.

O

Obamacare. "Patient Protection and Affordable Care Act" is the legislation proposed in 2010 by President Barack Obama to reform the health care system of the U.S.

Oligopoly. A market dominated by a small group of vendors.

Ontology. Branch of metaphysics that tries to answer questions such as: What is reality? Are there final causes?

Open Source. Denomination of rights for works and creations in which the authors give access to others such as the code in software or the electronic files of a book so other people can use, reuse and modify them without no charge.

Ostracism. Exile or expulsion of a person from a community.

P

Paywalls. Techniques for commercial hoarding that impede access to goods that could be of free access. In academia, publicly funded research isn't accessible without payment of a subscription to an information service.

Phishing. Electronic deception technique that attempts to capture the identity of a person or organization with destructive or criminal intent.

Pleonexia. Extreme greed for wealth or material possessions; avarice. Incapacity to reach a state of satisfaction. Insatiable.

Proactive. Person with initiative and capacity to get ahead of events.

Psychographic. Study of people's personality, values, opinions, attitudes, interests, and lifestyle with which interest groups discover consumer patterns.

Q

Quintile. Division of a population in five equal parts related to a variable (see decile).

R

Rentierism. Economic strategy that seeks to extract rents without innovation or creation of new products, services, or investment. In the West, it relates to the rent of land by aristocrats before the industrial age.

Resilient. Capacity of a material to return to its original shape once it has been deformed by an external force. In psychology, it is the capacity of a person to recuperate after a traumatic event.

Robber Barons. Name given to bankers and industrialists who monopolized markets in the late 19th century.

S

Slacktivism. Couch activism, attitude of constant complaint through electronic media without concrete action in the real world.

Stagflation. Economic phenomenon characterized by the simultaneous existence of high inflation and economic stagnation or regression.

Stakeholders. People affected by a potential transaction or actual transaction who can either gain or lose from a policy decision or transaction.

T

ToE. Ton of Oil Equivalent. Energy measurement unit expressed in a normalized ton of oil.

Top-down. Construction or configuration of a system from the apex to the base. E.g., a new factory starts with the decision of managers or shareholders and becomes a reality with activity by construction workers.

Trade-off. Compensated change; the change in one variable is linked to change in another variable. E.g., more volume, lower price.

Transcomputational. A problem to be solved that exceeds available computational power.

Transdiscipline. Research and problem-solving technique in which specialists from one discipline participate in fields other than their specialization.

Trendsetters. Person who establishes a tendency or a fashion.

Trolls. People who strive to create controversy and disgust in cyber-space, frequently with contentious opinions.

Trophic cascade. Changes suffered by an ecosystem when predators are added or removed from the trophic chain, e.g., the removal of wolves allows herbivores to increase their numbers. That, in turn, puts ecological pressure on the grasslands.

Trophic chain. It is the set of linkages biomass has as food within an ecosystem, e.g., herbivores, primary predators, secondary predators.

Trophic. Related to nutrition and nutrients in an ecosystem.

U

Upselling. Commercial technique that tries to hook a sale by an aggressive offering, but also that tries to harass consumers to acquire unnecessary or more expensive products once the consumer has shown interest in the less-expensive offering.

Y

Yuppie. Young Urban Professionals are the upper middle-class people between 20 and 43years of age focused on their personal and professional image.

Z

Zeitgeist. Spirit of the times. Is the cultural and social climate of an epoch.

Zoomass. Size of the physical volume of animals, expressed in weight units.

Works cited

1. **Hobbes, Thomas.** Leviathan. e-book. s.l.: The Project Gutenberg, 1651, XIII.
2. **Enciso, Froylán.** Entrevista con el doctor Leopoldo Salazar Viniegra. *Nuestra aparente rendición.* [Blog]. noviembre 2, 2011. http://nuestraaparenterendicion. com/index.php/blogs-nar/weary-bystanders/ item/715-el-gurú-de-la-legalización-de-las-drogas.
3. **Cedillo, Juan Alberto.** *La Cosa Nostra en México. Los negocios de Lucky Luciano y la mujer que corrompió al gobierno mexicano.* Monterrey: Grijalbo, 2011.
4. *Smallpox: Epitaph for a Killer?* **Henderson, Donald A.** 154, diciembre 1978, National Geographic, Vol. 6, pp. 796-805.
5. **Bourdain, Anthony.** Parts Unknown: Mexico (temporada 3, episodio 4). [Serie de televisión]. s.l.: CNN, 2014.
6. —. Under the Volcano. [En línea] 3 de mayo de 2014. http://anthonybourdain.tumblr.com/post/84641290831/ under-the-volcano.
7. **Esquivel, Gerardo.** *Desigualdad extrema en México: Concentración del poder económico y político.* México: OXFAM, 2015.
8. **Sharma, Ruchir.** Mexico's Tycoon Economy. *Breakout Nations. In Pursuit of the Next Economic Miracles.* Londres: Penguin Books Limited, 2012, pp. 73-82.
9. **Legatum Institute.** *Legatum Prosperity Index. Social Capital.* Londres: Legatum Institute, 2014.
10. **North, Douglass C., y otros.** *Limited Access Orders in the Developing World: A New Approach to the Problems of Development.* Policy Research Working Papers, Working Paper Series. Washington D.C.: World Bank, 2007.
11. **Wikipedia.** Timothy Morton. [Online] julio 21, 2016. http://en.wikipedia.org/wiki/Timothy_Morton.

12. **University of Southampton. School of Electronics and Computer Science.** Studying Complexity Science. *Complexity Science Focus* . [Online] 2015. http://www.complexity.ecs.soton.ac.uk/.

13. *Schools of fish and flocks of birds: their shape and internal structure by self-organization.* **Hemelrijk, Charlotte K. and Hildenbrandt, Hanno.** s.l.: The Royal Society Publishing, agosto 22, 2012, Interface Focus, pp. 726-737.

14. **Chirimuuta, Mazviita.** *Outside Color. Perceptual Science and the Puzzle of Color in Philosophy.* Cambridge: MIT Press, 2015.

15. **Hoffman, Donald D.** The Interface Theory of Perception: Natural Selection Drives True Perception to Swift Extinction. [ed.] Sven J. Dickinson, et al. *Object Categorization: Computer and Human Vision Perspectives.* Nueva York: Cambridge University Press, 2009, pp. 148-165.

16. **Wright Brothers Aeroplane Company.** The 1901 Wright Wind Tunnel. *Adventure Wing. The Virtual Hangar.* [Online] 2011. http://www.wright-brothers.org/Adventure_Wing/Hangar/1901_ Wind_Tunnel/1901_Wind_Tunnel.htm.

17. *Foundational Paradigms of Social Sciences.* **Tang, Shiping.** 2, junio 2011, Philosophy of the Social Sciences, Vol. 41, pp. 211-249.

18. **Wikipedia.** Thermodynamics. [En línea] 26 de agosto de 2016. http://en.wikipedia.org/wiki/Thermodynamics.

19. **Darwin, Charles.** *On the Origin of Species.* Londres: John Murray, 1859.

20. **Wikipedia.** Information theory. [Online] agosto 29, 2016. http://en.wikipedia.org/wiki/Information_theory.

21. **Katsnelson, Alla.** Researchers start up cell with synthetic genome. *Nature.* mayo 20, 2010.

22. **Teilhard de Chardin, Pierre.** *The Phenomenon of Man.* Nueva York: Evergreen, 1955.

23. *Constructal Theory of Generation of Configuration in Nature and Engineering.* **Bejan, Adrian y Lorente, Sylvie.** 4, 2006, Journal of Applied Physics, Vol. 100, pág. 041301.

24. *Cultural Evolution, Design and Philosophy: For the Change of Era.* **Viniegra Beltrán, Carlos.** 3, 2011, International Journal of Design & Nature and Ecodynamics, Vol. 6, pp. 171-212. DOI: 10.2495/DNE-V6-N3-171-212.

25. *Optimized by Evolution, Ants Don't Have Traffic Jams.* **Zyga, Lisa.** marzo 30, 2009, PhysOrg.com.

26. **Psicólogos Clínicos.** *Locus de control.* [Blog]. noviembre 30, 2010.

27. **Organización de las Naciones Unidas (ONU).** Declaración Universal de Derechos Humanos. [En línea] 10 de diciembre de 1948. http://www.un.org/es/documents/udhr/.

28. **Maquiavelo, Nicolás.** *Il principe.* Florencia: s.n., 1532.

29. **Kissinger, Henry.** La diplomacia. [trans.] Mónica Utrilla. México: Fondo de Cultura Económica, 1994, p. 56.

30. **Legal Information Institute.** Commander in Chief Powers. *Wex.* Ithaca, Nueva York, Estados Unidos: Cornell University Law School, 2002. https://www.law.cornell.edu/wex/commander_in_chief_powers.

31. **Chenoweth, Erica and Stephan, Maria J.** *Why Civil Resistance Works. The Strategic Logic of Nonviolent Conflict.* Nueva York: Columbia University Press, 2012.

32. **Liu, Eric.** Citizen University. [Online] 2012. http://www.citizenuniversity.us/.

33. **Slutkin, Gary.** Cure Violence. [Online] 2000. http://cureviolence.org/.

34. **Animal Político.** Gana en Nayarit candidato que dijo "sí robé, pero poquito". julio 7, 2014. http://www.animalpolitico.com/2014/07/gana-en-nayarit-candidato-que-dijo-si-robe-pero-bien-poquito/#axzz3AzGTxGoW.

35. *La fiesta de los 'dipu-tables'.* **Gutiérrez, Hugo.** agosto 11, 2014, Reporte Índigo.

36. **Arendt, Hannah.** *Eichmann in Jerusalem: A Report on the Banality of Evil.* Nueva York: The Viking Press, 1963.

37. **Wikipedia.** Elba Esther Gordillo. [Online] junio 2, 2016. http://en.wikipedia.org/wiki/Elba_Esther_Gordillo.

38. **García de León, Pedro.** *Education at a Glance* 2011. *OECD Indicators.* México: Organización para la Cooperación y el Desarrollo Económicos (OCDE), 2011.

39. *The 10 Most Corrupt Mexicans of 2013.* **Estévez, Dolia.** diciembre 16, 2013, Forbes.

40. **Barajas, Abel y Baranda, Antonio.** Dan golpe maestro. *Reforma.* 27 de febrero de 2013, pág. 1.

41. **Excélsior.** Fortuna de la maestra supera $100 mil millones, asegura ex asesor. 27 de febrero de 2013.

42. **Pinker, Steven.** *Better Angels of Our Nature: Why Violence has Declined.* Nueva York: Viking, 2011.

43. **Boyse, Kyla and Bushman, Brad.** Television and Children. *Your Child. Development & Behavior Resources.* [Sitio web]. s.l.: University of Michigan. Health System, agosto 2010.

44. **U.S. Department of Justice. Office of Juvenile Justice and Delinquency Prevention.** Data Analysis Tools. *Statistical Briefing Book. Law Enforcement & Juvenile Crime.* [Online] 2016. http://www.ojjdp.gov/ojstatbb/crime/data.html.

45. **U.S. Census Bureau.** Population Estimates. [Online] abril 2015. http://www.census.gov/popest/data/national/asrh/pre-1980/PE-11.html.

46. **Polyticks.com.** USA Homicide Rates. A Traditional Second Amendment Argument. [Online] 2015. http://polyticks.com/polyticks/beararms/liars/usa.htm.

47. **Organización de las Naciones Unidas (ONU).** Population by age, sex and urban/rural residence. *UN Data.* [Online] julio 11, 2016. http://data.un.org/Data.aspx?d=POP&f=tableCode%3A22#POP.

48. **Oficina de las Naciones Unidas contra la Droga y el Delito (ONUDD).** *Global Study on Homicide* 2013. *Trends, Context, Data.* Vienna: s.n., 2013.

49. *Fairness and Retaliation: The Economics of Reciprocity.* **Fehr, Ernst and Gächter, Simon.** 3, 2000, Journal of Economic Perspectives, Vol. 14, pp. 159-181.

50. **The World Justice Project (WJP).** *Rule of Law Index* 2014. Washington, D.C.: s.n., 2014.

51. **Haugen, Gary A. and Boutros, Victor.** *The Locust Effect: Why the End of Poverty Requires the End of Violence.* Nueva York: Oxford University Press, 2014.

52. **Instituto Nacional de Estadística y Geografía (INEGI).** Distribución por edad y sexo. Población total por grupo quinquenal de edad según sexo, 1950 a 2010. [Online] marzo 3, 2011. [Cited: agosto 24, 2016.] http://www3.inegi.org.mx/sistemas/sisept/Default.aspx?t=mdemo03&s=est&c=17500.

53. **Consejo Nacional de Población (CONAPO).** Proyecciones de la población 2010-2050. *México en cifras.* [Online] abril 25, 2014. [Cited: agosto 24, 2016.] http://www.conapo.gob.mx/es/CONAPO/Proyecciones.

54. **Instituto Nacional de Estadística y Geografía (INEGI).**
Encuesta Nacional de Victimización y Percepción sobre
Seguridad Pública (ENVIPE) 2014. [Online] septiembre 30, 2014.
http://www.inegi.org.mx/est/contenidos/proyectos/encuestas/
hogares/regulares/envipe/envipe2014/default.aspx.

55. *Which Professions Have the Most Psychopaths? The Fewest?* **Barker, Eric.** 21 de marzo de 2014, Time.

56. **Bilefsky, Dan and Clark, Nicola.** Fatal Descent of Germanwings
Plane Was 'Deliberate,' French Authorities Say. *The New York Times.* marzo 26, 2015.

57. **Olding, Rachel.** Germanwings plane crash: Murder-suicide
usually involves psychopathy or psychosis: experts. *The Sydney Morning Herald.* marzo 27, 2015.

58. **Pérez López, Juan Antonio.** *Fundamentos de la dirección de empresas.* Madrid: RIALP, 1996.

59. *The Natural History of Human Food Sharing and Cooperation: A Review and a New Multi-Individual Approach to the Negotiation of Norms.* **Kaplan, Hillard and Gurven, Michael.** Santa Fe: Santa Fe Institute, 2001. Conference on the Structure and Evolution of Strong Reciprocity. pp. 1-41.

60. **Orwell, George.** *Animal Farm.* Londres: Secker & Warburg, 1945.

61. **Martínez, Nurit.** Pide Gobernación a CNTE liberar Zócalo por fiestas patrias. *El Universal.* septiembre 12, 2013.

62. *Egypt's coup. The second time around.* **The Economist.** 6 de julio de 2013.

63. **Organización Mundial de la Salud (OMS).** *Female genital mutilation.* 2014.

64. **Pew Research Center.** *The World's Muslims: Religion, Politics and Society.* Washington, D.C.: s.n., 2013.

65. **Bazar, Emily.** Cockfighting's 'cultural tradition' kept alive in USA. *USA Today.* 23 de enero de 2007.

66. **Papini, Giovanni.** *El Diablo.* México: Porrúa, 1953.

67. **Wikipedia.** Minimum Wages by Country.
[Online] 12 2013. https://en.wikipedia.org/wiki/
List_of_minimum_wages_by_country.

68. **Weber, Max.** Politics as a Vocation. [Online] 1919.
http://anthropos-lab.net/wp/wp-content/uploads/2011/12/
Weber-Politics-as-a-Vocation.pdf.

69. *Estado y crimen.* **Zaid, Gabriel.** 1 de diciembre de 2014, Letras Libres.

70. **Friedman, Thomas L.** *From Beirut to Jerusalem.* Nueva York: Anchor Books, 1989.

71. **Universidad de las Américas Puebla (UDLAP).** *Índice Global de Impunidad* 2015. Puebla: Centro de Estudios sobre Impunidad y Justicia, 2015.

72. **Vélez Grajales, Roberto y Huerta Wong, Juan Enrique.** *Informe de movilidad social en México* 2013. *Imagina tu futuro.* México: Centro de Estudios Espinosa Yglesias, 2013. http://www.ceey.org.mx/site/ files/informe_mov_social_2013.pdf.

73. **Organización para la Cooperación y el Desarrollo Económicos (OCDE).** *Skills Outlook* 2015. *Youth, Skills and Employability.* 2015.

74. **Otero, Silvia.** Oficial: existe la hermandad en la SSP. *El Universal.* junio 15, 2002.

75. **El Economista.** Presentarán ante la SIEDO a "El Pozolero". enero 25, 2009.

76. **Quora.** How many bodies have been dissolved in acid on Breaking Bad? [Online] septiembre 3, 2012. http://www.quora.com/ How-many-bodies-have-been-dissolved-in-acid-on-Breaking-Bad.

77. **Animal Político.** Normalistas cumplen dos meses desaparecidos: cronología del caso Ayotzinapa. noviembre 26, 2014. http://www.animalpolitico.com/2014/11/ cronologia-el-dia-dia-del-caso-ayotzinapa/.

78. **Herrera, Claudia.** Exonera el tribunal electoral al PRI por caso Monex. *La Jornada.* febrero 19, 2015.

79. **Castillo García, Gustavo.** Ultimadas a muy corta distancia, 14 de las 22 víctimas de Tlatlaya. *La Jornada.* septiembre 26, 2014.

80. **Aristegui Noticias.** La casa blanca de Enrique Peña Nieto (investigación especial). [Online] noviembre 9, 2014. http://aristeguinoticias.com/0911/mexico/ la-casa-blanca-de-enrique-pena-nieto/.

81. **Ferriz de Con, Pedro.** *La razon de la caída Pedro Ferriz de Con.* [Video] julio 16, 2012.

82. **Univisión Noticias.** Aristegui denuncia que MVS prohibió reportaje de la casa blanca. marzo 22, 2015.

83. **Aristegui Noticias.** Video: Diputados del PAN convierten reunión plenaria en fiesta con escorts. [Online] agosto 11, 2014. http://aristeguinoticias.com/1108/mexico/video-diputados-del-pan-convierten-reunion-plenaria-en-fiesta-con-escorts/.

84. **Peña Nieto, Enrique.** *Conversaciones a Fondo.* [interv.] Pascal Beltrán del Río, et al. México, agosto 20, 2014.

85. **Excélsior.** Cierre de la Línea 12 es por desgaste ondulatorio en la vía: Joel Ortega. marzo 12, 2014.

86. **Villavicencio, Diana.** *Aún no libra Marcelo Ebrard responsabilidad por L12. El Universal.* septiembre 15, 2014.

87. **Pazos, Francisco.** Ebrard supo de peligro en L12. *Excélsior.* febrero 7, 2015.

88. **Aristegui Noticias.** "No me va a intimidar" campaña en mi contra del GDF y el PRI: Ebrard en MVS. [Online] enero 29, 2015. http://aristeguinoticias.com/2901/mexico/no-me-va-a-intimidar-campana-en-mi-contra-del-gdf-y-el-pri-ebrard-en-mvs/.

89. —. Mancera culpó a Ebrard ante Los Pinos por la 'casa blanca': Ricardo Raphael. [En línea] 30 de abril de 2015. http://aristeguinoticias.com/3004/mexico/mancera-culpo-a-ebrard-ante-los-pinos-por-la-casa-blanca-ricardo-raphael/.

90. *El TEPJF cobró a Ebrard "la afrenta" de la Casa Blanca: AMLO.* **Proceso.** mayo 1, 2015.

91. **Animal Político.** Estos son los 10 puntos que anunció Peña Nieto en respuesta al caso Ayotzinapa. noviembre 28, 2014. http://www.animalpolitico.com/2014/11/pena-nieto-acuerdo-seguridad-comision-anuncio-mensaje-palacio-nacional/.

92. *Funcionario encargado de combatir la pobreza usa reloj valuado en más de 3 millones de pesos.* **Esquivel, J. Jesús.** abril 1, 2015, Proceso.

93. **Delgado, René.** ¿Quién sigue? *Reforma.* marzo 21, 2015.

94. *Planet Hard Drive.* **Hidalgo, César A.** 14 de julio de 2015, Scientific American, Vol. 313, págs. 72-75.

95. **Huxley, Aldous.** *Brave New World.* Londres: Chatto & Windus, 1932.

96. **Diamond, Jared.** *Guns, Germs, and Steel. The Fates of Human Societies.* Nueva York: Norton, 1997.

97. —. *Collapse: How Societies Choose to Fail or Succeed.* Nueva York: Penguin Books, 2005.

98. **Johnson, Paul M. and Kenny, Paul J.** Dopamine D2 receptors in addiction-like reward dysfunction and compulsive eating in obese rats. [Online] 2010. [Cited: septiembre 10, 2015.] http://www.nature.com/neuro/journal/v13/n5/abs/nn.2519.html.

99. **Organización Mundial de la Salud (OMS).** *Preventing chronic diseases: a vital investment.* 2005.

100. **Norges Bank. Investment Management.** The Fund. History. [Online] [Cited: septiembre 1, 2015.] http://www.nbim.no/en/the-fund/history/.

101. **Nelson, Charles A., Fox, Nathan A. and Zeanah, Charles H.** *Romania's Abandoned Children: Deprivation, Brain Development, and the Struggle for Recovery.* Boston: Harvard University Press, 2014.

102. **Mischel, Walter.** *The Marshmallow Test: Mastering Self-Control.* s.l.: Little, Brown and Company, 2014.

103. *Children and the Internet: experiments with minimally invasive education in India.* **Mitra, Sugata and Rana, Vivek.** 2, 2001, British Journal of Educational Technology, Vol. 32, pp. 221-232.

104. **Wujec, Tom.** Marshmallow Challenge. Build the Tallest Freestanding Structure. [Online] febrero 4, 2015. http://www.tomwujec.com/design-projects/marshmallow-challenge/.

105. *Where Science Starts: Spontaneous Experiments in Preschoolers' Exploratory Play.* **Cook, Claire, Goodman, Noah D. and Shulz, Laura E.** 120, 2011, Cognition, pp. 341-349.

106. **Kaufman, Scott Barry.** Which Character Strengths Are Most Predictive of Well-Being? *Scientific American.* [Blog]. agosto 2, 2015.

107. *Prospect Theory: An Analysis of Decision Under Risk.* **Kahneman, Daniel and Tversky, Amos.** 2, 1979, Econometrica, Vol. 47, pp. 263-292.

108. **Wikipedia.** Heuristic. [Online] 09 28, 2015. https://en.wikipedia.org/wiki/Heuristic.

109. **Huang, Nellie S.** Lafite 1869: $232,692 a Bottle. *The Wall Street Journal.* octubre 30, 2010.

110. **Yale University.** Comparative Cognition Laboratory. [Online] 2016. http://caplab.yale.edu/publications.

111. **Dockser Marcus, Amy.** The Hard Science of Monkey Business. *The Wall Street Journal.* marzo 30, 2012.

112. **Pink, Daniel H.** *Drive: the surprising truth about what motivates us.* New York: Riverhead Books, 2009.

113. *Learning Motivated by a Manipulation Drive.* **Harlow, Harry F., Harlow, Margaret Kuenne y Meyer, Donald R.** 2, abril de 1950, Journal of Experimental Psychology, Vol. 40, págs. 228-234.

114. **Wikipedia.** Volkswagen emissions scandal. [Online] agosto 25, 2016. https://en.wikipedia.org/wiki/ Volkswagen_emissions_scandal.

115. *Financial Literacy and Subprime Mortgage Delinquency: Evidence from a Survey Matched to Administrative Data.* **Gerardi, Kristopher, Goette, Lorenz and Meier, Stephan.** 2010-10, abril 1, 2010, Federal Reserve of Atlanta Working Paper Series.

116. **Ariely, Dan.** Chapter 1: The Truth About Relativity. *Predictably Irrational by Chapters.* [Video]. s.l.: Duke University, 2016. http://danariely.com/resources/videos/.

117. —. *Predictably Irrational. The Hidden Forces That Shape Our Decisions.* Nueva York: Harper Collins, 2008.

118. *Interpersonal attraction in exchange and communal relationships.* **Clark, Margaret y Mills, Judson.** 1979, Journal of Personality and Social Psychology, págs. 12-24.

119. *Putting a Price Tag on Unpaid Housework.* **Covert, Bryce.** mayo 30, 2012, Forbes. http://www.forbes.com/sites/brycecovert/2012/05/30/ putting-a-price-tag-on-unpaid-housework/.

120. **Wikipedia.** Potlatch. [Online] agosto 18, 2016. https://en.wikipedia.org/wiki/Potlatch.

121. **Stiglitz, Joseph E., Sen, Amartya and Fitoussi, Jean-Paul.** *Report by the Comission on the Measurement of Economic Performance and Social Progress.* París: Institut national de la statistique et des études économiques (Insee), 2015. http://www.insee.fr/fr/publications-et-services/dossiers_web/ stiglitz/doc-commission/RAPPORT_anglais.pdf.

122. *China Makes Almost Nothing Out of Apple's iPads and iPhones.* **Worstall, Tim.** diciembre 24, 2011, Forbes.

123. *Manufacturing. When cheap is not so cheap.* **The Economist.** septiembre 2, 2014.

124. *Causal Entropic Forces.* **Wissner-Gross, A. D. and Freer, C. E.** 16, abril 19, 2013, Physical Review Letters, Vol. 110, pp. 168702 (1-5).

125. *Dynamic Horizontal Cultural Transmission of Humpback Whale Song at the Ocean Basin Scale.* **Garland, Ellen C., et al.** 8, abril 26, 2011, Current Biology, Vol. 21, pp. 687-691.

126. *Observational Learning in Octopus vulgaris.* **Fiorito, Graziano and Scotto, Pietro.** 5056, abril 24, 1992, Science, Vol. 256, pp. 545-547.
127. **Churchill, Winston S.** Blood, Toil, Tears and Sweat. [Discurso]. Londres: The Churchill Centre, mayo 13, 1940. [Traducción del autor].
128. **Reagan, Ronald.** Tear Down This Wall. Speech at the Brandenburg Gate (Berlin). s.l.: U.S. Air Force. Air War College, junio 12, 1987. [Traducción del autor].
129. *Metaphor, Morality, and Politics Or, Why Conservatives Have Left Liberals In the Dust.* **Lakoff, George.** 2, 1995, Social Research, Vol. 62. [Traductor desconocido].
130. *Faith, Certainty and the Presidency of George W. Bush.* **Suskind, Ron.** octubre 17, 2004, The New York Times Magazine.
131. **Locke, John.** *Two Treatises of Government.* Londres: Awnsham Churchill, 1689.
132. **Montesquieu.** *De l'esprit des loix.* Amsterdam: Chatelain, 1749.
133. **Lemon, Johanna.** The Great Stink. *Cholera and the Thames.* [Sitio web]. 2016. http://www.choleraandthethames.co.uk/cholera-in-london/the-great-stink/.
134. **Churchill, Winston S.** *The Second World War: Their Finest Hour.* Londres: Cooperation Pub. Co. [by] Houghton Mifflin, 1949. Vol. 2.
135. **León XIII.** *Rerum Novarum.* Ciudad del Vaticano: Libreria Editrice Vaticana, 1891.
136. **Francisco I.** *Laudato si'.* Ciudad del Vaticano: Libreria Editrice Vaticana, 2015.
137. **Obama, Barak.** Remarks by the President at Cairo University, 6-04-09. *https://www.whitehouse.gov.* [Online] 04 06, 2009. [Traducción del autor]. https://www.whitehouse.gov/the-press-office/remarks-president-cairo-university-6-04-09.
138. **Wikipedia.** List of countries by number of mobile phones in use. [Online] agosto 31, 2016. https://en.wikipedia.org/wiki/List_of_countries_by_number_of_mobile_phones_in_use.
139. **Helmrich, Brittney.** 33 Ways to Define Leadership. *Business News Daily.* abril 5, 2016.
140. **Dawkins, Richard.** *The God Delusion.* Londres: Bantam Books, 2006.
141. **Wikipedia.** Transcomputational. [Online] 03 16, 2016. https://en.wikipedia.org/wiki/Transcomputational_problem.
142. **Bacon, Francis.** *Meditationes Sacrae.* Londres: Excusum impensis Humfredi Hooper, 1597.

143. *The Role of Deliberate Practice in the Acquisition of Expert Performance.* **Anders Ericsson, K., Krampe, Ralph Th. and Tesch-Römer, Clemens.** 3, 1993, Psychological Review, Vol. 100, pp. 363-406.

144. *The 4 Rituals That Will Make You an Expert at Anything.* **Barker, Eric.** 15 de marzo de 2016, Time.

145. **Calvo A., Carlos.** Pleonexia. El apetito insaciable de cosas materiales. *Gestiópolis.* [Sitio web]. abril 16, 2010. http://www.gestiopolis.com/pleonexia-el-apetito-insaciable-de-cosas-materiales/.

146. **Anarchy Ensues.** Bush: go out and shop. [Online] 2006. https://www.youtube.com/watch?v=fxk9PW83VCY.

147. **Bacevich, Andrew J.** He Told Us to Go Shopping. Now the Bill Is Due. *The Washington Post.* octubre 5, 2008.

148. *Prosocial Spending and Well-Being: Cross-Cultural Evidence for a Psychological Universal.* **Aknin, Lara B., et al.** 4, 2013, Journal of Personality and Social Psychology, Vol. 104, pp. 635-652.

149. **Kondo, Marie.** *The Life-Changing Magic of Tyding Up.* Berkeley: Ten Speed Press, 2014.

150. **Gates, Bill.** *Gates' Microsoft Sell Strategy .* [interv.] CNBC. mayo 5, 2014. http://video.cnbc.com/gallery/?video=3000272555.

151. **Harper, Justin.** Here's The Real Reason There Are Abandoned Luxury Cars Around The UAE. *Business Insider.* septiembre 10, 2012.

152. **Sheehan, Michael.** The Sultan of Brunei's Rotting Supercar Collection. *Gizmodo.* marzo 15, 2011.

153. **Goldfarb, Zachary A.** 8 things millennials want—and don't want—show how different they are from their parents. *The Washington Post.* febrero 28, 2015.

154. *¿Constribuyen la ciencia y la tecnología a abatir la pobreza?* **Viniegra González, Gustavo and Viniegra Beltrán, Carlos.** 4, octubre-diciembre 2010, Ciencia. Revista de la Academia Mexicana de Ciencias, Vol. 61, pp. 46-55.

155. **Physiology Plus.** Total cross-sectional area of different vascular groups and its implication on the velocity of blood flow. [Online] febrero 15, 2016. [Cited: agosto 27, 2016.] http://physiologyplus.com/total-cross-sectional-area-of-different-vascular-groups-and-its-implication-on-the-velocity-of-blood-flow/.

156. *The Predator-Prey Power Law: Biomass Scaling Across Terrestrial and Aquatic Biomes.* **Hatton, Ian A., et al.** 6252, septiembre 4, 2015, Science, Vol. 349, p. 1070.

157. **Stiglitz, Joseph E.** *The Price of Inequality: How Today's Divided Society Endangers Our Future.* Nueva York: W. W. Norton & Company, 2012.

158. **Wikipedia.** Corporate Welfare. [Online] [Cited: 06 01, 2018.] https://en.wikipedia.org/wiki/Corporate_welfare.

159. **Bolio, Eduardo, et al.** *A tale of two Mexicos: Growth and prosperity in a two-speed economy.* México: McKinsey Global Institute, 2014.

160. *Our crony-capitalism index. Planet Plutocrat.* **The Economist.** marzo 13, 2014.

161. *The One Percent's Problem.* **Stiglitz, Joseph E. and Bilmes, Linda J.** mayo 31, 2012, Hive by Vanity Fair.

162. **Gibbs, Samuel.** How much are you worth to Facebook? *The Guardian.* enero 28, 2016.

163. **D'Onfro, Jillian.** Here's how much time people spend on Facebook per day. *Business Insider.* julio 8, 2015.

164. **Wikipedia.** Countries by Labour Force. [Online] 2013. https://en.wikipedia.org/wiki/List_of_countries_by_labour_force.

165. —. Facebook. [En línea] 25 de agosto de 2016. https://en.wikipedia.org/wiki/Facebook.

166. —. List of minimum wages by country. [Online] diciembre 2013. https://en.wikipedia.org/wiki/List_of_minimum_wages_by_country.

167. —. Japan. [Online] agosto 30, 2016. https://en.wikipedia.org/wiki/Japan.

168. **Common Sense Media.** *The Common Sense Census: Media Use by Tweens and Teens.* Estados Unidos: s.n., 2015. https://www.commonsensemedia.org/sites/default/files/uploads/research/census_executivesummary.pdf.

169. *Cognitive control in media multitaskers.* **Ophir, Eyal, Nass, Clifford and Wagner, Anthony D.** 37, septiembre 15, 2009, Psychological and Cognitive Sciences (PNAS), Vol. 106, pp. 15583-15587.

170. **ZF TRW Automotive Holdings Corporation.** Texting while driving now leading cause of US teen deaths. *Auto Safety. News and expert insight.* [Online] julio 10, 2013. http://safety.trw.com/texting-while-driving-now-leading-cause-of-us-teen-deaths/0710/.

171. **Bradbury, Ray.** *Fahrenheit* 451. Nueva York: Ballantine Books, 1953.

172. **Wikipedia.** Doomsday Clock. [Online] 04 7, 2016. https://en.wikipedia.org/wiki/Doomsday_Clock.

173. *Swarm Smarts.* **Bonabeau, Eric and Théraulaz, Guy.** 3, 2000, Scientific American, Vol. 282, pp. 72-79.

174. *The Social Brain Hypothesis.* **Dunbar, R.I.M.** 5, 1998, Evolutionary Anthropology, Vol. 6, pp. 178-190.

175. **Goldman, Alvin I.** Theory of Mind. [book auth.] E. Margolis, R. Samuels and S.P. Stich. *The Oxford Handbook of Philosophy of Cognitive Science.* Oxford: Oxford University Press, 2012.

176. **Yale University.** Gossip. [book auth.] D. Levinson and M. Ember. *Encyclopedia of Cultural Anthropology.* Nueva York: Henry Holt and Company, 1996, Vol. 2, pp. 544-547.

177. *Queen dominance and worker policing control reproduction in a threatened ant.* **Trettin, Jürgen, et al.** 21, 2011, BMC Ecology, Vol. 11. Disponible en BioMed Central.

178. **Wikipedia.** OSI Model. [Online] enero 30, 2017. [Cited: septiembre 8, 2016.] https://en.wikipedia.org/wiki/OSI_model.

179. *Emergence of Scaling in Random Networks.* **Barabási, Albert-László and Albert, Réka.** 5439, octubre 15, 1999, Science, Vol. 286, pp. 509-512.

180. *Robustness and network evolution—an entropic principle.* **Demetrius, Lloyd and Manke, Thomas.** 2005, Physica A, Vol. 346, pp. 682-696.

181. *Social Network Size in Humans.* **Hill, R.A. and Dunbar, R.I.M.** 1, 2002, Human Nature, Vol. 14, pp. 53-72.

182. *Assesing the Causes of Late Pleistocene Extintions on the Continents.* **Barnosky, Anthony D., et al.** 5693, octubre 1, 2004, Science, Vol. 306, pp. 70-75.

183. **Clark, Gregory.** *A Farewell to Alms: A Brief Economic History of the World.* Nueva Jersey: Princeton University Press, 2007. p.64.

184. **World Bank.** Agricultural land (% of land area). *DataBank.* [Online] 2000. http://data.worldbank.org/indicator/AG.LND.AGRI.ZS?end=2004&start=1983.

185. **Smil, Vaclav.** *Harvesting the Biosphere: What We Have Taken from Nature.* Cambridge: The MIT Press, 2012.

186. **Organización para la Cooperación y el Desarrollo Económicos [OCDE].** *Skills Outlook 2015. Youth, Skills and Employability.* 2015.

187. **World Bank.** Global Findex Database. *Financial Inclusion Data.* [Online] 2014. http://datatopics.worldbank.org/financialinclusion/.

188. **El Economista.** Peña Nieto celebra aprobación de reforma de telcos. *El Economista.* marzo 22, 2013. http://eleconomista.com.mx/sociedad/2013/03/22/pena-nieto-celebra-aprobacion-reforma-telecos.

189. **World Economic Forum.** Networked Readiness Index. *Global Information Technology Report 2016.* [Online] 2016. http://reports.weforum.org/global-information-technology-report-2016/networked-readiness-index/.

190. **Internet Live Stats.** Mexico Internet Users. [Online] 2016. http://www.internetlivestats.com/internet-users/mexico/.

191. **Wells, Georgia, McKinnon, John D. and Kim, Yun-Hee.** How Samsung Botched Its Galaxy Note 7 Recall. *The Wall Street Journal.* septiembre 16, 2016. http://www.wsj.com/articles/samsungs-management-of-recall-wounds-companys-image-1473928872.

192. **Mills, Mark P.** *The Cloud Begins With Coal. Big Data, Big Networks, Big Infrastructure, and Big Power. An Overview of The Electricity Used By The Global Digital Ecosystem.* Digital Power Group. s.l.: National Mining Association / American Coalition for Clean Coal Electricity, 2013. http://www.tech-pundit.com/wp-content/uploads/2013/07/Cloud_Begins_With_Coal.pdf?c761ac.

193. *Computers have a lot to learn from the human brain, engineers say.* **Greenemeier, Larry.** 2009, Scientific American. https://blogs.scientificamerican.com/news-blog/computers-have-a-lot-to-learn-from-2009-03-10/.

194. *Does Thinking Really Hard Burn More Calories?* **Jabr, Ferris.** 2012, Scientific American. https://www.scientificamerican.com/article/thinking-hard-calories/.

195. **Wikipedia.** Supercomputer. [Online] enero 19, 2017. https://en.wikipedia.org/wiki/Supercomputer.

196. —. Vilfredo Pareto. [Online] marzo 6, 2017. [Cited: marzo 5, 2017.] https://en.wikipedia.org/wiki/Vilfredo_Pareto.

197. —. Joseph Juran. [Online] abril 20, 2017. [Cited: marzo 5, 2017.] https://es.wikipedia.org/wiki/Joseph_Juran.

198. **Einstein, Albert.** *The Collected Papers of Albert Einstein. The Swiss Years: Writings,* 1900-1909. [ed.] Peter Havas. [trans.] Anna Beck. Nueva Jersey: Princeton University Press, 1989. Vol. 2. 0-691-08549-8.

199. **Wikipedia.** Distribución Boltzmann. [Online] mayo 10, 2017. [Cited: mayo 8, 2017.] https://es.wikipedia.org/wiki/Distribucion_Boltzmann#cite_note-landau-1.

200. *On Random Graphs I.* **Erdös, P. and Rényi, A.** 1959, Publicationes Mathematicae (Debrecen), Vol. 6, pp. 290-297.

201. **Facultad de Química, UNAM.** Fenómenos de superficie. Adsorción. *Departamento de Programas Audiovisuales. Administración de Manuales y Documentos.* [Online] 2017. [Cited: mayo 11, 2017.] http://depa.fquim.unam.mx/amyd/archivero/Unidad3Adsorcion_19664.pdf.

202. **Bible Hub.** Mateo 13:12. *Biblia Paralela.* [Online] 2004. http://bibliaparalela.com/matthew/13-12.htm.

203. **Webometrics, Cybermetrics Lab, Consejo Superior de Investigaciones Científicas (CSIC).** Ranking of scientists in Mexico Institutions according to their Google Scholar Citations public profiles. *Ranking Web of Universities.* [Online] noviembre 2016. [Cited: mayo 2, 2017.] http://www.webometrics.info/en/node/63.

204. *Money in Gas-Like Markets: Gibbs and Pareto Laws.* **Chatterjee, Arnab, Chakrabarti, Bikas K. and Manna, S. S.** s.l.: IOP Publishing, 2003, Physica Scripta, Vol. T106, pp. 36-38. 1402-4896.

205. **Chakrabarti, Bikas K. and Chatterjee, Arnab.** Ideal Gas-Like Distributions in Economics: Effects of Saving Propensity. [book auth.] Hideki Takayasu. *The Application of Econophysics.* Tokio: Springer, 2004, pp. 280-285.

206. **Nielsen, Jakob.** The 90-9-1 Rule for Participation Inequality in Social Media and Online Communities. *Nielsen Norman Group.* [Online] octubre 9, 2006. [Cited: marzo 5, 2017.] https://www.nngroup.com/articles/participation-inequality/.

207. **Euromonitor International.** *World Consumer Income and Expenditure Patterns* 2013. s.l.: Euromonitor International, 2013.

208. **Sachs, Jeffrey.** *The End of Poverty: Economic Possibilities for Our Time.* Nueva York: Penguin Books, 2006.

209. **Gómez Gil, Carlos.** *El colapso de los microcréditos en la cooperación al desarrollo.* Madrid: Catarata, 2016.

210. **Wikipedia.** World Population Estimates. [Online] enero 8, 2017. https://en.wikipedia.org/wiki/World_population_estimates.

211. —. Survivalism. [Online] enero 15, 2017. https://en.wikipedia. org/wiki/Survivalism.

212. *Before the Levees Break: A Plan to Save the Netherlands.* **Wolman, David.** 1, diciembre 22, 2008, Wired, Vol. 17. https://www.wired.com/2008/12/ff-dutch-delta/.

213. **Symons, Jeremy.** Trump Now Blames Scientists For Global Warming 'Hoax'. *The Huffington Post.* julio 27, 2016. http://www.huffingtonpost.com/jeremy-symons/trump-now-blames-scientis_b_11228538.html.

214. **Diamond, Jared.** *Collapse: How Societies Choose to Fail or Succeed.* Nueva York: Penguin Books, 2005.

215. *Israel Proves the Desalination Era Is Here.* **Jacobsen, Rowan.** julio 29, 2016, Scientific American. https://www.scientificamerican. com/article/israel-proves-the-desalination-era-is-here/.

216. *Here Are All the Billionaires Backing Donald Trump.* **Hackett, Robert.** agosto 3, 2016, Fortune. http://fortune.com/2016/08/03/trump-billionaire-backers-list/.

217. **Csikszentmihalyi, Mihaly and Seligman, Martin E. P.** Positive Psychology: An Introduction. [book auth.] Mihaly Csikszentmihalyi. *Flow and the Foundations of Positive Psychology.* Países Bajos: Springer, 2014, pp. 279-298.

218. **Kennedy, John F.** We Choose to Go to the Moon. [trans.] Carlos Viniegra. septiembre 12, 1962. https://er.jsc.nasa.gov/seh/ricetalk.htm.

219. **Wikipedia.** Transaction processing system. [Online] enero 26, 2017. https://en.wikipedia.org/wiki/Transaction_processing_system.

220. **Naím, Moisés.** *The End of Power: From Boardrooms to Battlefields and Churches to States, Why Being in Charge Isn't What It Used to Be.* Nueva York: Basic Books, 2013.

221. **Pilgrim, Sophie.** Smugglers work on the dark side of Rwanda's plastic bag ban. *Aljazeera America.* [Online] febrero 25, 2016. http://america.aljazeera.com/articles/2016/2/25/rwanda-plastic-bag-ban.html. http://america.aljazeera.com/articles/2016/2/25/rwanda-plastic-bag-ban.html.

222. **Unicef.** Salud y nutrición. *Unicef México.* [Online] 2016. http://www.unicef.org/mexico/spanish/17047.htm.

223. *Peña Nieto hace pública su afición por la Coca Cola Light.* **Celis, Fernanda.** *México: s.n., septiembre 9, 2016, Forbes. http://www.forbes.com.mx/pena-nieto-hace-publica-su-aficion-por-la-coca-cola-light/.*

224. **Gutiérrez, J.P., et al.** *Encuesta Nacional de Salud y Nutrición 2012. Resultados Nacionales.* Secretaría de Salud. Cuernavaca, México: Instituto Nacional de Salud Pública, 2012.

225. **WorldAtlas.** Countries With The Highest Levels Of Soft Drink Consumption. *Economics.* [Online] agosto 5, 2016. http://www.worldatlas.com/articles/countries-with-the-highest-levels-of-soft-drink-consumption.html.

226. **Caffeine Informer.** Caffeine Amounts in Soda: Every Kind of Cola You Can Think Of. [Online] mayo 13, 2015. http://www.caffeineinformer.com/caffeine-amounts-in-soda-every-kind-of-cola-you-can-think-of.

227. **Petrequin, Samuel.** France to bid adieu to plastic dishes with controversial ban. *Associated Press.* septiembre 12, 2016. http://bigstory.ap.org/article/54a14fa0bee742618906007606a39166/france-bid-adieu-plastic-dishes-controversial-ban.

228. **Legaleze.** Regulation of London cabs and PHVs. *Regulated businesses. Transport of passengers – hackney carriages and private hire vehicles (taxis, minicabs).* [Online] octubre 17, 2015. https://www.legaleze.co.uk/members/RB_passenger_transport_private_london_taxis.aspx.

229. **Wikipedia.** Taxicabs of New York City. [Online] enero 19, 2017. [Cited: septiembre 29, 2016.] https://en.wikipedia.org/wiki/Taxicabs_of_New_York_City.

230. *Uber just completed its two-billionth trip.* **Hawkins, Andrew J.** julio 18, 2016, The Verge. http://www.theverge.com/2016/7/18/12211710/uber-two-billion-trip-announced-kalanick-china-didi.

231. *Uber Loses at Least $1.2 Billion in First Half of* 2016. **Newcomer, Eric.** agosto 25, 2016, Bloomberg Technology. Uber Loses at Least $1.2 Billion in First Half of 2016.

232. **Banco de México.** Sistema de Información Económica. *Ingresos por Remesas.* [Online] 2010. http://www.banxico. org.mx/SieInternet/consultarDirectorioInternetAction. do?accion=consultarCuadro&idCuadro=CE81#.

233. **INEGI.** Censo de Población y Vivienda. [Online] 2010. http://www.beta.inegi.org.mx/proyectos/ccpv/2010/.

234. **Muñoz Ríos, Patricia.** El salario mínimo debería ser de 6 mil 500 pesos mensuales, según estudio. *La Jornada.* diciembre 5, 2011. http://www.jornada.unam.mx/2011/12/05/ politica/012n1pol.

235. **Bogage, Jacob.** How much Uber drivers actually make per hour. *The Washington Post.* junio 27, 2016. https://www.washingtonpost.com/news/the-switch/ wp/2016/06/27/how-much-uber-drivers-actually-make-per-hour/.

236. *Working with Machines: The Impact of Algorithmic and Data-Driven Management on Human Workers.* **Lee, Min Kyung, et al.** abril 18, 2015, CHI '15 Proceedings of the 33rd Annual ACM Conference on Human Factors in Computing Systems, pp. 1603-1612.

237. **Beekman, Daniel.** Uber deals put spotlight on Seattle showdown. *The Seattle Times.* mayo 10, 2016. http://www.seattletimes.com/seattle-news/politics/ uber-deals-put-spotlight-on-seattle-showdown/.

238. *Amazon's Jeff Bezos Doesn't Care About Profit Margins.* **Stone, Brad and Aley, Jim.** enero 8, 2013, Bloomberg. https://www.bloomberg.com/news/articles/2013-01-08/ amazons-jeff-bezos-doesnt-care-about-profit-margins.

239. *Uber's First Self-Driving Fleet Arrives in Pittsburgh This Month.* **Chafkin, Max.** agosto 18, 2016, Bloomberg. http://www.bloomberg.com/news/ features/2016-08-18/uber-s-first-self-driving-fleet-arrives-in-pittsburgh-this-month-is06r7on.

240. **Henry Ford Heritage Association.** The Five-Dollar Day—Jump-Starting the Middle Class. *Henry Ford, 150 years.* [Online] 2014. http://www.henryford150.com/5-a-day/.

241. **H Brothers Inc.** Inflation Calculator. *DollarTimes.* [Online] 2017. [Cited: octubre 4, 2016.] http://www.dollartimes.com/inflation/ inflation.php?amount=1&year=1914.

242. *What Is Code?* **Ford, Paul.** junio 11, 2015, Businessweek. https://www.bloomberg.com/ graphics/2015-paul-ford-what-is-code/.

243. *Nestle's Coffee Business Is Competing With Itself.* **Gretler, Corinne.** junio 27, 2016, Bloomberg. http://www.bloomberg.com/news/articles/2016-06-28/ nestle-leans-on-nespresso-s-kid-brother-as-coffee-growth-lags.

244. **AFP News.** Nespresso inventor says wife and Rome cafe inspired 'pod'. *The Local Ch.* agosto 21, 2016. https://www.thelocal.ch/20160821/ nespresso-inventor-says-wife-and-rome-cafe-inspired-the-pod.

245. **Nestlé.** *Annual Review* 2015. Suiza: Nestlé Ltd., 2015. http://www.nestle.com/asset-library/documents/library/ documents/annual_reports/2015-annual-review-en.pdf.

246. **Wikipedia.** Keurig. [Online] enero 31, 2017. https://en.wikipedia.org/wiki/Keurig.

247. **Crawford, Elizabeth.** Coffee pod sales growth slows, but emerging trends could expand category's reach, Packaged facts. *Food Navigator-USA.* [Online] enero 6, 2016. http://www.foodnavigator-usa.com/Manufacturers/Coffee-pod-sales-growth-slows-but-trends-could-expand-category-s-reach.

248. *Coffee Farmers Are Hurt by Single-Serving Pods Revolution in U.S.* **Javier, Luzi Ann and Pérez, Marvin G.** abril 15, 2015, Bloomberg. https://www.bloomberg.com/news/articles/2015-04-15/ the-coffee-revolution-is-just-too-efficient-for-hurting-farmers.

249. **Strand, Oliver.** With Coffee, the Price of Individualism Can Be High. *The New York Times.* febrero 7, 2012. http://www.nytimes.com/2012/02/08/dining/single-serve-coffee-brewers-make-convenience-costly.html?_r=1&ref=business.

250. **Alderman, Liz.** Nespresso and Rivals Vie for Dominance in Coffee War. *The New York Times.* agosto 20, 2010. http://www.nytimes.com/2010/08/21/business/ global/21coffee.html?_r=0.

251. **Ingraham, Christopher.** The stuff we really need is getting more expensive. Other stuff is getting cheaper. *The Wahington Post.* agosto 17, 2016. https://www.washingtonpost.com/news/wonk/wp/2016/08/17/the-stuff-we-really-need-is-getting-more-expensive-other-stuff-is-getting-cheaper/.

252. **Johnson, Carolyn Y.** Lawmakers grill Mylan CEO over EpiPen price hikes. *The Washington Post.* septiembre 22, 2016. https://www.washingtonpost.com/news/wonk/wp/2016/09/21/watch-live-lawmakers-to-grill-executive-who-hiked-the-price-of-lifesaving-drug-epipen/.

253. **Popken, Ben.** Mylan CEO's Pay Rose Over 600 Percent as EpiPen Price Rose 400 Percent. *NBC News.* [Online] agosto 23, 2016. http://www.nbcnews.com/business/consumer/mylan-execs-gave-themselves-raises-they-hiked-epipen-prices-n636591.

254. **Kuhns, Annemarie.** Growth in Inflation-Adjusted Food Prices Varies by Food Category. *United States Department of Agriculture, Economic Research Service.* [Online] julio 6, 2015. https://www.ers.usda.gov/amber-waves/2015/july/growth-in-inflation-adjusted-food-prices-varies-by-food-category/.

255. **Trading Economics.** United States Nonfarm Labour Productivity. [Online] 2017. [Cited: octubre 5, 2016.] http://www.tradingeconomics.com/united-states/productivity.

256. **Desilver, Drew.** For most workers, real wages have barely budged for decades. *Pew Research Center.* [Online] octubre 9, 2014. http://www.pewresearch.org/fact-tank/2014/10/09/for-most-workers-real-wages-have-barely-budged-for-decades/.

257. **Hamblin, James.** A Brewing Problem: What's the healthiest way to keep everyone caffeinated? *The Atlantic.* marzo 2, 2015. http://www.theatlantic.com/technology/archive/2015/03/the-abominable-k-cup-coffee-pod-environment-problem/386501/#article-comments.

258. **Wikipedia.** Airbnb. [Online] enero 31, 2017. https://en.wikipedia.org/wiki/Airbnb.

259. **Crook, Jordan and Escher, Anna.** A Brief History of AirBnB. *TechCrunch.* [Online] junio 28, 2015. https://techcrunch.com/gallery/a-brief-history-of-airbnb/slide/10/.

260. **Chafkin, Max and Newcomer, Eric.** Airbnb Faces Growing Pains as It Passes 100 Million Guests. [Online] julio 11, 2016. http://www.bloomberg.com/news/articles/2016-07-11/ airbnb-faces-growing-pains-as-it-passes-100-million-users. http://www.bloomberg.com/news/articles/2016-07-11/ airbnb-faces-growing-pains-as-it-passes-100-million-users.

261. **Wagner, Kurt.** Airbnb Is Approaching One Million Guests Per Night. *CNBC.* [Online] mayo 27, 2015. http://www.cnbc.com/2015/05/27/airbnb-is-approaching-one-million-guests-per-night.html.

262. *One Wall Street Firm Expects Airbnb to Book a Billion Nights a Year Within a Decade.* **Verhage, Julie.** abril 11, 2016, Bloomberg. http://www.bloomberg.com/news/articles/2016-04-11/one-wall-street-firm-expects-airbnb-to-book-a-billion-nights-a-year-within-a-decade.

263. **Coldwell, Will.** Airbnb's legal troubles: what are the issues? *The Guardian.* julio 8, 2014. https://www.theguardian.com/ travel/2014/jul/08/airbnb-legal-troubles-what-are-the-issues.

264. **Crunchbase.** Airbnb Acquisitions. [Online] 2017. [Cited: octubre 11, 2016.] https://www.crunchbase.com/organization/airbnb/ acquisitions.

265. —. Uber Investors. [Online] 2017. [Cited: octubre 11, 2016.] https://www.crunchbase.com/organization/uber/investors.

266. —. AirBnB Investors. [Online] 2017. [Cited: octubre 11, 2016.] https://www.crunchbase.com/organization/airbnb/investors.

267. *The Pure Theory of Public Expenditure.* **Samuelson, Paul A.** 4, s.l.: The MIT Press, noviembre 1954, The Review of Economics and Statistics, Vol. 36, pp. 387-389.

268. **Sanger, David E. and Savage, Charlie.** U.S. Says Russia Directed Hacks to Influence Elections. *The New York Times.* octubre 7, 2016. http://www.nytimes.com/2016/10/08/us/politics/us-formally-accuses-russia-of-stealing-dnc-emails.html.

269. *Putin Sees U.S., Goldman Sachs Behind Leak of Panama Papers.* **Rudnitsky, Jake and Arkhipov, Ilya.** abril 14, 2016, Bloomberg. http://www.bloomberg.com/news/articles/2016-04-14/ putin-sees-u-s-goldman-sachs-behind-leak-of-panama-papers.

270. **Leiner, Barry M., et al.** Brief History of the Internet. *Internet Society.* [Online] 2017. [Cited: octubre 13, 2016.] http://www.internetsociety.org/internet/what-internet/ history-internet/brief-history-internet.

271. **Nakamoto, Satoshi.** *Bitcoin: A Peer-to-Peer Electronic Cash System.* noviembre 1, 2008. https://bitcoin.org/bitcoin.pdf.

272. *Goldman Sachs Files Patent Application For Securities Settlement Using Cryptocurrencies.* **Cohen, Brian.** diciembre 1, 2015, Bitcoin Magazine. https://bitcoinmagazine.com/articles/goldman-sachs-files-patent-application-for-securities-settlement-using-cryptocurrencies-1449000967.

273. **Machlup, Fritz.** *The Production and Distribution of Knowledge in the United States.* Nueva Jersey: Princeton University Press, 1962.

274. **Comisión Económica para América Latina y el Caribe [CEPAL].** Declaración de Bávaro. [Online] enero 31, 2003. http://www.cepal.org/prensa/noticias/noticias/9/11719/ Bavarofinalesp.pdf.

275. **Amsden, Alice H.** *Asia's Next Giant: South Korea and Late Industrialization.* Nueva York: Oxford University Press, 1992.

276. **Organización para la Cooperación y el Desarrollo Económicos [OCDE].** E-government. *Glossary of Statistical Terms.* [Online] agosto 6, 2002. https://stats.oecd.org/glossary/detail. asp?ID=4752.

277. **Secretaría de la Función Pública.** *Acuerdo por el que se establece el Esquema de Interoperabilidad y de Datos Abiertos de la Administración Pública Federal.* septiembre 6, 2011. Diario Oficial de la Federación. http://www.dof.gob.mx/nota_detalle. php?codigo=5208001&fecha=06/09/2011.

278. **Internet World Stats.** Internet Users in the World by Regions. [Online] junio 30, 2016. http://www.internetworldstats.com/ stats.htm.

279. *Brexit Regret.* **The Economist.** octubre 12, 2016, The Economist. http://www.economist.com/blogs/graphicdetail/2016/10/ daily-chart-6.

280. **Wikipedia.** Colombian peace agreement referendum, 2016. [Online] diciembre 23, 2016. [Cited: octubre 12, 2016.] https://en.wikipedia.org/wiki/ Colombian_peace_agreement_referendum,_2016.

281. **CNN en español.** Colombia: los departamentos con más víctimas votaron mayoritariamente sí en el plebiscito. [Online] octubre 3, 2016. http://cnnespanol.cnn.com/2016/10/03/colombia-los-departamentos-con-mas-victimas-votaron-mayoritariamente-si-en-el-plebiscito/#0.

282. **BBC Mundo.** Qué dice de Colombia que haya habido 62% de abstención en el histórico plebiscito por el proceso de paz. [Online] octubre 3, 2016. http://www.bbc.com/mundo/noticias-america-latina-37539590.

283. **Obama, Barack.** *Memorandum on Transparency and Open Government.* Washington, D.C., Estados Unidos: s.n., enero 21, 2009. https://www.archives.gov/files/cui/documents/2009-WH-memo-on-transparency-and-open-government.pdf.

284. **Orszag, Peter R.** *Open Government Directive.* Washington, D.C., Estados Unidos: s.n., diciembre 8, 2009. https://fas.org/sgp/obama/opengov.pdf.

285. **Alianza para el Gobierno Abierto.** *Declaración de Gobierno Abierto.* septiembre 2011. http://www.opengovpartnership.org/es/acerca-de/declaración-de-gobierno-abierto.

286. **Sanyal, Sanjeev.** *The Random Walk: Mapping the World's Financial Markets* 2014. Hong Kong: Deutsche Bank AG, 2014. https://etf.deutscheam.com/DEU/DEU/Download/Research-Global/47e36b78-d254-4b16-a82f-d5c5f1b1e09a/Mapping-the-World-s-Financial-Markets.pdf.

287. **World Bank.** GDP (current US$). *DataBank.* [Online] 2016. [Cited: octubre 15, 2016.] http://data.worldbank.org/indicator/NY.GDP.MKTP.CD.

288. *Building a Better America—One Wealth Quintile at a Time.* **Norton, Michael I. and Ariely, Dan.** 1, s.l.: SAGE Journals, febrero 3, 2011, Perspectives on Psychological Science, Vol. 6, pp. 9-12.

289. **Organización de las Naciones Unidas [ONU].** *World Urbanization Prospects. The* 2014 *Revision, Highlights.* Population Division, Department of Economic and Social Affairs. Nueva York: s.n., 2014. https://esa.un.org/unpd/wup/.

290. *Manage Your Energy, Not Your Time.* **Schwartz, Tony and McCarthy, Catherine.** octubre 2007, Harvard Business Review. https://hbr.org/2007/10/manage-your-energy-not-your-time.

291. *Sleep Deficit: The Performance Killer.* **Fryer, Bronwyn.** octubre 2006, Harvard Business Review. https://hbr.org/2006/10/sleep-deficit-the-performance-killer.

292. *Stress and glucocorticoids promote oligodendrogenesis in the adult hippocampus.* **Chetty, S., et al.** 12, diciembre 2014, Molecular Psychiatry, Vol. 19, pp. 1275-83.

293. *Overloaded Circuits: Why Smart People Underperform.* **Hallowell, Edward.** enero 2005, Harvard Business Review. https://hbr.org/2005/01/overloaded-circuits-why-smart-people-underperform.

294. *You Can't Multitask, So Stop Trying.* **Atchley, Paul.** diciembre 21, 2010, Harvard Business Review. https://hbr.org/2010/12/you-cant-multi-task-so-stop-tr.

295. **National Transportation Safety Board.** *Controlled Flight Into Terrain, Korean Air Flight 801, Boeing 747-300, HL7468, Nimitz Hill, Guam, August 6, 1997.* Washington, D.C.: U.S. Government Printing Office, 2000. https://www.ntsb.gov/investigations/AccidentReports/Reports/AAR0001.pdf.

296. **Department of Homeland Security.** *The Role of Fusion Centers in Countering Violent Extremism.* Washington, D.C.: s.n., 2012. https://www.it.ojp.gov/documents/roleoffusioncentersincounteringviolentextremism_compliant.pdf.

297. **Maddison, Angus.** *Population, GDP and Per Capita GDP.* Groningen, Países Bajos: s.n., 2010. Historical Statistics of the World Economy: 1-2008 AD. http://www.ggdc.net/maddison/Historical_Statistics/vertical-file_02-2010.xls.

298. **Sartori, Giovanni.** *Homo videns: La sociedad teledirigida.* Buenos Aires: Taurus, 1998.

299. **Kurzweil, Ray.** *The Singularity Is Near: When Humans Transcend Biology.* Nueva York: Penguin, 2006.

300. *The end of Moore's law.* **S., L.** abril 19, 2015, The Economist. http://www.economist.com/blogs/economist-explains/2015/04/economist-explains-17.

301. **Guggenheim, Davis.** *Waiting for 'Superman'.* Electric Kinney Films, Participant Media, Walden Media, 2010.

302. **Wikipedia.** List of Coca-Cola slogans. [Online] noviembre 15, 2016. https://en.wikipedia.org/wiki/List_of_Coca-Cola_slogans.

303. **Benedikt Frey, Carl and Osborne, Michael A.** *The Future of Employment: How Susceptible Are Jobs to Computerisation?* Oxford, Reino Unido: Oxford Martin School, 2013. http://www.oxfordmartin.ox.ac.uk/downloads/academic/The_Future_of_Employment.pdf.

304. **Tesla Motors.** All Tesla Cars Being Produced Now Have Full Self-Driving Hardware. [Online] octubre 19, 2016. https://www.tesla.com/blog/all-tesla-cars-being-produced-now-have-full-self-driving-hardware.

305. *The least educated people in the world are in denial about how robots will take over their jobs.* **Martin, Will.** octubre 22, 2016, Business Insider. http://www.businessinsider.com/emolument-data-on-the-threat-of-robots-ai-artificial-intelligence-automation-to-jobs-2016-10.

306. **Edry, Ronny.** We Love You - Iran & Israel. *YouTube.* [Online] marzo 18, 2012. https://www.youtube.com/watch?v=mYjuUoEivbE.

307. **Wikipedia.** Ferrari P4/5 by Pininfarina. [Online] enero 5, 2017. https://en.wikipedia.org/wiki/Ferrari_P4/5_by_Pininfarina.

308. **Tidd, Joe and Bessant, John.** *Lego.* Case Studies, Innovation Portal. Reino Unido: Wiley, 2013. http://www.innovation-portal.info/wp-content/uploads/Lego1.pdf.

309. **Marshall, Ric and Lee, Linda-Eling.** *Are CEOs Paid For Performance? Evaluating the Effectiveness of Equity Incentives.* Nueva York: Morgan Stanley Capital International [MSCI], 2016. https://www.msci.com/documents/10199/91a7f92b-d4ba-4d29-ae5f-8022f9bb944d.

310. *Schumpeter. The look of a leader.* **The Economist.** septiembre 27, 2014, The Economist. http://www.economist.com/news/business/21620197-getting-top-much-do-how-you-look-what-you-achieve-look-leader.

311. **Abilla, Pete.** What I Learned from Jeff Bezos About Sales Management. *HireVue.* [Online] julio 28, 2015. https://www.hirevue.com/blog/coach-blog/what-i-learned-from-jeff-bezos-about-sales-management.

312. **Wikileaks.** *Someone has your password. The Podesta Emails.* [Online] 2016. https://wikileaks.org/podesta-emails/emailid/34899#efmAAGAAbAHLAIUAWxAXH.

313. **Krieg, Gregory and Kopan, Tal.** Is this the email that hacked John Podesta's account? *CNN Politics.* [Online] octubre 30, 2016. http://edition.cnn.com/2016/10/28/politics/phishing-email-hack-john-podesta-hillary-clinton-wikileaks/.

314. **Silverman, Craig and Alexander, Lawrence.** How Teens In The Balkans Are Duping Trump Supporters With Fake News. *BuzzFeed News.* [Online] noviembre 3, 2016. https://www.buzzfeed.com/craigsilverman/how-macedonia-became-a-global-hub-for-pro-trump-misinfo?utm_term=.yk0r5MxqY#.ledQEMo27.

315. **Wong, Julia Carrie.** Mark Zuckerberg accused of abusing power after Facebook deletes 'napalm girl' post. *The Guardian.* septiembre 9, 2016.

316. **Woolf, Nicky and Solon, Olivia.** Facebook profile glitch 'kills' millions. Even Mark Zuckerberg. *The Guardian.* noviembre 11, 2016.

317. **Lunden, Ingrid.** Facebook overhauls ad metrics, admits 4 bugs and errors led to misreported numbers. *TechCrunch.* [Online] noviembre 16, 2016. https://techcrunch.com/2016/11/16/facebook-overhauls-ad-metrics-admits-4-bugs-and-errors-led-to-misreported-numbers/.

318. **Knorr, Caroline.** 3 Places Families Should Make Phone-Free. *Common Sense Media.* [Online] abril 12, 2016. https://www.commonsensemedia.org/blog/3-places-families-should-make-phone-free.

319. **Duhigg, Charles.** *The Power of Habit: Why We Do What We Do in Life and Business.* Nueva York: Random House, 2012. 978-0-679-60385-6.

320. **Núñez, Ernesto.** Defiende Calderón gasto en seguridad. *Reforma.* diciembre 13, 2006.

321. *Metaphors We Think With: The Role of Metaphor in Reasoning.* **Thibodeau, Paul H. and Boroditsky, Lera.** 2, febrero 2011, PLoS ONE, Vol. 6, p. e16782.

322. **Ashoka.** Gary Slutkin. *Citation. The Person.* [Online] 2009. https://www.ashoka.org/en/fellow/gary-slutkin.

323. **Slutkin, Gary.** Let's treat violence like a contagious disease. *TEDMED.* [Online] abril 2013. http://www.ted.com/talks/gary_slutkin_let_s_treat_violence_like_a_contagious_disease#t-476653.

324. **Ransford, Charles, et al.** *The Relationship between the Cure Violence Model and Citywide Increases and Decreases in Killings in Chicago* (2000-2016). Chicago: Cure Violence, 2016.

325. **American Civil Liberties Union [ACLU].** *War Comes Home: The Excessive Militarization of American Policing.* Nueva York: ACLU Foundation, 2014. https://www.aclu.org/report/war-comes-home-excessive-militarization-american-police.

326. *How Jose Sokoloff demobilised guerillas with advertising.* **Reynolds, Emily.** octubre 15, 2015, Wired. http://www.wired.co.uk/article/jose-sokoloff-colombia-wired-2015.

327. **Sokoloff, José Miguel.** How Christmas lights helped guerrillas put down their guns. *TEDGlobal.* [Online] octubre 2014. http://www.ted.com/talks/jose_miguel_sokoloff_how_christmas_lights_helped_guerrillas_put_down_their_guns/transcript?language=en.

328. **Wikipedia.** Jaime Castro Castro. [Online] septiembre 17, 2016. https://en.wikipedia.org/wiki/Jaime_Castro_Castro.

329. —. Antanas Mockus. [Online] octubre 1, 2016. https://es.wikipedia.org/wiki/Antanas_Mockus.

330. —. Enrique Peñalosa. [Online] febrero 7, 2017. https://en.wikipedia.org/wiki/Enrique_Pe%C3%B1alosa.

331. *El capital social de la Ciudad de México: Una propuesta constitucional.* **Viniegra, Carlos.** 309, 2017, Este País.

332. **Parlamento Europeo; Consejo de la Unión Europea; Comisión Europea.** *Diario Oficial de las Comunidades Europeas.* Niza: s.n., diciembre 18, 2000. Carta de los Derechos Fundamentales de la Unión Europea.

333. *La buena administración como principio y como derecho fundamental en Europa.* **Rodríguez-Arana, Jaime.** 6, 2013, Misión Jurídica, Vol. 6, págs. 23-56.

334. *Estado de derecho y buen gobierno.* **Dermizaky Peredo, Pablo.** 2, 2000, Ius et Praxis, Vol. 6, págs. 145-151.

335. **Wikipedia.** TED (conference). [Online] enero 26, 2017. https://en.wikipedia.org/wiki/TED_(conference).

336. **Chen, Jane.** A warm embrace that saves lives. *TED India.* [Online] Noviembre 2009. https://www.ted.com/talks/jane_chen_a_warm_embrace_that_saves_lives.

337. **Savory, Allan.** How to fight desertification and reverse climate change. *TEDGlobal.* [Online] Febrero 2013. https://www.ted.com/talks/allan_savory_how_to_green_the_world_s_deserts_and_reverse_climate_change.

338. **Monbiot, George.** For more wonder, rewild the world. *TEDGlobal.* [Online] Julio 2013.

339. **Hari, Johann.** Everything you think you know about addiction is wrong. *TEDGlobalLondon.* [Online] Enero 2015. https://www.ted.com/talks/johann_hari_everything_you_think_you_know_about_addiction_is_wrong.

340. **Waldinger, Robert.** What makes a good life? Lessons from the longest study on happiness. *TEDxBeaconStreet* . [Online] Noviembre 2015. https://www.ted.com/talks/robert_waldinger_what_makes_a_good_life_lessons_from_the_longest_study_on_happiness.

341. **Liu, Eric.** Why ordinary people need to understand power. *TEDCity2.0.* [Online] Septiembre 2013. https://www.ted.com/talks/eric_liu_why_ordinary_people_need_to_understand_power.

342. **Cottam, Hilary.** Social services are broken. How we can fix them. *TEDGlobal.* [Online] Septiembre 2015. https://www.ted.com/talks/hilary_cottam_social_services_are_broken_how_we_can_fix_them.

343. **Wikipedia.** It's the economy, stupid. [Online] enero 26, 2017. https://en.wikipedia.org/wiki/It's_the_economy,_stupid.

344. **Reitman, Jason.** *Thank You for Smoking.* ContentFilm, Room 9 Entertainment, TYFS Productions LLC, 2005.

345. **Soderbergh, Steven.** *Erin Brockovich.* Universal Pictures, 2000.

346. **The Best Schools.** The 50 Most Influential Think Tanks in the United States. [Online] 2017. http://www.thebestschools.org/features/most-influential-think-tanks/.

347. **Willingham, Emily and Helft, Laura.** The Autism-Vaccine Myth. *NOVA.* [Online] septiembre 5, 2014. http://www.pbs.org/wgbh/nova/body/autism-vaccine-myth.html.

348. **Allday, Erin.** Failure to vaccinate fueled state's measles epidemic. *San Francisco Chronicle.* marzo 7, 2015.

349. **Wikipedia.** Citizens United v. FEC. [Online] febrero 7, 2017. [Cited: enero 21, 2010.] https://en.wikipedia.org/wiki/Citizens_United_v._FEC.

350. **Wallace, Gregory.** Voter turnout at 20-year low in 2016. *CNN Politics.* [Online] noviembre 30, 2016. http://edition.cnn.com/2016/11/11/politics/popular-vote-turnout-2016/.

351. **ChartsBin.** The Age of Current World Leaders. [Online] 2016. http://chartsbin.com/view/38561.

352. **Taylor, Ken and Perry, John.** What is an adult? *Philosophy Talk.* [Online] abril 10, 2011. https://www.philosophytalk.org/shows/what-adult.

Index

MASTERS,
LACKEYS
& SERFS